Revealing Deeper Meanings

Narratives from Veda to Purāṇas

Revealing Deeper Meanings

Narratives from Veda to Purāṇas

Dr. (Mrs.) Sindhu S. Dange

Aryan Books International
New Delhi

Revealing Deeper Meanings
NARRATIVES FROM VEDA TO PURĀṆAS

ISBN: 978-81-7305-562-1

Published in **2016** by
Aryan Books International
Pooja Apartments, 4B, Ansari Road, New Delhi-110 002 (India)
Tel.: 23287589, 23255799; Fax: 91-11-23270385
E-mail: aryanbooks@gmail.com
www.aryanbooks.co.in

Designed and Printed in India by
ABI Prints & Publishing Co., New Delhi

To

My Grandchildren

for

bringing so much joy

in

my life.

Preface

In my efforts to study the concept of *arthavāda*, this is my third book, which I am glad to present to the scholarly world. Here, I have viewed the concept of *arthavāda* in a wider perspective as applied to the narratives from Veda to Purāṇas. The *arthavādas* about Speech (Goddess Vāc) were dealt with by me in my first book *Aspects of Speech in Vedic Ritual* (Aryan Books International, New Delhi, 1996). The University Grants Commission gave me aid for my project titled "Arthavāda—A Study in Vedic Ritual Reasoning", under the scheme of 'Support for Major Research Project' (1991-1994). At the completion of my project, with the results got by me, related to the cultural history of the Indian society in Vedic times, I had my second book *Vedic Beliefs and Practices through Arthavāda*, in two volumes (Aryan Books International, New Delhi, 2005).

My study of *arthavāda* up to that time was restricted only to the Vedic sphere. But when I was invited to deliver the Keynote Address at the National Seminar on "Kathā in Sanskrit and Prakrit Literature", by the Department of Sanskrit and Prakrit Languages, University of Pune (Feb. 17-19, 2012), I again turned to the topic of *arthavāda*, but from a wider sphere with a new approach. I could find out that it is from the point of view of *arthavāda* that many narratives are given in the Veda, Epics and Mahāpurāṇas. These narratives try to explain the matter in hand, and are full of deeper meanings, which I have tried to reveal here, in my own way. I was rather happily surprised with the results arrived at.

I could know that for every 'change', though slight, in the ancient Indian society and for a new facelift of the society, in the sphere of the code of conduct (*dharma*), the best device has been *arthavāda* in the form of narratives mostly mythical accounts. I could also note that the concept of *arthavāda*, initially from the sphere of the Pūrvamimāṁsā system, where it is related only to *vidhi* (rite or ritual), has been a recourse of the Epics and the Purāṇas (mainly Mahāpurāṇas), to make their standpoint appealing to others, by giving narratives supporting it and glorifying it. Thus giving *arthavāda* in the form of narratives—I call it 'Arthavādaism'—has become a distinguishing mark of this literature. Even while presenting an individual case, the narratives have before them the society at large, its age-old norms as well as its phases. As seen this way, these narratives have functional value as per the needs of the very structure of the society of those times.

My thanks are to Dr. Madhavi Narsalay and Miss Mrunalini Newalkar for the information they gave me about the god Nṛsimha (Narasimha). Similarly, my discussions with Shri Ravindra Lad and Shri Arun Bhandare about the living tradition of the god Nṛsimha proved helpful to me. I thank them for this.

Dr. Brajkishore Swain, Puri, pointed out to me the exact meaning implied of the word 'daïta' in the context of the cult of Lord Jagannātha. Shri P.P. Ramachandran provided me information about the temples of god Brahmā, which, though very few, other than that at Pushkar (near Ajmer, Rajasthan), have to be taken into account. My thanks to these two for their help.

My thanks to Dr. Anjali Bhelande for her valuable suggestions for the book.

Dr. Ashwin Sawant and Dr. (Mrs.) Sucheta Sawant—Ayurvedic practitioners, and also studying for the Ph.D. Degree (in Sanskrit), in the Department of Sanskrit, University of Mumbai—ever ready to help, gave me information about the matters concerning Ayurveda. I have really no words to thank them.

(Mrs.) Ujwala Satam, Director, Accord Institute, Mumbai and Shri Rajiv Satam, Director, Accord Career Solutions and Training, have prepared an apt cover-design of the book, which can serve as a curtain-raiser to the contents inside. My hearty thanks to them, coupled with joy for the bond of friendship.

My sense of gratitude for the scholars whose works were of great help to me, though I have differed from them at many places.

I entrusted the work of publication of this book to Shri Vikas Arya (Aryan Books International, New Delhi), who has been publishing our books (mine and those of my husband (late) Dr. Sadashiv A. Dange) since 1994, with a sense of belonging. He has brought out this book also with the same feeling. I am thankful to him.

I shall feel rewarded if this endeavour of mine proves helpful in knowing the Indian way of looking at things—respecting the 'Old' and accepting the 'New', bridging the two—through narratives, coming as *arthavāda*.

19th May, 2016 **Mrs. Sindhu S. Dange**
Mumbai

Contents

Abbreviations

Āgniv. G.S.	*Āgniveśya Gṛhyasūtra*
Ait. Ār.	*Aitareya Āraṇyaka*
Ait. Br.	*Aitareya Brāhmaṇa*
Āpa. D.S.	*Āpastamba Dharmasūtra*
Āpa. Ś.S.	*Āpastamba Śrautasūtra*
Āśv. G.S.	*Āśvalāyana Gṛhyasūtra*
Āśv. Ś.S.	*Āśvalāyana Śrautasūtra*
AV	*Atharvaveda*
Baudh. D.S.	*Baudhāyana Dharmasūtra*
Baudh. G.S.	*Baudhāyana Gṛhyasūtra*
Baudh. Ś.S.	*Baudhāyana Śrautasūtra*
Bh. G.	*Bhagavadgītā*
Bhāg. P.	*Bhāgavata Purāṇa*
Bhār. G.S.	*Bhāradvāja Gṛhyasūtra*
Bhār. Ś.S.	*Bhāradvāja Śrautasūtra*
Bhav. P.	*Bhaviṣya Purāṇa*
Brah. P.	*Brahmāṇḍa Purāṇa*

Brahmav./Brahmavai. P.	*Brahmavaivarta Purāṇa*
Bṛhad. Up.	*Bṛhadāraṇyakopaniṣad*
Caraka	*Caraka Saṁhitā*
Chand. Up.	*Chāndogya Upaniṣad*
Gar. P.	*Garuḍa Purāṇa*
Gaut. D.S.	*Gautama Dharmasūtra*
Gop. Br.	*Gopatha Brāhmaṇa*
Hiraṇya/Hiraṇyakeśi G.S.	*Hiraṇyakeśi Gṛhyasūtra*
Jaim. Br.	*Jaiminīya Brāhmaṇa*
Jaim. Sū.	*Jaiminīyasūtra*
Kaṭh. G.S.	*Kāṭhaka Gṛhyasūtra*
Kaṭh. Sam.	*Kāṭhaka Saṁhitā*
Kāty. Sm.	*Kātyāyanasmṛti*
Kāty. Ś.S.	*Kātyāyana Śrautasūtra*
Kauṣ. Ār.	*Kauṣītaki Āraṇyaka*
Kauṣ. Br.	*Kauṣītaki Brāhmaṇa*
Kauṣ. Br. Up.	*Kauṣītaki-brāhmaṇa-upaniṣad*
Laṭ. Ś.S.	*Lāṭyāyana Śrautasūtra*
Mait. Sam.	*Maitrāyaṇī Saṁhitā*
Mān. G.S.	*Mānava Gṛhyasūtra*
Mān. Ś.S.	*Mānava Śrautasūtra*
Manu Sm.	*Manusmṛti*
Mārk. P.	*Mārkanḍeya Purāṇa*
Mbh.	*Mahābhārata*
Nir.	*Nirukta*
P.	*Purāṇa*

Pañc. Br.	*Pañcaviṁśa Brāhmaṇa*
Pār. G.S.	*Pāraskara Gṛhyasūtra*
Pūrva.	*Pūrvamīmāṁsāsūtra*
Rām.	*Rāmāyaṇa*
RV	*Ṛgveda*
Ṣaḍ. Br.	*Ṣaḍviṁśa Brāhmaṇa*
Śāṅkh. Ār.	*Śaṅkhāyana Āraṇyaka*
Śaṅkh. Ś.S.	*Śaṇkhāyana Śrautasūtra*
Śat. Br.	*Śatapatha Brāhmaṇa*
Sk. P.	*Skanda Purāṇa*
Suśruta	*Suśruta Saṁhitā*
SV	*Sāmaveda*
Tait. Ār.	*Taittirīya Āraṇyaka*
Tait. Br.	*Taittirīya Brāhmaṇa*
Tait. Sam.	*Taittirīya Saṁhitā*
Taitt. Up.	*Taittirīya Upaniṣad*
Up.	*Upaniṣad*
Vāj. Sam.	*Vājasaneyi Saṁhitā*
Vām. P.	*Vāmana Purāṇa*
Vas. D.S.	*Vasiṣṭha Dharmasūtra*
Vi. P.	*Viṣṇu Purāṇa*
Viṣṇu D.S.	*Viṣṇu Dharmasūtra*
Yājñ. Sm.	*Yājñavalkyasmṛti*
YV	*Yajurveda*
Comm./comm.	Commentary
Sāy.	Sāyaṇa

MODERN TITLES

ABORI	*Annals of the Bhandarkar Oriental Research Institute*
AIOC	All India Oriental Conference
BORI	Bhandarkar Oriental Research Institute
BSOAS	*Bulletin of the School of Oriental and African Studies*
CASS	Centre of Advanced Study in Sanskrit
Ency. PBP.	*Encyclopaedia of Puranic Beliefs and Practices*
ERE	*Encyclopaedia of Religion and Ethics*
GOS	Gaekwar Oriental Series
HDS	*History of Dharmaśāstra*
HOS	Harvard Oriental Series
JAOS	*Journal of the American Oriental Society*
SBE	Sacred Books of the East Series
VVRI	Vishveshvarananda Vedic Research Institute

Introduction

Narrative literature has a definite place in the history of any country. Coming from all strata of the society, which are wide apart from one another on several accounts, this literature presents a panoramic picture of its times and also the varied spheres, from which it has emerged.

On the Indian scene, we have the first prose narratives in the form of mythical accounts in the Vedic ritual-texts in their *arthavāda* sections. Hariappa believes that the practice of preserving the narrations of various events was prevalent in the period of the *RV*, or even earlier[1]. The mythical accounts in the form of long or short narratives, in the Vedic ritual-texts, are joined to the respective *vidhis*, glorifying them or even condemning them, if these *vidhis* are performed wrongly. Thus praise or condemnation (of the wrong *vidhi* i.e. rite or ritual) are the distinguishing characteristics of *arthavāda*. The narratives in the form of mythical accounts, figuring in the *arthavāda* sections, which the later age knew by the term *itihāsa* ('iti-ha-āsa'—'This was so' or 'This happened so') i.e. 'traditional account', were preserved by the Sūta-tradition. Dandekar proposes that right from the beginning, there have been two traditions—that of the *mantras* and the other preserved by the Sūtas.[2] The Sūta-tradition played an important role in the composition and preservation of the secular type of literature, narratives forming a part of this. The Sūta, turned into a Paurāṇika, modern day Purāṇika in India, requires special attention.[3]

As sacrifice was regarded as the origin of Ṛta (fr.√*ṛ*- 'to go on, move')—Order (concerning cosmic, sacrificial and moral contexts), the *arthavāda* portions did not swerve from their aim to extol sacrifice—the very womb (*yoni*—birth-place) of Ṛta. The same Ṛta developed into the concept of Dharma (fr.√*dhṛ*- 'to hold, sustain')—the code of conduct in the society, as per the stages (*āśramas*) in human life as well as the classes (*varṇas*) in the society. The narratives occurring in the two great Epics and the Mahāpurāṇas have this aim in view. In the Epics and the Purāṇas, there never are seen narratives which are purely for entertainment. Tales focussed on pure entertainment form part of the story-literature and Romantic Prose, the latter divided into two categories *viz. kathā* and *ākhyāyikā*—the earlier, denoting a romantic tale and the latter, a legendary tale based on some grain of historical truth. But chronologically these are of much later date.

We have said above that the mythical accounts in the ritual-texts, either of praise or condemnation of *vidhis*, are *arthavādas*, trying in their way to explain the efficacy of the *vidhis*. But the various accounts having at times a grain of historical basis or purely mythical accounts in the Epics and the Purāṇas (Mahāpurāṇas) also come as *arthavādas*. Every time there is no occasion of any rite or ritual (*vidhi*). Many times these tales or (long) narratives are in continuation of the earlier tales or narratives, given in the emboxing style, just to support them and the earlier tales or narratives are the ones, which lay down a rule of conduct. This has become so common in the Epics and the Purāṇas that the narratives here have formed their own style. A new term can be coined namely "Arthavādaism", which is for explaining to the people the matter in hand.

As we know on the ancient Indian scene are found people of diverse races and tribes and they got acculturated fully or partially with the Vedic-brahmanical Hindu Society. The narratives occurring as *arthavāda* throw much light on this and serve to bridge the seemingly inexplicable matters.

Next important topic is of sacrifice. As *arthavāda* is a term primarily dealing with the rites and rituals (*vidhis*) in sacrifice, the ritual-texts, especially the Brāhmaṇa-texts, are replete with *arthavāda*-accounts. An important detail to be noted from this context is of sacrifice or Agni running away from the gods, being bored and tired of the work of carrying oblations to gods. Though such *arthavāda*-accounts, sometimes are for introducing and then extolling a new idea or item in sacrificial performance, these mythical accounts certainly indicate the 'survival' of the fear of losing Fire (Agni), which was in the mind of the early man. Discovery of fire was a great step in the history of human civilisation. Hence, the fear of losing fire might have been reflected in such accounts. As Lang states '.... the savage and the senseless element in mythology is for the most part, a legacy from the ancestors of the civilized races'.[4] He has dealt with the 'survival' of savage mind in the Vedic myths of creation.[5] Though, he has not spoken about the myths of Agni or Sacrifice running away and the gods being desperate searching for it, we can say that here is seen the fear lurking in the ancient mind of losing Agni, which though dormant, is seen here in these myths in one form or the other. References to sacrifices, lasting for many years, even thousand years, occurring especially in the *Pañc. Br.* are not to be taken as speaking of imaginary sacrificies. They have to be taken as sacrificies lasting for the period of infinity. In the Vedic-brahmanical tradition, sacrifice though phenomenal in form, is conceptually eternal and ever-lasting and is the very womb (*yoni*)—the birth-place of Ṛta (Order).

The details of sacrifice of various types were lost or became obsolete in later times or were not thought to be very necessary to be given in a particular account, where that tale or account in Epics and Purāṇas had kept before it some definite purpose. When the Purāṇas state that a certain vow (*vrata*) or a visit to a certain holy place (*tīrtha*) bestows on a person the 'fruit' (i.e. the 'merit' gained) of the Aśvamedha or the Vājapeya sacrifice, the Purāṇas are not bound to give the details of these sacrifices, for their aim is to eulogise that particular vow or pilgrimage to a certain place.

Far behind is left the age of Śrauta rituals, and in the Epic and especially the Puranic Age, the code of conduct ("*dharma*") is seen as prone to get itself simplified and thus appealing and reaching the common masses, including women and *śūdras*, who were denied to study the sacred texts. In this critical period, the *Var. P.* seems to be a lone but bold fighter, prescribing the rite of initiation to the *śūdras* (chaps. 127-28) and somewhat laxity in restrictions for women.[6] Hence, the references to Vedic sacrificies (commonly mentioned being Aśvamedha and Vājapeya) and the 'fruits' of these promised by the Purāṇas for following the *dharma* of *dānas*, *vratas* and *visits* to *tīrthas* are to be taken into account with a proper understanding of those times.

The concept of *dāna*, *vrata* (vow), *upavāsa* and importance given to waters as the purifying agent has to be traced to the Veda, especially the Brāhmaṇa-texts. The ritual-texts speak of the *dakṣiṇās* to be given to the priests, acting as a precursor to the Puranic *dānas*, which are given not exclusively to the priests. The sacrificer consecrated for sacrifice is required to follow a vow with many rules and has to subsist on 'fast-milk' (*vrata-dughā* cow giving this milk). The waters form the indispensable purifying agent in the Vedic sacrifice and are also connected with the sacrificial fire as the Vasatīvarī, Praṇītā, Nigrābhyā and Ekadhanā waters.

When we come to the Epics and the Purāṇas, we find utmost importance given to these, supported and extolled by various mythical accounts, coming as *arthavāda*.

To note some examples of *dāna, vrata* (*upavāsa* included in it) and visit to holy places (*tīrthas*), most of which are on the banks of rivers.

A unique *dāna* is that of symbolic cows, of jaggery, ghee, sesame, sugar, milk, juice etc. The *Agni P.* (210.13 ab) says that for making the cows containing liquids, jars should be used, while for forming the cows containing solid matter like sesame, jaggery etc., heaps are to be formed. By the time of the Epic-Puranic Age, so much importance is seen attached to the cow that the very Mother Earth is said to have taken the form of a cow, when she is overburdened with the sinful persons. That the Mother Earth is regarded as a 'milch cow' can be seen in the mythical account of king Pṛthu, when he becomes a calf, milking the Mother Earth, making her yield all her treasures for the human race (*Bhāg. P.* IV, chap. 18). Another important *dāna* (giving away gift) is of the symbolic mountains, which are of eatables, precious metals and precious stones as also of elephants, cows, horses etc. The idea underlying the *dāna* of symbolic mountains is that of awe mixed with wonder felt for a mountain and can go back to the mountain-worshipping cult, indicated through the episode of the Govardhana mountain. Kṛṣṇa gave uplift to the folk-tradition of worshipping a mountain for getting rains, as against the age-old Vedic tradition of worshipping the Rain-god Indra, by offering him sacrifice.

From among the vows (*vratas*), two important ones can be named here. One is the Vaṭasāvitrīvrata, it being well known and practised in almost all provinces in India (even to this day) by the married women. Another one is the Kokilāvrata, in which a cuckoo is worshipped as a goddess. Observing a fast is generally accompanying a *vrata* (vow).

And to come to the point of pilgrimage (*tīrthayātrā*). The *Mbh.* and especially the Purāṇas are short of eulogising words for the places of pilgrimage, which mostly are on the banks of rivers. Here we have a mention of the Nāgatīrthas, which shows how the Nāgas were not only completely acculturated with the Vedic-brahmanical Hindu society, but also received homage by having places of pilgrimage.

The merit promised for giving the *dānas* or by having pilgrimage is said to be the same which a person can get after performing the Vājapeya and Aśvamedha sacrifices. Thus the efforts are to make the common masses, including women and *sūdras*, an important section of the social structure, which undoubtedly they were, but many times for namesake. Without actually spending any wealth or man-power on big sacrifices (small ones included), the common masses could aspire to get the 'fruit' (i.e. merit-*"puṇya"*) of these sacrifices, for *dāna* or pilgrimage was to be taken on individual level, involving less trouble and difficulties. In kind words, the Purāṇas say that even by listening to the importance of the *dāna* of the symbolic mountain or by simply observing that ritual, a poor person can go to heaven. Even reading the verses about the gift of mountains will nullify the effect of evil dreams and fear of mundane existence (*Matsya P.* 92.17-34; *Bhaviṣya P.* Uttara-parva 204.17cd-38).

Being confronted by the popularity of the Buddhist and Jain faiths, the old Vedic-brahmanical religion had to go in for new facelift. These two faiths were averse to priestly domination and class (*varṇa*) and caste (*jāti*) discrimination, giving stress more on purity of thought, speech and action rather than ritualdom. In such circumstances, the old Vedic-brahminical Hindu religion had to frame a new pattern for its code of conduct (*dharma*), which had its one foot in the old tradition and the other in the newly envisaged province, thus assuring one and all, the merit of sacrifices by going in for *dāna*, *vrata* (also *upavāsa*) and *tīrthayātrā*. These were the four pillars with the support of which, the old Vedic-brahmanical Hindu (from the Puranic period onwards, we can give the name 'Hindu') religion once again thrived well and became more prone to people. In this great task, the narratives or the mythical accounts in the *Mbh.* and the Purāṇas, coming as *arthavāda* (many times irrespective of any *vidhi*) proved to be of great help, by explaining to the listeners or readers the new face of the old *dharma*. While dealing with *dāna*, *vrata* (also *upavāsa*) and *tīrthayātrā*, only selected examples are taken note of and discussed in details, lest it would be too unwieldy an effort.

To come to the Curses, Boons and Oaths or Swearings. These figure in the mythical accounts as *arthavāda* but with definite purpose, not connected with any *vidhi* (ritual) and by no speck of imagination there could be any.

Actually these three — Curses, Boons and Oaths deal with 'spoken words'. The efficacy of the spoken word was no doubt preceded by the efficacy of emotion, of inarticulate wish or will.[7] While 'curse' springs from bad intention of doing harm to the other, 'boon' is given for other person's penance or service or devotion. And about 'oath', Westermarck notes—"An oath is essentially a conditional self-imprecation, a curse by which a person calls down upon himself some evil in the event of what he says not being true."[8] To put it in short, oath is a self-inflicted curse.

The Epics and Purāṇas abound in the accounts of curses, boons and on rare occasions, we have the accounts of oath or swearing. Though every mythical account of curse or boon will not divulge the secret of a historical fact, there are some *arthavāda*-accounts which serve as a pointer to historical fact or social phenomenon. The double-curse given to king Saudāsa—turned Kalmāṣapāda—can unearth an historical fact. The curse given by Bṛhaspati to Mamatā's—his elder sister-in-law's foetus (later on born as a blind child Dīrghatamas) speaks of a social custom of regarding 'a girl given in marriage as belonging to her husband's family'. The curse given to Yama (Dharma) by the sage Aṇimāṇḍavya is a strategy to give a logical explanation for the fact that even though a son of a maid-servant (*dāsī*), Vidura the wisest one from the Kaurava side, was in reality Dharma (a *brāhmaṇa*) reborn. The curse here thus tries to clear the contradiction between Vidura's low birth and his superb wisdom. Can we say that this is an 'apology' under the garb of a curse, as the caste-system had become deep-rooted in the then society by the Puranic period?

The curses given to Rāvaṇa are taken note of, for they can stand as evidence for the chastity of Sīta, when she was made to stay after being kidnapped, in the vicinity of Rāvaṇa's palace. Due to the curses Rāvaṇa could not dare even to simply touch her. He was cursed by the nymph Puñjikasthalā and then by Rambhā the wife of Nalakūbara, for he raped them. The curse was a stern warning that if Rāvaṇa ever even touched a woman (other than his wife), he would immediately meet his death. Again, the bitter prophecy from the mouth of Vedavatī, when Rāvaṇa molested her by pulling her hair was near to curse. She said that she would have, in her next life, unnatural birth and would be a righteous woman bringing death and destruction of Rāvaṇa, and she was Sītā, generations after generations taken to be 'Chastity' incarnate.

Curses flung on the sinners for disobeying elders, disrespecting preceptors, feeling proud of handsomeness or riches and becoming insolent thereby, are too common in the Epics and the Purāṇas to have a separate mention here. These are all dealt with in the V chapter.

Boons have also such an efficacy. In the *Rām.*, Rāvaṇa for practising penance gets a boon that he will be invincible and will not be killed by any human being. And he met his death by the arrow of Rāma, who though a human being was in fact god Viṣṇu taking birth as a human. This explains why Rāvaṇa could be so insolent and belligerent in his behaviour (obviously being assured by the boon).

Among oaths, the oaths taken by the sages in the *Mbh.* have been taken into consideration. These oaths are from the sages, when they were charged with the offence of stealing the lotus-stalks. It is seen that such a tale was current right from the times of the *Ait. Br.*, which mentions it in a *gāthā* (*Ait. Br.* V.30=25.5). As *gāthā* forms part of the secular tradition (Sūta-tradition), which is many times in the form of floating literature, the *Mbh.* could readily make use of it. The *gāthā* does not make mention of any specific persons, but the *Mbh.* coined a mythical account giving the names of persons, taking oath to prove their innocence.

The last chaper deals with miscellaneous points pertaining to gods and goddesses, the latter of various kinds and names. Of interest is the point of Father-god Brahmā, having very few temples, for he was admonished by lord Siva for his passionate nature and insolent behaviour, and was severely warned that he would not be offered any worship (*pūja*), nor will he have any temple of his. Hence, the only temple worth the name is at Pushkar near Ajmer in the Rajasthan State (India), and a couple of minor ones.

About god Śiva, his *gaṇas* (attendants-cum-associates) are framed on the lines of the *rakṣases* of grotesque appearance from the *AV*, and tailored on the *gaṇa* of the Maruts, the difference being that they are framed as becoming the devotees of lord Śiva sooner or later.

About the incarnations (*avatāras*) of Viṣṇu. The first three avatāras are from the secular or ritualistic tradition of beliefs about the inherent power of the creatures viz. fish, tortoise and boar. The dwarf-incarnation has certainly at its basis the belief about the extraordinary powers inherent in human beings of abnormal statures. Viṣṇu as a dwarf reminds us of this world-wide belief. Again the supreme powers possessed by a *baṭu* (a boy who has undergone initiation) are to be noted in this connection, for the dwarf Viṣṇu comes in the form of a *baṭu* to the royal palace of king Bali. The Nṛsiṁha or Narasiṁha incarnation dates from the *Mbh.* and the Purāṇas and speaks of the conditions granted to the *asura* Hiraṇyakaśipu on his word, when he was asking the boon of non-death. These conditions are practically the same as were asked by Namuci in the Brāhmaṇa-texts. However, a point to be noted in this connection is that in India, in the state of Maharashtra, right from 15th or 16th cent. AD or even prior to this period, in the writings of the Marathi saints, and even in the living tradition, Narasiṁha has been taken to be a ferocious deity, having mainly malevolent but when propitiated, benevolent traits.

About the tenth *avatāra* Kalki, who is presented as a warrior, coming with a sword in his hand, riding a horse and devastating all the *mlecchas*. Here, it is important to note the information provided by the work *Kālacakratantra*, quite wellknown in the tantric tradition of the Vajrayāna Buddhism. This Tantra is said to have been popularised by the king named Yaśa (Manjuśrīyaśa) of the Kalki gotra in the country Sambhala (*Kālacakra* I.26). The prophecy given here is that 800 years after this king, in the same family will be born, the king Raudracakrī, who will devastate all the *mlecchas*, and will bestow upon his friends *viz.* Rudra, Skanda, Gaṇeśa and Viṣṇu, who help him in his endeavour, horses, elephants, golden chariots and fighters (*ibid.*, I. 160-61).

Here, Kalki is said to be one, who has made *Kalka* i.e. perfect intermixture, of all the *varṇas* with their traits so amalgamated as to be beyond recognition. This etymology is certainly to criticise the Vedic-brahmanical Hindu view of the society based on *varṇa* (class) and caste (*jāti*). We have pointed out in the chapter in the context of the Kalki *avatāra* that Gonda has concentrated on the 'horse' of the rider, while we have taken Kalki riding the horse to be the representation of a king, wielding his power to vanquish and if need be to smash the evil forces. Even Jaiswal has maintained this stand regarding Kalki. The work *Kālacakratrantra* composed in the 11th cent. AD describing the heroic exploits of king Raudracakrī of the Kalki *gotra* and particularly the exploits of killing all the *mlecchas*, only follows this tradition about the Kalki incarnation and leaves no scope for any other interpretation.

The cult of Jagannātha is an interesting topic of study. Jagannātha later on is identified with Kṛṣṇa and Viṣṇu. It is near to certainty if we maintain that the very god in the form of Nīlamādhava ('Blue or Black Stone') and also in the form of wooden images is a gift from the aboriginal tribe of the Śabaras. The mythical tale of king Indradyumna coming as *arthavāda* in the Purāṇas only supports this. In this tale from the *Sk. P.* we note Brahmā telling through Nārada to the king Indradyumna to construct a Nṛsiṁha temple and perform a sacrifice in his honour. And even to this day the practice prevalent is of consecrating the 'new' ('reborn' at the Navakalevara rite) images with the 32-syllabic Mantrarāja of Nṛsiṁha and giving of offerings in the sacrificial fire with this Mantrarāja of Nṛsiṁha as well as the Pātāla-Nṛsiṁha. The temple of Nṛsiṁha is still existent in the precincts of the Jagannātha temple.

This makes us think a while on the role of Nṛsiṁha in the cult of Jagannātha. To say that Nṛsiṁha is one of the *avatāras* of Viṣṇu with whom lord Jagannātha is identified and hence importance of Nṛsiṁha in the rites and rituals of Jagannātha, is perfectly logical. But such a thought leads us to 'simple equation', leaving the problem not solved satisfactorily. Let us start from the mythical tale of Indradyuma again. As seen in it, there are two stages spoken of 1. Nīlamādhava—The Blue Stone; 2. As per the prophecy, it being disappeared, the installation of the new wooden images.

There is a folk-tradition, in which it is believed that actually these two, mentioned above, were two different cults, later on mingled together—one worshipping 'stone', another worshipping 'wooden image'.

The point is, how is it that of all the *avatāras* of Viṣṇu, Nṛsiṁha alone could be chosen here? Is it because of the tribal origin of the Jagannātha cult (as the mythical account of the king Indradyumna indicates) and the unusual shape (from the point of view of Indian iconography) and appearance of the images, that the fierce aspect of Viṣṇu in the form of Nṛsiṁha could be related here and could be the presiding deity of the important temple-rituals here? We have already seen that in the prevalent tradition of Maharashtra state, dating at least from the 15th cent. AD or even prior to that, Nṛsiṁha or Narasiṁha initially is taken to be a deity having malevolent traits. Was such a tradition prevalent when the cult of lord Jagannātha came to the fore-front at the time of the Purāṇas, especially the *Sk.P.*? Until we give a proper thought to this, the enigmatic problem will remain unsolved! In this very chapter, the tree-goddesses are taken note of. These are from the Purāṇas, by the time of which the science of Indian Medicine (Āyurveda), deep-rooted in the tradition from the Upaniṣadic period, had reached its zenith. It is the medicinal properties of these trees and plant like Tulasi[9] that made them have the 'cap' of the God-head and the mythical accounts coming as *arthavāda* are given to extol these.

Falling in line with the trees, are the rivers, which are regarded as goddesses, the principle of 'animism' working here prominently. The multiple use of waters, their quality to purify things and even wipe of sin—all these have made the rivers 'anthropomorphised' and thus showing some rivers as the wives of human heroes and giving them heroic sons.

The narratives or the mythical accounts, coming as *arthavāda* have at every place supported the issues discussed in the multi-faceted ancient Indian tradition from Veda to Purāṇas. In spite of *arthavāda* being a term strictly from the Pūrvamīmāṁsā context, glorifying only the ritual (*vidhi*) which is enjoined, it has assumed various dimensions, beyond remaining simply as a *vidhi*-oriented device. It figures at several places, where there is no reference directly to rite or ritual. Many times, one tale (of the nature of *arthavāda*) is given to support the previous tale and the previous tale comes to extol a particular norm of behaviour. All these mythical accounts or narratives are given mainly to support *dharma*—the code of conduct, which is to be practised. Thus in essence, it is the *'vidhi'* (of practising *'dharma'*), that is glorified by these *arthavādas*, in the form of narratives. But this *'vidhi-arthavāda'* relationship is beyond the pale of the strict ritualistic colour, envisaged in the Pūrvamīmāṁsa system of philosophy.

Thus, in the long journey of the ancient Indian Society, from the Veda to the Purāṇas, the narratives coming as *arthavāda* have become so indispensable due to their functional use as to form a style of their own of explaining matters to readers or listeners. Following the principles of 'Change' and 'Continuity', the (partial) switch over, undertaken in a gentle and soft way, from 'Old' to 'New' as per the structural need of the society at a particular period, has been possible only through narratives having their unique style, which we call 'Arthavādaism'.

NOTES AND REFERENCES

1. H.L. Hariappa, *Ṛgvedic Legends through the Ages*, Deccan College, Poona 1953, p. 132.
2. R.N. Dandekar, "The Mahābhārata: Origin and Growth", University of Ceylon Review, 12, 1954, p. 65.
3. See for this Appendix - A, Sūta-Chronicler, Composer and Narrator.
4. See A. Lang, *Myth, Ritual and Religion*, Vol. I, Longman's Green and Company, London, 1913 (1887), p. 35.
5. *Ibid.*, p. 230.
6. See Sindhu S. Dange, "Puranic Rules of Dharma and Human Rights for Śūdras and Women", *Dharmaśāstra and Human Rights*, (Proceedings of the National Seminar on 'Dharmaśāstra and Human Rights', CASS, University of Pune, 2010), ed. by Ujjwala Jha, New Bharatiya Book Corporation, Delhi, 2011, pp. 192-202.
7. J. Hastings (ed.), *ERE*, Vol. IX, 430a.
8. *Ibid.*
9. See for this Appendix B, Puranic Tree-goddesses—Their Medicinal Basis.

CHAPTER 1

Arthavāda as a Device

The fundamental trait of the Indian civilization has been described as a Harmony of Contrasts or as a Synthesis creating a Unity out of Diversity.[1] This synthesizing tendency is evolved from very ancient times, due to the presence on the Indian scene, of different people with their diverse languages and cultures and modes of living and thinking.[2] It was the Vedic period, which witnessed the creation of the Indian Man says Thomas.[3]

Though a creation of the Vedic times, the true picture of the Indian Man, mostly remaining the same in later times, can be seen only in the Epic and Puranic period, which saw the evolution of several new concepts and their practices, mingled in the old social structure. From that period onwards, the Indian Man has been following the *śrutismṛtipurāṇokta* tradition—the tradition coming from the Veda, Dharmaśāstra, the *Mbh.* to be coupled with this and the Purāṇas. But this tradition has never been rigid, for it was dependent on the concept of *dharma*—code of conduct—which was never static but invited change, never losing sight of continuity with the old.

Manu regarded to be the first law-giver, has laid down four norms for the practice of *dharma viz.* the entire Veda, which is the very root of *dharma*; the stored (i.e. remembered) knowledge and the conduct of the knowers of Veda; the practices of the righteous persons and; lastly one's own satisfaction, obviously based on one's own conscience (*Manu Sm.* II.6). Yājñavalkya adds one more —'the desire issuing forth from the right thought' (*Yājñ.Sm.* I.7). When Manu says that in the Kṛta Age (*yuga*), different were the *dharmas*, different again in the Tretā and Dvāpara Ages and still different in the Kali Age (*Manu Sm.* I.85), he intends to lay down that the practices even though once ideal, are prone to change with the passage of time. *Gaut. D.S.* points out that the *dharmas* pertaining to land, country caste and family are to be regarded as 'norms', if they are not opposed to the Veda (11.20). *Vas. D.S.* states that as per Manu's words, in the absence of any help from the Veda, the *dharmas* pertaining to country, caste and family be accepted (1.17). Manu goes to the extent of saying that the *dharmas* even of persons opposed to Veda (*pāṣaṇḍagaṇadharmas*) are to be taken into account (*Manu Sm.* I.118). *Āpa. D.S.* says that some *dharmas,* which cannot be traced to any text can be known from the women of all *varṇas* (II.11.19). This is obviously because women in the society are the source-books of living traditions. All these words coming from the ancient Indian law-givers clearly point out that the *dharma* in India has always been related to all strata of the society, for which it was meant. Apart from the *Śruti* (Veda) and *Smṛti* (Dharmaśāstra texts), the two more norms of *dharma,* which we have already noted above *viz.* the practices of the righteous persons (*Sadācāra*) in a particular period (in the society) and the decision taken according to one's own conscience, very well justify the changes in the practice of *dharma.* Hence there never has been any contradiction in the rules and practices laid down.

Here is taken into account a tale, which occurs in the Śāntiparvan of the *Mbh.* (chap. 272), which clearly points out how the concept of *dharma* centering round animal-sacrifice (in the Vedic ritual tradition) has totally changed and propounds the principle of non-injury (*ahiṁsā*), and that too from the mouth of Dharma incarnate. The tale runs as follows — There lived a *brāhmaṇa*, who followed *uñchavṛtti* (i.e. was living only on the grains, which naturally fell on the ground from the ears of corn). Once he wanted to perform a sacrifice, not having any desire whatsoever in his mind. Being intent on avoiding any kind of injury to any animal, he collected roots and leaves as the material for the sacrifice. A deer (who was Dharma himself and wanted to test the *brāhmaṇa*), staying nearby in that forest region saw this preparation of the sacrifice and approached the *brāhmaṇa*. He told the *brāhmaṇa* that the latter's sacrifice was devoid of any desire and was not having any sacrificial animal to be offered. So the deer requested the *brāhmaṇa* to make him (i.e. deer) the sacrificial animal. The *brāhmaṇa* strongly refused this. Then came out Sāvitrī from fire (Agni) and insisted that the deer's suggestion be followed. The *brāhmaṇa* again declined and Sāvitrī (displeased!) entered into the sacrificial fire. As the last attempt, the deer allured the *brāhmaṇa* by giving him a 'divine eye' to see the celestial nymphs and the aerial cars. Suddenly the desire to get the heavenly pleasures dawned upon the *brāhmaṇa's* mind and he gave the offering of the deer in his sacrifice. But the deer was Dharma himself, who (as noted above) wanted to test the *brāhmaṇa*. Thus committing injury by killing the deer, the *brāhmaṇa* lost all his stored merit. The *Mbh.* here declares that non-injury (*ahiṁsā*) is the only *dharma* and the *dharma* involving injury is bad. Here Dharma himself, who has appeared in the form of a deer, teaches this altogether different type of sacrifice, hitherto unknown, to the *brāhmaṇa* who interestingly is named 'Satya' (truth). This tale is significant, for it points out the new turn given to the old sacrificial *dharma*, which involved killing of the animal. The tale propounds the principle of non-injury (*ahiṁsā*) in sacrifice, on the background of the old thought of sacrificial killing of the animal, prevalent in the

Vedic period. In the Vedic period, sacrificial killing of the animal was regarded as a means of *dharma* (an oft-repeated statement-*yajñiyā hiṁsā dharmasādhanam* /). But in the changed times with the influence of the two faiths—Jainism and Buddhism—the old practice had to be discarded. The tale from the *Mbh.* noted above bears this very fact, validating Manu's words (*Manu Sm.* I.85) that in every Age, there ought to be changes in the *dharmas,* and hence they are different in every Age. Heesterman has missed this important point in the tradition of *dharma* in India, when he says—"The dharma's total dependence on the Veda is clearly a pious fiction. In some respects, the two are even incompatible. This is the case in the tangled matter of animal sacrifice, enjoined in Vedic ritual but against the dharma's rule of *ahiṁsā,* which prohibits the taking of any life", and further, "The solution is reasonable enough but, at the same time, it makes the gap between Veda and dharma all the more glaring".[4]

It is very patent that the tale from the *Mbh.* is ushered in, to explain to the listeners or readers of the new trend in the old sacrificial system. And here we come to the Indian way of explaining. The Indian way of explaining has been a unique one and it is of glorifying the prescribed matter in hand or condemning what is not according to the norm. This way of explaining dates back to the period of the Brāhmaṇa-texts, which are the ritual-texts and which employ this method under the name *arthavāda.*

The Veda is comprised of *mantras* and *brāhmaṇas.* The *mantras* make the performer remember the topics (*arthas*), which are invariably associated with the performance of the ritual.[5] The nature of the *brāhmaṇa*-portions is explained by the *Āpa. Ś.S.* as injunctions for performing the rites (XXIV.1.32). The instructions of such rites (*vidhis*) cannot be acquired from any other source except the *brāhmaṇa*[6]. The last part of the *brāhmaṇa*-portion is termed *arthavāda.*[7] *Arthavāda* is defined as a statement containing either praise (*prāśastya*) of the enjoined or condemnation (*nindā*) of the prohibited.[8] *Āpa. Ś.S* states four types of *arthvāda* and lays down with *prāśastya* and *nindā* two more types of *arthavāda viz. parakṛti* and *purākalpa* (XXIV. 1.33). *Parakṛti* states what has been done in the past by a single person, while in the *purākalpa* occurs what has been done in the past by two or more persons. All these four types stem from the sphere of sacrifice and the accounts occurring in them are obviously from the same context. In *parakṛti* we note the sacrificial performances of the celebrated ritualists and in *purākalpa* occur the olden accounts of the sacrifices performed by gods as well as men of antiquity. Śabarasvāmin has added eight more types of *arthavāda* under the *sūtra* (*Jaimini*. II.1.33), but they conform more to the manner of expressing the matter in hand and hardly differ in contents, which we have noted in the four types.

Arthavāda is broadly classified in three types *viz. Guṇavāda, Anuvāda* and *Bhūtārthavāda*.

1. *Guṇavāda* — e.g. *ādityo yūpaḥ*— 'The sacrificial post is the sun'. This statement, contrary to our direct perception, is to be understood by indication (*lakṣaṇā*) based on the quality (*guṇa*) of lustre, for both the sacrificial post and the sun are lustrous in appearance. This leads to their identification.
2. *Anuvāda—agnirhimasya bheṣajam* — 'Agni is a remedy against cold.' This statement simply confirms the quality of Agni, which is known to us by direct perception.
3. *Bhūtārthavāda—indro vṛtrāya vadham udayacchat*—'Indra raised the weapon i.e. thunderbolt, for striking Vṛtra'. Not coming into conflict with any means of knowledge, such as direct perception etc., this type simply embodies a statement of an event of past times.

The *arthvāda*-portions in the Vedic ritual-texts are not taken as expressing their meanings for their own sake. If they are taken so, it may lead to an occasion of undesirable contingency of having irrelevant portions in the Veda, which has only ritual in view. Whatever is not related to any ritual, will stand as irrelevant.[9] As the Vedic portions are to be recited daily as study (*svādhyāya*), all the Vedic portions have to be meaningful and also relevant. The *arthavāda*-portions also are to be regarded as meaningful and relevant. With this aim, the Mīmaṁsakas had to discuss at length the point of relevance of the *arthavāda*. Jaimini has dealt in details with the propriety and status of the *arthavāda*-portions of the Vedic ritual-texts (Pūrva. I.2.1-18). Sāyaṇa states that Jaimini had taken great pains to establish the authoritativeness of the *arthavāda*-portions.[10]

In this respect, it is necessary to take into account the doctrine of *ekavākyatā* (syntactical connection) used by the Mīmāṁsakas. Navathe has dealt with this topic in details.[11] The doctrine of *ekavākyatā* is taken by the older Mīmāṁsakas to denote *padaikavākyatā*, which takes place through a single word (*pada*) viz. *praśasta*—'commended'. The statement of injunction (*vidhi*) for example, from the animal-sacrifice, is—*vāyavyam śvetamālabheta bhūtikāmaḥ*. One desirous of prosperity should sacrifice a white (animal, normally a goat) to Vāyu.[12] Mādhavācārya, who accepts the *vākyaikavākyatā* of the *arthavādas* strongly rejects this view. The statement of injunction (*vidhivākya*) expects the ritual act enjoined by it to be commended, for this commendation would impel a person to undertake this act. On the other hand, the statement of *arthavāda* expects some ritual act (*vidhi*), as its very nature is to praise the *vidhi* or to condemn the prohibited *vidhi*. So it fulfils the expectation of the statement of *vidhi* of commending its ritual act. Thus the *arthavāda* has *vakytaikavākyatā* (syntactical relation through sentence) with the *vidhi* and stands as a part of the latter.[13]

While taking into account the texture of *vidhi* and that of its *arthavāda*, it has to be pointed out that they differ a lot. While the statements of *vidhi* are direct (being injunctions) and many times pithy, those of *arthavāda* are elaborate, for their very nature is declamatory. The statements of *arthavāda*, in spite of their ritual set-up, comprise etymologies, beliefs and practices prevalent in those times also those of olden times, mythical accounts, legendary accounts, ethical and moral rules, *gāthās*, *ślokas* etc. The secular tradition plays a vital role in bringing here most of these, which are pressed into service to help the Vedic ritual tradition of the *vidhis*, by commending them. Much can be said about the secular tradition which stems from the people at large, grows and flourishes independently. *Arthavāda* thus many times catches the finger of the secular tradition and comes to the profane level, never losing sight of its aim to commend the ritual, for which it is framed.

The 'secular' or 'profane' rendering help to the 'sacred' can be marked from a parallel from the western world. From the Middle Ages, England and France had groups of travelling entertainers, which were known to the French as *jongleurs*. The performances of these wandering groups attracted the attention of the Church, which thereafter started arranging religious plays drawn from the *Bible*, at first on the occasions of Christmas or Easter, suiting to those occasions. From the great storehouse—the *Bible*—inside the church were shown several other events in dramatic form.[14] The present author has discussed this topic in details in her book *Vedic Beliefs and Practices through Arthavāda*.

While tracing the history of the French epic, beginning about the middle of the eleventh century, perhaps a little later, Marc Bloch notes how the "Folk Memory" helped in spreading the epic gestes, which were in theory not intended to be read. They were made to be declaimed or rather chanted, and they went the rounds from castle to castle or from public square to public square with professional reciters called *jongleurs*. These performers were sometimes also the authors of the poems. Thus some *jongleurs* performed the compositions of someone else; others recited poems of which they were themselves the original 'inventors' (*trouvères*).[15] On the Indian scene, this phenomenon of transmitting the treasure of information to populace was in vogue through the Sūta-tradition, dating from the Vedic Times—nay even prior to that period, as we shall see further in this very chapter.

The point is of *arthavāda* commending and supporting the *vidhi*, at times validating the *vidhi*. It has to be noted here that condemning the prohibited *vidhi*, from another point of view, amounts to commending its opposite i.e. the prescribed *vidhi*. The role of *arthavāda* is thus functional, either by commending (*prāśastya*) or condemning (*nindā*).

Here is taken into account a concept parallel to *arthavāda*, from the western world, from the sphere of sociology and it is of 'Functionalism'. The first sociologist to think of this concept and its scope was Auguste Comte (1798-1857). Next comes Herbert Spencer (1820-1903) and thereafter Emile Durkheim (1858-1917). But the proper direction to the study of Functionalism was given initially by A.R. Radcliff-Brown (1881-1955) and then by Bronislaw Malinowski (1884-1942)—the social anthropologist—who collected the data for his studies by field-work.[16] Malinowski gained name due to his studies of the indigenous people of the Trobriand Islands off New Guinea (situated slightly north to Australia in the Pacific Ocean).[17] His stay there was from 1915-1918, in which period he noticed that the islanders had three kinds of stories *viz.* 1. Personal experiences; 2. Hearsay tales (legends, folk-tales etc.) for amusement; 3. Myths or Sacred tales, venerated and connected to social action and behaviour. In his opinion, this last type of tales is to be noted, as they serve as the validations of established practices and institutions or social action and behaviour. He pointed out that myths percolated to societies that could not be called primitive, and that like rituals, myths performed a specific function in the society, in which they were formulated and that whatever was their meaning, they could be grasped only by a functional analysis, which related them to social and economic institutions.[18] Thus, according to Malinowski, myths associated with the rituals can be understood on the basis of Functionalism or if they validate the rituals, being repeated regularly at the time of the rituals, they are to be interpreted on the basis of Charter-theory. Such validatory myths, which are repeated regularly at the performance of the rituals are the 'Charter-myths', according to him.

As a matter of fact, the word 'function' may simply give the idea of purpose and the types of function (purpose) occurring in myths or mythical accounts can be given as follows.[19]

A. Primarily narrative and entertaining;
B. Operative (Ritualistic); Iterative (Repetitive); and Validatory (Justificatory);
C. Speculative and Explanatory;
D. Eschatological.

These types of function can be applied not only to the myths or mythical accounts but also to several stories, narratives, in fact all matters which can be covered under the title *arthavāda*, the topic presently at hand. To deal with these types of function in details—

A. PRIMARILY NARRATIVE AND ENTERTAINING

Here are under this type, the works of Romantic Prose in Sanskrit *viz. Kādambarī, Vāsavadattā, Daśakumāracarita, Śukasaptati, Vetālapañcaviṁśati, Siṁhāsanadvātriṁśikā,* though in the latter three narrative works, together with entertainment is marked the 'didactic' purpose, as it is in the works *Pañcatantra* and *Hitopadeśa.*

As compared to this narrative literature, which has more or less 'entertainment' in view, the *arthavāda* as a device, springing from the Brāhmaṇa-texts for their rites and rituals, but having its span up to the Epics and Purāṇas and even further, is hardly for entertainment, for its sole aim is praise (*prāśastya*) or condemnation (*nindā*), as we have noted earlier. That there was no feature for pure amusement or relaxation in the Vedic ritual can be seen from the example of the Mahāvrata festival, which does not figure as an *arthavāda*-portion or even in the discussion about it. The Mahāvrata festival is held on the penultimate day in the Gavāmayana *sattra* and is specially meant for Prajapati. Several features from folk-culture figure in the Mahāvrata.[20] To see some significant features in short—the contest between an *ārya* and a *śūdra* for a white circular hide (symbol of the sun!) and the *ārya* to win it; a harlot and a *brahmacārin* abusing each other in the northern side of the altar; sexual union between a man and a woman, in a screened shade to the south of the Mārjālīya fire-place; beating of drums; the wives of the sacrificer singing in chorus; eight servants and maids or slaves and slave-girls, placing water-jars on their heads, dancing thrice round the Mārjālīya fire-place and singing popular songs in which cows (rain-showers!!) are lauded as 'mothers of ghee'. Though Kane rightly states that the Mahāvrata was some folk-festival in the hoary past and it was welded on to the solemn Vedic sacrifices[21], we cannot agree with him when he says that the Mahāvrata festival was for "relaxation after the weary days and months of sacrifices".[22] The various features noted above have the motif of fertility *viz.* the gain of the sun for getting the seasons at proper times, the sexual charms and the sexual act as an aid to fertility and the popular songs invoking in their own way the rain-showers ('mothers of ghee'-cows). Hence this particular rite was attached to the Gavāmayana rite, which is a series of Soma-sacrifices extending over twelve months and which is performed for various rewards such as prosperity (timely rains), progeny etc. Thus though not an *arthavāda*, the Mahāvrata festival points out that it was not for entertainment. In fact the ritual-texts (Veda), Epics and Purāṇas (the last type of literature in spite of its simple style) were never meant for entertainment, though Epics and Purāṇas were narrative in form.

To turn to the remaining types of function, which we have noted—

B. OPERATIVE (RITUALISTIC); ITERATIVE (REPETITIVE) AND VALIDATORY (JUSTIFICATORY).

Many *arthavādas*, attached to the rituals and hence figuring with them, starting from the period of the Veda (ritual-texts) and reaching up to and covering the Puranic period (and still on its march further) are of this type. These *arthavādas* in the form of mythical accounts, are repeated regularly at rituals or on ceremonial occasions. Thus, they are ritualistic ('Operative') and repetitive ('Iterative'). At times the accounts are told or recited regularly to justify the rituals. These are 'Validatory' in nature. They get the status of a 'charter'. To take some examples. The mythical account of the flood figuring Manu and the fish and Manu's daughter Iḍā-(*ghṛtapadī*-'ghee-footed) born from the sacrifice performed by Manu after the deluge, given in the context of the *iḍā*-offering. From the Puranic context, we take the Satyanārāyaṇa-vrata, which is very popular in Bengal and Maharashtra. It is described in the *Bhaviṣya P.* (Pratisargaparva chapters 24-29). It occurs in the Revā-khaṇḍa of the *Sk.P.* (Vaṅgavāsī ed.) but does not occur in the Venkateshvara Press edition. It is said that Nārada was told about this *vrata* by Viṣṇu himself. After worshipping Satyanārāyaṇa the performer has to listen to the stories and then partake of the *prasāda*.[23] The stories are about a *brāhmaṇa* who performed this *vrata* every month, of a vendor of wood, of a trader Sādhu with a ship full of merchandise and costly things and his daughter Kalāvatī. The stories are said to have been taken from the *Sk.P.* from its Revā-khaṇḍa.[24] These stories are the *arthavādas* validating the Satyanārāyaṇavrata and thus have the status of a 'charter'. There are several tales which are told or recited to justify the rituals of worship. We have the various stories (*kahāṇīs*) occurring as *arthavādas* in the worship of various gods and goddesses in the month of

Śrāvaṇa (in the Hindu almanac), prevalent in the state of Maharashtra, India. Several such stories (*kahāṇīs*) are published and are in print form.

But there are many stories which are folk-tales and which travel by word of mouth. Here is a tale current in the Vidarbha region (in the state of Maharashtra), which is told and heard (as a part of the ritual), every Sunday by women in the month Pauṣa (in the Hindu almanac), when they draw a circle of sandal-paste on a wooden plank to represent the sun and worship the deity Sun, at the end offering him the *naivedya* (food with sweets). The tale runs as follows:[25]

Once there was an old woman, who was very poor and had no support. But she was of good nature and a believer in god. She used to observe every year the *vrata* (mentioned above) on all the Sundays in the month of Pauṣa. On one such Sunday (in the Pauṣa month), when she had offered worship to the Sun-god and was about to take meals, a boy came and asked for meals, saying that he was hungry. The old woman offered him food, but he ate all the food leaving nothing for the woman. She then offered him a piece of betel-nut and the boy vanished. Two more Sundays and the same thing happened. On the last Sunday of the month, expecting the boy she prepared various sweets as per her resources. But this time she prepared more as to suffice for both of them. The boy came and he ate the whole of the food leaving the old woman completely baffled. But to complete the ritual of meal (as prevalent in India), she began to search for the nut. But the boy, stuffed to full capacity as he was, getting the piece of the nut ran for the door, shot through it, ran across the tiny court-yard and as the old woman rushed to where he ran, disappeared in the day-light. The old woman turned back only to be shocked to see that the boy had defiled the path in the court-yard by his excreta. Not being able to stand the sight of the dirt, she began to clean it with the broom. But to her surprise, the dirt was hard and began to glitter! It was gold and only gold everywhere!! The old woman got a second shock; but her lips quivered with smile and tears dropped from her eyes as she looked at the sky which had been lit up by the light of HIM (Sun), whom she had seen as a boy.

The tale, though crude, serves as an *arthavāda* for the ritual of sun-worship in the Pauṣa month. The association between gold and the sun is clear[26] and so it is between gold and Agni[27], the latter being called *hiraṇyaretas* (having gold as his seed). The *Śat.Br.* points out that when Agni united with waters, his seed became gold (II.1.1.5). Sun and Agni are the forms of one principle namely Heat.

C. SPECULATIVE AND EXPLANATORY

In the ritual-texts, the mythical accounts about creation are concentrated mainly on Prajāpati and they are speculative in nature, for the creation of the world is a matter of speculation. We have in the *RV* four myths of creation *viz. RV* X.129—the famous Nāsadīya-sūkta; X.90—the Puruṣasūkta; X.121—Hiraṇyagarbha Prajāpati, at the beginning of the universe and X.72-*sat* coming out of *asat* and Bṛhaspati blowing the birth of the gods, from whom the universe comes into existence.[28] These accounts in the *RV* are speculations about the creation of the universe. In the Brāhmaṇa-texts, we have the accounts of Prajāpati taking the form of tortoise and boar in the context of the creation of the earth.[29] The mythical account of Manu and the fish which we have noted earlier (in type B) also can be considered as speculative. The *Mbh.* and the Purāṇas repeat it with slight variations.[30] Purāṇas deal with the forms viz. tortoise and boar, taken by Viṣṇu to save many a situation.[31] In the context of creation, sometimes speculative type of mythical account occurs of the golden egg, which can be traced to the *RV*. In *RV* (X.121), it is said that Prajāpati, who was the Hiraṇyagarbha, was at the beginning of creation. The *Chānd.Up* (III.19) states that in the beginning, there was 'non-existent', which became 'existent'. It grew and then turned into an egg.

The *Chānd.Up.* points out how when the egg broke open, from it started the creation of earth, sky, mountains etc. Here we are reminded of the stand-point of Mercia Eliade, who says that myth (we can say the speculative myth) takes us to the 'Creative Era'—'the timeless Time'—*illud tempus*[32]—the Time, which is not clocked as it is the Time of God.

In this category, some mythical accounts are explanatory. The explicit etiologies (or aetiologies) of names, origin and purpose of plants, animals, men, cults, rituals etc. may appear to be superficial, but they form part of the mythical accounts coming as *arthavāda*.[33] Here we take an example from the *Sk.P.* A demon in the habit of spoiling conjugal union, was swallowed by Mātaṅgī, who was produced to subdue him. But the demon came out of her ear (*karṇa*), and so came to be called Karṇāṭa (*Sk.P.* III.2.18.98ff). Ultimately he was killed by Śyāmalā, Mātaṅgī's sister. The place where the demon came ultimately (when on the point of death) got his name (*ibid.*, 166-177).[34] The mythical account thus also serves to give the etymology of the name of the province Karnataka, now the Karnataka state (India).

D. ESCHATOLOGICAL

Here we have the mythical accounts coming as *arthavāda*, dealing with the concept of death or the world after death.

We take a mythical account from the *Mbh.*, which occurs at two places (Droṇa *parvaṇ* and Śānti *parvan*). Young Abhimanyu is killed and Yudhiṣṭhira in grief is inconsolable (Droṇa chaps. 51, 52). And here is given the account of the birth of Mṛtyu (goddess Death) from the mouth of Nārada. The god Brahmā created her to control the beings on the earth. Being told about this errand, she, full of the feeling of guilt, wept bitterly and her tears were collected by Brahmā (*ibid.* 53.23). Thereafter she went away to practise penance and that too rigourously. When she came back, Brahmā pacified her, telling that the drops of (her) tears collected by him in his (joined) palms would be the ailments or diseases born from the creatures themselves (*ibid.* 54.40b—*te vyādhayaḥ prāṇināmātmajātāḥ*), which would bring in their end and thus would kill them. She would thus incur no sin. The same account occurs again in the Śanti *parvan* of the *Mbh.* (chap. 257.15-22; chap. 258 entirely dealing with this), with a note that the tears of the goddess Mṛtyu (Death) turn into various diseases, which alone make persons die, absolving goddess Mṛtyu in this matter (*ibid.*, 258.34). The *Mbh.* at both the places refers to this account as *itihāsa*. The word *itihāsa* (*iti-ha-āsa* 'This was so' or 'This so happened') denotes traditional accounts preserved in the society by the class of the *sūtas*, which we shall see later. It is interesting to see that the idea of diseases and ailments of man himself bring about his death occurs in the tale "Death's Messengers" in the *Household Tales* from Germany.[35]

We have seen the types of functions and discussed them with examples from the Vedic to Puranic texts. Here is an example from the *Śat.Br.* The *arthavāda* here springs from the device of etymology for the *vidhi* of offering (that way in any sacrifice) and strikes an eschatological note with a tinge of philosophy. In the context of New-moon and Full-moon sacrifices, we have the word *āhuti* (offering). The offering given by the sacrificer becomes his body in the yonder world. When he departs from this world, that offering following him, calls out to him, "Come; I am here your body." As the offering thus calls out (*āhvayati* from √*hvā* or √*hve* —'to call out, invoke') it is called *āhuti* (*Śat.Br.* XI.2.2.6). The *arthavāda* based on etymology is brought in, to commend the *vidhi* of offering and is functional in nature, striking an eschatological note coupled with the belief based on the *karman*-doctrine.[36] The idea here is that the offerings given by the sacrificer in the sacrifice follow him to the other world and become his body, with which he can enjoy in the other world. It is this kind of belief that paved the way for the concept of *apūrva* or *adṛṣṭa*, which is a gift from the Pūrvamīmāṁsā system to Indian philosophical thought.

The device of *arthavāda* has been in effective practice in ancient India right from the Ritual Era and is used in the Epics and the Purāṇas. In fact it has travelled to the medieval times and has reached the modern age. The accounts (in writing or by word of mouth) regarding places, tribes, castes, places of worship and the gods and goddesses thereof etc. can vouchsafe for this.[37] All of these have one single aim and it is of explaining to people, either through praise of the matter in hand (many times with factual evidences) or condemning the prohibited matter.

Arthavāda being functional in nature, at times getting the status of 'charter', always has in view the social structure, may be in the form of individual units or as a collective whole. In the Vedic period, the institution of sacrifice was the distinguishing mark of the Aryan culture. It was a society, of which the very throb was sacrifice. With multitude of rites and rituals, the sacrificial institution attained its zenith. Naturally the statements of injuction (*vidhi*) required *arthavāda*-passages to commend them. This unit *viz.* sacrifice, of the society was supplemented and helped by the *arthavāda*. In the Āraṇyakas and more so in the Upaniṣads occur philosophical thoughts, which are at times stated in the ritual setting. There too are *arthavādas*, which commend these ritual details. But in the later era of the Epics and Purāṇas, in spite of the sphere of sacrifice left behind, *arthavāda* could fit in, nay it was a supporting factor to the data from the Epics and the Purāṇas. Even at times when there are sacrifices mentioned in the Epics and the Mahāpurāṇas, these texts seem to have forgotten the exact ritual details of the Vedic sacrifice. In fact this has been a separate topic of study of judging the role of Vedic sacrifice in the Epics and the Purāṇas.[38] In the *Rām.*, *Mbh.* and the Purāṇas, there are accounts of boons and curses, *ākhyānas* and *upākhyānas*, legends, tales etc., which justify the earlier incidents or the behaviour of persons. In the Purāṇas occur various vows (*vratas*) and festivals accompanied by the *arthavādas* commending them. The Puranic details can have some kind of relation with the ritual (*vidhi*), but the Epic-accounts emerge from the earlier ones in an emboxing style, the earlier and the later ones serving as *arthavādas*, not having any *vidhi* before them.

Now a pertinent question is – Whence came this non-ritualistic or secular literature, in the form of narratives, which occur at several places as *arthavādas*? We have noted the word *itihāsa*, which denotes 'a traditional account', very much keeping with its formation (*iti-ha-āsa*). Together with the word *itihāsa*, there occurs many times another word namely *purāṇa* which denotes 'an old tradition'. Sometimes these two words are given separate and at times both the words are found together. *Itihāsa* and *purāṇa*, comprising traditional accounts, dating at times from ages bygone, form the main treasure of secular literature. But what about the source of the secular literature? Attempts have been there to reach for it. Hariappa maintains that the practice of preserving the narrations of various events was prevalent in the period of the *Ṛgveda* or even prior to that.[39] Chakrabarti in his study of the Pāriplava (in the Horse-sacrifice) says that while some *ākhyānas* in the Pāriplava originated from the theologians, popular *ākhyānas* developed in all probability on the periphery of the sacred literature itself.[40] Dandekar has stated that right from the beginning there have been two traditions—that of the *mantras* and the other preserved by the *sūtas*.[41] This has given a clue to solve our problem. It seems that the source of traditional narratives and compositions was the Vedic secular tradition thriving simultaneously with the Vedic ritual tradition. The tradition of the *sūtas* composed and preserved the secular type of literature. The information from the *Mbh.* and the Purāṇas shed proper light on the role and status of the *sūta* and his indispensable position in ancient Indian narrative and in general, secular literature.[42] Sauti (Ugraśravas) the son of Lomaharṣaṇa narrated the *Mbh.* to the sages (Ādi. 1.5-21).

The fact of Sauti being one of the editors of the *Mbh.* can help us understand the nature of the *Mbh.* itself with all its *ākhyānas* and *upākhyānas* making it a compendium of knowledge. According to *Agni P.* (150.31), the *sūta* compiled the text of the Purāṇas due to the favour Vyāsa. This shows that *sūta* having a strong memory combined within himself the role of a chronicler, composer and narrator.

This secular or non-ritualistic tradition (not non-Vedic!) maintained mostly by the *sūtas*, was the fountain-head of the *arthavāda*-way of praising, justifying and explaining the matter in hand. In the Vedic ritual-texts the *arthavādas* are from the ritualistic circles, but at times they follow the pattern of the narrations, which emerge from the secular tradition. We have seen the words *itihāsa* and *purāṇa* which denote traditional accounts. When one turns to *nārāśaṁsīs*, *gāthās* and *ślokas*, one is convinced of the origin of this type of literature from the secular tradition. The *Ait. Br.* (VII.18=33.6) differentiates between a *ṛc* and a *gāthā,* calling the first *daiva* (divine) and the latter *mānuṣa* (human). The *Tait. Br.* (I.3.2.6) relates an old account that once the gods separated the dirty part from the divine speech as also from the food. The dirty part from the divine speech became the *gāthās* and the *nārāśaṁsīs*, while that of the food became wine. This shows that in the tradition of the Black *YV*, the *gāthās* and *nārāśaṁsīs* were not supposed to have respectable status like that of the Vedic mantras. But in the Ṛgvedic tradition, the *gāthās* had a respectable status, and there occur several *gāthās* in the *Ait.Br.* The Pāriplava cycle of legends, consisting of mini-cycles, each of ten days, mentioned in the context of Horse-sacrifice is worthy of taking note here. Thus while the sacrificial horse was away from the sacrificial enclosure, with the royal entourage, for a period of one year, when the Hotṛ priest had finished his daily ritual, at the end of it, a minstrel used to sing the deeds of the past kings, thus bringing the present sacrificer-king in line with the royal sacrificers of the past (*Śat.Br.* XIII.4.3.3-15). These songs may verge on *nārāśaṁsīs*. But they can better be called *gāthās*, as the latter is a term having a wider scope.

As noted above, there occur several *gāthās* in the *Ait.Br.* The *Ait.Br.* (VII.18=33.6) says that the story of Śunaḥśepa contains a hundred *gāthās.* However the extant legend of Śunaḥśepa in that text contains only ten *gāthās*, stating the importance of a son, as told by Parvata and Nārada to Hariścandra, who had no son. Some of these *gāthās* clearly appear to have come from the folk-tradition. The legend of Śunaḥśepa containing these *gāthās* comes as *arthavāda* in the context of Rājasūya sacrifice. Before we tun to the *yajñagāthās*, our final word about the *gāthās*. They may not be actually non-Vedic in character,[43] but it has to be accepted that their tradition was distinct from the Vedic priestly tradition. Horsch rightly points out that the anonymous stanzas (*gāthās*) originated mostly in secular and popular circles. According to him the *gāthā*-literature was derived from the non-hieratic or unorthodox sphere such as the *kṣatriya* milieu or the Vrātya community.[44]

Now about the *yajñagāthās.* Some of the *gāthās* in the *Ait.Br.* are termed *'yajñagāthā'*, obviously because they extol some sacrificial ritual or practice. This is the way Sāyaṇa has explained the term *yajñagāthā.* He says that *yajñagāthā* is one which is sung by all the ritualists having in view a sacrifice.[45] There is no doubt about the fact that the *yajñagāthās* were formed on the basis of the *gāthās*, which had a secular and popular origin. The *yajñagāthās* came from the ritualistic circles on the pattern provided by the *gāthās.* This is how the 'sacred' takes the help of the 'profane', catching its finger, and ultimately bringing even the latter (i.e. 'profane') in its fold. Falling in line with the *yajñagāthās* are the *ślokas*, which occur at several places in the Brāhmaṇa-texts. The *ślokas* in the Brāhmaṇa-texts form a part of the traditional lore, which is preserved in the ritualistic tradition. Macdonell and Keith say that it is not possible to tell the exact meaning of the word *śloka*, but it can be said that the word *śloka* denotes such *mantras*, the different varieties of which are preserved safe in the Brāhmaṇa-texts and are termed *ślokas*.[46] Though recorded in the Brāhmaṇa-texts, the *gāthās*, *nārāśaṁsīs*, *itihāsa* and *purāṇa* and *ślokas*[47] formed part of the floating mass of literature, which Winternitz calls 'literary public property'.[48] *Itihāsa* and *purāṇa* (traditional and legendary accounts) are replete in the Epics and the Purāṇas, the latter adding accounts of varied nature supporting the vows, holy places, rituals, festivals etc. and also giving the details of mythology grown around mountains and rivers.

The word *purāṇa* and the concept underlying it require some attention. Dange has dealt with this topic elaborately.[49] Purāṇa is first mentioned in the *AV* (XI.7.24), along with *ṛcs*, *sāmans*, *chandases* (metres) and *yajuses*. At other place in the same text, it is mentioned with other types of lore such as *gāthās*, *nārāśaṁsīs* and also *itihāsa* (XV.6.11, 12). The *Śat.Br.* mentions its recitation (part by part) in the 'ten-day' mini-cycles of the Pāriplava, at the Horse-sacrifice (XIII.4.3.13), on the ninth day, when the people of the Bird tribe were assembled. There were the bird-catchers also. This shows that the type of lore called Purāṇa was meant for common people. The language of this lore must have been simple. This can be vouchsafed from the language of the extant Purāṇas, which at many places, diverges from the 'Sanskrit' written or spoken as per the norms of the Pāṇinian rules.[50] The so-called 'lapses' (if we can call them so!) in the language of the Purāṇas cannot be ascribed to the mistakes made by the scribes, as the work of copying a Purāṇa was done with utmost care and devotion. As the deity of the Purāṇa was believed to be present in the Purāṇa, copying a Purāṇa manuscript was for propitiating the deity of the Purāṇa and for gaining virture. The common method was to copy the whole or part of a Purāṇa and gift it to a *brāhmaṇa* or keep it in a temple. This is why several manuscripts are found of one and the same Purāṇa, spread over in different areas. Regular assemblages of reading and hearing of the Purāṇas were arranged, the most popular being of the *Bhāgavata Purāṇa*, the cycle of reading which comprised of seven days (*saptāha-sapta*—'seven'+*ahan*—'day'—a term carried to the present times).

The Purāṇika (Purāṇika of the earlier times) as also the listeners of the Purāṇa were required to observe certain strict rules of celibacy and purity.[51]

For the analysis of the concept behind the word *purāṇa* and of the nature of the lore called Purāṇa, Dange directs us to Yāska who explains the word *purāṇa* as "*purā navam bhavati*"—'the lore which is called Purāṇa is both *purā* and also *nava*' (*Nir.* III.19). He further explains the word '*nava*' as 'brought forward' (*ānītam bhavati*). This gives a clue to know the exact nature of the Purāṇa. It is brought forward in the tradition and it is never entirely new. This indicates that Purāṇa is as old as the Veda and is developed side by side with the Veda. Hence the *Śat.Br.* (XIII. 4.3.9-13) calls the lores Sarpavidyā etc., including Purāṇa, as Veda. Dange gives the following statement about Puraṇa, which marks the main characteristics of this type of compositions—"Purāṇa is ancient traditional knowledge that assumes ever new gloss, being on par with the Veda, for the common people."[52] Dange further points out that one foot of the Purāṇa lore is in the Vedic lore, while the other touches new fields. The latter foot treads on contemporary ground, while the earlier one brings with it the vestiges of the past. It, thus, assumes the nature of a compendium of the old and the new, or Vedic and popular new factors—customs, manners, rites and so on. Here, the Purāṇa gets the status of Itihāsa. This is the reason, why at many places, the words Itihāsa and Purāṇa are spoken of as being together.[53] The main reason for assuming the nature of a compendium by the lore of the Purāṇa was the social conditions of those times, when the women, *śudras* and the general masses of the people were denied the study of the sacred texts and were seeking an easy and rightful approach to knowledge and information. In spite of its style being loose and far from exactitude, not paying heed to grammatical rules at times, the lore of the Purāṇa attained the status of *vidyāsthāna* as also of *dharmasthāna*,[54] for the people at large. The lore of Purāṇa in this endeavour made the maximum use of the device of *arthavāda*, as that was the easiest way to reach the masses.

Though a part of the ritual-texts, especially the Brāhmaṇa texts, *arthavāda* waded through the two Epics and covered the gamut of the Purāṇas so much so that it became a way of justifying and explaining. While carrying out this function, it presents a panoramic picture of ancient Indian society, where the 'Old' in tradition, though with a slow pace, accepted the 'New', with the changes justified by several evidences in the form of tales, accounts etc., which are convincing in the setting of those ages. *Arthavāda* thus has become not only a way of explaining and justifying but has also become a system, which we can designate as 'Arthavādaism'—an altogether new term!!

In the pages to follow, we deal with 'Arthavādaism' through narratives from Veda (ritual-texts) to Epics and Purāṇas (Mahāpurāṇas). Examples from these texts can be multiplied. Hence, only accounts with specific importance are taken up for discussion such as of acculturation of various tribes and their loan, in some matters to the indigenous people; rites and rituals, curses and boons, beliefs and practices of people at large, Epics-Puranic gods and goddesses, at times searching for the unbroken line (wherever possible)—ultimately to come to the Indian Man, who follows the continuity of *dharma* (code of conduct) but also welcomes and accepts changes in it, 'continuity' and 'change' being the marks of any healthy society.

NOTES AND REFERENCES

1. Address of Suniti Kumar Chatterji (General President), *Proceedings,* All India Oriental Conference, XVII Session, Ahmedabad, 1953, published by the Local Secretary, XVII AIOC, Gujarat Vidyasabha, Ahmedabad, p. 23.
2. *Ibid.*

3. F.W. Thomas, *Indianism and Its Expansion*, University of Calcutta, Calcutta, 1942, p. 7.
4. J.C. Heesterman, *The Inner Conflict of Tradition*, Essays in Indian Ritual, Kingship and Society, Oxford University Press (first published by University of Chicago Press), ed. for South Asia by Oxford University Press, Delhi, 1985, pp. 82-83.
5. S.M. Paranjape (ed.), *Arthasaṅgraha*, Bombay, 1927, p. 51.
6. *Ibid.*
7. *Ibid.*; also *Āpa. Ś.S.* XXIV.1.33— *brāhmaṇaśeṣo' rthavādaḥ*।
8. *Arthasaṅgraha*, p. 353—*prāśastyanindānyataraparam vākyamarthavādaḥ*।
9. Jaimini's *Pūrvamīmāṁsāsūtra* I.2.1; also see Abhyankar Vasudevashastri (ed.), *Mīmāṁsānyāyaprakāśa* of Āpadeva, Government Oriental Series, BORI, Poona, 1937, pp. 14-16.
10. Sāyaṇa's Introduction (*bhūmikā*) to his comm. on the *RV*. See Ṛgveda I *maṇḍala*, pub. by the Vaidika Samshodhana Mandala, Poona, 1933, p. 10—*arthavādabhāgasya prāmāṇyam mahātā prayatnena jaiminiḥ samarthayāmāsa*।
11. P.D. Navathe, "On the Mīmāṁsā Doctrine of Ekavākyatā", *Proceedings* of the Winter Institute on "Ancient Indian Theories on Sentence-Meaning", University of Poona, Pune, 1980, p. 190.
12. See P.D. Navathe, *op.cit.*, p. 192. The *arthavāda* eulogising Vāyu as the swiftest deity, stated by the *Tait. Sam.* (II.1.1.1) serves to commend the ritual act of sacrificing to the deity Vāyu, enjoined by the *vidhi* in the Kāmyapaśukāṇḍa.
13. *Pūrvamīmāṁsāsūtra* I.2.7, 22; *Jaiminīyanyāyamālā* I.2.1.1-3.
14. See W. Turner (ed.), *Hamlet* (Intrn.), The Educational Publishing Company, Bombay, June 1959, Intrn. p. i f; also see Sindhu S. Dange, *Vedic Beliefs and Practices through Arthavāda*, Vol. I, Aryan Books International, New Delhi, 2005, Intrn. pp. xx-xxiii.
15. Marc Bloch, *Feudal Society* (tr. from French by L.A. Manyon), Routledge and Kegan Paul Ltd., London, 1961, p. 94.
16. See A. Jonathan Turner, *The Structure of Sociological Theory*, reprint, Rawat Publication, Jaipur, 1995 (the first Indian edn. 1887), pp. 39-52.
17. Paul Theroux, "Under the Spell of the Trobriand Islands", *National Geographic*, July 1992, pp. 117-136.
18. For his theory, see Malinowski Bronislaw, "Myth in Primitive Psychology", in *Magic, Science and Religion and Other Essays*,

ed. by R. Redfield, London, 1992 (1925); also his *Myth in Primitive Psychology*, London, 1926.

19. G.S. Kirk, *Myth—Its Meaning and Functions in Ancient and Other Cultures*, Cambridge University Press, 1970, p. 253 ff.
20. P.V. Kane, *HDS*, Vol. II, Pt. II, 2nd edn., BORI, Poona, 1974, pp. 1244-45.
21. *Ibid.*, p. 1245. Pierre Rolland also holds the view that the Mahāvrata had an independent existence, before it was absorbed in the Soma-sacrifice. See Pierre Rolland, "A Study of A Solemn Vedic Ritual—The Mahāvrata", *Journal of Bihar Research Society*, Vol. 58, 1972, pp. 79-82.
22. P.V. Kane, *HDS*, Vol. II, Pt. II, p. 1245.
23. For the detailed information of this *vrata*, see P.V. Kane, *HDS*, Vol. V, Pt. I, 2nd edn., BORI, Poona, 1974, p. 437.
24. *Ibid.*
25. The tale has come to the author from her mother-in-law (the late) Kashibai and has been verified from many sources. It was recorded by the author for the first time in her book—*The Bhāgavata Purāṇa—Mytho-Social Study*, Ajanta Publications, Delhi, 1984, p. 287f. (Appendix D—The Sun-Boy).
26. In the ritual-texts, we often meet the statement (whenever gold plate etc. of gold is used)— 'We are making the very form of his, who is dazzling afar' (i.e. the sun). In tradition, gold is regarded a solar metal.
27. In the Agnicayana rite, a small golden image of a man is placed in the lowest layer of the Great Fire-altar, while it is being built. Here the golden man represents Agni-Prajāpati the very deity of sacrifice.
28. For full treatment of these hymns, see Sindhu S. Dange, "Ṛgvedic Accounts", *Myths of Creation (Proceedings of the Seminar)*, University of Bombay Publication, Bombay (Mumbai), 1987, pp. 7-11.
29. *Śat. Br.* VII.5.1.5— Prajāpati assuming the form of tortoise in the process of creating the earth; *Tait. Br.* I.1.3.5-6—Prajāpati assuming the form of a boar, diving into the waters and piercing the earth by means of his tusk and taking it out. In the *Śat Br.* (XIV.1.2.11) this boar is called Emuṣa. In fact this can be traced to the *Tait. Sam.* (I.10.8), where the earth is said to have been uplifted by a black boar with thousand arms.

30. *Mbh.* Vana.187. 6-56; *Matsya P.* I and II; *Bhāg. P.* II.7.12; also VIII.24.7-57.
31. *Vi.P.* I.9.88 (Viṣṇu taking the 'tortoise' form supporting the Mandara mountain); *Bhāg. P.* II.7.13 (for 'tortoise' form of Viṣṇu); *ibid.* III, chaps. 17-19 (for 'boar' form of Viṣṇu).
32. Ninian Smart, *Dimensions of the Sacred—An Anatomy of the World's Beliefs*, London, 1996, pp. 146-47.
33. See Sindhu S. Dange, *Vedic Beliefs and Practices through Arthavāda*, Vols. I and II, which have an exhaustive treatment of many of these topics.
34. For full account, see Sadashiv A. Dange, *Ency. PBP*, Vol. II, Navrang, New Delhi, 1987, p. 407f.
35. Wilhelm Grimm, *Household Tales* (1864; 1884), Eng. tr. by Margaret Hunt, Vols. I and II; The tale "Death's Messengers", *Household Tales*, Vol. II, Tale No. 177, p. 277 ff.
36. The doctrine of *Karman* can be traced to the *RV* (X.14.8), where the (recently) dead person is asked to unite in the heaven with the fathers *(pitṛs)* and with Yama, with the merit (accumulated) of his sacrifices and that of his good works. Leaving his blemish behind, the dead person is asked *to come back to his house again* (*ibid.* 8c—.............................. *punarastamehi*) and unite with his body in full vigour. Macdonell has missed this point, as he takes the word *ehi* as 'go back'. In the Padapāṭha actually, the word *ehi* is divided as *ā* and *ihi*, with a *daṇḍa*, and thus means 'come back'. See A.A. Macdonell, *A Vedic Reader for Students*, Oxford University Press, 14th Impression of the reprint in India 1951, Madras, 1988 (England 1917), p. 170(his tr. of *RV* X.14.8c). In fact, such a thought about the dead's coming back also occurs in *RV* X.16.5, which supports our interpretation.
37. The various Jātipurāṇas and the Sthalapurāṇas are being studied, but many works of these categories are still unearthed and invite attention.
38. See Madhavi Narsalay, *Epics and Mahāpurāṇas on Vedic Sacrifice*, Aryan Books International, New Delhi, 2015.
39. H.L. Hariappa, *Ṛgvedic Legends through the Ages*, Deccan College, Poona, 1953, p. 132.
40. Samiran Chandra Chakrabarti, "A Study of the Pāriplava", *Indo-Iranian Journal*, 32, Kluwer Academic Publishers (printed in the Netherlands), 1989, p. 262.

41. R.N. Dandekar, "The Mahābhārata: Origin and Growth", *University of Ceylon Review*, 12, 1954, p. 65,
42. Sindhu S. Dange, "Sūta—The Paurāṇika", *Purāṇa*, Varanasi, Vol. XL, NO. 2, July 1998, pp. 83-91; also see Appendix-A, "Sūta—Chronicler, Composer and Narrator.
43. According to St. Petersburg Dictionary, as compared to *ṛc*, *yajus* and *sāman*, the *gāthās* are not Vedic. See A.A. Macdonell and A.B. Keith, *Vedic Index of Names and Subjects* under "Gāthā".
44. Paul Horsch, *Die Vedische Gāthā und Śloka-Literatur*, Francke Verlage, Bern, 1966, III part of the book-chapters on origin and development of *gāthās*.
45. See Sāyaṇa on *Ait. Br.* III.43=14.5; V.6=22.1; VII.8=32.7; VII.9=32.8 etc.
46. A.A. Macdonell and A.B. Keith, *op.cit.*, under "Śloka".
47. See Sindhu S. Dange, "Songs from Secular Tradition", *Aspects of Speech in Vedic Ritual*, Aryan Books International, New Delhi, 1996, pp. 206-30 (the detailed treatment of the topic).
48. See M. Winternitz, *History of Indian Literature*, Vol. I (Intrn., Veda, National Epics, Purāṇas and Tantras), Munshiram Manoharlal, New Delhi, 2nd edn., 1972, (University of Calcutta, 1927), p. 314.
49. See Sadashiv A. Dange, "Purāṇa and Śāstra", *Gleanings from Vedic to Puranic Age*, ed. by Sindhu S. Dange, Aryan Books International, New Delhi, 2002. pp. 165-77.
50. See Sindhu S. Dange, *Puranic Etymologies and Flexible Forms*, Viveka Publications, Aligarh, 1989, pp. 122-32. Thus verbs are used with their *pada* changed (the Parasmaipada changed to Ātmanepada and the vice-versa); are declined incorrectly; nouns or their forms incorrect; forms of gerund incorrect. Some colloquial expressions come very close to those in later times, in vernacular languages, and some words newly find a place in the language of the Purāṇas.
51. See Sadashiv A. Dange, "Purāṇa and Śāstra", *Gleanings from Vedic to Puranic Age*, p. 170f.
52. *Ibid.*, p. 168.
53. *Ibid.*
54. *Yājñ.Sm.* I.3.

[CHAPTER 2]

Acculturation of Ancient Tribes and Clans

In the Vedic period, there are noted several tribes which appear to be from the Vedic fold itself or were away from and at times antagonistic to the Vedic Aryans, which however were recognised and accepted in the Vedic fold. Here the efforts will be to see how the device of *arthavāda* has explained this process of acculturation of various tribes to the Aryan fold or better to say—Vedic-brahmanical Hindu fold as this process spreads over to the Puranic times or even further.

A reference to some tribes together with their lores is made in the context of Horse-sacrifice, in the Pāriplava cycle of legends, consisting of mini-cycles, each of ten days. The Pāriplava cycle lasted for one year, while the sacrificial horse with the royal entourage was away from the sacrificial chamber. Apart from the Vedas *viz. RV, Yajus-Veda, Veda of the Arharvans, Veda of the Aṅgirases* and *Sāmaveda*, here are specifically mentioned Sarpavidyā (lore of the Sarpas) on the fifth day, Devajanavidyā (lore of the Rakṣases) on the sixth day, Māyāveda (lore of the Asuras) on the seventh day, Itihāsaveda to be told to the people of Matsya tribe and fisher-men (*matsyahanaḥ*) on the eighth day and Purāṇaveda to be told to the people of the Bird-tribe and men acquainted with the science of birds on the ninth day (*Śat.Br.* XIII.4.3.3, 6-14). While the lores like the Sarpavidyā, Devajanavidyā and Māyāveda are from the non-Vedic tradition, Itihāsaveda and the Purāṇaveda are from a-Vedic tradition. Portion from the respective lore is enjoined to be narrated by the Hotṛ priest at the end of the day after finishing his regular duty. The mention of these lores along with the regular Vedas speaks of their assimilation in the Vedic ritual tradition. A question which naturally crops up is—In which language the Sarpavidyā, Devajanavidyā and Māyāveda were composed? In case they were composed in the respective local languages, we have to suppose that the Hotṛ priest knew these languages or on his behalf there was a narrator from the respective tribe. What the text of these lores was, has never come to light, as it is buried deep in the layers of history as to go into oblivion. However a clue for the lore 'Sarpavidyā' could be got, as it is mentioned with respect to the people 'Sarpavidaḥ' who were present there (*ibid.* XIII.4.3.9). They were the 'knowers of Sarpas' i.e. the lore of nullifying the snake-poison'. The *Mbh.* mentions 'Viṣaharī Vidyā', given by Brahmā to Kaśyapa (*Mbh.* Ādi I.20.16). The serpent-worshippers knew this *vidyā*. In the beginning, mention is made of the lores of the tribes *viz.* Sarpas, Rakṣases, Asuras and also other tribes. These tribes might have been on the periphery of the Aryan civilization and some of them like the Sarpas were acculturated in the Vedic fold.

The acculturation of the Sarpa tribe which was a totemistic tribe in the Vedic Aryan fold is an epoch-making step in the history of ancient Indian culture. In the *RV*, we have three hymns in praise of the grinding stones in the ritual of Soma-pressing. The two hymns go on the name of two seers from the Sarpa tribe *viz.* Jaratkarṇa, the son of Irāvat (*RV* X.76) and Arbuda Kādraveya (*ibid.* X.94). The third hymn is by the son of Arbuda, named Ūrdhvagrāvan (*ibid.* X.175). It is interesting to note that in the mythical account, occurring in the *Ait. Br.*

(VI.1=26.1) as *arthavāda,* the seer Arbuda Kādraveya (the son of Kadrū, who is known as the mother of serpents)[1] is the main personality. The two seers having the same name (Arbuda Kādraveya) appearing in the two texts (*RV and Ait. Br.*) have to be obviously different. But in the account occurring in the *arthavāda* of the *Ait. Br.,* Arbuda Kādraveya carries out the same work and it is of praising the grinding-stones in the ritual of Soma-pressing. Can one say that 'Arbuda Kādraveya'—the name—especially the matronymic epithet (from the name 'Kadrū'—the serpent-mother) Kādraveya—is a 'cap' given to any Sarpa seer for praising the grinding-stones in the ritual of Soma-pressing? That the *Ait.Bir.* follows the Ṛgvedic tradition, hence the same name, can be a plausible explanation, though the two texts are chronologically apart.

To turn to the ritual of Soma. Soma is said to be coming from a very far off place.[2] The rite of purchasing Soma hints that it originally belonged to a non-Vedic (non-Aryan) clan. This same is ritually enacted and Soma is purchased from a *śūdra* or a *brāhmaṇa* of a lower status called Kautsa, who is then driven away.[3] The trend of acculturation is clearly seen in the ritual of Soma-pressing. The mythical account occurring in the *Ait.Br.* (VI.1=26.1) as *arthavāda* explains to us about it. It speaks of a sacrificial session of the gods, which remained unsuccessful as the sacrifice was lacking in a detail and the gods could not destroy the evil. At that time came a seer named Arbuda Kādraveya, who advised the gods to invoke the grinding (or pressing) stones (*grāvans*) at the midday pressing and wipe off the evil thereby. Arbuda Kādraveya himself invoked the pressing stones for the sake of the gods. But the gods being apprehensive of the Sarpa-seer looking at Soma and thereby putrefying it, wrapped his eyes with his head-wear. It has to be marked that the same practice of wrapping the eyes with the head-wear, while invoking the pressing stones at the midday pressing, became a part of the Vedic ritual tradition. In this sacrifice, when Soma (juice) was maddening the gods, they thought it to be the effect of the Sarpa seer's chants, while invoking at the midday pressing. Hence the gods mixed his chants with their *ṛcs*.

The *arthavāda* in the form of the mythical account noted above, points out certain additions, which were made to the already existing Soma-ritual. They are:

1. Practice of invoking the pressing stones in the midday Soma pressing;
2. This practice is coupled with that of wrapping the face with the head-wear at the time of midday pressing;
3. At this pressing, a mixture of the chants of the Sarpa-seer and the *ṛcs* (of the gods), to be used as the praise-formulas;
4. The emergence of and the establishment thereafter of the office of the Grāvastut priest, whose duty has been to praise the pressing stones;
5. The rite called 'Grāvastutpraiṣaḥ' in the Agniṣṭoma sacrifice, in which at the midday pressing, on the word from the Adhvaryu priest, the Abhiṣotṛs calling the sacrificer request him to go to the Grāvastut priest (obviously for calling him to invoke the pressing stones);
6. At this midday pressing, a rite of giving a turban as a gift to the Grāvastut priest (*grāvastute uṣṇīṣapradānam*).[4]

Now about the practice of invoking the grinding or pressing stones (at the midday pressing), with which the Sarpa seer Arbuda Kādraveya seems to have been familiar. This leads us to the method of extracting juice from the Soma-shoots. In this regard, there occur two methods in the *RV viz.* one, by pounding the Soma-shoots with a pestle and mortar (*RV* I.28.1-4), and the other is grinding the Soma-shoots with stones. The first method appears to be the older and may go back to the Indo-Iranian age, on comparison of the Vedic Soma ritual with the Haoma ritual of the Parsis. It has to be pointed out that the Zoroastrian ritual, following the *Avesta*, of preparing Haoma (=Soma) followed even in modern times, requires mortar (*hāvanīm*) and pestle (lālā).[5] The method of pressing the Soma shoots with the pressing (or grinding) stones appears to be somewhat of late emergence. Most probably this method was prevalent among some people, may be Sarpas, who were other than the settled Aryans. The seer of the Sarpa tribe (Arbuda Kādraveya) was familiar with this method. Hence, his advice to the gods to invoke the grinding stones so that the latter would give more Soma juice. In fact the method of pressing the Soma shoots with the pressing or grinding stones appears to be somewhat crude as compared to the older method involving the implements. This method using the grinding stones though adopted by the Vedic ritualists, required the invocation of these stones as a supplement, which the Sarpa seer suggested and which later on became an indispensable part of the Soma ritual.

Thus, the *arthavāda* occurring in the *Ait.Br.* (VI.1=26.1) convinces us of the acculturation of the Sarpa tribe in the Aryan fold. In fact, this process had started right from the Ṛgvedic times. At the beginning, already are mentioned by us the hymns by the seers of the Sarpa clan (*RV* X.76; 94; 175). One hymn has the Sarparājñī (of the Serpent tribe) as the female seer (*ibid.*, X.189), and also the deity as stated by Sāyaṇa, who also points to Sūrya as an alternate for the deity. The deity Sarparājñī was identified in the Vedic ritual with the Earth, as a queen of what creeps (Sāy. on *Ait.Br.* V.23=24.4; *Kauṣ.Br.* XXVII.4). In fact, the serpents are commonly believed to be '*autochthonous*' i.e. sprung from the soil (see German- '*autochthon*'—'sprung from the soil'—*chthon, chthonos*—'soil'). This belief reiterates the identification of the deity Sarparājñī (Queen of serpents) with the Earth, who is also 'Queen of serpents'. The *Ṛgvidhāna* points out that the recitation of the hymn (*RV* X.189—Sarparājñī), mentioned above, wards off all fear from the serpents. We have already referred to the lore — Sarpavidyā-coming from the Sarpa tribe (*Śat.Br.* XIII.4.3.9), and the *Gop.Br.* mentions the *vyāhṛti* (sacred word) 'Vṛdhat' coming from the Sarpaveda (I.1.10).

From this point of view, of interest will be the details regarding a sacrificial session performed by the Serpents, which occurs in the *Pañc.Br.* (XXV.15.1-4). It is said that through this *sattra* the Serpents gained a firm support in these worlds (*ibid.* 2). Then is given an exhaustive list of the Serpents (Sarpas) who worked as priests in this session (*ibid.* 3). The nomenclature of the priests reminds us of the same in the Vedic sacrifice. Some of these could be seen here—Brahman, Udgātṛ, Hotṛ, Maitrāvaruṇa, Prastotṛ, Pratihartṛ, Acchāvāka, Agnīdh, Adhvaryu and so many, to make the list complete. Interestingly Arbuda figures as the Grāvastut priest. There are mentioned the Sarpas (Nāgas—in later times) as carrying out the duties of all the priests, mentioned above. The list is found in the *Baudh. Ś.S.* (XVII.18) and *Baudh. G.S.* (III. chap. 10). According to Baudhāyana, these were the kings and princes of the Sarpas, who at Khāṇḍavaprastha, in human form, performed this *sattra*, desirous of obtaining poison. It is said that 'because it consists of ten-and ten-(*daśa*) versed lauds, therefore the Sarpas (serpents) are biting'.[6] It is said that at the middle day (in this *sattra*) the *sāmans* of the Sarpas are applied.[7] The Gṛhya ritual of Sarpabali also called Śravaṇā or Śravaṇākarma enjoined for the propitiation of the serpents has to be taken note of here.[8]

By the time one comes to the period of the *Mbh.*, the Sarpas, subsequently called Nāgas, were quite acculturated in the Vedic-brahmanical fold. That Arjuna had married Ulūpī the Nāga-princess is quite well known. In their early years of boyhood, when Duryodhana giving poison in food to Bhīma, throws him into the Gaṅgā, the latter reaches Āryaka the Nāga in the Nāgaloka (*Mbh.* Ādi 127.55-59), and receives from him the boon of having the strength of 1000 elephants (*ibid.* 63-71). The *Mbh.* here says that Bhīma was the great great grandson of Āryaka (from the side of Bhīma's mother Pṛthā i.e. Kuntī)—*dauhitradauhitra* (*ibid.* 65).

But there are reasons to believe that the relations between the Nāgas and the people of the Aryan fold might not be at times smooth. The account of burning the Khāṇḍava forest can vouchsafe for this (*ibid.* Ādi. 221-26 chaps.). Again king Parikṣit's curse, given to him by the sage Śṛṅgin to avenge the insult of his father at the hands of the king, is a knotty point. That curse or boon is a mythological arrangement to account for an incident, which has already taken place, is too well-known a phenomenon. King Parikṣit insulted the sage Śamīka by hanging a dead serpent round the sage's neck, for he did not give any reply to the king's query about the deer, which ran away after being shot by the king. Hence the curse of the sage's son Śṛṅgin to king Parikṣit that the king would meet his death being bitten by a serpent (*ibid.* Ādi. 40.10-32; also *ibid.* chap 41). The curse came to be true and Parikṣit met his death at the hands of the Nāga Takṣaka (*ibid.* Ādi 42.23-32; also chap. 43). In this regard Mahalingam expresses a strong possibility of a plan hatched for killing Parikṣit.[9] A folktale from Punjab can support this, for it speaks of the living tradition. According to it, king Parikṣit kidnapped the daughter of the Nāga Bāsaka (Vāsuki). The Nāgas extremely angry at this, with full preparation for a battle, invaded the Indraprastha city and in that, king Parikṣit was killed.[10] The *Mbh.* narrates how Parikṣit's death was followed by the famous Sarpasattra of Janamejaya, the son of Parikṣit, who as a revenge was bent upon killing all the serpents (Nāgas). Ultimately this sacrifice of the Sarpas (Nāgas) was stopped by the sage Āstīka.[11] The sage Āstīka was born from the parents, both of whom had the same name i.e. 'Jaratkāru' (*ibid.* Ādi. 14.2-7). Though the sage Jaratkāru, Āstīka's father, was of the Yāyāvara *brahmaṇa* family (*ibid.* Ādi 13.11), his mother Jaratkāru was a Nāga (Sarpa tribe) and a sister of the Nāga Vāsuki. The name 'Jaratkāru' is to be tallied with the name Jaratkarṇa—Sarpa seer—in the *RV*, the 'seer' of a hymn (*RV* X.76).

About the cult of serpent-worship or about serpent or snake as such, there has been a detailed study.[12] That serpent (especially 'cobra') was once a 'totem' can be seen from the practice followed by the Bhils and Bhillas. They worship the python and never injure it. In June, the Gonds try to kill a cobra and then cut off its head and tail, which are offered to Nāga Deo ('Serpent-god') inside the house, while they cook and eat the body, with the idea that by this, they will be protected form the effects of eating any poisonous substance throughout the year.[13] This practice is more or less the same as followed by a totemistic tribe. The chief serpent-worshipping race in ancient India is known as the Nāgas, who appear both in history and folklore. Oldham points out that the Sarpas, Asuras, Nāgas all represent hostile tribes, who opposed the Aryans. Others speak of the race of the Nāgas as of trans-Himalayan origin, who adopted snake as their national emblem and give their name to the cobra. Nāgas appear to have been foreign perhaps non-Aryan people chiefly in North India, but occupying other parts of the country. They were powerful in Central and South India. In Buddhist tradition, folklore and art, there are frequent references to the Nāgas and the Nāga kings.[14]

By the time one comes to the Purāṇas, one finds that Serpent especially the deadly venomous one Cobra-Nāga, getting the name from the Nāga clan, came to be revered in the Vedic-brahmanical Hindu tradition. The various vows and festivals occurring in this connection and the stories told to convince, have to be taken note of. In the month of Āṣāḍha as per the Hindu almanac, on the fifth day in the bright half, Manasā the Serpent-goddess is to be worshipped (*Brahmavi. P.* Prakṛtikhaṇḍa, 46.134). This cult of Manasā is even now prevalent in Bengal. There the cult of Manasā or Bishahari (Viṣaharī) holds the foremost place. She is worshipped by placing an earthen pot marked with vermillion under a tree; clay images of snakes are arranged round it and a trident is driven into the ground. A special shrine or a room is dedicated to the goddess where snakes abound.[15] In this context the story of Behulā is very famous in Bengal. Behulā the newly-wedded young wife brought back to life her husband, who was bitten by a snake. This she could do due to the favour of the Snake-goddess Manasā only on the condition that Behulā should make her father-in-law worship Manasā, as he was averse to the goddess. The father-in-law accepted this saying that he would offer flowers to Manasā by the left hand turning his face away from her idol. Mansā agreed to this. This shows the goddess Manasā being accepted in the Vedic-brahmanical Hindu fold of gods and goddesses at a loss of her prestige. This story is recorded by Thomas.[16] The story of Behulā is clearly an *arthavāda* which points out the greatness of the Serpent-goddess Manasā, but her inclusion in the fold of the gods, permitted somewhat reluctantly.

In the month of Śrāvaṇa, which falls in the rainy season, one of the most famous festivals is of Nāgapañcamī. The *Sk.P.* mentions it as being held at Kāśī, where a *kuṇḍa* (a circular pit for preserving water or fire—here water) is referred to as dedicated to the serpent-god Vāsuki (IV.66.7-16). The *Bhav.P.* gives a detailed account of the Nāgapañcamī festival, which according to this Purāṇa comes in the dark half of the Bhādrapada month, which also falls in the rainy season (*Bhav. P.* Brahma 32.44ff). The description of the festival in short is—On this day, figures of various types of serpents in various colours are mentioned to be drawn on the ground or they may be made of gold, wood or clay. They, generally five in number, should be worshipped with red flowers and sandal-wood paste to be applied to them. Brāhmaṇas are to be fed with sweet balls (*modakas*) and preparation from milk. The yearly vow of twelve *pañcamīs* (fifth dark of every month) is to be observed, each being auspicious and hence allotted to each of the twelve Nāgas (serpents) *viz.* Ananta, Vāsuki, Śaṅkha, Padma, Kambala, Karkoṭaka, Aśvatara, Dhṛtarāṣṭra, Śaṅkhapāla, Kāliya, Takṣaka and Piṅgala.[17] We have already mentioned the sacrificial session performed by the Serpents (*Pañc. Br.* XXV.15.1-4; especially *ibid.* 3, where the names of the serpents with the duties of the respective priests allotted to them are mentioned). Among them are noted the names Dhṛtarāṣṭra and Takṣaka, which occur in the description of the Nāgapañcamī festival given by the *Bhav. P.* as seen above. The *Bhav. P.* states that at the end of the yearly vow (of twelve *pañcamīs*), a figure of a serpent made from red chalk is to be offered to a *brāhmaṇa* and to the priest guiding the vow, a gold *nāga*-image is to be offered. The *Bhav. P.* also states that in the month of Āśvina figures of serpents from Kuśa grass are to be worshipped (Brahma 38.1, 2).

It has to be noted that the festival of Nāgapañcamī is celebrated even in modern times in the state of Maharashtra (India), on the fifth day of the bright half in the month of Śrāvaṇa in somewhat the same way as stated in the *Bhav. P.*, the details of which have been noted above. A couple of ritual details to be added are—One should not cut anything (even vegetables, fruits etc.) on this day, with an iron (nowadays steel) instrument; one should not use frying pan or cauldron made of iron,—the black metal being associated with 'evil powers'[18], and one should hear the *kahāṇī* (*kathanī=kathā*) i.e. the tale of the Nāgas (serpents). One of the *kahāṇīs* tells how the Nāgas first becoming angry, come to the house of a householder to kill him and all the inmates of the house by their poisonous bite, but are immediately pacified after seeing the worship of their figures drawn on the ground or wall or on a wooden plank. These *kahāṇīs* are folktales from the floating mass of literature, spreading by word of mouth but now many of them being in print form. But they serve as *arthavāda* to the *vidhi* (ritual) of worshipping the serpent-figures, which are nine, signifying the nine prominent, families of the Nāgas. They are—Ananta, Vāsuki, Śeṣa, Padmanābha, Kambala, Śaṅkhapāla, Dhṛtarāṣṭra, Takṣaka and Kāliya.[19] At times the name—Nāga Karkoṭa appears with these. The *kahāṇīs* referred to above are repeated every year at the time of the worship and are thus validatory in nature, so as to become 'Charters' to convince people of the importance of Nāga worship. In Andhra Pradesh (an Indian State), the serpent-worship is observed on the fourth day of the month by going to an ant-hill and offering milk there. The day is known as Nāgulacaviti (i.e. Nāgacaturthī).[20] The work *Vratarāja* mentions Nāgadaṣṭoddharaṇa-vrata, which is a *kāmya* vow (i.e. a vow observed as per the desire-*kāma*-of a person and it is not a regular-*nitya*-vow). This is observed on the fifth day in the bright half of the Bhādrapada month and it is for warding off the bite of a venomous serpent.[21] Now to come to a very interesting festival-Nāgadīpāvalī or Nāgadivāḷī, which comes on the first or fifth day in the bright half of the Mārgaśīrṣa month i.e. practically one month after the 'Festival of Lights' (Dīpāvalī), which is celebrated all over India. Nāgadivāḷī is not a regular feature of every household but is celebrated as a custom and practice of the family. This festival is commonly celebrated in the Vidarbha-Nagpur region in the state of Maharashtra and lasts for one day. In the name of each male member (who is alive) of the family, one sweet preparation is made. So as per the number of the male members mainly and also children, the sweets are there and they are different from one another. The same number of wicks are lighted in the lamps. The lamp which is lighted stands for the life. Nāga is taken to be the oldest ancestor of the family. In his honour is this festival celebrated, the chief aim being to ensure long life for all the members in the family.[22]

These are the rituals concerning serpents (Nāgas), some traced from the Purāṇas and some from prevalent practices. Sometimes the *kahāṇīs* (tales) support them, at times there are beliefs (e.g. 'Lamp which is lighted'=Life) which work as the convincing factor. On the whole, serpent-worship having its roots in totemism or originating independently of it, got its access to the Vedic-brahmanical Hindu fold and the process of acculturation of the serpent or Nāga tribe in the Vedic-brahmanical Hindu fold, started from the Vedic times, became complete in the Puranic period, reaching even the recent times, and in all this process the role of 'Arthavādaism' has to be reckoned.

To come to the *asuras,* who often figure with the gods in the Vedic ritual texts. Many a mythical account in the Vedic ritual texts (especially the Brāhmaṇa texts) start with the expression that the gods and *asuras* were in conflict. The *asuras* are constantly spoken of as being the offspring of Prajāpati and on par with the gods.[23] Shendge has tried in her own way to identify the *asuras*.[24]

It will be interesting to see the original concept of the word '*asura*'. In the *Avesta,* Ahura (=Asura) is the name of the highest god. In the *RV* it is particularly associated with the gods Varuṇa or Mitrā-Varuṇā (dual deity), whose *māyā* or potential power (Macdonell—'occult power') is described. But the word *māyā* in the sense of 'craft' is also applied to hostile beings (*RV* X.124.5; 138.3). According to Macdonell, towards the end of the Ṛgvedic period, the application of the word to the gods began to fall into disuse. The popular etymology recognising a negative in the word (i.e. *a* + *sura*) might have helped here.[25] In *AV* and later works, *asura* always meant a 'demon'. In the ten-day cycles of the Pāriplava *ākhyāna,* the 'Māyāveda' is said to be of the *asuras* (*Śat.Br.* XIII.4.3.11). Here the Veda of Māyā is to be taken as the 'lore of craft' (used against the gods), belonging to the *asuras.*

We have seen above that both gods and *asuras* are said to be the offsprings of Prajāpati-the creator. Thus the quarrelling parties or forces inimical to each other are closely connected. This relationship can be explained on the principle of phratry, which is described as 'curious hostile friendship between two parties'.[26] In such relationship, both groups, seemingly divided but forming in effect a totality, together constitute a unity—the oneness of the tribe.[27]

The *asuras* are to be distinguished from *rakṣases, yātudhānas, piśācas, arātis, kimīdins* and several other evil spirits, the latter group being the enemies of mankind. The *asuras* in the Vedic ritual-texts are seen to be the enemies of gods, always trying to outshine them in the performance of sacrifice and the fruits to be gained thereby. Men, i.e. human beings, as a rule, seem to be excluded from their sphere of action.[28]

Indra is said to have come into conflict with several demons, some called *asuras* and some *dāsas*.[29] Here we take into account three *asuras*, who are not seen causing any menace to the humans directly, but who try to disturb the 'Cosmic Order', in which they do not succeed and get vanquished. These three *asuras* are—Śuṣṇa, Svarbhānu and Vṛtra.

Śuṣṇa is regarded as a demon of drought (fr. the root √*śuṣ*—'to dry').[30] There is a mention of his strong forts (*RV* I.51.11) and also of his moving fort (*ibid.* VIII.1.28). Indra releases the waters when he shatters these forts (*ibid.* I.51.11; VIII.40.10). In the *Kāṭh.Sam.*, in the context of *savas*,[31] we have an *arthavāda* in the form of a mythical account. It is, as follows—Śuṣṇa, was in possession of nectar. In order to have that, Indra became a lump of honey and laid in the path of Śuṣṇa, who saw it and devoured it. Indra entered Śuṣṇa and came out of his mouth with the nectar (XXXVII.14).[32] Here, nectar stands for the rain-waters hoarded by Śuṣṇa, the original Ṛgvedic concept as seen above, remaining unchanged.

Another such *asura* is Svarbhānu, who hides the sun but whose efforts are foiled by the seer Atri. Atri is said to have found the sun with the *turīya mantra*[33] and to have placed him in the sky (*RV* V.40.6, 8; *AV* XIII.24.12, 36). This myth also figures in the *Pañc. Br.* (IV.5.1,2; IV.6.12, 13; XIV.11.12, 14). Here not Indra but the seer Atri (*RV* and *AV*; *Pañc. Br.* XIV.11.12, 14) or the gods (at the remaining two places in the *Pañc.Br.*) repel the darkness to make the sun shine again. Here Svarbhānu disturbs the Cosmic Order (*ṛta*) by capturing the very source of light, which however is re-established. This proto-myth of the *RV* travelled further to the *Mbh.* and the Purāṇas and got developed in the full-fledged myth of the demon Rāhu (Ketu) swallowing the sun and the moon. In the mythologies the world over, instead of a demon at times a fierce beast chases the sun or the moon.[34] It was Tilak who stated that an eclipse of the sun was then first observed by the seer Atri.[35] The present author has dealt with this myth in details in her book.[36]

Finally, to come to the *asura* Vṛtra, the prominent and the oft-mentioned *asura,* for whose slaying, Indra is said to have been born (*RV* VIII.78.5; 10.55). The epithet *vṛtrahan* (slayer of Vṛtra) exclusively belongs to Indra, whose constant conflict and fight with Vṛtra and the eventual slaying of Vṛtra is frequently referred to as *vṛtrahatya*. The word *vṛtra* many times is used to denote plural number and that too always in neuter gender.[37] But here we take the word *vṛtra* as of the masculine gender denoting singular number.

The word *vṛtra* for us denotes the *asura* Vṛtra who tries to disturb the Order (*ṛta*), which is brought back. It was Yāska, the composer of *Nir.* who made the first effort to know the meaning of the word *vṛtra* and the nature of Vṛtra. Yāska mentions two schools, *viz.* (1) Nairukta—Etymological school, to which, Yāsaka himself belongs. He derives the word *vṛtra* from the root √*vṛ* —'to cover, envelop'. Vṛtra is the one, who has enveloped all the waters of the universe in his body, as is seen at several places in the *RV*. It is Indra, who vanquishes and smashes Vṛtra and releases streams of water. (2) Aitihāsika—School of Aitihāsikas—the legendists—who maintain *itihāsas* i.e. the traditional accounts—from the word *itihāsa* meaning 'This was so' (*iti-ha-āsa*). The Aitihāsikas narrate the *itihāsa* that Vṛtra was an *asura*, the son of Tvaṣṭṛ. They have preserved many such *itihāsas*, which at times appear fanciful.[38]

But Yāska does not stop at these two schools. He gives a third and that too an important observation of his. He says that in the *mantras* and in the accounts (obviously *arthavādas*) from the Brāhmaṇa-texts, Vṛtra is spoken of as a serpent (*Nir.*

II.17—*ahivat tu khalu mantravarṇā brāhmaṇavādāśca/*). This points out that the nature of being a serpent is superimposed upon Vṛtra. Here, a mythical element is superimposed upon an independent entity. Thus Yāska as early as the seventh century BC shows the knowledge of the process of 'myth' being formed and proves to be the first theorist to lay his hands on the process of myth-making and that too most probably on comparative basis. The statement of Yāska seen above echoes the belief commonly found in folklore and mythology that certain creatures such as frog, crocodile etc. are the controllers of waters on the earth.[39] The Frog-hymn—Maṇḍūka-sūkta (*RV* VII.103) is regarded as a rain-charm, the underlying belief being that the frogs have control of all waters, which they release and so we get rains.[40] On the same lines, Vṛtra the controller or enveloper of waters was believed to be a serpent. To regard Vṛtra as a serpent may appear to be a metaphor. But one has to remember that the worldwide mythical belief as noted above is at the basis of it.

Dandekar takes a note of the monographs by E. Benveniste and L. Renou, in which they have discussed the linguistically cognate words *vṛtra* in the *RV* and *vṛthra* in the Avesta. According to them, these two words have to be derived from the root √*var*—'to resist'. Dandekar agreeing with these scholars opines that the original sense of the word *vṛtra* is merely 'resistance'—an abstract idea! The historical hero—the national war-god—Indra, overcame a number of human foes who had 'resisted' the onward march of the Vedic Indians. These human foes, thus naturally came to be looked upon as the Vṛtras. At the later stage of the Ṛgvedic mythology, the historical human Vṛtras were collectively transformed into the one 'demon', who prominently opposed Indra the great god. When naturalistic elements came to be regarded as the rain-god, there was a corresponding naturalistic transformation of Vṛtra's personality so that he came to be looked upon as the cloud-demon.[41]

Dandekar's stand-point regarding the historical nature of Indra is quite acceptable. The present author has maintained that even the famous hymn (*RV* II.12) is clearly a panegyric of the human hero Indra, who came to be regarded as a godhead. The hymn reminds us of the ballad-poetry of later times. Even in the times of the *RV*, a class of *sūtas* used to preserve the accounts of the hero's exploits as well as several other accounts of important events, which were recited or sung by them at times in a particular sacrifice. This famous hymn (*ibid.*) praising Indra, was (most probably) recited, may be quite often, at the Soma-sacrifice.[42] When rain became a dire necessity for the settled pastoral life of the Vedic Aryans, Indra the embodiment of valour, was regarded as a rain-god. He also became the god of fertility.[43] with his consort—Indrāṇī—who stood for the Great Earth.[44] With Indra as the rain-god, his principal adversary naturally and logically became a cloud demon. Many Ṛgvedic passages teeming with the descriptions of thunder, lightning, mist, hail and downpour confirm the 'cloud'-nature of Vṛtra.[45]

From the point of view of mythological setting, the oft-repeated rain-myth in the *RV* has to be regarded as the counter-part of the combat-myth. Hence, Vṛtra, the adversary of Indra can be placed on a larger canvas of other mythologies. In the Egyptian mythology, Horus the sun-hawk, fights Set the serpent. While the wordy battle raises high, Horus plants his semen in Set, which comes out of the latter's ears and this causes the river Nile to flood.[46] In the *Avesta*, Tishtrya is said to bring rain, while Apaosha tried to keep the rain away. When the terrible fight ensues between the two in the cosmic ocean Voura-Kasha, that ocean is caused to bounce, and there is formed rain in the shape of clouds through the vapours, caused by Tishtrya's movements (Tir *yashta* 20-30). The Chinese common belief is that the dragons fight and then it rains. In Nepal, it is believed that on the Nāgapañcamī day (which falls in the rainy season), it rains the heaviest, for on that day the fight between Gaurḍa and the serpents rages high.[47] Indra-Vṛtra fight can be viewed through this perspective also.

In fact the Indra-Vṛtra fight leads us to a twin-concept of an archetypal hero and an archetypal demon. Just as we have an archetypal hero in all mythologies with only the face changed of them,[48] we have the archetypal demon, controlling and not releasing the life-sap of the whole world. And it is the hero who fights him and releases the treasure for mankind. Vṛtra in the *RV* stands for such a demon (*asura*), who is to be ultimately vanquished to maintain the Order (*ṛta*). The Order (*ṛta*) works on three levels *viz.* cosmic, sacrificial and moral. The rain-myth in the *RV* centering round Indra and Vṛtra pertains to the cosmic level, where the Order disturbed by Vṛtra is brought back by Indra.

We come to the sacrificial level, where in the ritual texts, we mark the same trait of Vṛtra. In the *Śat.Br.* occurs the *arthavāda* in the form of a mythical account that when Indra cut off the three heads of Tvaṣṭṛ's elder son Viśvarūpa, Tvaṣṭṛ becoming furious offered into fire whatever pure Soma[49] was left there, for Indra though uninvited had already consumed practically all the pure Soma. The Soma offered by Tvaṣṭṛ, as it was to reach fire, developed into a human form, and it was Vṛtra. Vṛtra (thus) became possessed of Agni and Soma, all sciences, all glory, all nourishment and all prosperity. When Indra pleaded to Agni and Soma, they came over to him, followed by sciences etc., leaving Vṛtra powerless. Indra then cut off Vṛtra into parts, making that part which was of the Soma content turned into moon.[50] Here we find Vṛtra possessing Soma and Agni—Moist and Heat (*ārdram ca śuṣkam ca*) — the only two important principles (and no other as the third!) in the universe (*Śat.Br.* I.6.3.23) and Indra subsequently gaining them. These two principles are indispensable for the Order (*ṛta*) on the cosmic level. But these two are important even on the sacrificial level and hence are brought here to maintain the Order (*ṛta*) on that level. The *Śat.Br.* mentions that Vṛtra agreed to be the food of Indra (*ibid.* I.6.3.17). Thus the 'eater-eaten' relationship exists between Indra=Sun and Soma (Vṛtra)=moon. Dange has discussed this in details convincingly, pointing out the exact implication of it.[51] The eating and again letting out of the moon by the sun is a monthly drama in the cosmos, which is enacted at the Soma ritual. In the Agniṣṭoma sacrifice, the Śukra cup of pure Soma stood for the sun and Indra; the Manthin cup for the moon and Vṛtra. The latter was eaten and released by the former involving the principle of complementation in rivalry and seeming enmity, with a step further .... Indra=sun-Śukra (cup)—the eater'; Vṛtra=moon=Manthin (cup)—the 'eaten' (*ibid.* I.2.1.3ff; I.6.3.17; III.9.4.2; *Jaim.Br.* I.82). Dange maintains that the two—the 'eater' and the 'eaten'—are complementary to each other, suggesting the ultimate wholeness of the two.[52] Indra-Vṛtra fight is thus a regular and indispensable feature of the Order (*ṛta*). It is conceptualised on the cosmic level but is brought also on the sacrificial level.

The principle of complementation in this fight gets the colour of reconciliation, when we take a note of the Vṛtra-myth in the *Mbh.* Here Vṛtra is said to be born from Danāyu, the wife of Kaśyapa (*Mbh.* Ādi 65.33), and not from Dānu as the *RV* mentions.[53] Following the ritual-texts that Tvaṣṭṛ was the creator of Vṛtra, the *Mbh.* at one place mentions Vṛtra as born from the Abhicāra-fire (fire kindled for malevolent purpose) of Tvaṣṭṛ (*ibid.* Udyoga 9.48) and speaks of the peace-agreement with Indra on the words of the great seers (*ibid.* 10.27-31). The *Mbh.* is conversant with the significant Ṛgvedic trait of Vṛtra controlling the life-sap of the world. Hence, at one place, it is said that Vṛtra took possession one by one of the five Great Elements (Earth, Water, Lustre, Wind and Ether), which were the substrata of smell (*gandha*), taste (*rasa*), form (*rūpa*), touch (*sparśa*) and sound (*śabda*) resp., and Vṛtra was to be smashed by Indra with the thunderbolt. When Vṛtra entered Indra, Indra killed him with the 'unseen' thunderbolt (*ibid.* Āsvamedhika 11.7-19). However, the *Mbh.* sounds a note of reconciliation between Indra and Vṛtra and that too in a unique way. It is said that Vṛtra goes to the world of Highest Bliss after hearing the advice of Sanatkumāra (*ibid.* Śānti 280.57-59). Elsewhere it is said that when Indra attacked Vṛtra with the thunderbolt, Vṛtra died but went to Viṣṇuloka.[54]

By the Puranic period, many more mythological details were gathered round the name of Vṛtra. The *Brahma P.* calls Vṛtra and his elder brother Viśvarūpa *vṛjinodbhava*—'born of *vṛjina*......... (i) *vṛjina*—'hair' or (ii) 'sin', this latter meaning may be referring to the sin of *brahmahatyā* (killing a *brāhmaṇa*). This 'sin' stuck to Indra for killing the treacherous Viśvarūpa, the son of Tvaṣṭṛ and *asura's* sister. Viśvarūpa though a *brāhmaṇa* priest of the gods, secretly contrived to let the oblations go to the *asuras* (*Tait. Sam.* II.5.1.1). *Mārk.P.* (5.1ff) and the *Sk.P.* (V.2.35.5ff) mention the birth of Vṛtra from the hair of Tvaṣṭṛ Prajāpati, which the latter offered in the fire to give rise to Vṛtra. The *Sk.P.* having its doctrinal pro-Śiva colour, is quick enough to add that Indra worshipped the *liṅga* and having thus propitiated Śiva, killed Vṛtra with the foam of water, obviously by the prowess of *liṅga* (*ibid.* 29). The *Padma P.* (Bhūmikhaṇḍa 23.1ff) also states Vṛtra's birth from fire when Marīci's son Kaśyapa threw his hair in it. But sticking to the Puranic image of Indra as sending nymphs to seduce the sages, the *Padma P.* here adds that Indra sent the nymph Rambhā to allure Vṛtra to drink wine in so much excess that with his strength reduced and balance gone, Vṛtra was killed by Indra. Interestingly, the *Sk.P.* and the *Bhāg. P.* mention that Vṛtra was a *gandharva* in his former birth,[55] and due to the curse of Pārvatī was born as a demon.[56] Thus the original mythological concept of Vṛtra as a demon holding all waters on the earth was presented by the *Mbh.* and the Purāṇas (not all Purāṇas mention Vṛtra) with added layers of mythical accounts (*arthavādas*). Following the words of Peter Munz we can say that this is "embroidery' to the original myth.[57]

In spite of the Śaivite colour of the *Sk.P.* in narrating the myth of Vṛtra, the reference to Indra's propitiating Śiva by worshipping the *liṅga*, getting prowess and by that, smashing Vṛtra, the son of Tvaṣṭṛ Prajāpati is worthy of taking note. It goes back to the strife between Rudra (the proto-type of Śiva) and Prajāpati, recorded in the Vedic ritual-texts. As Prajāpati being enamoured of his daughter ran after her, Rudra, on the words of the gods, to punish Prajāpati pierced him with a dart (*Śat.Br.* I.7.4.1-3). The *Ait. Br.* makes this a star-myth. It says that Prajāpati transformed himself into a roe-buck (*ṛśya*) and approached his daughter, who assumed the form of a doe (*rohita*).[58] Bhūtavat (i.e. Rudra) fashioned by the gods to punish Prajāpati, pierced the latter with an arrow. Prajāpati bounded up to the sky and became the constellation Mṛga, his daughter the asterism Rohiṇī and the arrow became the constellation called 'the three-knotted arrow' i.e. the girdle of Orion (*Ait. Br.* III.33=13.9). The note of enmity of Rudra (=Śiva) with Prajāpati in Vedic mythology is thus very old.[59] The *Sk.P.* being Śaivite in texture and nature is too ready to take the help of this myth to weave one more layer to the myth of Vṛtra. Thus the Vedic-brahmanical Hindu tradition—Hindu tradition materialising from the Epics and Purāṇas onwards—has convincingly preserved the myth of this archetypal *asura* Vṛtra, with his adversary—the great warrior-god Indra never lost sight of.

Oldham notes a tradition prevalent among the Kafirs of the Hindu Kush which reminds us of the Indra-Vṛtra (serpent) myth. It maintains that the Bashgul Valley was once held by a great serpent, who would devour the passers-by and who eventually was killed by Imra or Indra.[60] This myth, though can come under "Hero-myths", dealing with the exploits of a Hero-here Indra, the under-current of Indra-Vṛtra strife running through it cannot be denied.

We have noted above the two references from the *Mbh.*, which point out that after hearing Sanatkumāra's advice Vṛtra goes to the world of Highest Bliss or after death goes to Viṣṇuloka. It speaks of the complete surrender of the demon to the god, so much so that after death the demon is to get the next birth in the Viṣṇuloka, which is allotted to the righteous people. Such a thought proved to be a great help to the Puranic literature, in which is marked the principle of *Virodha-bhakti* (Devotion springing from Enmity). It is this principle on the lines of which the demon (*asura*) gets redeemed and is ultimately united with the divinity. A simple stroke of god's hand showers the favour and the ultimate annihilation of the demon gives to him the same reward as is for the normal devotees.[61]

We have noted at the beginning of this topic dealing with the *asuras* that the *asuras* in the Vedic texts are opposed to gods and not to humans. The enemies of mankind are the evil forces such as *rakṣases*, *yātudhānas* etc.[62] The *AV* has mainly these in view when it prescribes the remedies against them based on magic and medicine. Here we take into account two demons (*asuras*) whose identity has been an unsolved riddle in spite of many efforts. One is Araru, who is mentioned only twice in the *RV* (I.129.3; X.99.10), also by *AV* (VI.46.1, where Dream is said to be Araru), later on by the *Mait. Sam.* (IV.1.10), *Śat. Br.* (I.2.4.17) and *Tait.Br.* (III.2.9.3-4). He is said to have spread himself on the earth. When driven away from there, he flew to the mid-region and then to the sky. He was four-footed and hence agile. According to Dange, Aruru, from all descriptions (though meagre), appears to be a super-human mythical evil being, to drive away whom Indra had to use his *māyā* i.e. special power (*RV* X.99.10). Another demon (*asura*) is Nārmara, who is mentioned only once in the *RV* (II.13.8). Indra, for the sake of Pṛkṣa and Dāsaveśa, is said to have vanquished Nārmara with his wealth, by dragging him to the mouth of (the river?) Ūrjayantī. However, he is not said to have died and he was only thrown in the mouth of Ūrjayantī. Dange has identified (as per his opinion—a modest hypothesis) Nārmara with the Egyptian King Narmara, who ruled after the king Zaru. Zaru ruled over Egypt prior to the rule of the royal Dynasty. Narmara was formerly in the Middle-east, may be of the city Uruk (<Uruj<Ūrjayantī in the *RV*?), and later on moved to Egypt. In the Bible is mentioned Erech, which place was at the mouth of the river Euphrates, near Persian Gulf. Was Nārmara (of the *RV*) dragged by Indra to this place? According to Dange, Nārmara could be a real powerful person (king) as was Śambara, both having some historical truth about them.[63]

The *asuras viz.* Śuṣṇa, Svarbhānu and Vṛtra form a different category, for they try to disturb the Cosmic Order (*ṛta*), holding the world as though to ransom, and hence are to be annihilated. But when we come to the *Mbh.* and the Purāṇas, we find the concept of *asura* somewhat changed. In the *Mbh.*, even Vṛtra except at one place (*Mbh.* Āśvamedhika 11.7-19), which we have already noted, is not connected to cosmic order, but has only 'one-to-one' bitter relationship with Indra, who is his born enemy. Like a human being, aspiring for the Highest Bliss or Viṣṇuloka, he gets the Ultimate Bliss, which is aspired by the righteous people.

In the accounts of Kṛṣṇa as a cowherd-boy, we find several *asuras* coming in various forms to cause fatal harm to Kṛṣṇa, but ultimately are themselves annihilated. The tenth *Skandha* of the *Bhāg. P.* is replete with many such examples. The names of some of the demons, mentioned here, also occur in other Purāṇas. To name some demons (*asuras*) from the *Bhāg. P.*

(i) The child-murderess Pūtanā, who came to suckle the infant Kṛṣṇa, besmearing deadly poison to her breasts;[64]
(ii) Tṛṇāvarta, the demon coming in the form of a cyclone;[65]
(iii) Vatsāsura coming in the form of a calf;[66]
(iv) Bakāsura in the form of a big crane;[67]
(v) Aghāsura in the form of a big python;[68]

(vi) Ariṣṭa in the form of a bull;[69]
(vii) Dhenuka in the form of a big ass;[70]
(viii) Pralamba in the form of a cow-herd;[71] and
(ix) Vyoma in the form of a cow-herd.[72]

In the Purāṇas, especially the *Bhāg. P.*, as Kṛṣṇa reaches the status of divinity, all forces headed by Kaṁsa that are against him form a united front and get the name *'asura'*. And as per the principle maintained by the Purāṇas, all these *asuras* are to be 'redeemed', and the way Kaṁsa acts, it appears he is the agent himself seeking final redemption. We have pointed out the principle of 'Virodha-Bhakti' (Devotion through Enmity or Opposition) seen in the Purāṇas. It is this principle that redeems the demon and unites him with the divinity. The Purāṇas are quite convincing here, for even from the psychological point of view, their justification stands to reason. Thus not actual worship, not paying homage, not having even the desire to look at the divine hero, but the enmity itself with the divinity takes a major portion of the thoughts of the *asuras,* thus actually dominating their lives, making them constantly think about the 'ultimate truth' which is 'divine' and thus an aspect of god. This is a step that leads them to a particular position of advantage prior to their redemption, which is an actual contact with the god. A graphic description of the condition of Kaṁsa, who is haunted by the divine Kṛṣṇa (Śrīkṛṣṇa) occurs in the *Bhāg. P.* Thus we note—"As he (i.e. Kaṁsa) disturbed in his mind, while drinking, speaking or moving about, sleeping, breathing, always (in his mind) saw before him that Lord (god Śrīkṛṣṇa), with (his emblem) the Sudarśana-disk, he (i.e. (Kaṁsa) got the same form (i.e. of Śrīkṛṣṇa)—the form which was difficult to attain." (*Bhāg. P.* X.44.39). Kaṁsa is only one of those, real or mythological villians that get the title of an *'asura'* and finally await redemption by the highest principle personified by Śrīkṛṣṇa. He is not an *'asura'* by birth, but the bad quality of being *'asura'* is seen in him by the Purāṇa. Whoever is against the hero (now a 'divinity') is an *'asura'*. And the god himself thinks about such *'asuras'* keenly though from a stand, which is different from the one meant for the other normal devotees. The final annihilation of these *'asuras'* at the hands of the god is their redemption, and in the Puranic expression, their becoming 'one' with the god or their merging into the very form of the god. Many stand in the line of Kaṁsa in the vaults of the Puranic literature. Thus Hiraṇyākṣa gets rolled to the divinity.[73] Hiraṇyakaśipu follows the same path and Śiśupāla and the like do not lag behind in this.[74] Even Pūtanā—the child-murderess—who came to suckle the infant Kṛṣṇa applying deadly poison to her breast, obviously with the intention of killing him, but was sucked by Kṛṣṇa of her life, is said to get, after her death, the world meant for the righteous people (*Bhāg. P.* X.6.35 cd). Though a *yātudhānī* (a female evil spirit), she attained the heavenly world, the 'fortune' of a 'mother'—*jananīgati* (*ibid.* 38 ab), as she suckled the child Kṛṣṇa. Her burning funeral pyre was emitting so much fragrance as to make the residents of Vraja returning to their place, curious of knowing the cause (*ibid.* 41).

The concept of *asura* is related to three levels *viz.* cosmic, sacrificial and moral. We have seen the *asuras* which tried to disturb the cosmic level. The same concept is seen on the sacrificial level in the form of the constant strife between gods and the asuras. The concept travels further to the *Mbh.* and the Purāṇas, where the *asuras* are seen in the human form, who commit grave sins against the god, became his dire enemies, but are finally redeemed. The mythical accounts about the *asuras*, evil spirits etc. occurring in the Purāṇas, are no doubt *arthavādas*. They are given by the Purāṇas with the purpose of projecting Kṛṣṇa as a child endowed with divinity and later on as a God—Personal God—which was the need of the society in those times. The *Bhagavadgītā*, which forms part of the *Mbh.* (Bhīṣma. chaps. 25-42) after elucidating the concepts of Jñāna and Karma in earlier chapters, deals with the path of

Devotion from the ninth chapter onwards, where we see Lord Śrīkṛṣṇa emerging as a Personal God. It was the Purāṇas who reached the common masses. For back was left the age, which saw Gārgī, Maitreyī and several other learned females (some of them the *ṛṣikās* in the *RV*)[75] and also the flexibility in *varṇa*-system, when even a learned non-*brāhmaṇa* was taken to be a *ṛṣi* and a *brāhmaṇa*, as is seen from the example of Kavaṣa Ailūṣa.[76] The institution of Paurāṇika (modern day Purāṇika associated with the temple), taking its sap from the *sūta* tradition, came to the forefront to impart the knowledge of the Purāṇas, which were orally told, though they were also in written form. In the changed circumstances, in order to propagate the old Vedic-brahmanical religion, with several changes introduced suiting to the practices of the righteous people in the then society (*sadācāra*), the Purāṇas resorted to the principle of Arthavādaism, which succeeded in convincing the people. The *arthavāda*-accounts, which we have noted, are given to glorify the Lord in every little detail, as they are enshrined in the doctrine of Devotion (Bhakti, that too Saguṇa-Bhakti).

Here we take into account the story of a *brāhmaṇa*, named Ajāmila, who had taken a slave girl as his wife. He had ten sons from her, the youngest being named 'Nārāyaṇa' (the name of Viṣṇu). The *brāhmaṇa* (Ajāmila) was very much attached to Nārāyaṇa. As Ajāmila attained the age of eighty and was seriously ill, the servants of Yama (the god of Death) came to take him away. Being excessively fond of his son Nārāyaṇa, Ajāmila's last letters which he uttered, were *nā-rā-ya-ṇa*. Hearing this four lettered word *nārāyaṇa*, which stands for Viṣṇu's name, there came the attendants of Viṣṇu to carry him to the Viṣṇuloka (*Bhāg.P.* VI.1.21ff-31). They were not ready to hand over Ajāmila to the attendants of Yama. Their pleading on behalf of Ajāmila was—'As Ajāmila has uttered the four-lettered word (*nārāyaṇa*) at the moment of death, he though a sinner throughout his life, has all his sins wiped off (*ibid.* VI.2.8). In fact, uttering the name of Viṣṇu acts as a perfect expiation (*suniṣkṛta*) in the case of —thief; drinker of wine; one who deceives a friend; killer of a *brāhmaṇa;* one who spoils the 'bed' of his preceptor (by approaching the preceptor's wife); one who kills a woman or a king or his own father or a cow; and other grave sinners (*ibid.* VI.2.9, 10). This mythical account coming as *arthavāda* tries to convince the common people of the importance of the path of Devotion (of Viṣṇu—(*Bhāg.P.* being a Vaiṣṇavite Purāṇa), the first step of it being 'simply uttering the name of Viṣṇu', which can instantaneously wipe off all the grave sins. Taking into account the age-old fact that the *Bhāg.P.* is the most read and heard of the Purāṇas in the Saptāhas (seven-day sessions) in the temples or in the homes, the popularity of such an *arthavāda* account bringing out the importance of Devotion, falls short of any more words for explanation!!

The *RV* refers to Dasyus or Dāsas many a time.[77] They were rich and affluent. Among them were Ilibiśa, Cumuri, Dhuni, Pipru, Śambara and Varcin. One Dāsa king named Balbūtha is said to have performed a sacrifice, in which he gives *dakṣiṇās* to his priest, who was the descendant of the Kaṇva family (*RV* VIII.46.32ab). But it is generally observed from the text that they were not following the sacrificial cult (*ibid.* VIII.6.3; 70.11; X.22.8) of the Vedic people. Their residence seems to be of a *pur* (fort)-type (*ibid.* II.20.8). They are spoken of as of dark skin (*ibid.* I.130.8; IX.41.1) and as snub-nosed (*ibid.* V.29.10). Sāyaṇa takes the word *anāsaḥ* meaning 'without mouth' (*an-āsaḥ*) i.e. unable to speak the Vedic language.[78] They are said to be *mṛdhravācaḥ* (*ibid.*) i.e. 'of indistinct speech.' Here we are reminded of the *arthavāda* occurring in the *Śat.Br.* (III.2.1.18-24). The gods had Sacrifice and the *asuras* Speech. The gods asked Sacrifice to call Speech to him. When Speech on the word of Sacrifice[79] came to the gods, they separated her from the *asuras* and offered her in fire as a holocaust. Being deprived of Speech and thus undone, the *asuras* cried 'he' lavaḥ!', 'he lavaḥ!'[80] The *Śat.Br.* says that they uttered this unintelligible speech and he who speaks thus is a *mleccha* (barbarian). The *Śat.Br.* (III.2.1.24) calls the language of the *asuras* 'Mleccha', which is the language of the *mlecchas* (barbarians). Richter-Ushanas Elbert points out that Ṛbhus[81] were the originators of the language of the *mlecchas*[82]. The speech of the Dāsas or Dasyus might have been different from that of the Aryans. Indra is said to have subdued and killed Śambara, Pipru, Namuci, Dhuni, Cumuri and Varcin (normally taken as demons) who are at times called Dāsa excepting Dhuni and Cumuri, who always figure as Dāsas.[83]

It cannot be decided whether the Dasyus or Dāsas were non-Aryan. The word *dāsa* has a sense of servant in the Vedic language. Vasiṣṭha calls himself a *dāsa* of Varuṇa (*RV* VII.86.7). Yāska gives the etymology of the word *dāsa* from √*das*—'to diminish, to be exhausted' (*Nir.* II.17). A mythical account occurring as an *arthavāda* in the context of the Aponaptrīya hymn can be helpful in this respect. Kavaṣa Ailūṣa, the son of a *dāsī*, was driven away by the priests from their Soma-sacrifice and was thrown away in the desert, as he was an *abrāhamaṇa* ('not a *brāhmaṇa*). But when they witnessed his 'seeing' the Aponaptrīya hymn (which was the invocation and praise of the god Apām Napāt) and the miracle of the river Sarasvatī (It was the desert, where Kavaṣa Ailūṣa was thrown!) rushing forth, surrounding Kavaṣa Ailūṣa from all sides, they invited him in their fold (*Ait. Br.* II.19=8.1; cf. *Kauṣ.Br.* XII.3). This shows that the Dāsas or Dasyus were regarded as being on a different footing, when compared to the Aryans—that too the upper class of the Aryans. The insult meted out to the son of a *dāsī* and later on his inclusion with respect among the *brāhmaṇas* shows the flexibility of the *varṇa*-system in the Vedic age.

Let us see the opinions of some scholars, who have tried to trace the identity of the Dāsas. Das regards the Dāsas as the first Aryan settlers.[84] Buddhaprakash maintains that the

Dāsas were the affluent Aryans against whom the majority of the Aryans living in villages stood in revolt.[85] Asko Parpola is of the firm opinion that the Aryans and the Dāsas, or Asuras (according to him, the words Dāsas, Dasyus, Asuras and also *śatru* being alternate with each other) were two different clans. Varuṇa was the lord of the Dāsas or Asuras and later on this principal deity of the subdued Asuras was incorporated by the Aryans in their pantheon.[86] Thus according to Parpola, there was amalgamation of the Aryan and the dāsa religions. Though the question cannot be solved decisively, it seems that the Dāsas or Dasyus had their distinct identity, only to get themselves acculturated in the Vedic fold. But as most of them probably were poor and employed for menial work, the word Dāsa came to mean 'a servant.'

This invites again the case of the *asuras*, though we have already dealt with it. We regard Dāsas or Dasyus and *asuras* different unlike the opinion of Parpola noted above. The mythical account of the *asura* king Bali[87] and also that of Hiraṇyakaśipu[88] indicate that by the Puranic times, the *asuras* were completely acculturated in the Vedic-brahmanical Hindu fold, thus echoing the old Vedic note that the *asuras* were the brothers of gods, both being born from Prajāpati and the word *'asura'* stood only for an evil tendency.

Among the tribes, Paṇis seem to be important, being wealthy. But they seem to be keeping themselves away from the sacrificial religion by not performing sacrifices and not giving any gifts (*dakṣiṇās*) to the priests. Hence they have all derogatory words heaped on them. "O wise god (Pūṣan) pierce the hearts of the Paṇis with your saw' (*RV* VI.53.5) says one seer, who again requests, "O Pūṣan! cut and loosen the hearts of the Paṇis" (*ibid.* 7). "Paṇi verily is the wolf" remarks another seer (*ibid.* VI.51.14). The intense desire of the priests was that the Paṇis should perform sacrifices and give *dakṣiṇās* (*ibid.* I.180.7).

A prominent trait of the Paṇis was that they were money-lenders (*bekanāṭa*).[89] But in spite of earning wealth the Paṇis seem to be stingy as can be seen from their not performing sacrifices and not giving *dakṣiṇās*. Bṛbu the head of the Paṇis however is an exception, who is said to be spacious in donation as the bed of the river Gaṅga, for he gave 'thousands' (*rātiḥ sahasriṇī*) to the priest (*ibid.* VI.45.31, 32). Here Bṛbu is praised in three *mantras* (*ibid.* VI.45.31-33). In the same *maṇḍala* of the family of Bharadvāja, we mark the keen desire of the seer to win the Paṇis over. Thus we have the words—"Soften, O God! even Paṇi's mind" (*ibid.*. VI.53.3).

The significant trait of the Paṇis is their association with the cows. The expression—"The rains have been held up as cows by the Paṇi"(*ibid.* I.32.11), shows that they might be cattle-traders or keeping cows in large quantities. An elaborate mythical account occurs in the *Jaim.Br.* (II.440-442). They are called *asura* and are said to be the cow-herds of the gods (*ibid.* II.440—*atha ha vai paṇayo namāsurā devānām gorakṣā āsuḥ*). This mythical account occurs as the *arthavāda* of the Abhiplava (Ṣaḍaha) rite which is performed for six days and is repeated in each of the twelve months (in a year) in the Gavām-ayana *sattra. A sattra* is a series of sacrifices (Soma-sacrifices) lasting for twelve days to a year or more. Gavām-ayana is a series of Soma-sacrifices extending over 361 days and is regarded as a *prakṛti* (i.e. norm) of *ayanas. Ayana* means advancing, particularly the advancing of the sun to the north and south of the equator, the Viṣuvan. Gavām-ayana, therefore, is a sacrificial rite confined to one year's period, with its middle-most day called Viṣuvan and with two wings of the series of sacrifices at each side. It is, as it were, the replica of the year. Gavām-ayana derives its name from the *arthavāda* that the rite was first performed by the cows (*Pañc.Br.* IV.1.4). As the word 'go' also denotes the rays of the sun, the rite is related to the course of the sun.[90]

The *arthavāda* in the *Jaim.Br.* (II.440-442) brings out how the Paṇis—the cow-herds of the gods—carried away the cows of the gods to the nether region and were crafty in bribing the bird Suparṇa sent by the gods in search of the cows. Eventually Suparṇa was punished and the faithful bitch Saramā was sent on this errand, who did not fall prey to the cunningness of the Paṇis. She was given a boon[91], as she brought the news of the cows to the gods. This *arthavāda* is functional, as it is used to justify the gain of the 'cows' (those in the *arthavāda* of the *Jaim.Br.* only secondarily)—but initially the gain of the rays of the sun (the word 'go' also denotes the sun's ray)—then the sun—and later on the year (Saṁvatsara).

The mythical account coming as *arthavāda* looks like a folk-tale[92], where—Suparṇa (the beautiful-winged bird) and Saramā (the bitch)—two creatures figure. Though Suparṇa can be traced to the Śyena-Suparṇa of the Veda[93], the 'bitch' is purely a loan from the area of the folk-tale, even admitting the mention of Yama's two dogs (*RV* X.14.10-12). The mythical account does not speak anything of the Paṇis further. Most probably by the time of the *Jaim.Br.*, the Paṇis had gone into oblivion and their memory remaining only in this account or they were acculturated in the Vedic fold, not requiring any special mention hereafter.

A note has to be taken of the Vrātyas, who seem to be on the periphery or outside the pale of the Aryan society.[94] One whole *kāṇḍa* (XV) of the *AV* eulogises the Vrātya and speaks of the hospitality given to him.[95] His epithet *mahādeva* (XV.1.4) and his description as having black (*nīla*) belly and red (*lohita*) back (*ibid.* 7), remind us of the later god Śiva, who is said to be Mahādeva and *nīlalohita*. A passage from the *Pañc.Br.* enables us to know some details about the Vrātyas. The Vrātyas were leading the life of a joined group, were destitute and were left behind. They were not given to the study of the Veda, did not till the land and were not engaged in trade. Dyutāna was the chief or the 'House-holder' (Gṛhapati) of the Vrātyas (*Pañc. Br.* XVII.1.7).[96] The behaviour of the Vrātyas was somewhat abnormal and at times quite despicable. They ate food which was meant for the *brāhmaṇas*. They called good words bad; used to strike a person with a stick, who did not commit any act punishable; though not initiated spoke the language of the initiated.

However, a convincing means was found out by the ritualists, who, we have to admit, were also social thinkers. This means was in the form of the Vrātyastomas, by performing which sacrifices, even the Vrātyas could be acculturated in the Vedic fold. The *Pañc.Br.* enjoins the four Vrātyastomas, which are one-day sacrifices (ekāhas).[97] The sixteen-versed *stoma* is employed in each of these Vrātyastomas and the first of these is enjoined for all the Vrātyas (*ibid.* XVII.1.2). The *Jaim.Br.* speaks of three Vrātyastomas (II.221-225). The *Kāty.Ś.S* deals with Vrātyastoma (XXII.4.1-28). The *Āpa.Ś.S* (XXII.5.4-14) and the *Pār.G.S.* (II.5) also have dealt with it. The *Pār.G.S.* clearly points out here that from among the Vrātyas, those desirous of having the proper *saṁskāras* after performing the Vrātyastoma sacrifice, can study as per their wish and become worthy of keeping contacts with (for up to that time, they were out-cast). The *Pañc.Br.* in fact has dealt with this topic of the Vrātyas in an elaborate manner. Actually, the four Vrātyastomas enjoined by it have taken into account different types of people in the society, noting their tendencies and ages, who have turned Vrātyas and are desirous to join again the bigger group of the Aryan fold.[98]

A detail from the *Pañc.Br.* points out that the Vrātyas were the adherents of a certain 'Deva' (God) and not of the usual gods.[99] The Vrātyas held a sacrificial session with Budha as their *Sthapati*. They consecrated themselves without having previously begged of Varuṇa a place for divine worship. Varuṇa cursed them that they would not know the path leading to the gods and would be devoid of a share in the sacrifice. Hence, the other priests do not take sacrificial substance (rice, barley etc.) nor (a draught of) Soma for them to sacrifice it on their behalf. But the *Pañc.Br.* specifically mentions that after the sixty-one-day sacrifice performed by the Vrātyas, the herbs, milk etc. acquired essence and became full of lustre and juice.[100] This mythical account coming as *arthavāda* is stated to glorify the sixty-one-day rite. The *Pañc.Br.* here states that a libation be offered in the Gārhapatya fire, with a request to Varuṇa to give a place of worship (*Pañc.Br.* XXIV.18.8), for it was due to the curse of Varuṇa that the Vrātyas were earlier reduced to a low position, as it has been noted before by us.

It seems that as the Vrātyastomas were a subsequent and necessary development in the history of the Vrātyas, by which they could be assimilated in the Vedic Aryan fold, the sixty-one-day rite of the Vrātyas (the adherents of the 'Deva') included in the series of rites laid down by the *Pañc.Br.*, is a clear indication of the acculturation of the Vrātyas in the Vedic Aryan fold. The role of *arthavāda* in this process has to be noted.

The work *Vrātyatāśuddhisaṅgraha* of later times points out how the attitude towards the Vrātyas was slowly becoming softened. It says that the Vrātyastoma like the penance for an *avakīrṇin* or the Niṣādasthapati is to be performed in the ordinary fire (*laukika agni*) and the Vrātya could be purified even after twelve years of celibacy or if he is an ordinary person, simply after bath only once in a day, which is accompanied with the Pāvamanī hymns addressed to Soma.[101] The later concept of Patitasāvitrīkas from amongst the Aryans termed as Vrātyas is based on the earlier concept of the Vrātya community. The Patitasāvitrīkas or Sāvitrīpatitas were those, in whose case even the upper limit of their age for undergoing the initiation rite was over. Yājñavalkya, having in view the Vrātyastomas prescribed by the ritual-texts and noted by us, states that Sāvitrīpatitas remain Vrātyas, unless a Vrātyastoma sacrifice is performed by them, after which they could have the initiation-rite performed in their case.[102]

A reference to Niṣādas occurs in the *YV*.[103] The work *Suparṇādhyāya* mentions the Niṣādarāṣṭra with many divisions (VII.16).[104] The *Rām.* mentions a kingdom of the Niṣādas on the bank of the river Gaṅgā. Guha, a Niṣāda, who was the *Sthapati*—the lord of the Niṣāda tribe—was ruling there.[105] The *Mbh.* mentions the region of the Niṣādas on the verge of or as adjacent to the sea (*Mbh.* Ādi 28.1). The opening to the country of the Niṣādas was at a place, where the river Sarasvatī is said to have disappeared in the desert due to the sins of the Niṣādas, with the thought, 'May not the Niṣādas know i.e. see me' (*ibid.* Vana 130.3, 4). There is a reference to Garuḍa eating the Niṣādas, when he is on his march to bring nectar from the heaven. This reference occurring in the works *Suparṇādhyāya* and the *Mbh.* has to be taken as symbolic of the defeat and acculturation of the Niṣādas in the Vedic Aryan fold.[106]

The *Bhāg.P.* traces the origin of the Niṣāda tribe joining it to the account of Veṇa, the king[107], who tortured his subjects, but ultimately met his death at the very 'Huṅkāra' of the sages. Becoming aware of the calamity of kingless state (*arājaka*), the sages created king Pṛthu with Arcis after churning Vena's two hands.[108] But prior to this, they cleaned Vena's (dead) body of the black 'evil' (sin) he had gathered. For this, they churned one of Vena's thighs and on came a dwarfish person, dark in complexion and short in stature, with a big chin. When he asked "What should I do?", they ordered him, "Be seated (*niṣīda*)". The 'dark' person, who took upon himself all the 'black' sins of Vena (the 'black' colour figuring in both) and his descendants are called the 'Niṣādas'[109] (from the apparent similarity between the two words *viz. niṣīda* and *niṣāda*). In the account from the *Mbh.*, the founder of the Niṣāda-clan is said to rise from the right thigh of the king Vena (*Mbh.* Śānti. 59.95-97) and Pṛthu was churned from his right hand (*ibid.* 98). Aryans seem to have married the Niṣāda girls as is seen in the work *Suparṇādhyāya* (X.18.5.......*dvijastu saniṣādīkaḥ sasutaḥ.....*). By the time of the Smṛtis and the *Mbh.* the Niṣādas were totally acculturated in the Vedic Aryan fold.[110]

The term *pañcajanāḥ* is generally explained as *niṣādapañcamāḥ*, Niṣādas being included after *śūdra*. Yāska quotes the remark of Aupamanyava—*catvāro varṇāḥ niṣādaḥ pañcamaḥ* (*Nir.* III.7), indicating the inclusion of the Niṣādas in the Vedic fold—the process of which had been there long before Yāsaka.

Here we come to the Brāhmaṇa-texts which enjoined a temporary stay among the Niṣādas, for the sacrificer in the Viśvajit sacrifice.[111] This 'compulsory dwelling has two motifs in view *viz.* (i) The sacrificer (king) is reminded of his duties towards the Niṣādas, who form a part of the kingdom; (ii The Niṣādas are convinced of their being accepted in the Vedic Aryan fold, as the sacrificer (-king) stays with them.

The *Pañc. Br.* (XVI.6.7) while laying down for the Viśvajit-sacrificer a dwelling (though for three days!) among Niṣādas, says that the latter are handed over to the earth and hence the sacrificer obtains the food found on the earth. This shows that the sacrificer was required to consume the wild eatables such as wild rice etc. (Lāt. Ś.S. VIII.2.8-9) from the Niṣādas, who solely subsist by the earth. This 'three days' stay among the Niṣādas, along with nine days stay (three days each) at three other places comes as a means to remove the bad consequences of giving away all the property in the Viśvajit sacrifice.[112] This is simply *arthavāda*. The 'stay' is prescribed, to make the king aware of his duties towards these strata of the society. Nevertheless it has also become a means to point out how the Niṣādas were acculturated in the Vedic Aryan fold. As we have already noted, the great legendary ancestor of the Niṣāda clan (though it is a mythical account) is 'born' (through a limb) of the *kṣatriya* Arya king Vena, pointing out that the Niṣāda clan is from none other but the Aryan fold itself. The Pūrvamīmāṁsā-sūtra goes to the extent of laying down the Raudra-*iṣṭi*, which could be performed in the case of (or on behalf of) the Niṣāda-*sthapati* (VI.1.25...........*etayā* (*raudreṣṭyā*) *niṣāda-sthapatim yājayet*).

We have seen the efforts of the Aryan fold to acculturate the Niṣāda clan in it. However, a probe in their origin in interesting, though it is hidden in the hoary past. Suniti Kumar Chatterji has dealt with this issue in details. He says that the Niṣādas were the old Austric people of India. India received all her human inhabitants, who came in successive waves from abroad. After the Negroids, who were the oldest people to come to India, there came to India from the west, from Palestine, proto-Australoids, some of whom passed out of India and still have their descendants living in Australia as aborigines. Those who stayed on in India evidently became characterised into the Austic people and developed their language and culture on the soil of India. These were known in ancient India as Niṣādas. They were a dark-skinned people and were spread all over India and formed the most important element among the lower classes or castes throughout the country. Being lost into an Aryan-speaking people, they lost their name and language. They gave some basic things, like the stick or hoe cultivation of wild rice, of some plants and vegetables etc.[113] Here we are reminded of the references from the *Pañ.Br.* (XVI.6.7) and *Lāt. Ś.S.* (VIII.2.8-9), which we have noted above, and which point out that the Viśvajit-sacrificer in his 'compulsory' 'three days' stay among the Niṣādas is required to eat the wild eatables, related to the earth. Prior to Chatterji, there have been efforts to know the origin of the Niṣādas.[114] All these views, including that of Chatterji, which plainly speaking is quite convincing (from the point of view of the study of races), are unanimous in pointing out that the Niṣādas were different from the Aryans but later on were acculturated in that fold. This historical fact is convincingly brought out by the ritual-texts, which have been noted above.

The Kirātas are mentioned as *pañcama varṇa*, staying in the caves of the mountains.[115] Even the Niṣādas are said to be the *pañcama varṇa* (the fifth *varṇa* added to the already four existing *varṇas*), as we have noted early. This shows that many non-Aryan tribes were, after acculturation, included in the Aryan fold as forming the *pañcama varṇa,* which subsequently was merged in the fourth i.e. *śūdra varṇa,* the total number of *varṇas* thus seen as four only. According to Suniti Kumar Chatterji, the Mongoloid peoples, with a number of different racial elements possessing certain common physical characteristics came into India probably before the Aryans, who knew them as Kirātas. They formed wide settlements throughout Assam, Bhutan and Nepal and also in East and North Bengal, North Bihar and the regions to the south of the Himalayas on North India right up to Kashmir.[116] Manu mentions several tribes, among which figure the Kirātas (*Manu Sm.* X.44). He says that all these tribes were from the *kṣatriya varṇa* formerly; but due to their not having the proper *saṁskāras*, they were 'fallen' and became *śudras* (*ibid.* 43). This shows the effort on the part of the social thinkers of those times to include all tribes in the Vedic Aryan fold.

The elevated status of the Kirātas, after acculturation, can very well be recognised from the account in the *Mbh.* Vana chaps. 27-41), in which god Śiva is said to present himself as a Kirāta, while testing Arjuna's devotion and sincerity in penance for getting the Pāśupata missile. Though Kirāta is commonly understood as Bhil, the very name 'Kirātā' (of a tribe and an individual, here Śiva) is important from our point of view. In the sixth century AD, the poet Bhāravi wrote his famous epic named *Kirātarjunīyam* of eighteen cantos, based on the episode seen above from the *Mbh.*

This trend of acculturation is seen all the more patent in the legend of Śunaḥśepa, which occurs in the *Ait. Br.* (VII.13-18=33.1-6). When Viśvāmitra accepted Śunaḥśepa as his son, his fifty sons older to the son Madhucchandas, did not approve of this act of Viśvāmitra, while the fifty sons who were younger to Madhucchandas accepted Śunaḥśepa as their brother. The fifty sons who did not agree with Viśvāmitra were cursed by him that their descendants would resort to the lowest castes. They became Andhras, Puṇḍras, Śabaras, Pulindas and Mūtibas. It is said that most of the Dasyus are the descendants of Viśvāmitra (*ibid.* VII. 18=33.6). The *Ait. Br.* here tries to point out that all these tribes once belonged to the Aryan fold. Some of these actually merged in the Vedic Aryan fold and then were admitted in the *pañcama varṇa*.

When we come to the age of the *Rām.*, we find that the Vedic Aryans had by then established their big colonies. To the south of the Vindhya mountain, there were several tribes which were trying to assimilate in the Vedic fold. However, the Rākṣasa tribe, having its stronghold in Laṅkā (today's Srilanka) was totally opposed to the Vedic culture. In spite of the *Mbh.* and the Purāṇas mentioning at several places the Rākṣasas, the graphic picture of their culture is mirrored in the *Rām.* The *Rām.* mentions three different families of the Rākṣasa tribe. The first one was the Virādha family, which stayed at the northern end of the Daṇḍaka forest. Virādha—the head of this family—maintained that the family came from the couple Java and Śatahṛdā (*Rām.* Araṇya 3.5). When Virādha caught hold of Sītā and was not ready to release her from his clutches, Rāma and Lakṣmaṇa had to cut off his arms (*ibid.* 4.5-7). When Virādha was nearly crushed to death, he asked Rāma to place him in a deep pit, for that had been the practice followed by the Rākṣasas to get a good world after death (*ibid.* 4.22-23). Virādha here confesses that out of infatuation, he could not recognise Rāma, who has by fatally attacking him, released him from the Rākṣasa form. And here comes the account of the curse given to Virādha by Vaiśravaṇa. Virādha in former birth was the *gandharva* Tumburu, who was cursed by Vaiśravaṇa to be a Rākṣasa. When propitiated by Tumburu, Vaiśravaṇa said that the former would come back to the heavenly world, only when killed by Rāma in the fight (*ibid.* 4.14-18). Another family of the Rākṣasas was that of the Dānavas, who were the descendants of Danu. Kabandha was the son of Danu. Kabandha with his largely expanding arms, caught hold of Rāma and Lakṣmaṇa, when they were on the search of Sītā. Kabandha was formerly cursed by the sage Sthūlaśiras for his insolence, but was to get his form back, only when his large arms were to be cut of by Rāma (*ibid.* 71.1-7). The curse in the case of Virādha and the one in the case of Kabandha are clearly a mythological strategy, which is employed to justify the defeat of these two Rākṣasa families by the Aryans and their subsequent acculturation in the Aryan fold.

It was with the third family of the Rākṣasas that the Aryans came into conflict, especially with Rāvaṇa, the lord of Laṅkā. The Uttarakāṇḍa of the *Rām.* (chaps. 4-11) gives much information about the ancestors of Rāvaṇa, who was from the family, which started from the couple Vidyutkeśa and Sālakaṭaṅkaṭā (*ibid.* 4.17ff). The name of the female—Sālakaṭaṅkaṭā—makes us surmise of the aboriginal trace in it. Rāvaṇa born in this family practised penance and getting a boon from the god Brahmā made Kubera leave Laṅkā and himself became the lord of it. Thus came into being the kingdom of the Rākṣasas with Laṅkā as its hub. Sage Agastya as is believed, was the first (Arya) person to go to the south crossing the Vidhya ranges and to have some colonisation on the northern bank of the river Godāvarī, near Janasthāna in the Daṇḍaka forest.[117] Thereafter came many sages to stay there. The Rākṣasas were already staying in the Janasthāna, which they had monopolised. Thus started a series of conflict between the Aryans and the Rākṣasas. With the arrival of Rāma and Lakṣmaṇa in the Daṇḍaka forest, the sages therein got some relief as they had then a strong support. The harsh words followed by the cruel punishment meted out to Rāvaṇa's sister Śūrpaṇakhā resulting into the kidnapping of Sītā by Rāvaṇa was the climax of the Arya-Rākṣasa tussle. Rāma's invasion of Laṅkā and the subsequent terrible Rāma-Rāvaṇa battle form the latter part of this conflict. In spite of Bibhīṣaṇa—the brother of Rāvaṇa—getting the kingdom of Laṅkā after Rāvaṇa as per Rāma's wish, the Rākṣasa tribe practically became extinct from the political history of the Āryāvarta.

Now about the grotesque appearance and the cannibalistic tendency of the Rākṣasas, which are deep-rooted in the 'collective mind' in the tradition, and which could be true to some extent. Even to this day, there are Palaeolithic tribes and some such ones are in the Andaman islands, and the tourists are not allowed to enter those areas. Some such tribes might have been there in the age of the *Rām.* The descriptions of Tāṭakā (*Rām.* Bāla 25.13), Ayomukhī (*ibid.* Araṇya 69.11, 12) and the Rākṣasīs guarding Sītā in the Aśoka-vana (*ibid.* Sundara 17) point out that not only males (for ex. Kabandha *ibid.* Araṇya 69.26-32), but even the females of the Rākṣasa tribe were terrible in appearance and bloodsucking in thought. How far these descriptions are true cannot be decided as the very tribe (Rākṣasa) has gone into oblivion long back. May be, this was the conventional way of describing the Rākṣasas, who were totally opposed to the infiltration and supremacy of the Vedic Aryans in the southern part of India. Nevertheless, it seems that Rākṣasas were good to look at, except for their black complexion. There were beautiful Rākṣasa women in Laṅkā (*ibid.* Sundara 18.26); Hanumān saw beautiful Rākṣasa women at the night time (*ibid.* 2.20); Hanumān could notice Mandodarī (Rāvaṇa's wife) from her bewitching beauty (*ibid.* 10.50-52). Even Rāvaṇa's stature was quite imposing (*ibid.* Yuddha 111.34-36). Rāvaṇa's epithets *viz.* Daśānana, Daśagrīva, Daśaśiras, Viṁśatibhuja, denoting his ten faces and twenty hands, need not be taken in the literal sense and are indicative of mythological layers added to him.

The ethical concepts of the Rākṣasas seem to be similar to those of the Aryans, the noteworthy examples being of Mārīca and Bibhīṣaṇa. It was Mārīca who advised Rāvaṇa not to kidnap Sītā and take enmity with Rāma, who was a pious prince; moreover it was an unrighteous deed to carry away anybody's wife (*ibid.* Araṇya chap. 37, especially vv. 14-22 in it). There seems to be much similarity between the practices of the Rākṣasas and those of the Aryans. Rāvaṇa's rigorous penance; Hanumān seeing the Yātudhānas (Rākṣasas) engaged in the Vedic studies and reciting *mantras* (*ibid.* Sundara 4.13); the Brahmarakṣases knowing the six Vedāṅgas (auxiliary sciences of the Veda), offering oblations in sacrifice and uttering Brahmaghoṣas (*ibid.* 18.2); sacrifice to Nikumbhilā by Indrajit, the son of Rāvaṇa (*ibid.* Yuddha chaps. 84-85); the 'Svastyayana'[118] performed by Rāvaṇa prior to march; the sacrifices performed by him etc., reflect the cultural life of the Rākṣasas. Hence there is a trend to believe that the Rākṣasas were originally a clan of the Aryans. But being deviated from the original source, they went to south and there established big and wealthy colonies, the pride of which led them to excess of enjoyment and cruelty.[119] This can be corroborated from the *Rām.* itself, which has used the strategy of curse. Thus originally a Yakṣiṇī, Tāṭakā, due to her cruelty is turned into a Rākṣasī by the curse of Agastya, who also cursed Mārīca to be a Rākṣasa (*ibid.* Bāla 25.12). Kalmāṣapāda out of mistake served human flesh to Vasiṣṭha and hence became a Rākṣasa (*ibid.* Uttara 65.28).

But in fine, it is better to regard the Rākṣasas as from a tribe, which had its establishment to the southern end of India and Srilanka. Having come into contact with the Aryavarta land, the Rākṣasas tried to adopt the practices of the Aryans. Those who studied the Vedas, were known as 'Brahmarakṣases' and some like Bibhīṣaṇa and Mārīca were genuinely good. But initially they could not be assimilated in the Vedic Aryan fold, as they were totally opposed to the Vedic Aryan culture.

Another important tribe from the *Rām.* is of the Vānaras (monkeys), which had their habitat to the south of the Vindhya mountain in the forest. Vāli is called by Rāma a *śākhāmṛga*—a creature staying on the branch of a tree (Kiṣkindhā 18.42), which might have been the usual way of addressing or referring to Vānaras. May be the Vānaras were carrying with them the reminiscence of their totemistic origin, which became patent through their attire and speech. Though they differed from the Aryans with respect to many matters, they welcomed the Aryan culture and became friends with Rāma and Lakṣmaṇa and helped them in defeating the Rākṣasas, who could not be acculturated in the Vedic Aryan fold.

A full chapter of the *Rām.* (Bāla chap. 17) is devoted to the birth-account of different heroes of the tribes *viz.* Vānara, Gopuccha (a kind of monkey) and Bear (Ṛkṣa). The point to be noted is that these heroes are said to have been born from the Aryan gods to the females of these tribes. The whole chapter is an *arthavāda*, which tries to justify the acculturation of these totemistic tribes in the Vedic Aryan fold. Thus the important Vedic gods are pressed into service here, the list containing the names of the gods as well as that of the Vānaras is quite a long one. The principle underlying here is—As was the form (*rūpa*-appearance), attire and valour of the god, so was that, of the individuals from the Ṛkṣa, Vānara and Gopuccha tribes (*ibid.* 17.19, 20), indicating the process of *aryanisation* of these tribes, which were totemistic. The chapter mentions several other tribes, such as Nāgas and Kiṁpuruṣas. Vāli was the chief of the tribes *viz.* Vānara, Gopuccha and Ṛkṣa. We have noted above that the heroes from these tribes are said to have been born from the Aryan gods and it is an *arthavāda* which tries to account for the acculturation. In order to show that the *arthavāda* does not forget even small details, here we take a couple of examples. Thus Vālī was born from Indra, and Sugrīva from the Sun (Bāla 17.10). As Vālī and Sugrīva are seen as the enemies of each other, so are their generators (fathers) *viz.* Indra and Sūrya (Tapana) in conflict with each other right from the *RV*.[120] In fact the *Rām.* has chosen the antagonistic pair of Indra and Sūrya purposefully to indicate the in-born enmity of Vālī and Sugrīva, there too Vālī (born from Indra) was defeated and killed (by Rāma, from a dynasty traced to the Sun)[121] and this was for Sugrīva (born from the Sun). A mythological justification indeed! Indra and Sūrya are again the gods, from whom is traced the birth of Arjuna and Karṇa respectively, who stood as dire enemies of each other in the *Mbh* (Ādi 63.116; 63.98; 110.18).

The *Ram.* passingly mentions several tribes (*ibid.* Araṇya 14.16ff). One such tribe like the Vānaras, was a totemistic tribe of the Gṛdhras (Birds), Jatāyu a Gṛdhra heading it. Garuḍa's brother Aruṇa is said to have got two sons—Sampāti the elder and Jaṭāyu, both from Śyenī (a female hawk—but we can take it here to mean a female bird). This is told by Jaṭāyu to Rāma, with a promise to protect Sītā in the forest in the absence of Rāma and Lakṣmaṇa, he being a friend of Daśaratha (*ibid.* 31.34). Even this tribe was acculturated in the Aryan fold. Jaṭāyu was deadly wounded by Rāvaṇa, when the latter was carrying away Sītā, and Jaṭāyu was trying to release her from Rāvaṇa's tight grip. When Rāma came searching for Sītā, he saw the Bird Jaṭāyu, who was holding his last breath only to tell Rāma about the whole incident, after which he did not survive. While placing the body of Jaṭāyu on the funeral pyre, the words uttered by Rāma are important. He says that the Bird Jaṭāyu will get, after death, the same reward, which is acquired by the *āhitāgni* persons (the persons who maintain the three fires), persons who perform sacrifices, warriors who do not return (i.e. run away) from the battlefield and those who give away lands as gifts (*ibid.* Araṇya 68.29-30). Here Rāma is viewing the sacrifice made by Jaṭāyu (in trying to save Sītā) with great respect and giving him the same status as that of the Aryans, who perform the righteous deeds. It also indicates the acceptance of the members of the Bird tribe in the Vedic Aryan fold.

A reference to the members of the Bird tribe occurs in the *Śat Br.* in the context of the Horse-sacrifice, which we have referred to earlier (*Śat.Br.* XIII.4.3.13). Thus Purāṇaveda was to be told to the people of the Bird tribe and men acquainted with the science of Birds, on every ninth day of the mini-cycles of ten days in the Pāriplava cycle of legends. Here King Tārkṣya is taken by Macdonell probably originally to represent the sun in the form of a divine horse.[122] But Macdonell also notes that in one or two later Vedic texts Tārkṣya is, however, referred to as a bird, and in the epic and subsequent literature, he is identical with the swift bird Garuḍa, the vehicle of Viṣṇu.[123] The *Śat.Br.* (XIII.4.3.13) takes the word Tārkṣya as denoting a bird and that too king or chief of the Birds. Here the word *vāyovidvika* is taken by Eggeling to denote 'bird-catchers', though he has given the literary meaning—'men acquainted, with the science of birds.'[124] The *Śāṅkh.Ś.S.* (16.2.25-27) also mentions this instruction of reading out the Purāṇaveda on the ninth day in the mini-cycles of the Pāriplava *ākhyāna*, to the Birds who are the people of Tārkṣya Vipaśyat. It gives the explanation (alternative?) of Birds as 'religious students' (*brahmacāriṇaḥ*). According to the Comm. on the *Śāṅkh. Ś.S.*, it is the *Vāyu P.* (*purāṇam vāyuproktam*) that is to be recited and not the *RV* (X.130)—*tasya vedaikadeśatvāt*.

The two brothers *viz.* Jaṭāyu and Sampāti, referred to in the *Rām.* are said to be born from a *syenī* (female hawk or female bird), with Aruṇa (Garuḍa's brother) as their father. The mention of the father could be mythological; but the mention of *śyenī* speaks of their totemistic character as of the Bird tribe. The *Śat. Br.* mentions such a Bird tribe, as we have noted above and supports the existence of such Bird tribes at the time of the *Rām.* They might be nomadic tribes, with Gṛdhra or Tārkṣya as their totem.[125] They had their own rites and rituals. Sampāti, the elder brother offers water in obsequies to Jaṭāyu (*Rām.* Kiṣkindhā 58.35; 60.1). Whether this practice was adopted by them from the Aryans cannot be proved convincingly.

The *Rām.* refers to a woman—Śabarī—from the Śabara tribe (Araṇya chaps. 73 and 74). These Śabara people are seen to be staying on the bank of the Pampā lake and earning their livelihood by the forest-activities particularly hunting, gathering fruits etc. Śabarī was a *śramaṇī* (a female recluse), who after meeting Rāma, which was her cherished desire, cast away her body in fire and got release from the cycle of birth and death (*ibid.* 74.32-33).

According to an account in the *Padma P.*, a Śabara was a devotee of Viṣṇu and wore on his body, the two distinguishing things characteristic of the Vaiṣṇavite faith *viz.* the stone Śālagrāma (woven in a garland or necklace?) on his chest and the leaves of the Tulasī plant on his head. At the hour of his death, the attendants of Yama were about to take him to the other world, but having seen these two objects on his body, they left him (*Padma P.* Pātālakhaṇda 20.45-75). This shows that by the time of the Purāṇas, even the aboriginal Śabaras became the devotees of Viṣṇu and thus were completely acculturated in the Vedic-brahmanical Hindu fold.

Śabarī in the *Rām.* and Śabara in the *Padma P.* are the devotees of Rāma and Viṣṇu resp. Though the two works are far away from each other chronologically, the two god-heads are very near. In fact, in the Bālakāṇḍa and the Uttarakāṇḍa (regarded as having many interpolated portions) of the *Rām.*, Rāma is shown to be attaining status very near to that of a god, and there too that of Viṣṇu. In fact Rāma is regarded and often spoken of as Viṣṇu, who has taken birth on the earth.

The name of the famous commentator of Jaimini's Pūrvamīmāṁsāsūtras—'Śabarasvāmin'—invites attention, as it seems connected to Śabara, though no convincing evidence can be given. A legendary account says that his original name was Ādityadeva, but when tortured by the Jains for his tenets, he stayed in the disguise of a Śabara for his protection, thus getting the name 'Śabarasvāmin'. A verse from the floating mass of literature states that Śabarasvāmin took four wives, one each from the four *varṇas* and had six sons from them *viz.* Varāhamihira, Bhartṛhari, Vikrama, Haricandra, Śaṅku and Amara. Such accounts hardly have any grain of truth and keep the 'name' puzzling as before, nevertheless throwing some dim light on the acculturation of the Śabaras.

The *Mbh.* mentions the creation of many non-Aryan (*mleccha*) tribes such as Śabara etc. from the cow belonging to Vasiṣṭha (*Mbh.* Ādi 174.38-40; Droṇa 26.17). It states that Nandinī created Śabaras on the order of Vasiṣṭha (*ibid.* Śalya 40.21), and that they used to earn their livelihood in the kingdom of Māndhātṛ[126] (*ibid.*, Śānti 65.13-15). Lord Śiva himself took the form of a Śabara (*ibid.* Anuśāsana 14.141). Dange has rightly pointed out that here the cow Nandinī is a symbol of the very Earth, who stands as a 'mother', from whom we have origin of several tribes *viz.* Pallava, Drāviḍa, Yavana, Śabara, Pauṇḍra, Kirāta, Siṁhala, Barbara, Khaśa, Cibuka, Pulinda, Cīna, Hūṇa, Kerala, Mleccha.[127] The Earth was milked by Pṛthu, the former becoming a cow and the latter making several persons successively a calf (*Bhāg.P.* IV chap. 18).[128] We have seen the account of King Vena in the context of the Niṣāda tribe. Pṛthu and Arcis came out after churning (dead) Vena's hands (*Bhāg.P.* IV.14.44; IV.15.1). The *Mbh.* specifically mentions that Pṛthu was churned from Vena's right hand (*Mbh.* Śānti 59.98). This account tallies with that of the cow Nandinī to some extent. In one account the cow (Nandinī) is a symbol of the Earth; in the other account the Earth becomes a cow, but in both the accounts cow stands as a source of production of several tribes or of many things of enjoyment.

We have referred to many tribes coming from the body of the cow Nandinī. Many of these got acculturated in the Vedic-brahmanical society, their acculturation being justified by the mythical accounts coming as *arthavāda*. The social structure of ancient India prone to assimilating these tribes needed such *arthavāda* accounts. Many of these tribes came to be reckoned as the 'fourth *varṇa*' (*śūdras*), which was the only *varṇa*, to which entry was easy, for the upper three *varṇas* (*brāhmaṇa, kṣatriya* and *vaiśya*) were bound by the rules and regulations and hence could not accommodate and admit any new entrants.

Here we take a note of certain tribes, which are mentioned in the *Mbh.* and which were acculturated in the Vedic-brahmanical fold. In the Bhīṣma *parvan* of the *Mbh.*, there occurs a long list of countries, where reside these tribes or groups of people, some of them not from the Vedic-brahmanical fold, while with some of them and their names we are conversant (*Mbh.* Bhīṣma 9.39-70). Mārkaṇḍeya says that in the Kali age, the groups of *mlecchas* such as Ābhīras, Śakas etc. will rule over certain parts of (the then) India (Vana 188.35-36). The Ābhīras resided on the banks of the river Indus and Sarasvatī and were conquered by Nakula (Sabhā 32.9-10). It is pointed out in the *Mbh.* that the Ābhīras formerly were *kṣatriyas*. But being afraid of Paraśurāma, who had sworn to kill all the *kṣatriyas*, they resorted to the caves of the mountains as hiding-places and left off their duties, reducing their descendants to the state of *śūdra* (Āsva. 29.16). This clearly indicates that they were assimilated in the *śūdra varṇa* in the Vedic-brahmanical fold.

Karṇaprāvaraṇa was a tribe staying close to the southern sea and was defeated by Sahadeva (Sabhā 31.67). Megasthenes—the Greek historian—has mentioned in his records this tribe, by stating that the people of this tribe used to cover their body with their ears and hence were named; Karṇaprāvaraṇa' (*karṇa*—'ear'; *prāvaraṇa*—'covering'). May be right from the upper part of their body (starting from ears), they might be covering their whole body with a long blanket or their (ear) lobes might be very much elongated as we mark even in this age in the case of some tribals, who wear big ear-ornaments, hanging from their ear-lobes. The *Mbh.* records that these tribesmen had come to meet Yudhiṣṭhira with gifts for him (Sabhā 52.19).

The *Mbh.* notes that from Vasiṣṭha's cow Nandinī were created the tribes such as Kerala, Hūṇa etc., which are termed *mleccha* (Ādi 174.38). There is mentioned the tribe Kolisarpa, which though *kṣatriya* formerly, was reduced to the status of *śūdra,* not getting the sanction from the *brāhmaṇas* (Anu. 33.22). This is justifying the entry of the tribe Kolisarpa in the Aryan fold though in the *śūdra varṇa,* simultaneously convincing us that the tribe in the past was *kṣatriya* and from the Aryan fold itself. Here we are reminded of the legend of Śunaḥśepa which occurs in the *Air.Br.* and to which we have already referred. There several tribes are said to be formerly the sons of Viśvāmitra but because of disobedience to him became the various tribes (*Ait.Br.* VII.18=33.6), indicating the all-pervasive nature of the Vedic-brahmanical fold.

The case of the Pauṇḍras is the same as that of the tribe Kolisarpa, which has been noted above. They are said to be staying in the kingdom of the king Māndhātā (Mbh. Śānti 65.14). It is pointed out that they were first from the *kṣatriya* fold (i.e. upper *varṇa*), but due to the anger and displeasure of the *brāhmaṇas* for them, they became *śūdras* (*ibid.* Anu. 35.17-18). The *Mbh.* mentions the origin of the Pahlava tribe from the tail of Nandinī—Vasiṣṭha's cow (*ibid.* Ādi 174.36) and that of Barbara tribe, again from the same cow (*ibid.* 37), the cow standing for the Earth, as we have already noted. But it is the cow of Vasiṣṭha—an Āryan—indicating the all-pervasive hold of the Vedic-brahmanical fold, the fact again and again pointed out through *arthavāda*-accounts

That this process of acculturation of various tribes has been a constant phenomenon, can be noticed from a reference to the 'Pāñcajanya' Agni, which occurs in the *Mbh.*. Agni (Fire) is regarded to be the son of five *viz.* Kāśyapa, Vāsiṣṭha, Prāṇa, Āṅgirasa and Cyavana (*Mbh.* Vana 220.1, 5). This Agni (Pāñcajanya) born from the five above-mentioned *ṛṣis* (seers) was the origin of five families, taking the names of these *ṛṣis* (*ibid.* 5 *pāñcajanyaḥ ...... pañcavaṁśakaraḥ....*). The concept can be traced back to the *RV*, where Agni of Bharata is spoken of (*RV* VII.8.4). The very name 'Pāñcanjanya' leads us to the concept of *pañcajanas* and also to that of the 'Niṣādapañcama' society, consisting of the four *varṇas* and the Niṣādas (and many such tribes which were acculturated) as the fifth *varṇa*. The *Mbh.* states here an interesting detail. It says that the Pāñcajanya god (Agni) generated gods Śiva, Indra etc., the progeny of the Pitṛs Praṇidhi, Bhānu etc. (Vāna 220.6-10). Moreover he created persons, who (even now) are stealing or carrying away sacrifice i.e. nullifying or destroying the 'merit' of sacrifice, performed by the sacrificers (*ibid.* 11ff). But the Agni established (on the altar-here the Great Fire-altar is probably referred to)[129] injures them with his wings and being 'pacified' with the *mantras*, they do not (dare to) steal the 'merit' (*iṣṭam*) of sacrifice (*ibid.* 16, 17). The word 'Pāñcajanya' is self-eloquent of its all-pervading character. Dange has rightly pointed out that this concept of 'Pāñcajanya' Agni speaks of the effort on the part of the *Mbh.* to bring all clans and tribes under the banner of 'sacrifice.'[130]

In the age of the Epics and the Purāṇas, there have been sects following the Śaiva, Vaiṣṇava and Śākta faiths, the information of which is too well-known[131] and hence is not recorded here. Moreover, these are from the Vedic-brahmanical Hindu society and have been a part of this very social structure, not requiring any justificatory explanation for their being in this structure. Same is the case of the sects following Tantrik or other such practices.

Apart from these sects, here we take into account the sect of the Magas—later on called the Maga *brāhamaṇas*—which has become a part of the Indian society from very early times and needs a detailed treatment.

Maga is a priest of the sun-god. Magas along with Bhojakas[132] are referred to at several places in the *Bhav.P.* The origin of the Magas is given by the *Bhav. P.* at two places in two different ways. According to one account they are said to be the mind-born sons of the sun-god (*ibid.* Brāhma. 177.11-35), while in the other account they are said to be the sons of Agni (*ibid.* 139.44). The first account differing in detail, occurs in the *SK.P.*, where they are said to be the *brāhmaṇas* (*viprāḥ*) born out of the sun's body (*Sk.P.* VI.147). The second account in the *Bhav.P.*, combining the Sun and Agni—the two agents—is quite interesting. It says that Nikṣubhā, the daughter of the sage Sujihva, always attended upon the fire (Agni), as told by her father. Once the Sun-god, seeing her became passionate. In order to enjoy her, he entered fire and became the son of Agni (the Fire-god). Once, accidentally, the Sun-god could catch her, when she inadvertently crossed over the fire. Showing his real form and blaming her for insulting the fire, he took her by hand and united with her. The son born to her was called Jaraśabda (*Bhav.P.* Brāhma 139.32-33). From him came the Magas. According to one legend, Magas sprang from Jarṣabha, the son of the Sun-god from Nikṣubhā, who was the daughter of the sage Sujitvan of the Mihira *gotra.*[133] Mihira is the name of the Sun. According to the *Padma P.* there are four sects of the Magas *viz.* Maga, Māmaga, Mānasa and Mandaga, corresponding to the four *varṇas—brāhmaṇa, kṣatriya, vaiśya* and *śūdra* (*Padma P.* Svargakhaṇḍa 9.34). The *Mbh.* gives the word Maṅga for Maga (*Mbh.* Bhīṣma 11.36). It says that in the Śākadvīpa, there are four well-known *janapadas* (countries) namely Maṅga (populated mostly with the *brāhmaṇas*), Maśaka (with righteous and generous *kṣatriyas*), Mānasa (with persons having their livelihood by the *vaiśya* way) and Mandaga (with *śudras*, following with faith their code of conduct). There is neither a king, nor a rod of punishment, or an executive meting out the punishment (*ibid.* 35-39). The story of the immigration of the Magas from Śākadvīpa is narrated differing in some details given in the Purāṇas such as *Bhav. P.* (Brāhma. 139ff), *Sāmba P.* (3, 24, 26), *Brahma P.* (20) and *Varāha P.* (177).[134] Ajay Mitra Shastri pointing to Hazra for support states that this story is given for accommodating the special features by the

Magas in solar worship and for improving the social status of the Maga *brāhmaṇas*.[135] The account runs as follows. Sāmba, the son of Kṛṣṇa from Jāmbavatī, who had been afflicted by leprosy due to Nārada's curse, got cured of the disease by worshipping the sun (Sūrya) and installed the image of the sun in a large temple built by him at Mūlasthānapura (modern Multan) on the bank of the river Candrabhāgā (Chenab). When no *brāhmaṇa* priest was available locally, to conduct the Sun-worship in its new form, he brought on the advice of Gauramukha, Ugrasena's priest, from Śākadvīpa eighteen families of Maga priests, who are said to be the descendants of the Sun (Sūrya) from Nikṣubhā, the daughter of Sujihva.

We have already noted the account from the *Bhav. P.* (Brāhma. 139.32-33) regarding Nikṣubhā and her son Jaraśabda and the Magas coming from the latter. Ajay Mitra Shastri, on the basis of the *Sāmba-purāṇa* (XXII and XXIX.2) states that the Magas were probably responsible for popularising the anthropomorphic representation of the Sun-god, who was earlier worshipped in the symbolic form and the emergence of the Sun-worshipping (Saura) sect.[136] Shastri notes that Varāhamihira, the author of the work *Bṛhatsaṁhitā* was a Maga priest.[137] Varāhamihira prescribes that the Magas were the proper persons to consecrate the Sūrya image (*Bṛhatsaṁhitā* LIX.19), and also furnishes the description of the icons of the Sun (*ibid.* LVII.46-48). The Magas are referred to in numerous inscriptions and literature up to the 12th cen. AD.[138] The Magas are still present in various parts of India—in Bihar and Uttar Pradesh where they are called Śākadvīpin Brāhmaṇas; in Bengal where they are known as Graha-vipras (for their interest in astrology and the lore of planets) and Ācārya Brāhmaṇas in Rajasthan where their nomenclature is Sevaka or Bhojaka.[139]

Shastri traces the Magas to the Sun-worshipping Magi priests, who were originally inhabitants of Medea, later on gradually spread over the whole of Achaemenian world, particularly Iran, some of them finding a foothold in Zoroastrianism.[140] He has also referred to several opinions, in this respect.[141] The issue of Magi priests and their spread to Zoroastrianism has been debatable, which is passed over here as it is not directly concerned with the issue of the Maga *brahmaṇas*. That the Magas came from outside (from the Śākadvīpa, as the *Mbh.* states clearly) is proved conclusively. They have been accepted in the social structure as *brāhmaṇas*[142] that too Sun-worshipping priests. Moreover the Purāṇas, by weaving the tale of Sāmba have justified their status in the society, carving out a place of respect for them.

Thus right from the Ṛgvedic times (or even prior to that period) spreading over to medieval and even to later age, there has been the process of assimilation in India of various tribes,[143] clans and sects in the society. These units at times are seen to have their own *vratas* (vows to follow), festivals, gods and modes of worship, in most of the cases identical with those in the Vedic-brahmanical Hindu society, sometimes bearing only similarity and at times totally different. The Vedic, Epic and Puranic accounts coming as *arthavāda* have justified this process of assimilation. This way of justifying and explaining, which we have designated as 'Arthavādaism', was the need of the social structure, which followed this for its own working.

By the Puranic period, we have this structure of the society, which though initially to some extent was multi-ethnical in character, by this age became a unit, complete in itself, to be known as the Ancient Indian Society. In the pages to follow, it will be seen how the process of Arthavādaism has helped the various facets of this society the prominent of them being 'Sacrifice' (*yajña*), which though remained in later times in a changed form, has ever been a hub of all religious and ritualistic activities, howsoever small or big they may be!

NOTES AND REFERENCES

1. In the *Mbh.*, in the Garuḍa legend, Kadrū is seen as the mother of serpents, while her co-wife Vinatā has two sons, the illustrious one being Garuḍa.
2. The ritual of Soma dates back to the Indo-Iranian period. In both the *RV* and the *Avesta*, Soma or Haoma is said to grow on mountain and it is believed that it descends to earth from its mythical region in heaven. For details, see Nawaz R. Guard, *Ritual Drink in the Iranian and Indian Traditions (From Avestan and Sanskrit Sources)*, Thesis, University of Bombay, Bombay(=Mumbai), 1991. For Haoma-ritual, pp. 223-43; 421-39; for identifying the Soma-Haoma plant, pp. 425-31.
3. P.V. Kane, *HDS*, Vol. II, Pt. II, p. 1141 note 2546.
4. *Śrautapadārtha-nirvacanam*, by an unknown author, pub. by Yudhishthira Mīmāṁsaka, Bahalgarh (Sonepat, Haryana), 1984, pp. 268-69.
5. See A.A. Macdonell, *Vedic Mythology*, Motilal Banarsidass, Reprint, Delhi, 1995, (Strassburg, 1898), p. 106; also J.J. Modi, *The Religious Ceremonies and the Customs of the Parsees*, Bombay, 1937 (1922), p. 253.
6. See *Pañcaviṁśa Brāhmaṇa*, tr. by W. Caland, 2nd ed., Sri Satguru Publications, Delhi, 1982 (Calcutta, 1931), p. 641f (tr. of *Pañc. Br.* XXV. 15.3). The explanation is *daśa* (ten)> daṁś (to bite) and so the serpents are 'biting' (*daṁśuka*).
7. Caland points out that the ten *sāmans* of the Sarpas are registered in the Araṇyageyagāna (*SV*. Calcutta, ed., Vol. II, pp. 417-21). See W. Caland, *op.cit.* p. 641. He says that out of these ten, the first three are intended here. This shows how the Sarpa-*sāmans* got entry into the *SV*.
8. See Sindhu S. Dange, "Sarpa-Bali", *Hindu Domestic Rituals—A Critical Glance,* Ajanta Publications, Delhi, 1985, pp. 88-94.
9. T.V. Mahalingam, "The Nāgas in Indian History and Culture", *Journal of Indian History*, University of Kerala, Trivandrum, Vol. XLIII, Pt. I, April 1965, Serial No. 127, p. 11.
10. C.F. Oldham, *The Sun and the Serpent*, London, 1905, p. 58.
11. *Mbh.* Ādi 50.33-54; 51.6-7; 56.4-26; chap. 58.
12. Many beliefs are gathered round serpent or snake *viz.* as controlling water and hence haunting rivers, lakes etc.;

representing ancestors; guarding treasures, which are buried; identifying and protecting the kings or heroes, healing diseases of all sorts and most important is giving children by its favour to the childless. For detailed information see *ERE*, Vol. XI, pp. 414a and 415b.

The worship of snake or serpent seems to have originated independently of totemism. Descent from the snake, the use of its name as a title, the taboo which prevents its slaughter and the respect paid to it when dead all appear in India. See *Ibid.*, p. 416b. For a detailed study see *ibid.* 412ff; also C.F. Oldham, *op.cit.*; also T.V. Mahalingam, *op.cit.*

13. *ERE*, Vol. XI, p. 413a.
14. *Ibid.*, p. 414a & b.
15. *Ibid.*, p. 413 a.
16. See P. Thomas, *Epics, Myths and Legends of India*, 9th edn., Bombay. For the full story see, Sadashiv A. Dange, *Myths from the Mahābhārata—Quest for Immortality*, Vol. I, Aryan Books International, New Delhi, 1997, p. 150 note 398 and Appendix C—"The Story of Behulā and the Snake Goddess" pp. 284-85. The figure of Manasā is shown with a seven-hooded serpent above her head. See A.H. Longherst, Humpi *Ruins*, Delhi, 1933, p. 30, figs. 8 and 9.
17. These twelve Nāgas are obviously the twelve famous Nāga families and they are remembered here in the yearly vow and shown respect by observing the twelve *pañcamīs* (every fifth day in the dark half of the twelve months of a year).
18. The classical explanation of the power and danger of iron is that of Tylor and it is of the spirits's fear of iron, for they are essentially creatures belonging to the ancient Stone Age and the new metal is hateful and hurtful to them. See for this, E.B. Tylor, *Primitive Culture*, Vol. I, London, 1903 (1871), p. 140.

    On the other hand, J.A. Canon Macculloch, thought that the spirits' dislike of iron was simply a human dislike transferred to them—what men feared, spirits would also fear. See J.A. Macculloch, *Folk-Lore*, Vol. XLIII, pp. 372 ff.

    In fact, this issue of 'Iron' as connected to 'Magic' is dealt with by Verrier Elwin, in details. See Verrier Elwin, *The Agaria*, Oxford University Press, Reprint, Indian Branch, first published in 1942, pp. 130-68.

19. See Mahadevashastri Joshi (ed.), *Bhāratīya Saṁskṛti Kośa* (Marathi), Vol. 4, Pune, 1970, p. 738a.
20. *Ibid.*, p. 755b.
21. *Ibid.*, p. 734b.
22. *Ibid.*, p. 735a. This festival used to be celebrated every year (for one day) in the house of the author (of the present book) till recent times and hence the information is correct and authentic.
23. A.A. Macdonell, *Vedic Mythology*, p. 156.
24. Malati J. Shendge, *The Civilised Demons—The Harappans in the Ṛgveda*, Abhinava Publications, New Delhi, 1977.
25. A.A. Macdonell, *op.cit.*, p. 156.
26. G.J. Held, *The Mahābhārata*, London, Amsterdam, 1935, p. 300.
27. *Ibid.*, p. 296.
28. *ERE*, Vol. IV, p. 392 a.
29. A.A. Macdonell, *op.cit.*, pp. 158-62.
30. *Ibid.*, p. 160.
31. See J. Gonda, *The Savayajñas* (*Kauśikasūtra* 60-68, tr., Intrn. and Comm.), N.V. Noord—*Hollandsche Uitgevers Maatschappu*—Amsterdam, 1965, p. 13.
    "......a *sava* may be described as a "solemn, consecration" (*abhiṣeka-*) for special ceremonies of considerable variety. ....*sava* is the name of special religious ceremonies of the one day because in them one undergoes the process *su*, i.e. is anointed (consecrated) with lordship (supremacy)." Here the context is of Indrasava."
32. This process or motif of swallowing (something) and making it disgorged is seen in the legend of Kaca, where Kaca enters the stomach of Śukrācārya, when the ashes of the former after killing him are mixed in wine and are administered by the *asuras* to Śukra. Śukra teaches the Sañjīvanī lore to Kaca, who comes out breaking the right side of Śukra, who dies but is brought back to life by Kaca. For a detailed study of this see, Sadashiv A. Dange, *Myths from the Mahābhārata—Quest for Immortality*, Vol. I, "Kaca and Śukra", pp. 153-229, especially pp. 162-73.
33. For details, see Sindhu S. Dange, "Solar Eclipse and the 'Fourth' Mantra of Atri", *Journal of the Asiatic Society of Mumbai*, Mumbai, Vol. 82 for 2008 (New Series), 2009, pp. 7-11.

34. G.V. Davane, "The Rāhu-Ketu myth", *Perspectives in the Vedic and the Classical Sanskrit Heritage,* D.K. Print World (P) Ltd., New Delhi, 1995, pp. 135-38.
35. B.G. Tilak, *Orion*, published by Tilak Brothers, Poona, 1893, p. 159.
36. See Sindhu S. Dange, *Vedic Beliefs and Practices through Arthavāda,* Vol. II, Aryan Books International, New Delhi, 2005, pp. 406-08.
37. Macdonell takes the word *vṛtrāṇi* (Neuter Nom. Plu.) as referring to terrestrial foes. It applies to both—'human enemies' as also 'celestial demons'. The term must have been based on an earlier meaning such as 'obstruction'—then 'obstructor'. See A.A. Macdonell, *op.cit.*, p. 159.
38. One example of such *itihāsas.* The account about Viśvarūpa, the elder son of Tvaṣṭṛ, whose three heads were cut off by Indra, with the result, three different birds came out of these three heads. See Tait. Sam. II.5.1.1ff; *Jaim.Br.* II.156.
39. Andrew Lang, *Myth, Ritual and Religion,* London, 1913, pp. 42-44, where in three different stories, a frog controls all waters. Also Donald Mackenzie, *Myths of Pre-Columbian America,* The George Gresham Publishing Company, London, year not mentioned, p. 241, where fish, frog etc. are regarded as the terrestrial forms of Tlaloc the Mexican god of rain.
40. *RV* VII.103 is regarded as a rain-charm. See M. Bloomfield, "The Frog-hymn", *The Journal of The American Oriental Society,* Vol. XVII, p. 173f; also Norman Brown, "Some Notes on the Rain-charms", *New Indian Antiquary,* Vol. II-2, May 1921.
41. R.N. Dandekar, "Vṛtrahā Indra" *Vedic Mythological Tracts,* Ajanta Publications, Delhi, 1979, pp. 173-76.
42. Sindhu S. Dange, "Ṛgveda II.12 and Sūta-tradition", *Śrījagannāthajyotiḥ, Shri Jagannatha Journal of Indology,* Puri, Vol. 10 (Silver Jubilee Vol.), 2005, pp. 49-53.
43. E.W. Hopkins, "Indra as the God of Fertility", *The Journal of the American Oriental Society,* Vol. XXXVI, New Haven, U.S.A.
44. Sadashiv A. Dange, *Vedic Concept of 'Field' and the Divine Fructification.* University of Bombay Publication. Bombay (Mumbai), 1971, pp. 16-17, 71.
45. A.A. Macdonell, *op.cit.*, pp. 58-60, 158.

46. R.T. Rundle Clark, *Myth and Symbol in Ancient Egypt*, Thomas and Hudson, London, 1959, p. 205.
47. For details, see Sadashiv A. Dange, *Pastoral Symbolism from the Ṛgveda* (Bhau Vishnu Ashtekar Vedic Research Series, Vol. No. 111), University of Poona Publication, Poona (Pune), 1970, p. 15.
48. See Joseph Campbell, *The Hero with a Thousand Faces*, Bollingen Series XVII, Princeston University Press, Princeston, New Jersy, 3rd print, 1973 (1949).
49. Soma-juice is mixed with barley or cow's milk or curds, the mixture getting the name *yavāśira, gavāśira* and *dadhyaśira* resp. But here it is pure.
50. *Śat. Br.* I.6.3.1-17; repeated *ibid.*, V.5.4.2-12; and already has been recorded in the *Tait. Sam.* II.4.12.1
51. See Sadashiv A. Dange, *Images from Vedic Hymns and Rituals*, Aryan Books International, New Delhi, 2000, p. 126f.
52. *Ibid.*, pp. 127-28.
53. A.A. Maddonell, *op.cit.*, p. 158.
54. *Mbh.* Vana 101.14-15; Udyoga 10.39; Śānti 282.9; for Viṣṇuloka 283.59-60.
55. *Sk.P.* I.1.16.53; also I.1.17.93-101—*gandharva* Citraratha; *Bhāg.P.* VI.9.11 ff—*gandharva* Citraketu.
56. For details, see Sadashiv A Dange, *Ency. PBP*, Vol. II, pp. 421-22.
57. Peter Munz, *When the Golden Bough Breaks*, Routledge and Kegan Paul, London and Boston, 1973, p. 40. Peter Munz applies the historical method to get the meaning of any myth.
58. This was obviously to hide himself from the sight of the gods, who however could spot him out and thought of punishing him.
59. This myth has a double character that of the incest of Prajāpati with his daughter and that of the *Prāśitra* (the small portion of Prajāpati's flesh stuck to Rudra's arrow or dart), which was eaten by the god Bṛhaspati. In the sacrifice, it is a small portion (like a Peepal berry or a barley grain) of the sacrificial cake, which is eaten by the Brahman priest. For the detailed treatment of this myth, see Sindhu S. Dange, "Prāśitra in Myth and Ritual," *Prabhākara-Nārāyaṇa-Śrīḥ (Dr. Prabhakara Narayana Kawthekar*

Fel. Vol.) Studies in Indology and Musicology, Pratibha Prakashan, Delhi, 1993, pp. 81-86.

60. See C.F. Oldham, *op.cit.*, p. 118.
61. See Sindhu S. Dange, *The Bhāgavata Purāṇa—Mytho-Social Study*, p. 196.
62. For details of these evil forces of several kinds see, A.A. Macdonell, *op.cit.*, pp. 162-65.
63. See Sadashiv A. Dange, "'Araru' āṇi 'Nārmara'" (Marathi), Vidarbha Samshodhana Mandala, Nagpur, *Annual* No. 1997, pp. 10-20.
64. *Bhāg. P.* X.6; *Brahmāṇḍa P.* IV.29.124; III.73.100; *Vāyu P.* 9.97; 98.100; *Vi. P.* V.4.1; 5.7-11, 23; 6.23; 15.2; 29.5; *Brahmav. P.* IV.10; *Brahma P.* chap. 184.
65. *Bhāg. P.* X.7.20-32; *Brahmāṇḍa P.* IV.29.124; also *Brahmav. P.* IV.11.2-7.
66. *Bhāg. P.* X.11.41-44.
67. *Ibid.*, X.11.47-52; *Brahmav.P.* IV.16.4ff-11.
68. *Bhāg.P.* X.12.13-38.
69. *Ibid.*, X.36.1-14; *Vi.P.* V.14 (whole chapter); also 15.1; 29.4 etc.; *Brahmāṇḍa P.* II.73.100; IV 29.124.
70. *Bhāg.P.* X.15.20-40; *Vi.P.* V.8 (whole chapter); *Brahma.P.* chap. 186; *Brahmav. P.* IV 22.2 ff-95.
71. *Bhāg. P.* X.18.17-29; *Brahmāṇḍa P.* III.6.15; IV.29.123; *Vāyu P.* 68.15; *Vi.P.* V.9.13 to the end of the chapter; *Brahma P.* chap. 187.
72. *Bhāg. P.* X.37. 29-33.
73. *Ibid.*, III.19.28.
74. *Ibid.*, X.74. 45, 46.
75. See Sindhu S. Dange, "Women in Smṛtis: Issues of Inheritance," *History of Science, Philosophy and Culture in Indian Civilization*, Vol. IX Part 2, *Women in Ancient and Medieval India*, ed. by Bhuvan Chandel, Centre for Studies in Civilizations, New Delhi, 2009, pp. 125-27.
76. The well-known story of Kavaṣa Ailuṣa, the son of female slave, who was driven away from the sacrificial session, but was invited to join when he 'saw' the hymn Aponaptrīya. See *Ait.Br.* II.19=7.1; also *Kauṣ.Br.* XII.3.
77. A.A. Macdonell, *op.cit.*, p. 157f.
78. Also see K.F. Geldner, *Der Rig-Veda*, HOS, Vol. 34, Cambridge (Massachusetts), London, 2nd print, 1978, p. 26 for *RV* V.29.10d.

79. Here Sacrifice (*Yajña)* stands for a male and Speech (*vāc*) for a female. The case thus is of a male calling a female to him and the female comes to him.
80. According to Sāyaṇa the words *he'lavaḥ* (by *sandhi* with the following words *he'lavaḥ)=he'lavo* stand for *he'rayo* i.e. *he arayaḥ* meaning 'Oh! The spiteful enemies!' (*la* standing for *ra* — the change in the letter). The *asuras* being deprived of Speech could not utter the words *he arayaḥ* in a correct manner, their words thus becoming unintelligible.
81. Ṛbhus are the three brothers (a triad) often mentioned together, have wonderful exploits to their credit and are raised to the status of semi-gods. For details see, A.A. Macdonell, *op.cit.,* pp. 131-34; also see Félix Nève, *An Essay on The Myth of the Ṛbhus,* tr. from French into English by G.V. Davane, Ajanta Publications, Delhi, 1985.
82. See Elbert—Ushanas Richter, *The Indus Script and the Ṛgveda,* Motilal Banarsidass, Delhi, 1997, p. 17.
83. See A.A. Macdonell, *op.cit.,* pp. 161-62.
84. A.C. Das, *Ṛgvedic Culture,* Calcutta, Madras, 1925, p. 94.
85. Buddha Prakash, *Ṛgveda and the Indus Valley Civilization*, VVRI, Hoshiarpur, 1966, pp. 83-98.
86. Asko Parpola, "The Coming of the Aryans to Iran and India and the Cultural and Ethnic Identity of the Dasas, "the paper originally pub. by Finnish Oriental Society, Helsinki and later on pub. in *Studia Orientalia,* 64, Helsinki, pp. 227-29.
87. For the account of the *asura* king Bali and the Vāmana incarnation, see *Bhāg. P.* VIII. chaps. 18-23.
88. For the account of the *asura* Hiraṇyakaśipu—*Ibid.*, VII. chaps. 3-8; that of his brother Hiraṇyākṣa, *ibid.* III. chaps. 17-19.
89. *Nir.* VI.26—*bekanāṭāḥ* as *kusīdinaḥ*—'money-lenders'; also *ibid.* II.17—The word *'paṇi'* explained as *vaṇik* i.e. 'trader'—*paṇirvaṇig bhavati, paṇiḥ paṇanāt.* This explanation is based on etymology.
90. See T.N. Dharmadhikari, "Gavām-ayanam", *Sacrifice in India—Concept and Evolution,* ed. by Sindhu S. Dange, Proceedings of the UGC National Seminar, Department of Sanskrit, University of Mumbai, Viveka Publications. Aligarh, 1987, pp. 30-36.
91. Saramā the bitch was given the boon that she would breed her species ((obviously 'strong' like herself). The *Jaim. Br* points out

that this is the reason why in Vidarbha regions (now in the state of Maharashtra, India), the dogs—to be exact 'hounds' (which pounce like robbers—*mācalāḥ sārameyāḥ*)—kill (even) the tigers (*Jaim. Br.* II.442). Here the boon, which is a mythological strategy, brings out the fierce nature of the hounds.

92. See the opinion of Ruth Benedict, *Encyclopaedia of the Social Sciences*, 1930-1935, Vol. II, p. 179. "For the purpose of methodology, there is no difference between a folk-tale and a myth."

93. For the references to the myth of Soma brought from heaven by the Śyena-Suparṇa (the beautiful-winged *Śyena*—'hawk' or as per Macdonell 'eagle'), see A.A. Macdonell, *op.cit.*, pp. 111-12. For the myth fully dealt with, see *RV* IV.26; 27.50.

94. Bloomfield says that the *vrātya* seems to be a kind of *brahmacārin*, or at any rate one who has entered the Brahmanical community after having converted from an Aryan, but non-Brahmanical tribe. See M. Bloomfield, *The Atharvaveda*, Strassberg, 1899, p. 94.

95. Sāy. on *AV* (XV.1.1) says that the description of the Vrātya does not apply to all Vrātyas, but only to some very powerful, universally respected and holy Vrātya, who was, however, not in the good books of the *brāhmaṇas* that were solely devoted to their own rites and sacrifices.

96. The equipment of the 'House-holder' included a turban, a bow without arrow, a rough vehicle covered with board, a garment with black fringes, two goat-skins—one white, one black—, a silver ornament. See *Pañc. Br.* XVII.1.14. According to Caland the silver ornament was worn around the neck. See W. Caland, *Pañcaviṁśa Brāhmaṇa*, 2nd ed., Sri Satguru Publications, Delhi, 1982 (1931), p. 457.

97. The *Pañc. Br.* speaks of four Vrātyastomas (XVII. 1-4). The first Vrātyastoma is for those who lead the life of a joined group, are destitute and are left behind. They do not study the Veda or plough or trade (*ibid.* XVII.1.2). The second Vrātyastoma is for those, who being mean and censured lead a Vrātya-life. (*ibid.* XVII 2.1) The third Vrātyastoma is for those who are the youngest and lead a Vrātya-life (*ibid.* XVII 3.1), and the fourth one is for those, who being the oldest lead a Vrātya-life (*ibid.* XVII 4.1).

98. *Ibid.*

99. See W. Caland, *op.cit.*, p. 621 note 2 on *Pañc. Br.* XXIV. 18.2.

100. *Pañc. Br.* XXIV. 18.3—

Before the sixty-one-day rite, there was neither juice in the herbs, nor butter in the milk, nor fat in the flesh, nor hair on the skin, nor leaves on the trees. But after the said rite, since that time all these acquired these potencies.

101. See P.V. Kane, *HDS*, Vol. II, Pt. I, 2nd ed., BORI, Poona, 1974, p. 387, also note 928 on the same page.

102. *Manu Sm.* II.38-40; *Yājñ.Sm.* I. 37-38 and the comm. Mitākṣarā on v.38.

103. *Tait. Sam.* IV.5.4.2; *Vāj.Sam.* XVI.27; *Kāṭha Sam.* XVII.17.

104. J. Charpentier, *Die Suparṇa-sage*, Uppsala, 1920.

105. *Rām.* Ayodhyā 50.35 ff upto the end of the chapter; also *ibid.* 51.1-7, where Guha, the Niṣāda-sthapati speaks to Lakṣmaṇa.

106. See Sadashiv A. Dange, *Legends in the Mahābhārata*, Motilal Banarsidass, Delhi, 1969, p. 6; also 2nd ed. *Myths from the Mahābhārata*, Vol. I, *Quest for Immortality*, Aryan Books International, New Delhi, 1997, pp. 50-51.

107. *Bhāg. P.* IV.14 (the whole chap. and partly the 13th chap.).

108. *Ibid.*, IV 15.1.

109. *Ibid.*, IV.14.44-46. Yāska (*Nir.* III.8) explains the word *niṣāda* as 'one who has sin settled in him'—*niṣādaḥ kasmāt niṣaṇṇam asmin pāpam iti /*

110. The comm. Mitākṣarā on *Yajñ.Sm.* (I.91) says that a Niṣāda is one, born of a *brāhmaṇa* from a *śūdra* wife. Niṣādas are said to stay on the bank of a river and having their livelihood by catching fish. See *Mbh.* I.28.2; *Sk.P.* IV.50.64.

111. *Kauṣ. Br.* XXV.15; *Pañc.Br.* XVI 6.7; *Lāṭ. Ś.S.* 8.2.7-9.

112. See W. Caland, *op.cit.*, p. 437. Note 2 in the tr. of *Pañc. Br.* XVI 6.1.

113. See *Proceedings and Transactions of the All India Oriental Conference*, 17th Session, Ahmedabad, Oct.-Nov. 1953, published by the Local Secretary, 17th AIOC, Gujarat Vidyasabha, Ahmedabad, p. 25 (Presidential Address of Dr. Suniti Kumar Chatterji, General President of AIOC, 17th session, Ahmedabad).

114. Mahīdhara commenting on the *Vāj. Sam.* (XVI. 27) says that Niṣādas are mountain-dwellers Bhils. Weber from the ritual of the Viśvajit-sacrifice deduces that the Niṣādas were settled aborigines, for to be able to reside with them, as is required by

the ritual, their close association with the Aryans and accepting the influence of the latter is necessary. See for this, A.A. Macdonell, and A.B. Keith, *Vedic Index of Names and Subjects,* under "Niṣāda". Macdonell and Keith believe that the term 'Niṣāda' refers generally to all non-Aryan tribes and no particular tribes as such.

The *Rām.* mentions Niṣādas, see G. Ramdas, "The Aboriginal Tribes in the Rāmāyaṇa", *Man in India,* Vol. V, 1925, p. 28 ff. The *Bṛhatsaṁhitā* (XIV.10) refers to the kingdom of the Niṣādas, as does the *Rām.*

According to Mukherji, the Niṣādas along with the Śabaras were the inhabitants of the South. See R.K. Mukherji, *Ancient India,* Allahabad, 1948, p. 72.

115. *AV* X.4.14; *Vāj. Sam.* XXX.16; *Tait. Br.* III.4.12.1.
116. S.K. Chatterji, *op.cit.* p. 25; for details see note 113 supra.
117. See Sadashiv A Dange, *Myths from the Mahābhārata,* Vol. 3, *Probe in Early Dim History and Folklore,* Aryan Books International, New Delhi, 2002, p. 17f. Here Dange points out that who actually was the one to cross the Vindhya is not known. The haloed personality of Agastya, through various myths and the Agastya star rising to the southern quarter of the sky was anthropomorphised as the ancient sage of that name and the myth of the sage crossing the Vindhya got floated, and got elaborated with additions in the later period, as indicated by the narrations in the *Mbh.*
118. 'Svastyayana' is a means of averting of evil by the recitation of *mantras* or performance of expiatory rites. It also signifies the benediction of a *brāhmaṇa* after presentation of offerings.
119. K.S. Ramaswami Shastri, "The Aryan Colonies of Kiṣkindhā and Laṅkā," *Indian Culture,* Vol. V, p. 195 f.
120. A.A. Macdonell, *op.cit.*, p. 63.
121. *Raghuvaṁśa* I.2, where we have the mention of Rāma's *vaṁśa* (dynasty) as *sūryaprabhavaḥ* (starting from the sun).
122. A.A. Macdonell, *op.cit.*, p. 149. Macdonell points to two references in the *RV* (I.89.6; X. 178.1), which are the only references to Tārkṣya in the *RV*, and which point to his being a horse.
123. A.A. Macdonell, *op.cit.*, p. 149.

124. See J. Eggeling, *The Śatapatha Brāhmaṇa*, Part V, SBE Vol. 44, Reprint, Motilal Banarsidass, Delhi, 1978 (1900), p. 369 note 5, tr. of *Śat. Br.* XIII 4.3.13. Eggeling has given here the word as *vāyovidyika*.
125. See A.C. Das, *Ṛgvedic Culture*, Calcutta, 1925, p. 148.
126. This is near about the town Māhiṣmatī, near the place Māndhātā—Oṁkāreśvara in the Vindhya mountain.
127. Sadashiv A. Dange, *Hindu Dharma āṇi Tattvajñāna*, published by the Maharashtra University Book Production Board, Shri Lekhan Vachan Bhandar, Pune, 1973, p. 20; 2nd edn., Continental Prakashan, Pune, 2016, p. 23; also see *Mbh.* Ādi 174. 36-38.
128. See Sindhu S. Dange, "the Earth-Cow and Pṛthu's Dart", *Purāṇa*, All India Kashiraj Trust, Varanasi, XIII-i, January 1971, pp. 79-81.
129. *Mbh.* Vana 220.17. Here most probably the Great Fire-altar is referred to. It is built in the shape of a bird, which is in the position of flying, with the wings spread. The *Śat. Br.* deals extensively with the rite of Agnicayana (*kāṇḍas* VI to X).
130. See Sadashiv A. Dange, *Hindu Dharma āṇi Tattvajñāna*, p. 296; 2nd edn., p. 327.
131. *Ibid.*, 2nd edn., pp. 334-41, for detailed information.
132. See, for the information about the Bhojakas, Sadashiv A. Dange, *Ency. PBP*, Vol. I, Navrang, New Delhi, 1986, pp. 124-26.
133. *Ibid.*, p. 126.
134. D.R. Bhandarkar, "Foreign Elements in Hindu Population", *Indian Antiquary*, XL, 1921, pp. 17ff.
135. Ajay Mitra Shastri, *Varāhamihira and his Times*, Kusumanjali Prakashan, Jodhpur, 1991, p.11. Also see R.C. Hazra, *Studies in the Upapurāṇas*, I, p.32; also by him, "the Sāmba-Purāṇa, a Saura work of Different Hands", *ABORI*, XXXVI, Pune, 1955, pp. 62 ff.
136. See Ajay Mitra Shastri, *op.cit.*, p. 11; also p. 27 note 80.
137. *Ibid.*, p. 10.
138. *Ibid.*, p. 28 notes 86 and 87.
139. *Ibid.*, p. 12; also p. 28 note 88, which refers to Debala Mitra, "Foreign Elements in Indian Population," *The Cultural Heritage of India*, II, pp. 614-15.
140. Ajay Mitra Shastri, *op.cit.*, p. 10f.
141. *Ibid.*, p. 27 note 77.

142. One such Maga *brāhmaṇa*, an high Executive Officer in the service of the Government of India studied for his Ph.D degree on "Solar Lore in the Purāṇas with special reference to the Skanda Purāṇa "(Ph.D. degree was awarded in 1978, by the University of Mumbai). The said Maga *brāhmaṇa* (Dr. Naval Kishor Sharma) studied under the guideship of late Dr. Sadashiv A. Dange, R.G. Bhandarkar Professor and Head, Department of Sanskrit, University of Bombay (now Mumbai).

143. Various tribes are mentioned in the Purāṇas. *Kūrma P.* I.45.39-42; *Brahmāṇḍa P.* I.2.31.82 ff. The *Vām.P.* gives tribes as they existed in various regions as from Madhyadeśa; Uttarāpatha (Northern); Eastern; Dākṣiṇātya (Southern); Western; those termed Vindhyamūlasthāna (Residing at the foot of the Vindhyas).

For detailed information, see Sadashiv A. Dange, *Ency. PBP*, Vol. V, Navrang, New Delhi, 1990, pp. 1479-80, under "Tribes".

CHAPTER 3

Sacrifice—Concept and Phases

The word 'sacrifice' is closely associated with such words as sacred, sacrament, sanctum etc. and is traced to its Latin origin 'sacrificium' ('sacer'—holy; 'facere'—to make), the concept of something pure and holy, and also out of the normal routine. But this stride to what is 'beyond', nevertheless is connected with the routine. Sacrifice which falls in the sphere of routine is a device to connect the divine with the mortal existence. It is an objective link between man and the spiritual world.[1] Sacrifice of any land or tribe has this inherent principle. Sacrifice is a close involvement between the god to whom sacrifice is offered and the one who offers. The Sanskrit word for sacrifice is *yajña* or *yāga* (fr. √*yaj*—'to sacrifice'). The three constituents of sacrifice are—material to be offered (*dravya*), deity to which material is offered (*devatā*) and the ritual of offering (*tyāga*).[2]

The old principle by which the concept of sacrifice can be explained is the rule *'do-ut-des'*—'I give that thou mayest give'. Prayer forms an important part of sacrifice. Tylor points out that both prayer and sacrifice go hand in hand. The suppliant who bows before his chief, laying a gift at his feet and making his humble petition displays, at once, the anthropomorphic model and origin of sacrifice and prayer.[3] The Vedic sacrifice is not only an act of worship on the part of the human beings, but also an act of providing assistance to the gods, for the offerings given in sacrifice, accompanied by the uttering of holy prayers, give strength to the gods, who, in turn help the human beings by fulfilling their desires. The Saṁhitās and the Brāhmaṇa-texts give importance to two factors *viz.* ritual of sacrifice (*vidhi*) and the appropriate chants or prayer (*mantra*), recited along with the ritual. The ritual comprising offerings of materials make the gods strong and the chant or prayer infuses them with good cheer, as the gods also need praise. Several *ṛcs* can be pointed out in this respect.[4] G.van der Leeuw, while discussing in general about sacrifice, says that it is no longer a mere matter of bartering with gods and no longer homage to the god, but it is an opening of a blessed source of gifts. It is quite impossible to say who is actually the donor and who the recipient. The pivot of the sacrificial act is always the gift itself: it must be given, that is to say, be set in motion. The principal feature is not that someone or other should receive something, but that the stream of life should continue to flow. And thus instead of rationalistic *do-ut-des*, we must say: *do ut possis dare*—'I give in order that thou mayest be able to give': I give thee power that thou mayest have power, and that life may not stagnate because of any lack of potency.[5] The Vedic sacrifice goes far beyond this idea and is joined with Ṛta (Order), which we will see, after noting some more opinions on the origin of sacrifice.

Hopkins points out that sacrifice originates in various fears and desires, to get, to get rid of, to propitiate, to commune, to atone.[6] Tylor, who at the end of the nineteenth cent., was the first to enter the field of scientific investigation of the concept and rite of sacrifice, says that sacrifice originally was a gift offered to supernatural beings to secure their favour or minimise their hostility.[7] William Robertson Smith (a Scottish scholar 1846-94) was inspired by the discovery of totemism and was the first to give a plausible reasoned explanation of sacrifice.[8] He saw in the practices of the totemic cult the root origin of sacrifice. The oldest stratum of sacrifice consisted in the communal banquet of sharing in the sacrificial victim. It was a precious time when humanity and divinity 'sat at the same table' and enjoyed their kinship with each other. The god (in the totem animal), the victim and the totemistic group belonged to the same kin. He showed how expiatory (*piaculum*), mechanical, materialistic, priest-ridden conceptions were later than the kind of sacrifice he felt was primitive in the 'purest' levels of biblical religion. Sacrifice if given the proper conditions, could develop into the lofty ethical ideas of altruism. Smith formed this view-point following his German mentor Julius Wellhausen.[9] For Hubert and Mauss, 'Sacrifice is a religious act which, through the consecration of a victim modifies the condition of a moral person who accomplishes it or that of certain objects with which he is concerned'.[10] According to E. Westermarck, as the supernatural beings were supposed to have human appetites and human wants, there came the practice of offering sacrificial gifts to them by men. It was also believed that in the absence of offerings, these beings became feeble and powerless.[11] Frazer, who is regarded as the first to form the principles of magic ('the law of similarity' and 'the law of contact or contagion'),[12] maintains that the sacramental communion is simply a magical act. Durkheim holds that both the essential forms of evolved sacrifice namely the act of oblation and the act of communion,[13] are found in germinal form in *intichiuma* rites.[14]

Again prior to discussing the main idea underlying the 'sacrifice' in India, let us see the main ideas generally connected with sacrifice—

1. COMMUNION

The most rudimentary forms of sacrifice have this fundamental principle underlying them. This is prominently marked in totemism, in which there is a sacramental eating of the (divine) totemistic animal or plant, thereby physically imbibing the supernatural qualities of the totem and thus having a union with it.

The same idea of communion is seen in the rites and rituals concerning the dead. This was effected by eating the body of the deceased or holding a feast in his name in the funeral rites. A practice which occurs in the funeral rites is of cutting or tearing the hair and burying it with the body of the dead. Even scratching one's body especially the face, causing it to bleed also formed a part of the rite of mourning.[15]

2. CONCILIATION

After fear for the deities, there arose the idea of conciliation, which gave rise to the piacular or propitiatory rites. To take the examples from the worldly life—Building or entering a new house or canoe; starting on a war or trade expedition; sowing or reaping of new crops; offering of the first born man and beast. Offering the sacrificial victim, which serves as a scapegoat also falls in line with this, for the victim wipes off the guilt of a person.

3. HONORIFIC OFFERINGS

These offerings are in grateful recognition of the goodness and beneficence of the deity. The offerings of first fruits and many other gift-sacrifices fall in this category.

The ideas noted above in the three categories there too in the communion-category, are the main to be marked in the early sacrifices and the ethical notions of self-sacrifice etc. are noticed in the higher religions of later times.[16]

Having taken a note of these theories or view-points regarding the origin and nature of sacrifice in general, when we turn to the sacrifice in India, we feel that it cannot be covered in its entirety exclusively by any of these view-points. Hopkins is right in pointing out this fact, when applied generally.[117] The sacrifice in India, like sacrifice in any other land, is an example in this respect, as it has been evolving, with the passage of time bringing new trends in it, which are suiting to the changes in the social structure. And here we find the role played by the device of *arthavāda* (Arthavādaism), which is the stand-point maintained, while writing the present work.

Though efforts have been made to trace the origin and nature of sacrifice in the *RV*[18], it has to be pointed out that in spite of being known, the types of sacrifice can be marked only in the *YV* tradition. Though we may surmise that fire was established in the three altars (*RV* II.36.4 .... *ni ṣadā yoniṣu triṣu*), the names of three fires (Gārhapatya, Āhavanīya and Dakṣiṇa) are not mentioned. Ritual indications such as 'cooking of a fat bull' or 'cooking of a fat ram' (*ibid.* X.27.2c, 17a) are marked, but they do not tally with the ritual details of later times. The *RV* mentions a ritual of cooking of a spotted bull, with a note that these were the rituals of bygone times (*ibid.* I.164.43 cd), but lost afterwards.[19] Again we find that *ukṣans* (stud bulls, kept for procreation fr. √*ukṣ*—'to sprinkle'), *ṛṣabhas* (=*vṛṣabhas*—virile, sprinkler bulls fr. √*vṛṣ*—*varṣ*—'to sprinkle') and *vaśās* (barren cows) are offered to Agni (*ibid.* VI.16.47). However, a definite ritual of sacrificially killing a bull cannot be maintained in the ritual of the Brāhmaṇa-texts. The information about the Śūlagava-rite, in which a bull is sacrificed to Rudra, occurs in the *Āśv. G.S.* (IV.9.1-40). This tradition is much later than the ritual-tradition of the Brāhmaṇa-texts. Dange rightly says that about what was the nature of Vedic ritual of the period of the *Ṛgveda*, there is very little help.[20]

We have already taken a note of the three indispensable constituents of sacrifice, namely, *dravya* (material of offering), *devatā* (deity, to which offering is made) and *tyāga* (ritual of offering).[21] *Dravya* or material which is offered in sacrifice, could be in the form of an animal or a simple corn-offering in the form of sacrificial cake or *caru* (rice, boiled with ghee) etc.

Both, the animal and the sacrificial cake are said to be having five constituents[22]—*pāṅkta*. In the case of animal-offering, it has to be pointed out that there cannot be found any trace of totemism even in the earliest phase of sacrifice in India, and obviously in later phases also reaching the modern age. In the Vedic sacrifice, the animal offered is regarded as closely connected with the god, at times through its colour or form. And as the offering of the animal is given in fire (Agni), it could be taken as the very form of Agni or Agni-Prajāpati (sacrifice incarnate in the form of god).[23] A mythical account, which occurs as *arthavāda* in the *Śat.Br.* explains this in clear terms. Prajāpati thought of Agni's forms (*agnirūpāṇi*). He searched for Agni, who had entered different forms, which were five different animals *viz.* man (*puruṣa*), horse, bull, ram and he-goat. Prajāpati was convinced about their being Agni and slaughtered to place them in himself, as Agni's forms (*Śat.Br.* VI.2.1.1-6, 18). Hence in the rite of building the Great Fire-altar (Agnicayana), the heads of these five animals are placed in the lowest layer. However it has to be pointed out that slaughter of man is a debatable point. The *Tait. Sam.* makes a mention of four heads, that of man, horse, bull and serpent (V.2.9.2-5). Though the *arthavāda* passage in the *Śat.Br.* mentions only five animals as the forms of Agni, all the animals,[24] of which the oblations are offered in fire, can be regarded as standing for the very sacrifice or Agni-Prajāpati as his alter-morphs.

Though animals (mainly goat) are offered to individual gods,[25] the predominant note in this context is that animals belong to Agni and therefore are offered to him. A mythical account coming as *arthavāda* states that once Agni went away from the gods and they searched for him by means of different kinds of cattle, with a thought that as Agni himself is (cattle or) an animal,[26] he will become manifest unto his own form (*Śat.Br.* VI.3.1.22). The gods deposit all their beasts, both domestic and wild, with Agni (*ibid.* II.3.4.1, 2). The *Ait. Br.*

states that the sacrificial victim was not willing to go to gods, as it saw death before it. It asked somebody to go before it and Agni went before it. Therefore, it is said that every animal is connected with Agni, for it follows Agni and submits to it (*Ait.Br.* II.6=6.6). In the Vedic ritual tradition, the animals to be sacrificed are closely connected with Agni or Agni-Prajāpati and are regarded as his alter-morphs and no individual animal stands as an exclusive symbol of Agni-Prajāpati or any other god, such as Viṣṇu, Bṛhaspati, Soma, Vāyu etc. Thus there is no trace of zoomorphism or theriomorphism in the Vedic sacrificial tradition. Again no trace of totemism is found in this tradition. The sacrificial victim only when consecrated has a changed status (of being regarded as holy), that too for a while. The whole species of that victim is never regarded as holy and forbidden for being killed. Even in the case of the sacrificial victim, there was a practice of not offering certain parts of the victim (in fire) to the god, as can be seen from an *arthavāda* account, which occurs in the context of Agniṣṭoma (Soma-sacrifice with animal-offering). It is said that when the gods seized an animal for offering it in the sacrifice, Tvaṣṭṛ first spat upon its head, thinking that the gods, taking the animal to be dirty and hence impure, would not touch it, for animals belonged to Tvaṣṭṛ. The spittle of Tvaṣṭṛ became the brain in the head and the marrow in the neck bone of the victim. The *Śat.Br.* here says that one must not eat that part of the animal, as it was spitten by Tvaṣṭṛ (*Śat.Br.* III.8.3.11). The *Śat.Br.* further says that as the *asuras* made portions of the head, the shoulders, the neck and the hind-thighs of the animal for being offered, one should not do so (*ibid.* III.8.3.29). This indicates the difference between the Vedic and *asura* practice of offering the animal in sacrifice. The Vedic practice most probably was to bury the parts of the beast, including the head, not used as offerings, at the Śāmitra-enclosure.[27] The severed head of the sacrificial beast, being buried and regarded as 'lost' gave rise to the myth of sacrifice itself losing its head, on the basis of the equation at many places between the sacrificer, sacrificial beast and the sacrifice and has been a cause of the effort to replace the head of sacrifice.[28] It has to be noted that the blood of victim was not offered in sacrifice. It was to be cast away in blind darkness and was regarded as the share of the *rakṣases*, with no fire for this offering. This is brought out by an *arthavāda*, which occurs in the context of the New-moon and Full-moon sacrifices (*Śat.Br.* I.9.2.35). This seems to be the belief among ancient Greeks also, who offered to the earthly lower spirits their special animals, pigs and dogs, whose blood flowed into the earth and their carcasses were burned. Thus blood was poured into a trench for ghostly heroes.[29]

Together with the animal-offering, the dough-offering figured in the Vedic ritual tradition, with all the details regarding the sacrificial cake (*puroḍāśa*). Such a cake, baked on a particular number of *kapālas* is connected to a particular deity. Here the concept of 'number' plays an important part, with respect to the potsherds to be used for baking the cake. It seems that there was a firm belief about the cake to be offered to a deity and the number of potsherds to be used for that cake.[30] Regarding the shape of the cake (*puroḍāśa*), a mythical account coming as *athavāda* in the context of New-moon and Full-moon sacrifices, has to be taken into account. It runs as follows. The tradition of sacrifice can be traced from times immemorial, for the gods having performed sacrifice reached the heavenly world. The gods tried to hide the sacrifice from men, as they were afraid of the latter knowing it and by performing it, reaching the heaven. Hence, the gods sipped the sap of the sacrifice, drained it and effaced the traces of it by the sacrificial post. The seers praised and toiled in pursuit of sacrifice like the gods. They came to the place of sacrifice and found the sacrificial cake (*puroḍāśa*), which had become a tortoise. To that creeping tortoise (*puroḍāśa*) the seers asked to stand still for Aśvins, Sarasvatī and Indra. Only when they pleaded for Agni, it stopped. The seers offered it entirely in the fire and the sacrifice shone forth to them. They produced it and spread it. Thereafter the same sacrifice (i.e. science of sacrifice) is taught by the father to the son, by the former to the latter (*Śat.Br.* I.6.2.1ff). The *arthavāda* already has occured in the *Tait. Sam.*, where instead of the mention of the gods, we have Aṅgirases and the gods by whose names the tortoise (sacrificial cake) is asked to stay still, are Indra, Bṛhaspati and All-Gods. Only when told to be firm for Agni, it became firm (*Tait.Sam.* II.6.3.2,3). The *arthavāda* poses some questions, which are—Was there a practice of offering a live tortoise (that too the entire one) in the sacrificial fire? Though not directly mentioned as sacrificed, the tortoise could be taken so, for it is said to be originally a sacrificial cake, which is offered to the gods. This could be supported from a detail in the rite of Agnicayana, in which a live tortoise is enjoined to be kept at the lowest level (*Śat. Br.* VII.5.1.1).[31] Another question is—Was the sacrificial cake (*puroḍāśa*) of the size of a tortoise? It might have been of such size in the hoary past. But by the time of the *Śat.Br.*, we have a clear instruction that the sacrificial cake should not be too broad, for in that case, it would be a 'human' i.e. a common cake, on the profane level. Some ritualists say that it should be of the size of a horse's hoof.

But even this size also cannot be decided. Hence he should make it of such a size as in his own mind he does not think it too broad (*ibid.* I.2.2.9, 10).

We have noted in the beginning that ritual of offering (*vidhi*) and prayer in the form of *mantra* are the two important features of sacrifice. The chant or *mantra*, which is a potent form of Speech, is an integral part of sacrifice (*yajña*).[32] The *mantra* (chant or prayer), appropriate to the ritual makes the sacrifice perfect in form (*rūpasamṛddha*). This thought occurs in the *Nir.* (I.16) and prior to that several times in the *Ait. Br.*[33] The *RV* contains the *mantras* (in the form of *ṛcs*), the ritual use of many of them is pointed out by Sāyaṇa with the help of the later tradition, especially that of the Śrautasūtras. Wherever, ritual use of the *mantra* cannot be traced, Sāyaṇa is modestly frank to say *gato viniyogaḥ* ('The ritual use is lost' i.e. cannot be traced). It is interesting to note that the importance of the *mantra* or *mantras*, accompanying any ritual or *pūja* (worship) has remained an ever-lasting and unaging phenomenon in the Indian tradition, up to this day.

We have noted already that the offerings and the *mantras* give strength to the gods, who being pleased, send timely rains and seasons, for the human beings. The same thought is marked in the *Avesta*, the hoary tradition of which and that of the *RV*, can be traced to the same proto-Indo-Iranians, who later on got separated and came to be identified as two distinct peoples having two separate traditions. In the *Avesta*, Tishtrya outdone by Apaosha cries to Ahura Mazda, "O Ahura Mazda! Men do not offer me with sacrifice and praise; should they worship me with sacrifice and praise, they would bring me the strength of ten horses, ten bulls, ten mountains, ten rivers" (*Yasht* VIII.23, 24). In yet other *Yashts*, we see the gods, being pleased with sacrifice and prayer, ready to help the human beings.[34] This exactly tallies with the Ṛgvedic thought.

In the context of prayer or *mantra*, a mention has to be made of *gāthās*, *yajñagāthās* (occurring in the *Ait. Br.*) and *ślokas*. The role of these compositions is similar to that of *mantras*, as far as the aspect of giving firm basis to the ritual goes.[35] This is clearly seen with regards to the *gāthās* in the domestic rituals which are enjoined in the Gṛhyasūtras. As these rituals were performed by the house-holder, with or without the help of the priest, the singing of the *gāthās* was equal to the reciting of the *mantras*, for on some occasions specific *mantras* are not enjoined.[36] On the pattern of these *gāthās*, several *gāthās*, ritualistic in essence but popular in form, were composed by the priestly class and these occur as *yajñagāthās* in the Brāhmaṇa-texts. Such *yajñagāthās* are recited in a particular sacrifice or sacrificial rite in lieu of the *mantras*.[37] Falling in line with the *yajñagāthās* are the *ślokas*, which occur at several places in the Brāhmaṇa-texts. In spite of the fact that in few cases, the secular tradition could be traced, the *ślokas* mostly are composed by the Vedic priestly class, which considered them to be important as *mantras*. In fact, Sāyaṇa calls some of the *ślokas* as *mantras*.[38]

The ritual texts enjoin the recitation of these compositions, which serve as *mantras*. In fact, the *gāthās* were sung (fr. √*gai*—'to sing', √*gai+tha* (the suffix) giving the word *gāthā* feminine gender, cf. √*vac*—'to speak', *vac>uc>uk+tha*—*uktha*—the spoken word), by the sacrificer or the ritualists. Singing of the *gāthās* formed part of the sacrificial rituals as also of some domestic rituals, laid down in the Gṛhyasūtras.[39] Kane says that the domestic rite Sīmantonnayana is mainly of a social and festival nature.[40] This suggestion is hardly acceptable, for no ritual detail, here, including the *gāthā*, in praise of King Soma, by the two lute-players, sung with the accompaniment of the instrumental music, can simply be for entertainment or festivity. Festivity could be an added motif. The vocal and instrumental music serve as a charm as effective as the actual *mantras*—aspects of the Divine Speech.[41] In fact, this has been a living tradition in India for any occasion of performing a ritual or worship, reaching the modern times both in urban as well as rural areas. The expression of Speech in the form of prayer, *mantra*, vocal and instrumental music (including the beating of drum)[42] gives a throb of life to the ritual or worship, which otherwise being mute would appear lifeless.[43]

With the phenomenal aspect comprising offerings and prayers (*mantras*), the sacrifice in the *RV* and the ritual-texts may appear to be a simple 'give-and-take' practical business between man and god. But right from the Ṛgvedic times, there has been deeper thought regarding sacrifice. This becomes patent when we lay our hands on the Puruṣa-sūkta (*RV* X.90).

Here we have the concept of the Great Cosmic Puruṣa, having thousand heads, thousand eyes, thousand feet. He is the Lord of Immortality (*ibid.* 2c). From Him, through Virāj[44] (a female principle) is created another Puruṣa, who is the replica of the Cosmic Puruṣa. The gods (who are already there!) perform a sacrifice, taking this (second) Puruṣa as a victim and from his body split into different parts, the gods create everything in this universe.[45] The Great Cosmic Puruṣa is the *adhyakṣa* (*adhi+akṣa*)—Supreme Supervisor, and the second Puruṣa is his agent. The latter is the Primeval Man, from whose limbs creation comes into existence, and he has become the beast (sacrificial victim) to be sacrificed.

From the 'sacrifice' of the Primeval Man (Puruṣa), mentioned with all the details pertaining to the 'created' universe, we cannot say that there was human-sacrifice at the Ṛgvedic times. This is a conceptual human sacrifice. As Wendy Doniger O' Flaherty says, it is not a true blood sacrifice, but a dismemberment and distribution; not an actual creation of something out of nothing, but rater a rearrangement.[46] Such a concept of splitting up of the body of a Creation-Being is universal. Lang notes various trends in the savage myths of creation, one of them being that the world or its various parts, had been formed out of the body of some Supernatural Being, a god or a giant or a member of some mysterious race.[47] Lang refers to the paper read by Haug in 1871 about the Puruṣasūkta, which states that the ideas which the hymn contains are certainly of a primeval antiquity.[48] The concept of universe created from the dismemberment of a Primordial Man occurs in other mythologies also, let alone the tribal ones. The Chinese myth of P'an-ku's sons cutting him into three parts, from which arise three parts of China; the Babylonian myth of Marduk killing the female dragon Tiamat and creating heaven and earth from her two jaws; and several other such myths can be noted in this regard.[49]

The Puruṣasūkta (*RV* X.90) is a myth and that too a 'creation myth'. 'Myth' according to Mercia Eliade takes us to the 'Creative Era'—'the timeless Time'—*illud tempus*[50]—the Time, which is not clocked as it is the Time of God. This view-point of Mercia Eliade is all the more applicable to the 'creation myth'—Puruṣasūkta—, for this myth also, takes us back to a hoary past, when sacrifice, only in a crude form, was prevalent. Sāyaṇa in his comm. on this hymn says at the beginning, that the ritual use of this hymn cannot be traced; it has gone into oblivion. But the hymn, presenting a creation myth, has to be regarded as having functional use and the colour of *arthavāda*, though the latter concept has emerged in the ritual-texts and the system of Pūrvamīmāṁsā in still later age gave it a scientific treatment. The last *ṛc* (verse) in the Puruṣasūkta *(RV* X.90.16) says—"With the sacrifice, the gods performed (their) sacrifice; these were the first ordinances (*prathamāni dharmāṇi*)." The sacrifice of the Primordial Man served as a pattern. It was a cosmic sacrifice, in which the spring season was offered as melted butter (*ājya*), the summer its fuel (*idhma*) and the autumn its oblation (*haviḥ*). Even the sacrificial grass (*barhis*) is mentioned on which they sprinkled as sacrifice the Puruṣa (Primordial Man). The reference to the clotted butter (*pṛṣat-ājya*) collected at the end of that sacrifice also is not left out (*ibid.* vv. 6-8). The fifteenth *ṛc* mentions seven enclosing sticks (*paridhayaḥ*), thrice seven (i.e. twenty-one) faggots (*samidhaḥ*) and the binding of the Puruṣa as a victim. This shows that the cosmic sacrifice here had the basis of the materialistic sacrifice (*dravyayajña*), and the gods themselves performed their sacrifice following the pattern of this (cosmic) sacrifice, in which the Primordial Man (replica of the Cosmic Puruṣa) was offered. These are said to be the first *dharmans* i.e. fixed rules, from √*dhṛ*—'to sustain, to hold' (*ibid.* 16b-*tāni dharmāṇi prathamāni āsan*), with respect to the sacrifice (*yajña*), if we can say so. The point to be noted is that at the end of this sacrifice, the powers or forces (*mahimānaḥ*), obviously produced by the sacrifice, reached the heaven, where the ancient Sādhyas and the gods had their stay (*ibid.* 16 cd). Sāyaṇa takes the word *mahimānaḥ* to mean *mahātmānaḥ* (the great souls) who reached the heavenly world. Geldner translates the word as "Mächte", meaning powers or forces.[51] Macdonell also has taken it to mean "powers."[52] This shows that even after the sacrifice,[53] the effect produced by it is recorded in the heaven. The Pūrvamīmāṁsā system of philosophy thought of the concept of *apūrva* or *adṛṣṭa,* which most probably can be traced from such Ṛgvedic concept. The etymology of the word *āhuti* (offering given in fire) occurring as *arthavāda* in the context of the New-moon and Full-moon sacrifices, also breathes this same thought. The offering given by the sacrificer becomes his body in the yonder world. When he departs from this world, that offering follows him and calls out to him, "Come; I am here your body". As the offering thus calls out (*āhvayati* from √*hvā* or √*hve*—'to call out, invoke'), it is called *āhuti* (*Śat.Br.* XI.2.2.6). The *arthavāda* in the form of etymology is functional in nature as it commends the *vidhi* of offering and strikes an eschatological note, tinged with ethics, and speaks of a belief based on the *karman*-doctrine.

Thus right from the beginning, the concept of sacrifice has been to rise to the cosmic level, offerings and prayers figuring as only the phenomenal aspects of it. The ritual-texts, now and again, try to stress this stand-point. To take a couple of examples. The *yūpa* (sacrificial stake or post) is required in the Soma-sacrifices, rather in animal-sacrifices *viz.* Nirūḍhapaśubandha or Paśubandha and Horse-sacrifice, for the sacrificial animal is immolated only at the *yūpa.* Though fixed on the terrestrial plane (in the sacrifice), the *yūpa* is understood to reach the region of the gods.[54] The *Tait. Sam.* explains how the sacrificial stake touches all the three regions *viz.* the nether, earth and through mid-region the heaven. The lowest portion of the *yūpa,* which is unchiselled, is fixed in a pit, which symbolises the nether region, belonging to the *pitṛs.*

What is above the part dug in, up to the girdle of the *yūpa* belongs to men; the girdle to the plants, these parts symbolising the region of the earth. What is above the girdle up to the top, to Viśve Devāḥ (All Gods); the top to Indra, the rest to the Sādhyas, these parts standing for the heavenly region (*Tait. Sam.* VI.3.4.6, 7). The post is set up to discern the world of heaven (*ibid.* VI.3.4.8). This is about the sacrificial post (*yūpa*), which is said to be the banner i.e. emblem, of sacrifice (*RV* III.8.8........ *adhvarasya ketum*).

Another instance which we take is of *āsandī* seat (or generally translated as throne-seat). It is prescribed for the sacrificer at the Vājapeya and Rājasūya sacrifices, as also for placing the Soma-shoots, Ukhya Agni (i.e. the fire kept in the fire-pot) and also the pot at the Pravargya ceremony. The height of the *āsandī* in each of these cases differs. But the *āsandī* in each case is more or less high and certainly above the ground, indicating the two levels maintained in the rites and rituals,—one earthly and the other divine. When the sacrificer performs a sacrifice, he goes near the gods to the divine level. Hence the use of *āsandī* (for him or for the things used in sacrifice.[55]

That the divine plane is maintained in the sacrifice can be seen from two details (out of many others!) from the code of conduct prescribed for a sacrificer. As the sacrificer, consecrated for the sacrifice, is believed to be one among the gods, the 'fast'-milk (*vrata*) is cooked i.e. heated, for him, which he partakes in the Agniṣṭoma sacrifice and does not offer it in fire, for the sacrificial food of the gods is cooked and not uncooked (*Śat.Br.* III.2.2.10). Again, the gods do not sleep. The sacrificer, being a mortal requires sleep. So he sleeps, but commits himself to Agni, who would awaken him from sleep for Agni is the Lord of vows and is always wide awake (*ibid.* 22).

The same divine plane is maintained with respect to the speech, mentioned in the ritual tradition. Though uttered by the human beings (the consecrated sacrificer or priest), it is used for the sacrificial purpose and in the precincts of the sacrifice. It is clearly distinguished from the ordinary human speech as well as that of the birds, beasts etc. Here we point to the injunction (*vidhi*) of litany (Prātar-anuvāka). The *Kauṣ. Br.* clearly states that the priest should begin to recite, when night is far advanced, but before the time when cattle, ordinary men and birds take up to speech (XI.8). Prātar-anuvāka may begin immediately after mid-night and conclude as soon as day-light appears. In this hour, there is sought to be no other sound heard, for fear of contamination, except that of the recitation of the hymns and some detached verses.[56]

In the sacrificial context, the concept of speech is never thought to be other than that of truth. The *Ait.Br.* states in clear words that the consecrated sacrificer has to speak truth only. As the gods are established in truth and human beings are prone to falsehood, the *Ait.Br.* raises a doubt here as to how a mortal man be able to speak truth in all contexts. It suggests a way that the consecrated sacrificer should utter *vicakṣaṇavatī vāk* (I.6). Sāyaṇa, while explaining the expression (here) *'vicakṣaṇavatīm vācam vadet'*, says that the consecrated person (i.e. sacrificer) has to use the term *vicakṣaṇa*, when he utters any sentence. Thus he should say, 'Devadatta, *vicakṣaṇa*, bring the cow'; 'Yajñadatta, *vicakṣaṇa*, tie the cow' etc. Dange has explained this expression, catching its import. He says that comprehending the real meaning of the word *vicakṣaṇa*, we have to take into account the expression that follows in such cases: *satyam vai cakṣuḥ* (*Śat.Br.* I.3.1.27 and *Ait.Br. loc.cit.*). Hence by addressing Devadatta or any other person, the sacrificer actually transfers his own responsibility of seeing the truth on somebody else, for he himself cannot move out being consecrated, nor can he talk to others during this period. The one who is addressed as *vicakṣaṇa* serves as the 'eye' of the sacrificer (*Ait.Br.* I.6..... *cakṣur vai vicakṣaṇam*.......) and takes up the responsibility of fetching correct (*satya*) things.[57] There are several such occasions when the ritual-texts try to stress the divine level of sacrifice as separated from the earthly level.[58] This distinction between the two levels is also maintained in the Purāṇas, when the rules of daily behaviour are laid down by them in the context of various vows (*vratas*) to be followed. Such vows are prescribed for the worship of specific deties as also for a specific period. Dange has made a detailed study of these at a great length.[59] To give succinctly, the rules in a vow concern bath, worship, limited and specific food, that too totally avoiding salt, honey, anything pungent, wine and flesh (*Agni P.* 175.10 ff). Just as the Vedic ritual-texts give stress on the quality of 'truth', which we have noted, the Purāṇas also give importance to the inward purity of a person following a vow. The *Brahma P.* says that together with the food to be taken only once a day, a person should be devoid of evil will or cunning and egoism (*Brahma P.* 216.43).

From the Vedic to the Puranic times, the ritualism, though materialistic in form, has always aimed at taking the 'mortal' level reach the 'divine' or 'higher' level. This aim may seem to be very high at the beginning. But the purpose of the rules of conduct for a consecrated sacrificer or a person following any vow (*vrata*) is to train the mind of the performer for good behaviour and that too permanently! In spite of weakness, so common to human beings, the institution of ritualism, either in the form of sacrifice or Puranic *vrata*, impels a man to make a start and behave according to a particular code of conduct at least for a short duration. Thus ritual paves a way to the all-pervading eternal Truth-Satyam-the Ṛta.

In the context of the Puruṣasūkta, we have noted the expression 'first (fixed) ordinances' (*RV* X.90.16b..... *dharmāṇi prathamāni.....*), which indicates some kind of definite 'Order'. And here we come to the concept of Ṛta. The word Ṛta (from √ṛ- 'to go', thus the 'ever-going' course of things) signifies the cosmic order or law prevailing in nature, which is governed by the highest gods. Mitra and Varuṇa are lords of order and are the upholders of order (*ibid.* I.23.5). Varuṇa and the Ādityas are sometimes called guardians of order (*ṛtasya gopā*), but even Agni and Soma are also at times eulogised by this term. The epithet *ṛtavān*, is mainly applied to Agni, for he is the 'observer of order', as he maintains perfectly the order of sacrifices. But this epithet is also applied to Varuṇa and Mitra. Varuṇa is said to be *dhṛtavrata*—'whose ordinances are fixed' (i.e. firmly held or borne by him). The Ṛta here is concerning the order in the cosmos, the movements of the sun and the moon, of day and night, the arrival of seasons at the proper time in a year and so on. Another aspect of Ṛta concerns the sacrificial sphere and in this, Ṛta signifies the very sacrifice and the rites and rituals coming with it. The third aspect of Ṛta is connected to the moral sphere, where are found the concepts of 'truth' and 'right'. The concept of 'Asha' in the Zoroastrian tradition (in the *Avesta*) can well be compared with that of Ṛta. Even 'Asha' meaning 'order' is related to the three spheres, which we have noted in the context of Ṛta.

Ṛta in the Vedic tradition is only conceptual in form, not having any pictographical record, unlike the Mayet of the ancient Egyptians. Mayet, the symbol of 'order' is noticed in the form of a 'figure'. When the priest in ancient Egypt raised a small figure of Mayet before the image after worship, it meant that order was established.[60] Dange suggests that on Indian side, Swastika could be taken as the corollary of Mayet or of Ṛta (√*ṛ*-'to go on'). Again the solar disk could very well be taken as the visible Ṛta (*RV* I.139.2), whence came the disk of Viṣṇu.[61]

We have seen that Ṛta in the cosmic sphere is governed by certain gods. In the moral sphere Ṛta developed to sustain the social order and is seen in the concept of Dharma (from √*dhṛ*-'to hold, sustain'), and in later ages, the king is called 'the protector of *dharma*' (*dharma* meaning 'which sustains the society'—*dhārayati iti dharmaḥ*), and the 'rod of punishment' (*Daṇḍa*) coming to the help of the king in his duties.[63] Here we have to take note of the word 'Satya', which is mentioned with the word 'Anṛta' (*RV* VII.49.3). Dange points out the exact distinction between the two concepts *viz.* Ṛta and Satya. Ṛta symbolised constant activity; Satya stood for stability, which is very essential for the building of a social order. But Ṛta and Satya had the identical status. An act against the Satya (established law) was Anṛta. Moreover, it went against the general cosmic order—Ṛta.[64]

Ṛta concerning the two spheres *viz.* cosmic and moral,[65] was somewhat superseded by the Ṛta, which centred round the concept of sacrifice, as sacrifice was the distinguishing mark of the Aryan culture. The *RV* points out that both Ṛta (concerning cosmic sphere) and Satya (related to moral sphere) have their origin from Tapas (*RV* X.190.1—*ṛtam ca satyam cābhīddhāt tapaso' dhyajāyata*). The word *tapas* (from √*tap*—'to shine, to be hot' etc.) initially is connected with the concept of 'toiling' and 'mortifying' the body in the context of sacrifice, for the sacrificer has to observe a strict code of rules. Thus 'sacrifice' (order—Ṛta—in the sacrificial sphere) stands above the Ṛta pertaining to the cosmic as well as the moral spheres. Hence, sacrifice is eulogised in the highest terms. It is the 'womb of good deeds' (X.61.6..... *sukṛtasya yonau*). Sacrifice is said to be the womb of Ṛta (*Śat.Br.* I.3.4.16...... *yajño vā ṛtasya yoniḥ........*).

The tradition of sacrifice in India has been from times immemorial. The Puruṣasūkta (*RV* X.90) takes us to the age of creation. Already are noted the *arthavādas* fro the *Śat.Br.* (I.6.2.1ff) and the *Tait. Sam.* (II.6.3.2, 3), where it is marked that the sacrificial cake (*puroḍāśa*) becoming a tortoise, is offered in sacrifice. Most important source of sacrifice is Prajāpati, who is said to have discovered sacrifice and saw many sacrifices. To give one example. From the *Śat.Br.*, as an *arthavāda,* we have a mythical account. The gods were passing upwards to the heavenly world, but the *asuras* enveloped them with darkness. The gods started a sacrificial session of a hundred Agniṣṭomas and could dispel some of the darkness. They then entered upon a sacrificial session of a hundred Ukthyas, but could not dispel the entire darkness. When they approached Prajāpati, he asked them to perform a sacrificial session (*sattra*) of a hundred Atirātras. This worked and the gods could dispel the *asuras*, darkness and all evil. The gods found the heaven after that (*Śat.Br.* XI.5.5.1-6). Indra is said to have given the knowledge of certain sacrificial rites to seers. To see briefly, knowledge of the Stomabhāgas to Vasiṣṭha (*Pañc.Br.* XV.5.25; *Gop. Br.* II.2.13); of expiations to Vasiṣṭha (*Śat.Br.* XII.6.1.38ff); of Uktha to Viśvāmitra (*Saḍ.Br.* I.5.1) etc. It has to be noted that as Indra was a 'human' hero in reality, later on deified[66] the recipients of his gift of knowledge about sacrifices and the details thereof were human (seers). The role of seers in the search of sacrifice and the propagation of the knowledge about it cannot be set aside. We have already noted how they came to the place where gods had performed the sacrifice. When they offered the sacrificial cake in the form of tortoise, the sacrifice shone forth to them. From the former to the later, from the father to the son, the knowledge about sacrifice travelled through ages (*Śat. Br.* I.6.2.1 ff). Some seers 'saw' some unique sacrifices and so were additions made to the list of sacrifices. Such sacrifices are Catuṣṭoma of Gautama (*Jaim.Br.* II.173), Catūrātra of Atri (*ibid.* II.281), Jāmadagnya of Jamadagni (*ibid.* II.284) etc. Sacrifice in India thus has a hoary tradition and its origin is lost in the deep layers of history. Even in the Brāhmaṇa-texts, final form of sacrifice is not seen and one feels that it is still in the making.[67] It is in the Śrautasūtras that the rules regarding the procedure of sacrifices are seen codified; there also certain variations occur in the Śrautasūtras.

It is noted earlier that Prajāpati discovered sacrifice. In fact Prajāpati is also said to have offered himself as an oblation in sacrifice. Sacrifice was his own image (*Śat.Br.* XI.1.7.8). Even elsewhere the *Śat.Br.* identifies sacrifice with Prajāpati

(IV.3.4.3). Thus Prajāpati is identified with both the sacrificer as well as the sacrifice. The Brāhmaṇa-texts untiringly try to show the importance of sacrifice, which is connected to the cosmic level. The concepts of Time and Space are joined with sacrifice. Thus Prajāpati comes to be identified with the Father Time —Samvatsara—Year. In the *RV*, we have the image of a Divine Wheel (Year), which takes one full year for its single rotation (*RV* I.164.11). This is the undecaying and ever-rotating wheel, having twelve spokes (i.e. months) and wherein rest seven hundred twenty sons (offsprings), each two forming a pair (days and nights in a year). To take only one example from the Brāhmaṇa-texts for seeing the concept of Time related to Prajāpati. The Great Fire-altar which is built with five layers of bricks in the rite of Agnicayana,[68] stands for the body of Prajāpati, who became disjointed having created the cosmos.[69] Prajāpati is also related to another important concept and it is of Space. The *Tait. Sam.* states that sacrifice finds support in Dyauḥ-Heaven and Pṛthivī-Earth (II.6.3.5). The *Ait.Br.* in this regard describes the marriage of Dyauḥ and Pṛthivī and connects them with the *sāmans*. The mythical account (in short) goes as follows. These two worlds, once joined together, later on got separated. As a result, there were no rains, no heat (i.e. no sun) and the people suffered. So the gods brought these two worlds together and contracted their marriage. By means of the Rathantara *sāman*, this Earth incites Heaven; by the Bṛhat *sāman*, heaven incites Earth; by Naudhasa *sāman* this (Earth) incites that; by the Śyaita *sāman* that (Heaven) incites this (Earth). Earth gave the place of sacrifice (to Heaven) for the gods. Hence there a dark (place i.e. spot) as it were in the moon. Therefore, in the bright half of the month, they sacrifice (This is obviously because the dark spot on the moon in the waxing fortnights can be easily marked). Heaven placed saline soil[70] (*ūṣāḥ*—'salt' is a wrong translation) in the earth (*Ait. Br.* IV.27=19.5). In the *Tait.Br.* in the context of Agnyādhāna (the rite of setting up the sacred fires), there occurs a mythical account coming as *arthavāda,* as follows. Heaven (Dyauḥ) and Earth (Pṛthivī) once closely joined together, got separated. But while separating, the two decided to exchange their best parts worthy of sacrifice (*yajñiyam*). Heaven gave saline soil on Earth, while Earth gave the black spot on the moon (*Tait. Br.* I.1.3.2, 3). This *arthavāda* occurs for explaining the importance of the *vidhi* in the Agnyādhāna rite. The officiating priest (Adhvaryu) places the saline soil in the pit of the Ahavanīya fire and while doing so he has his mind upon the black spot of the moon. By this he sets up the fire (Āhavanīya) on both *viz.* Heaven and Earth. Thus is sacrifice related to the two worlds and through them Space.[71] As sacrifice is the birth-place or origin of Ṛta (Order), it is very much connected to the concept of creation itself. Now creation cannot be without 'pairing' (*mithuna*). Hence everything, small or big, is said to have a pairing with the other unit of different or of its species, the concept covering oblations, ladles, chants (*mantras*), substances like ghee, the wife of the sacrificer etc. In fact, it is a thought-provoking study made by Dange, about *mithuna.* He has dealt with several rites and rituals, pointing out the sexual symbolism underlying them.[73] Through the details of (sacrificial) rites and rituals of the material sacrifice (*dravya-yajña),* the Vedas have built up the science of sacrifice, taking sacrifice to the divine level, ultimately to become one with the all-pervading eternal Ṛta-Order. Thus material sacrifice, with its inevitable materialistic details, is only a means to know the higher eternal sacrifice, leading to Ṛta-cosmic as well as moral spheres.

The Brāhmaṇa-texts try to explain this concept through mythical accounts (as *arthavādas*). The *Śat.Br.* in the context of the Agnicayana rite gives an *arthavāda.* Once the gods performed several sacrificial rites, even the building of the Great Fire-altar. But all these could not make them immortal. Prajāpati instructed them on the proper way of building the Great Fire-altar in the Agnicayana rite, which when built made the gods, immortal. Then came Death complaining that if the men also constructed such a Great Fire-altar and became immortal, there would not be any share left to him of them (whom can he overpower?). The gods while pacifying him said that thereafter no one would be immortal with body. Only when Death had taken man's body as his share, the man would become immortal through his knowledge and holy work. The *arthavāda* quickly explains that here knowledge is of the Great Fire-altar and the holy work is the construction of it (*Śat.Br.* X.4.3 3-9). We are here reminded of the dialogue between Yājñavalkya and Ārtabhāga from the *Bṛhad. Up.*, regarding man's existence after death and that too connected with his *karman* (action). And Yājñavalkya's final word is — "A man remains (even after death) known to be righteous due to his rigtheous deed (*puṇyena karmaṇā*) and sinful due to his sinful deed" (*Bṛhad.Up.* III.2.13). The *arthavāda* in the *Jaim.Br.* has earlier touched this point in the context of the Agnihotra rite and that too in a very lucid style. It is as follows. When the Agnihotrin (a sacrificer, who maintains the three fires—Gārhapatya, Dakṣiṇa and Āhavanīya, and daily attends on them) dies and goes to the other world, the Father and the Forefathers come to him and with displeasure say that he has not brought anything with him from the terrestrial world. To them he should reply that whatever merit he has accumulated belongs to them. The *Jaim.Br.* makes a division in a clear cut way. It says that his sons take his property, his good deeds the Fathers (ancestors—near and distant ones) and his evil deeds the enemies. Having divided all his belongings in this threefold way, he goes to have a stay with him, who shines yonder (*Jaim.Br.* I.50). That the stay in the Ādityaloka (domain of the Sun) has been the highest aim of a mortal is reflected in Manu's words, when it is said that by seeing the great grandson (*putrasya pautreṇa*), a man reaches the highest world of Sun—*bradhnasya viṣṭapam* (*Manu S.* IX.137).

The concept of sacrifice, according to the ancient ritualistic thinkers, is so wide that the sacrifice, with its materialistic details, could be continued in the next world also, after the death of the sacrificer. Thus when the Agnihotrin dies, all the three fires (mentioned above) are to be carried to the cremation ground and the *yajñapātras*,[74] excepting the grinding stones used for pressing the Soma shoots and the iron instruments as well as the earthen pots, are to be kept on the body of that man (*Āśv. G.S.* IV.2.1; IV 3.1-23). This is no doubt a later tradition and one may be led to draw a conclusion that as the sacrificer (Agnihotrin) was associated with the three fires as also the *yajñapātras*, so should he be with them at the cremation, indicating their extinction with his. But it is not so, when we turn to a verse from the *RV* (X.14.16).

The verse (*RV* X.14.16) is the last of a hymn to the manes.[75] The important expression here (*ibid.* 16a) is *trikadrukebhiḥ patati*—'he flies (*patati*) with the *trikadrukas*. Opinions are divided on the subject of the verb 'patati' (flies). It is understood as Soma by Macdonell,[76] as Yama by Sāyaṇa and by Geldner as 'the dead one'.[77] Sāyaṇa understands the expression to mean that it is Yama who flies for the protection of the *trikadrukas*, which he understands as the three special sacrifices in the Soma-sacrifice, they being termed as Jyotiṣṭoma, Goṣṭoma and Āyuṣṭoma. Geldner translates the expression as meaning that the Dead (sacrificer?) flies to the Trikadruka-days (*An den Trikadrukatagen*), obviously suggesting the tradition of the three last days of the special Soma ritual already hinted by Sāyaṇa. But even then Geldner puts a question-mark after the word *Trikadrukatagen* (?).[78] The present author has discussed this expression in details and has given her interpretation, with the help of the *Pañc.Br.* (XVI. 1-3), which records that the *'trikadrukāḥ'* are three in number, having the same names *viz.* Jyotiḥ, Gauḥ and Āyuḥ. But they are not the names of sacrifices, but of the *stomas*. It says—'These (three) *stomas* (together) are the *trikadruka stomas......'* (*Pañc.Br.* XVI.3.8).[79] Thus the expression *trikadrukebhiḥ* would mean with the *trikadruka* chants or formulas. The chants or *mantras* have significance, for they are said to save a person from the fear of death (*Jaim. Br.* II.381). This is to be remembered when Sāyaṇa glosses (on *Āśv. Ś.S* VI.10) that five *ṛcs* (*mantras*)—from this hymn (*RV* X.14.7-12, excluding X.14.9) are to be recited in case the sacrificer died in the middle of the sacrificial session (*sattramadhye dīkṣitamaraṇe*). Though this gloss does not pertain to the verse in question (*RV* X.14.16), the purport of the verse is beyond doubt, for it clearly suggests the sacrificer to go to the abode of Yama, along with the sacrifice, and with the help of the Trikadruka formulas.[80] The concept of sacrifice in the Vedic Texts, thus, takes in its gamut, the other world also, where the once started sacrifice can be continued by the sacrificer, without any hindrance. As sacrifice is considered to be the birthplace or origin (*yoniḥ*) of Ṛta (both cosmic and moral, sacrificial Ṛta being inherent in the sacrifice itself), it is thought of to have such large dimensions.

In this light, we can view the sacrifices enjoined by the *Pañc.Br.* in its last chapter. We have Twelve years *sattra* (*Pañc.Br.* XXV.6); Thirty-six years *sattra* (*ibid.* 7); Hundred years *sattra* (*ibid.* 8); Thousand days *sattra* (*ibid.* 9); Three years *sattra* (*ibid.* 16); Thousand years *sattra* of Prajāpati (*ibid.* 17); Thousand years rite of the Viśvasṛjs (*ibid.* 18). Simply taking these to be 'imaginary' will not take us to the real concept of sacrifice. The 'numbers' of the years, pointing out the duration of sacrifice, occur as a part of *arthavāda*. Each number is joined with a certain concept on the principle of imitative or mimatic magic, the principle being 'Like produces like.' To take the number 'Hundred'. It is joined with the normal term of man's life, which is thought to be of hundred years—in a way immortality which the man achieves. Again the number 'Thousand' is joined with the highest Virāj (metre), for the highest Virāj is of a thousand syllables (*ibid.* XXV.9.4). Caland rightly points out that the word *virāj* (fr. *vi* + √*rāj*—'to shine brilliantly;) stands for 'splendour'.[81] The numbers mentioned in the ritual contexts are for complementing the sacrifice or its procedure through the magic of 'Number'.[82] Again as sacrifice for the Vedic ritual thinkers is believed to be the origin or birthplace of Ṛta, such large numbers of years, occurring in the context of sacrifices, to be performed, indicate the concept of 'Infinity' related to sacrifice, in the ancient Vedic mind. For the Vedic ritualists, 'hundred' or 'thousand' could be an expression, eloquent of Infinity'.[83] 'Infinity' is not simply a concept born out of imagination and so are the sacrifices enjoined for large numbers of years not imaginary. These sacrifices try to justify the unending cycle of sacrifice, which is the birth-place of Ṛta.

Here we take only one example, which aptly shows the invariable relation between sacrifice and Ṛta. It is the rite of Agnihotra, which is regarded as the hub of Vedic ritualism. It is conceptually built up on the basic idea that when the sun sets, he enters Agni (Fire) which is his womb, and from the womb, the sun comes out in the morning. So the rite of Agnihotra is mainly, nay, solely connected with the sun, who is the source of heat and lustre—an aspect of cosmic Ṛta.

Here we are reminded of the last king of the XVIII dynasty in ancient Egypt—Amenhotep IV (1375-1358 BC)—who substituted the worship of the multiplicity of gods by that of one god—Aton i.e. the Sun—and even changed his own name (Amenhotep, which meant 'Amen rests') to Akhnaton ('Aton is satisfied'). The king was so overwhelmed with the sun that he used to catch the rays of the sun in his hands to imbibe the solar energy. In the Vedic context, we cannot forget Max Müller, who betrays unmistakable bias for the solar phenomenon, which according to him is present in practically all the Vedic deities.[84] The anthropologists and the ethnologists called him 'solarist' and even nicknamed him as 'Sun' (with such an expression as "Here comes the Sun").[85] We cannot wholly agree with the stand-point of Max Müller and as

Dandekar has pointed out, most of the mythological identifications proposed by Max Müller are now generally rejected.[86] Nevertheless, the influence of the sun on the life of the Indians, reaching even the modern era, cannot be gainsaid.

The rite of Agnihotra vouchsafes for this belief and the *arthavādas* occurring in the ritual-texts validate the rite. The *Śat.Br.* (II.3.1.30, 36) states that when the sun sets and goes down, Agni is the light. When the sun rises, Sūrya is the light. Therefore, in the evening, while offering libation, the *mantra* is —'Agni is the light (*jyotiḥ*); the light is Agni, Svāhā!' In the morning, the *mantra* recited while giving offering, is—'Sūrya is the light; the light is Sūrya, Svāhā!' (for the *mantra, Vāj Sam.* III.9, 10). The *Jaim.Br.* treats this topic fully (I.1-65). It brings all the important details from the Soma-sacrifice as being on par with the various details in the Agnihotra rites and states that with the two evening oblations as well as with the two morning oblations, he performs all sacrifices (*sarvairetairyajñakratubhir-iṣṭm bhavati*) the *mantra* is *agnirjyotirjyotiragniḥ svāhā* (*Jaim.Br.* I.4). Whatever sin is committed by a person during daytime, that the sun makes him to do and the sin committed by him in night, that Agni wants him to do (*ibid.* 9). Sūrya and Agni, both being important, each of them decides to offer his own self to the other. When the sun sets, he offers himself to Agni. Agni follows the sun, when the latter rises. Thereby Agni offers himself to the sun (*ibid.*). The *Tait.Br.* states that as oblations were offered for Agni, the sun desired to have such oblations. So both Agni and the Sun came to agreement and decided that the evening offering would be for Agni and the morning one for the sun (II.1.2.6). The *Tait.Br.* further states that if one offers prior to sunrise in the morning and has already offered at the previous evening to Agni, both these offerings virtually belong to Agni. So the morning offering to the sun should be after the sun has arisen (*ibid.* 7). This point is elaborately discussed by the *Ait.Br.* which comes to the conclusion that the evening offering should be in the night (when after the sunset, darkness sets in), while the morning offering should be when the sun is actually seen (*Ait.Br.* V.31=25.6). That the Agnihotra rite is prescribed to maintain and help the regular daily course of the sun is vouchsafed by the *Jaim.Br.*, when it records the view of Nagarin Jānaśruteya that the sun enters fire in the evening that is his womb. When a person offers the two oblations in the evening, that is his womb. When a person offers the two oblations in the evening, he stands on the back of the sun and when he offers the two oblations in the morning, he causes the sun to rise thereby (*Jain.Br.* I.11). The *Śat.Br.* states—"While he sacrifices in the morning before the sunrise, he causes him to be born—really, he (i.e. the sun) would not rise, if he does not sacrifice his offering to him i.e. Agni" (*Śat.Br.* II.3.1.5). The *Kūrma P.* says that the fruit of the performance of Agnihotra rite is the lustre of the sun (*Kūrma P.* II.8.53). This is how the relation of the sun and Agnihotra rite has percolated even upto the Puranic times. The Śrautasūtras enjoin daily offering of morning and evening Agnihotra for a man, who has established his (three) fires, as also for a man, who has no fires.[87] The *Kaus. Br.* gives stress on *sandhi* (joint) as the exact hour of giving offering in fire. It states that one should offer to the sun when he is about to rise and has not as yet arisen. The evening offering should be when the sun has set. Thus the offering should be at the joint of day and night (or of night and day), which is the *sandhi* or the *sandhyākāla* (*Kauṣ Br.* VII.9). A note has to be taken of the mythical account, figuring as *arthavāda* in *Kāṭh. Sam.* which gives an explanation for the rite of offering—that too milk-offering-in fire. The account runs as follows. Sun and Agni came from the same womb. From that birth-place the Sun went upwards and his semen fell down, which was taken by Agni. Agni made it thick and placed it in the cow. It became the milk of the cow, with which is offered the Agnihotra (*Kāṭh. Sam.* VI.3).

The Agnihotra rite being so important, the *arthavādas* are stated to justify it. It has to be pointed out that the curiosity to know the sojourn of the sun when he sets and the anxiety mixed with apprehension for his return on the next morning certainly lie at the basis of the Agnihotra rite. The Purāṇas also weave *arthavādas* in this regard. The Purāṇas speak of the demons Mandeha, who try to devour the sun at sunset every day (*Brah. P.* I.2.21.11ff). According to the *Gar.P.*, the Mandehas are three and half crores in number (I.205.61). The *SK.P.* says that due to the curse given to these demons by Prajāpati, they die every day, yet their bodies remain in tact (I.2.37.17, 18). When the *brāhmaṇas* throw at these demons the water consecrated by the Gāyatrī *mantra* at the *sandhyā*-ritual, they get burnt (*ibid.* I.2.38.19). The *Gar. P.* also says the same. A person who does not perform *sandhyā* kills the sun i.e. he helps the demons to kill the sun (*Gar.P.* I. 205.62).[88]

In ancient mythologies, other than Indian, also, occur the ideas of sun's night journey, his disappearance, efforts to bring him back and several rites to give him strength for his daily routine.[89] In fact, the cosmic drama of the sun's disappearance and his rise in the next morning has been a universal myth and so are the rites and rituals associated with it. However we are not agreeing here with the theory that all myths are derived from the rituals, for there can be a myth without a ritual associated with it and vice-versa. The idea of 'ritual giving rise to myth' was originally thought of by W. Robertson Smith but it achieved near-immortality when it was adopted by his friend and admirer J.G. Frazer and became the basic presupposition of Frazer's monumental work *The Golden Bough*.[90]

On the Vedic scene, the disappearance of the sun and his rising in the next morning has not developed as a full-fledged myth but has been a proto-myth.[91] But later on the Purāṇas developed this proto-myth into myth or meta-myth by the 'embroidery'[92] of mythological details of the Mandeha demons, which we have noted above.

The whole edifice of the Agnihotra rite is built up as connected to the sun, his setting and rising in the next morning, on the whole an important and regular feature of Ṛta on the cosmic level. The Agnihotra rite is also connected with Ṛta on the moral level. We point out here a small detail which occurs in the *Ait. Br.* While enjoining the evening offering in the fire, when the sun sets and the darkness spreads, the *Ait. Br.* quotes a *gāthā*, which is in the form of swearing on the part of certain person (V.30=25.5). The *gāthā*, though coming from folk-tradition[93], assumes the role of a Dharmaśāstra text and points out that a person stealing lotus-stalks would incur a series of sins, one of them being that which a person commits while turning away a guest arrived at the evening time. The *Ait.Br.* at this place calls the sun *eka-atithiḥ* (Sāyaṇa—'One living in a foreign land, without any relatives', though the word can also mean 'an excellent guest', like *eka-vīraḥ*—'unparalleled warrior'), residing among the sacrificer's oblations which are being offered. The sun being a guest is to be given hospitality and is not to be turned away[94], as the *gāthā* likes to indicate. In later times, the *Manu S.* enjoins a rule that a guest coming in the evening should not be turned away, for he is sent by the sun (*Manu S.* III.105). Thus the setting of the sun for his nocturnal sojourn and the offering given in fire for his return in the next morning, as we have seen in the Agnihotra rite, has laid down a certain norm in the Indian tradition, which has reached even the modern age. The rite of Agnihotra has been studied by many scholars.[95] Even in this age, when water, held in the joined palms, is offered to the sun in the morning with prayers, at the sunrise and a lamp (preferably an oil-lamp) is lit in the evening at the setting of the sun (when the darkness just sets in), it is only the celestial luminary—the Sun—the maker of seasons and year—that we bow down to, which is the inherent idea in the rite of Agnihotra, which couples it with the offerings given in fire (Agni) for the Sun.

That sacrifice is regarded as the birthplace (*yoni*) of Ṛta (on the cosmic level) can be seen from the rite of Agnihotra, which is related to the sun. Nevertheless there are several rites and rituals in various sacrifices which are related to the Ṛta on the cosmic level, Agnihotra rite being only one of them. Sacrifice is also the birthplace of Ṛta on the moral level. This is seen prominently from the code laid down for the sacrificer. The ritual-texts expect the sacrificer to emerge as a 'better' man, after performing the sacrifice. For this a definite code of conduct is laid down, comprising the rules of consecration (*dīkṣā*)[96]; toiling (*tapas*) or fervour or austere devotion[97]; inculcating such qualities as faith (*śraddhā*), gratitude, humility, truth (*satya*); giving gifts (*dakṣiṇās*) etc.[98]

Sacrifice thus joined with cosmic as well as moral spheres stood as a pivot in ancient Indian life and the ritual-texts with several *arthavādas* ushered in, extol this. Here, we come to an interesting point and it is of the running away of sacrifice for a small duration and the means to catch hold of it. We can take some of the *arthavādas*, connected with this, which also explain the additions made to the already existing ritual. But prior to these, the point to be discussed is—why such accounts should crop up in the ritual-texts. The foremost reason is to bring out the importance of sacrifice, to know and master the secrets of which, both the gods and the *asuras* are seen striving hard. The conflict of these two groups for victory through sacrifice—either of these winning or getting a score over the other—occurs so many times that it has become a regular feature of the ritual-texts. Hence, the anxiety of the gods for protecting sacrifice, which should be exclusively in their possession! If we probe this point still further, it takes us to the 'discovery of fire' in ancient times, which has been an important landmark in the history of human civilisation. Fire was so important that the fear of losing it always lurked somewhere in the ancient mind. The *arthavādas* stating 'the running away' of sacrifice or Agni can be understood in this light. As Lang has pointed out, the savage and the senseless element in mythology is, for the most part, a legacy from the fancy of ancestors of the civilized races.[99] The accounts of sacrifice or Agni running away, hiding somewhere, wandering etc. can be taken as 'survival' of some such belief, which cannot be dated but is seen percolated in the ritual-texts.[100] We can take into account some *arthavādas* in this regard, each of which is given with a unique motif. The *Śat.Br.*, in the context of the New-moon and Full-moon sacrifices, while laying down the use of the black antelope skin, gives a mythical account, according to which sacrifice once escaped from the gods and roamed in the form of a black antelope. The gods found it, stripped it of its skin and brought the skin away with them (*Śat.Br.* I.1.4.1; also *Tait.Br.* III.2.6.1, 2). Here the importance of the skin of the black antelope is unique, for the beast is identified with the sacrifice or Prajāpati. Dange maintains that the beast was sacrificially killed in far ancient times and the skin was worn on special ritual-occasions. This was prior to the fuller development of the Vedic ritual tradition and hence is not mentioned in any of the extant ritual-texts.[101] The *Pañc.Br.* also speaks of sacrifice running away. Taking the form of the beautiful-winged bird (Suparṇa), it wandered and the gods had to catch hold of it by the Sauparṇa *sāman* (*Pañc.Br.* XIV.3.10). Though the *arthavāda* here is for glorifying the Sauparṇa *sāman*, the anxiety to catch hold of the runaway sacrifice cannot be gainsaid. The *Ait.Br.* has explained several such factors connected with sacrifice, in the context of Soma-sacrifice. These are—*praiṣas*-directions, by which the gods sought to start the sacrifice (*pra* + √*iṣ*); *purorucas-mantras* (according to Sāyaṇa—7 in number), by which they made the sacrifice radiant (*pra+*√*ruc*—causal); altar (*vedi*) in which they found the sacrifice (*anu+*√*vind*); when found, they took the sacrifice (√*grah*) with cups—*grahas*; they made it known (*ni+*√*vid*—causal) by Nivids (short formulas of addressing the gods). Here, 'etymology' works for explaining these names related to sacrifice, 'etymology' coming as *arthavāda*. But the whole issue starts with the note that 'sacrifice went away from the gods' (*Ait.Br.* III.9=11.9). To point out the importance of Aśvavāla grass (*Saccharum spontaneum*), of which the *prastara* (a bunch of grass, here Aśvavāla grass) is made, there occurs an *arthavāda* that once sacrifice went away and wandered in the form of a horse. The gods rushed, took hold of that horse's tail, tore it out and threw it down in a lump, from which we have the shoots of the Aśvavāla grass (*Śat.Br.* III.4.1.17). In the Vedic ritual tradition, the horse which is mentioned is a white horse, which has as it were, a scorched mouth (Sāyaṇa says—'a reddish mouth'). In the *Śat.Br.* there occurs an *arthavāda* which states that once Agni went away from gods and entered water. Prajāpati becoming a horse went in search of him. When Prajāpati found Agni on a lotus-leaf and eyed him, Agni scorched his mouth (*Śat.Br.* VII.3.2.14). The *Ait.Br.*, in the context of Rājasūya sacrifice, gives an *arthavāda* which is important on many accounts. Prajāpati created sacrifice and thereafter Brahma (holy power) and Kṣatra (lordly power), also both kinds of offsprings—those who eat the oblations (i.e. *brāhmaṇas*, as Sāyaṇa says) and those who do not eat the oblations (*rājanyas, vaiśyas* and *śūdras*, according to Sāyaṇa). From these offsprings, sacrifice departed. But both Brahma and Kṣatra pursued it, with their weapons. The weapons of the Brahma were the utensils of sacrifice (*yajñāyudhāni* needed for sacrifice), while those of the Kṣatra were horse-chariot, corslet, the bow and arrow. Sacrifice was afraid of Kṣatra's weapons and started trembling. The Brahma followed the sacrifice and obtained it (*Ait.Br.* VII.19=34.1). The *arthavāda* in the form of the mythical account brings forth the importance and the indispensable nature of the *yajñāyudhāni.*[102] The same *arthavāda* ends in saying that the *kṣatriya* (lordly power) has to lay aside his weapons, when he has to be a sacrificer and having the holy power (Brahma), taking the weapons of the holy power (utensils of sacrifice), thus becoming the holy power, he can come to perform sacrifice (*ibid.*) This shows the broader outlook of the ritual-texts. This can be corroborated from an injunction (*vidhi*) occurring in the *Śat.Br.* The Adhvaryu (officiating) priest, while striking the grains in the mortar, utters a call to the *haviṣkṛt* (preparer of the oblation), whose duty is to further pound the (rice) grain. The *Śat.Br.* mentions the call in four ways in anticipation of the *haviṣkṛt* (or sacrificer) being of any one of the four *varṇas*—even of the *śūdra varṇa* (*Śat.Br.* I.1.4.12). The *Śat.Br.* here suggests that any *śūdra* could perform a sacrifice.[103] May be this is like the Niṣāda-sthapati (lord of the Niṣādas), in whose case the Raudra *iṣṭi* (sacrifice) is laid down.[104]

In fact, the relationship between man and Agni in unique as they depend upon each other. The *Śat.Br.* explains this in the context of Agni-upasthāna rite (homage to the fires), which comes in the Agnihotra rite. The *arthavāda* relates that Prajāpati, in creating living beings, created Agni. As soon as born when Agni sought to burn everything on the earth, the creatures tried to crush him. Agni approached man for help, and appealed to him saying, "Having reproduced me, maintain me in this world, so will I reproduce and maintain thee in the yonder world" (*Śat.Br.* II.3.3.1, 2). When the man establishes the two fires (Gārhapatya and Āhavanīya), he reproduces Agni and then maintains him (*ibid.* 3). When the householder (Agnihotrin) dies, they place him on the funeral pyre, from where he is reproduced out of fire (Agni). As long as the householder is alive, Agni is his son, for the former produces him by the Agnyādhāna rite. But when the householder dies, Agni reproduces him, thus becoming his father (*ibid.* 5). Thus the discovery of fire, which was a milestone in the history of man has reached its culmination in the sacrificial philosophy of the Vedic people, in that man and Agni (fire) are shown so intimately related for the working of Ṛta.

Here, to take into account some rites and rituals which are not strictly Vedic. Nevertheless, they occur in the Brāhmaṇa-texts, with the *arthavādas* glorifying them. We have already discussed the point of acculturation of various tribes in the Vedic Aryan fold in the earlier chapter. These tribes had their own rituals and rites, which naturally found space in the Vedic tradition.

It is already seen that the *asuras*, formed a clan other than that of the *devas*. Though the Brāhmaṇa-texts tell us that the *devas* and the *asuras* were 'brothers' being born of Prajāpati, the former are said to have vanquished the latter. The mythical accounts figuring as *arthavāda* are of great help in knowing the non-Vedic rituals or non-Vedic elements in the Vedic rituals, which have come from outside. Here, we take up the example of Rauhiṇa. In the context of constellation Citrā, the *arthavāda* occurs in the *Śat.Br.*(II.1.2.13-17). The gods and *asuras* vied for supremacy. The *asuras* thought of constructing a fire-altar, named Rauhiṇa, to ascend the heavenly world. Indra thought that if the *asuras* become successful, they would go to heaven and overpower the gods. So, taking the guise of a *brāhmaṇa*, Indra went to the *asuras* with a brick of his own requesting them to lay it on the rising fire-altar, which they were constructing. The *asuras* agreed, and Indra placed his brick there on the layer of the altar. The altar went on rising with the bricks placed on the layers one after the other. As the altar was about to be completed, Indra pulled out his brick and down came the alter tumbling! From the bricks that fell helter-skelter, Indra created several bolts and cut the necks of the *asuras*. The gods, who saw this spectacle, exclaimed with surprise, "O, what a wonder (*citram bata*)! We have killed so many *asuras*." As the brick (of Indra) created the wonder (*citram*), it got the name Citrā. It is said that a person who knowing this, sets up his fires under the Citra constellation slays his rivals, and especially a *kṣatriya* should think of this as he is anxious to strike and vanquish his enemies. Almost a similar account is recorded by the *Tait.Br.* (I.1.2.4-6), where the *asuras* are named Kālakañjas. It is said that the *asuras*, who tumbled down became the spiders and two of them, who flew up, became the heavenly dogs.

From this Citrā-brick episode, extolling the setting up of fires on the Citrā constellation, the fact that comes to the surface is that the "rising" (*rauhiṇa*) fire-altar was a speciality of the *asuras*. Before we discuss the point in details, it would be better to set aside the opinion that fire-worship itself was adopted by the people (*devas*) form the *asuras*.[105] This opinion presupposes that there was no fire-worship anywhere apart from the people known as *asuras*. It is very well known that fire-worship, like the worship of the sun, obtains in regions far and wide.[106] To turn to the point of altar-brick, which Indra placed and those which *asuras* were placing on the altar. On the basis of pottery-techniques found out by the archeological surveys of India, Converse suggests that the use of bricks in altars, like the Agnicayana ("laying down the fire-altar') was adopted by the Vedic priests from the indigenous culture, by which he means the Harappans.[107] The reasons put forth are:

1. The Harappans used millions of fired bricks; but, the Ṛgveda does not even refer to bricks—it has no word for brick.
2. The Agnicayana is the only rite which used bricks, the other Vedic altars being of packed earth. This view is refuted by Naama Drury, on the basis of a passage from the *Śat.Br.* (VI.2.1.10), which brings out the difference between the *iṣṭakās* and the *aniṣṭakās*. The *iṣṭakās* are those that are seen by one, after offering (*iṣṭvā*) an animal, thus getting associated with the animal-sacrifice, and *aniṣṭakās* are those which have no such connection. Drury surmises that the baked bricks were used only at the Agnicayana rite or there was a distinction between the baked bricks themselves, these called *iṣṭakās* being used or seen after an animal-sacrifice. According to Drury

there is much Vedic content in Agnicayana which could not prove its origination from a non-Vedic society.[108] It has to be pointed out here that the passage from the *Śat.Br.* (VI.2.1.10), which Drury mentions is an *arthavāda* explaining the term *iṣṭakā* from the word *iṣṭvā*, etymology coming to help here. How far this *arthavāda* is useful in establishing the indigenous nature of the Agnicayana rite is doubtful, for this issue requires some more evidence.

Apart from the question whether the Agnicayana was or was not, of the Vedic origin, the point to be noted is that the fire-altars made by the Vedic Aryans were not much above the ground. The *mekhalā* of the later period also was not for making the altar high; it was only for decoration and to make the altar look like a woman[109]. In all cases, the altar shows a pit in the earth,[110] or it was a surface-to-surface structure in the main. But here we have the Rauhiṇa going up, as the very name (fr. √*ruh*—'to grow, go up') and the account show.

The Rauhiṇa of the *asuras* recalls to memory the 'Tower of Babel.' Frazer records two versions of it. According to one version, in the early days of the world, all mankind spoke the same language. When they came to Shinar or Babylon, they settled and gradually started building a tower, with the idea that any one who might wander afar may see that tower and come to the place. But the sight of the tower, which was coming up, displeased God and he decided to split the unity of men, by confounding their language. The result was that people left the work and the place was called 'Babel'.[111] According to another version, some wished to scale heaven and there wage war with the Almighty or set up their own idols in his stead. At last the tower went so high that the brick layer took a whole year to be placed on the tower. When the brick layer fell down, everybody was sorry for the loss of one year. The God confounded their language and due to confusion, the tower remained incomplete.[112] Frazer has noted two more such stories—one African and the other Bambola.[113] The story of the Ashantees comes very close to the story of the Citrā-brick, which we have noted. The story runs as follows. God lived among men but withdrew to heaven being insulted by an old woman. Men resolved to find him. So they collected all the porridge pestles and piled them up. But when the tower was thus nearly completed, they found that the supply of the pestles ran short. They were, otherwise, near heaven. A wise (!) man stood up and said, "It is quite simple. Take the lowest pestle and put it at the top." This was done and the whole pile collapsed and ruined were the men, who could never ascend to heaven.[114]

In connection with the Rauhiṇa, we may compare a fire-altar from about the same region of the Tower of Babel (first version from Babylon i.e. modern Iraq). This is the structure excavated at Pasargadae, Iran, capital of Cyrus, and is thought to have been built about the 9th cent. BC. In the photograph are seen two massive flat-topped plinths, nearly joined to each other, of white stone bordered with black (a style characteristic of early stone work at Pasargadae). One has stone-steps leading up to its top, and it is suggested that the king (or chief magus) might have ascended this plinth and offered worship before a great gathering in the presence of fire on the other plinth.[115] Both the plinths (one with steps and the other as the fire-altar) seem (as seen in the photograph) to be quite high. Could the fire-altar on the flat-topped high plinth excavated at Pasargadae be a later modification of the Rauhiṇa? In any case, in the face of the mythical accounts occurring in the *Śat.Br.* and the *Tait.Br.* and the fire-altar on the high plinth (the fire-altar itself now raised!), we can strongly maintain that Rauhiṇa definitely was a ritual-artifice of the *asuras.*

With this, we now go back to the *RV*, which mentions the word *rauhiṇa* twice. At both the places, Sāyaṇa and almost all translators understand the word *rauhiṇa* to mean an *asura*.[116] At one of the places (*RV* II.12.12), Rauhiṇa is said to be ascending the sky, much like the fire-altar Rauhiṇa in the *Śat.Br.* A difference to be marked between Rauhiṇa on the one hand, and other *asuras* on the other, is that the latter do not appear as names of objects, as is the case with the Rauhiṇa. Some of the mythological *asuras* figure in the context of the Vedic ritual, but only symbolically, some objects in many cases standing for some part of the body of the so-called *asura*.[117] On the other hand, Rauhiṇa appears as the name of the fire-altar of the *asuras*, which was a raised altar as against the Vedic one that was practically close to the earth. It has to be noted that the account of even this *asura*-altar is brought into service by the Vedic ritualists, which glorifies setting of fire on the Citrā constellation for vanquishing one's enemies.

Next we come to the ritual of Soma itself, which has much non-Vedic influence, at times seen through the *arthavāda*. Soma is said to be coming from a far off place and the rite of purchasing Soma indicates that it was borrowed from a non-Vedic (or non-Aryan) clan. The same is reflected when Soma is said to be ritually purchased from a *śūdra* or from a person of a lower status, called Kautsa who was then forced out (*Śat.Br.* III.3.3.7; *Tait.Sam.* I.2.7). The contribution of the Sarpa-tribe and their acculturation in the Vedic fold, right from the *RV*, spreading over to the ritual-texts and running over to the modern times are the points already noted by us in the earlier chapter. The mythical account coming as *arthavāda* in the *Ait. Br.* (VI.1=26.1) has a definite function in this regard, which we have discussed in the earlier chapter. The *arthavāda* from the *Ait.Br.* indicates not only the loan of the methodical ritual but also of the chants, not unmixed with a sense of rivalry, both from the Sarpa tribe.

We now turn to the mythical account in the Śat.Br. (X.5.1.1-17). Purūravas is already a figure in the *RV*, along with Urvaśī (X.95). At another place in the *RV*, Purūravas is said to be *su-kṛt* i.e. "the performer of a ritual" (*RV* I.31.4). It has to be noted that both these references to Purūravas occur in the later part of the *RV*. The *Śat.Br.* gives the account in detail. It points out that Purūravas learnt a new method of sacrifice from the *gandharvas*. At first, they give him fire in a fire-pan for the sake of sacrifice. But, on the way, that fire is lost; but, the *gandharvas* say that what was the fire is now an Aśvatha tree and what was the fire-pan is now the Śamī tree. To gain the fire back, the *gandharvas* suggest two methods—(i) cooking of a mess of rice, sufficient for four persons; then, taking each time three fire-sticks from the Aśvattha tree, anointing them with ghee and placing them on the (ordinary) fire, with the verses (*mantras*) having the words *samit* and *ghṛta* (*ibid.* 14)[118] (ii) making the upper *araṇi* (fire-stick of the Aśvattha and the lower one of the Śamī wood (*ibid.* 15). The *gandharvas* say that both these methods have become recondite (*parokṣam iva vā etat*) and they tell him the third method, in which both the *araṇis* are prepared from the wood of the Aśvattha tree. The fire that would result from these two *araṇis* of the same wood (of the Aśvattha) is said to be the old one that had been lost! Here, we have a clear evolution of the kindling method, and it is indicated that the final method was told by the *gandharvas* to Purūravas. Nevertheless, the earlier method of churning the fire from the lower *araṇi* made of Śamī continued, in spite of the great status that Purūravas gained in the Vedic ritual tradition, which identified him and Urvaśī with the upper churn-rod and the lower *araṇi*, of the Aśvattha and the Śamī trees resp. (*Vāj. Sam.* V.2; *Śat. Br.* III.4.1.22; *Kāty. Ś.S* V.1.28-30).

Even with the importance of Purūravas in the Vedic ritual tradition, there is reason to believe that he was not entirely an authority, nor was he respected totally. In the *Mbh.*, Purūravas is called Aila, born from Ilā, wife of Budha and the daughter of Vaivasvata Manu. Ilā after becoming a man is named Sadyumna (*Mbh.* Ādi 75.16; Anuśāsana 147.26). Thus, Ilā is both the mother and father of Purūravas (*Mbh.* Adi 75.18, 19), who hence is named Aila. He tyrannaised the *brāhmaṇas* so much that ultimately the latter killed him (*ibid.* 20-22). The

Puranic tradition has something to add. On the one hand it says that Purūravas introduced three fires in the place of the original one fire (*Brahamāṇḍa P.* II.3.66.19). It should be noted that the *RV* does not mention three fires, as they are known later. The word *gārhapatya* occurs thrice (*RV* I.15.12; X.95.27 and 36), but does not denote the ritual-fire of that name.

Certain Purāṇas, on the other hand, say that Purūravas was beaten by the *brāhmaṇas* of the Naimiṣa region.[119] With these details from the *Mbh.* and the Purāṇas in hand about Purūravas, the question that stares us is, who was Purūravas in the origin?[120] We have noted that his birth is shrouded in mythological mystery, as seen in the *Mbh.* May be he was an individual, fallen astray from his original tribe and wanted to join that tribe again-the tribe of the *gandharvas*—by performing a sacrifice as per the new method told by the *gandharvas*, which later on was followed in the Vedic tradition. In that case, the tribe of the *gandharvas* influenced the Vedic ritual immensely, itself going into oblivion, merging into the mist of myths. The mythical account coming as *arthavāda*, of Purūravas and Urvaśī[121], given in the *Śat. Br.* (XI.5.1.1-17), shows that the tradition of the ritual remained Vedic, but the tribes that loaned certain details to it got mythical. But this 'welcome' attitude towards 'change' is exactly the proven characteristic of the Vedic priestly class, which continued even in later times.

Here, we take into account an interesting practice of offering, which, though non-Vedic, finds place in the *Śat. Br.* and the *Kauṣ.Br.*, with its origin traced in the *RV*, as the *RV* mentions it for the first time. The seer in the *RV* says to Indra. "O Indra! you attacked with your own *māyās* (occult powers) those (*asuras*)—knowers of *māyā*—who used to offer oblation in their own mouth." (*RV* I.51.5ab).[122] The important word in this *ṛc* is *śuptau*. Neither Yāska in his *Nirukta* nor Macdonell and Keith in their *Vedic Index of Names and Subjects* have taken a note of this word. Geldner while translating this *ṛc* takes the word *śuptau* (original word is *śupti*) as meaning *Schulter* i.e. 'shoulder',[123] which cannot fit in the context of offering oblations, for 'shoulder' cannot be a place where the oblations can be offered. Sāyaṇa takes the word *śuptau* as meaning *mukhe* i.e. mouth, having before him the mythical account coming as *arthavāda* in the *Śat.Br.* at two places and in the *Kauṣ.Br.* at one place. These mythical accounts coming as *arthavāda* are important from our point of view. In the *Śat.Br.* in the context of the Vājapeya sacrifice (*Śat.Br.* V.1.1.1, 2) and in the context of the Darśa-pūraṇamāsa *iṣṭis* i.e. New-moon and Full-moon sacrifices (*ibid.* XI.1.8.1, 2) occurs the same mythical account, which is as follows—The gods and the *asuras* were performing sacrifice. The gods gave offerings to one another, while the *asuras*, due to their ego (*atimāna*), gave oblations into their own mouths (*sveṣu āsyeṣu*). The sacrifice of the gods was successful, but the *asuras* could not succeed in their sacrifice and were defeated.

The same mythical account, with slight changes, occurs in the *Kauṣ.Br.* (VII.3), in the context of the consecration-rite in the Soma-sacrifice. A sacrificer consecrated for the Soma-sacrifice has not to give the daily offering of milk (in fire) in the Agnihotra rite till the completion of the Soma-sacrifice. The mythical account here relates that once in a Soma-sacrifice in the rite of Agnihotra, the *asuras* gave the offerings in themselves (i.e. in their mouths). But the fire in their mouths had already extinguished. Hence, they were defeated. The gods, on the other hand, established the fire of vital breaths (*prāṇāgni*). In this *prāṇāgni*, at both the times (morning and evening) the offering of milk is given. In short, the sacrificer partakes of the milk, which is given as offering. Thus in the Soma-sacrifice, the daily Agnihotra-offerings are given in the *prāṇāgni* (Here also figures *agni* i.e. the fire of vital breaths).

We have taken note of the *māyins* from the RV (I.51.5ab) and also of the *asuras* from the Brāhmaṇa-texts, as seen above. In the *RV* itself, we have the mention of *śrutapā* i.e. one who drinks (partakes of) the oblation himself (not offering to any deity) and also *anindra =an-indra* not having Indra i.e., who does not believe in Indra (*RV* VII.18.16; also X.27.6). These were obviously the persons, not believing in the Vedic sacrifice. In the society of the Vedic times, there might have been such individuals or small groups of people. Barth points out that though the higher Vedic religion may not have admitted images or sacred places, there must have been a lower stratum of Animists, who did not confirm their worship to the deities of Nature.[124] Fergusson presses this point too further and states that—"It may become an interesting investigation to inquire whether the Greeks were not the first who taught the Indians idolatry.[125]

The Vedic people did not have idol-worship, as there is no reference to any idol of gods. However, there is a mention of the idol of Indra at two places in the *RV.* At one place the seer Vāmadeva clearly asks—"Who will purchase this Indra of mine for ten milch cows; when will he kill the enemies and give him (i.e. my Indra) back to me?" (*RV* IV.24.10). At another place, the seer, after making mention of large amounts, says that even for such wealth he will not sell him i.e. Indra (*ibid.* VIII.1.5). The hymn (and obviously the *ṛc*) is addressed to Indra, thus indicating that it might be the idol or image of Indra, which is meant here. These two references indicate that in the Ṛgvedic times people might be keeping an idol or image of Indra made of wood or stone. Probably such an idol or image of Indra was kept in the house as 'fetish'.[126] This is indicated in the words of the seer Vāmadeva (*ibid.* IV.24.10), for he knows that a person having the idol of Indra with him has the power of killing the enemies. It has to be noted that in the entire *RV,* there are only two references to the idol or image, and those too of Indra only. This is obviously because Indra initially was a human hero—a warrior par excellence—who later on was deified in the times of the *RV.*[127] In the Epic-period, we see references to temples, idols or images of gods and also the temple-keepers (*devalakas*).[128] Interestingly, the *Garuḍa P.* (I.134.1, 2) mentions the image of Śakra (i.e. Indra) made of dough, before which the king had to take bath on the Mahānavamī day (the day prior to the Dussera day).

We have taken a note of idols or images of stone or wood. But prior to these, there were rude stocks of stone, which gradually developed into anthropomorphic images, which at times were given the masks of silver[129] etc. Initially there might have been the rites of blood-sacrifice offered to a deity. A survival of such rites appears in the custom of smearing rude stones and images with red paint, which might have come as a substitute for an older practice of feeding a god by smearing the face and especially the lips of an idol with the blood of a sacrificial victim. Such practices were not there among the Vedic people, who believed only in the sacrificial rituals. Among these sacrificial rituals there never was the practice of offering blood to a god, who never was in the form of an idol. The blood of a sacrificial victim (sacrificial animal) was dropped outside, taking it to be the share of the *asuras*.[130]

To come to the *RV* (I.51.5ab), which mentions the *māyins*, and the ritual-texts (*Śat.Br.* V.1.1.1, 2; XI.1.8.1, 2 and *Kauṣ.Br.* VII.3), the *asuras*, who used to offer the sacrificial offering in their own mouth, without offering it into the sacrificial fire— This detail if not taken literally may refer to the practice which we have noted, of feeding the idol or image of a god, by smearing its face, especially its lips with the blood of the sacrificial victim. The Vedic tradition, as per the practice which was prevalent and was followed from ages, firmly believed in giving offering in the fire alone. Those who did not follow this and were against it, were attacked by Indra with his occult powers (*RV* I.51.5ab) or faced defeat as the Brāhmaṇa-texts point out, which we have noted already. The mythical accounts from the Brāhmaṇa-texts are obviously given to eulogise the Vedic practice of offering. Nevertheless they indicate the non-Vedic practice also and are thus important from the cultural point of view.

The above-mentioned non-Vedic practice of sacrifice reminds us of a unique sacrifice and it is of a deer. In the very first chapter, while noting the changing phase of the Vedic brahmanical religion, we have noted the story of the *brahmaṇa* named Satya, who was allured by the very Dharma, coming in the form of a deer, in order to test the *brahmaṇa*. The deer (i.e. Dharma) advised the *brāhmaṇa* to offer the former (i.e. deer) in sacrifice, which ultimately the *brāhmaṇa* did, becoming greedy for the heavenly pleasures. As a result the *brāhmaṇa* had to face the destruction of his merit accumulated by him over the years (*Mbh.* Śānti chap. 272). This story apart from teaching the principle of *ahiṁsā* (non-injury to the living beings), makes us ponder over the sacrifice of the deer—that too as a holocaust. The questions cropping up in this regard are—was the sacrifice of a deer a regular or familiar feature with the hermit-dwellers in the forest? Or is it that the deer was at hand and was the *brāhmaṇa's* companion and there too on the encouraging words of the deer, the *brāhmaṇa* sacrificed him? Again the offering in fire of the deer as a holocaust poses a question. Was the *brāhmaṇa* conversant only with this practice of sacrifice and not the Vedic practice, for he did not see any lacuna in his sacrifice or did not feel any kind of remorse over that? The whole idea of the *brāhmaṇa* was to offer the deer in the sacrifice and as the story is given to teach the principle of *ahiṁsā* (non-injury to living beings), we are required to connive at the lacunae in the sacrificial procedure, which ought to have been as per the Vedic norm.[131]

But the sacrifice mentioned in the *Rām.* (Ayodhyākāṇḍa) needs still more attention. In the early phase of exile, Rāma and Lakṣmaṇa make in the forest a dwelling from leaves (*parṇaśālā*). To follow the ritual of 'pacification of the dwelling place' (*vāstuśamana*) Rāma asks Lakṣmaṇa to hunt a black antelope so that it could be offered in sacrifice and the exact traditional rite in this regard could be performed (*Rām.* Ayodhyā 56.22 ff). Lakṣmaṇa as per Rāma's instruction hunts a black antelope and throws it into the fire. When it is completely roasted and the blood is dried up, Rāma takes bath and offers the portions of the black antelope to gods and manes. He then establishes the various fireplaces and the altars (*ibid.* 26-32). With Rāma's offering to the manes, we are reminded of a reference from Bhāsa's *Pratimānāṭaka* (Act V. verse 10 and the passage preceding it), which points out that the *pitṛs* are satisfied when flesh of 'Kāñcanapārśva' (type) of deer is offered to them.

On the face of it, it is very clear that this whole procedure of sacrificing the black antelope is very crude and not according to the norm laid down by the Vedic ritual-texts. Nevertheless it is said to be according to the *śāstradṛṣṭo vidhiḥ* (*ibid.* 23b) and figures in the *Rām.* and that too not in the (so-called) interpolated portion. The crude nature of this ritual of sacrifice may lead us to the conclusion that its source might have been a tribal ritual, which was practised by Rāma, as there was no other way left for him.[132] But, we have no evidence for this.

The sacrifice of a black antelope for the pacification of *vāstu* (residence i.e. the deity ruling the residence) takes us to the deity Vāstoṣpati. The *vāstus* (places of residence) of Viṣṇu (*RV* I.154.6) and also those of Mitra and Varuṇa (*ibid.* VIII 25.5) are mentioned in the *RV*, but these gods are not the deities of those *vāstus*. The deities Tvaṣṭṛ and Rudra rule over the *vāstus*. But the exclusive lord of *vāstu* is the deity Vāstoṣpati, who is a separate deity.[133] In the *Āśv. G.S.* (II.7 to II.9), there is a separate section called *athāto vāstuparīkṣā*, concerning *vāstu*, right from choosing the land upto the ritual of offering. Thus when the newly built house is ready, the *sthālīpāka* is to be prepared and four offerings of it accompanied by four *mantras* (*RV* VII.54.1-3 and VII.55.1), are to be given (in fire) in the middle of that house. Feeding of the *brāhmaṇas* is laid down and the *brāhmaṇas* are to be asked to say *śivam vāstu śivam vāstu* ('Let the place of residence be auspicious'—i.e. beneficial to the residents).

According to the Purāṇas, Vāstupuruṣa is having the form of a demon. His figure was to be laid in the foundation of a building. Various deities which spring from his body are to be worshipped by the person, who undertakes to construct his building, failing which the Vāstupuruṣa would devour the inmates of the house.[134]

Thus, the deity Vāstoṣpati is an age-old one. As seen above, the tradition of pacifying the deity of *vāstu,* by giving some kind of offering dates back from olden times, at least from the period of the Gṛhyasūtras, running over to the Purāṇas. But the sacrifice of black antelope by throwing it in fire (as holocaust) mentioned in the *Rām.* stands unique, and takes us to the period of antiquity, when 'silencing' the sacrificial animal and then 'immolating' it were unheard of, they being the parts of the later developed sacrificial ritual. Here we are reminded of a couple of passages from the *RV*, which may have a bearing of offering (the whole animal) in sacrifice.[135] But we cannot say a definite word about them. As Dange has rightly pointed out the sacrifice of black antelope—that too as holocaust—was the most ancient form of sacrifice.[136] This point gets support from the fact that a black antelope or a deer is a beast found more in the wild region (deer at the most in hermitages) than in the urban area. So these beasts figure in the story of the *Mbh.* as well as in the *Rām.*, and here too the sacrifice of the black antelope reminds us of the nomadic stage which the human civilisation has left far far back. This is the 'legacy' or 'survival' of the olden times, as Lang has said in the context of myths, but the term we can very well apply here.[137]

We have taken into account the concept and practice of sacrifice from the ritual-texts as well as practices from non-Vedic sources. Here, we come to a stage, which though reckoned as 'philosophical', survives mainly on the sacrificial imagery. As the sacrificial institution held its influence on the society for a very long time and persisted even in later times, the philosophical texts propounded their tenets couched in the ritual setting.

The Āraṇyakas which were meant to be mere books of instruction to be given in the forests (the very name *āraṇyaka* fr. the word *araṇya*), independent of ritual, could not sever themselves from ritual. In fact, conceptually the term *āraṇyaka* is a generic one, denoting the texts, which were to be studied in the forests. Hence, the Upaniṣads containing philosophical doctrines formed part of these texts, as they are the culmination of the respective Āraṇyakas.[138] The Āraṇyakas many a time adopt the style of the Brāhmaṇa-texts and try to glorify the matter in hand by *arthavāda*. We can take some examples. The VII chapter of the *Kauṣ. Ār.* deals with *Saṁhitopadeśa*. It is also called *Saṁhitopaniṣad*.[139] It is actually the knowledge (*upaniṣad*) of the *saṁhitā* (relation or relativity), which is shown to exist between all entities—animate, inanimate, even abstract concepts such as *vāc, manas, satya* etc. The *arthavāda* here is that one who knows *saṁhitā*, is joined (*saṁdhīyate*) with offsprings, cattle, success, spiritual lustre, heavenly world and attains the entire span of life (*Kauṣ. Ār.* VII.1-8, 12, 14). That a person born in this world has to make his life fruitful is beautifully brought out by an allegory of *daivī vīṇā* and *mānuṣī vīṇā*. *Daivī vīṇā* is the *śarīravīṇā*—human body imagined to be a lute and the *mānuṣī vīṇā* is the lute (as an instrument) made by a man. The similarity between these two *vīṇās* is graphically described with all the minute details, associated with a lute. It is said that one who knows the *daivī vīṇā* well and handles it efficiently, becomes well-known in this world (*ibid.* VIII. 9 & 10). To take some examples from the *Tait. Ār.*, which has a large canvas to express its thoughts. It states four kinds of Death and the worlds acquired thereof (I.8). It describes the place of Yama and here we have four kinds of Hell (I.19). they are:

1. Visarpin —in the south-east direction;
2. Avisarpin—in the south-west direction;
3. Viṣādin—in the north-east direction, and
4. Aviṣādin—in the north-west direction.

The explanation given by Sāyaṇa in each case indicates that these hells are stated as a part of ethical teaching. In fact, in a much later period, we see that the Purāṇas have taken this task upon themselves to describe various hells and the torments therein to the sinners. As the Purāṇas were composed to reach the common masses in the society, it is but natural if they are seen imparting such ethical teachings as a code of conduct, through accounts, stories etc. The *Tait.Ār.* mentioning four kinds of Death and four kinds of Hell is seen getting connected to the 'man' in the society.

This is all the more patent when we see the five great sacrifices—Mahāyajñas—dealt with by the *Tait. Ār.* (II. 10). It is pointed out that unlike other sacrifices, these sacrifices are to be performed daily. They are—Devayajña (offerings to be given in fire to the gods); Pitṛyajña (offerings to the *pitṛs*); Bhūtayajña (offerings to all the beings); Manuṣyayajña (offering food to men)........and lastly Brahmayajña (daily study of scriptures—may be a *ṛc* or *yajus*). The *Śat.Br.* has already dealt with the five sacrifices, which we have noted earlier (XI.5.6.1). the *Śat.Br.* has connected these sacrifices (except Bhūtayajña) with the four debts, which a person has to pay off during his lifetime (*ibid.* I.7.2.1-5).[140] Of all these five sacrifices, Brahmayajña is considered to be the best sacrifice. The *Tait.Ār.* has discussed here a vital point. Is the Brahmayajña to be suspended, in the event of there being the natural phenomena such as the whirling wind, thunder, rain, lightning etc.? The *Tait.Ār.* straightway says 'No' to this, and describes metaphorically these natural phenomena as follows—cloud as *havirdhāna*; lightning as Agni; rain as *havis*; rumbling of the cloud as the sound Vaṣaṭ; thundering of the cloud as the Anuvaṣaṭkāra; wind as the *ātman* (breath); the New-moon day as the Sviṣṭakṛt (Agni). When a person studies his *svādhyāya* (daily study of scriptures), it is verily his *tapas*-toiling-, which he practises (*ibid.* II.14). The *Tait. Ār.* here has given a line of metaphors, in order to point out the importance and indispensable status of Brahmayajña in the life of man. The *Śat.Br.* has already called these natural phenomena as four

Vaṣat-calls *viz.* the sound of the blowing wind; of lightning-fall; of thundering; and of rumbling and has prescribed the Brahmayajña even on these occasions (*Śat. Br.* XI.5.6.9). It has to be noted that in later times, the Sūtras prescribe suspension of the study of sacred texts when the natural phenomena, such as those mentioned above, occur.[141]

The Āraṇyakas though treaded on the path of philosophical thought, were very hesitant to leave the support of ritualistic system and its method of convincing through *arthavāda*. Here we take an example from the *Ait. Br.* of the Niṣkevalya *śastra*[142], which is to be recited in the Mahāvrata rite. The *Ait. Ār.* here treats first the three regions *viz.* Pṛthivī, Antarikṣa and Dyauḥ from the *ādhidaivika* (concerning the deity) point of view and the same regions from the *ādhyātmika* (concerning self or person as individual) point of view as Pṛthivī (Earth)=Mouth (Speech); Antarikṣa (Mid-region)=Nose (Breath) and Dyauḥ (Heaven)=Forehead (with the Sun as the Eye). The importance of *upāsanā* (meditation) is stated and that is of Prāṇa. It has to be noted that even while speaking of the importance of Prāṇa, the Niṣkevalya *śastra* (from the ritual context) is not lost sight of. It is stated that the *uktha* (Niṣkevalya *śastra*) is to be meditated upon as Prāṇa (*Ait. Ār.* II.1.2, 4). But the metaphysical thought prevails that all the *ṛcs*, all the Vedas, all sounds have only one *vyāhṛti* namely Prāṇa (*ibid.* II.2.2).

Thus in the Āraṇyakas are strewn the gems of metaphysical thoughts, while they themselves are seen catching the finger of ritual, because they thrived in a society which was breathing the very air of sacrifice. Hence, the Āraṇyakas could not settle down as philosophical texts, which they became in most parts but that too in the form of the Upaniṣads, thus serving as a link between ritual and philosophy.

The Upaniṣads are generally taken to be in clear contrast to the Brāhmaṇa-texts, which are the manuals to know the ritual-tradition. But a critical study of the Upaniṣads points out that the Upaniṣadic thinkers had to propound their highest doctrine only through the medium of the ritual-tradition, for the society at large was teeming with the ritualistic atmosphere, and sacrificial terminology was the only keyword for reaching it. This is also the method of *arthavāda*, by which the metaphysical thought is justified or glorified by the details from the sacrificial tradition.

The famous *Kaṭha Up.* starts with the story of Naciketas (I.1.13-19). Yama gives three boons to Naciketas. By the third boon, Naciketas insists on Yama to enlighten him on the future of human being after death. And Yama not ready to impart this highest knowledge to Naciketas, ultimately has to bend to wish of Naciketas, being committed to grant the boon. This highest philosophy of Ātman is the very pivot of the *Kaṭha Up.* Interestingly, by the second boon Naciketas asks Yama as to how the sacrifice leading to the heavenly world should be established. Yama gives him proper instructions about the new fire and the sacrifice and declares that the new fire would bear the name of Naciketas (*Kaṭha Up.* I.1.15, 16 and 19). This indicates the acceptance by the then society of a new type of fire and eventually a new sacrifice, as we have noted from the mythical account in the *Śat.Br.*, the gain of new fire by Purūravas from the *gandharvas*. The two accounts can be compared in this light. The account of Naciketas suggests that the new sacrifice itself can be a means of reaching the god (here Yama) who can impart the Highest knowledge.

The idea well-rooted in the Vedic ritual-tradition is that a *ṛc* (Ṛgvedic *mantra*) or a *yajus* (sacrificial prose formula from the *YV*) helps the ritual attain its full form.[143] There is an invariable connection between a *ṛc* and a *sāman* (*Ait. Br.* VII.12=32.11). The *sāmans* have an important place in the Vedic sacrificial tradition. The *Chānd. Up.* (being attached to the Sāmaveda) deals with the *sāmans* exhaustively. It refers to the five-fold *sāmans* (II.1-7), the seven-fold *sāmans* (II.8-10) and several other *sāmans* (II.21; II.24.3, 4; II.24.7-10; II.24.11-15). The mention of the three pressings of Soma (II.24.6-16), the identification of the metre Gāyatrī with Brahman (III.12.5, 6) and the various *stobhas* (I.13.1-4) can be taken into account here.

These are the clear references to the sacrificial ritual, stationed in the Upaniṣads. But many a time the Upaniṣadic philosophy is couched in the sacrificial imagery. The Kaṭha Up. speaks of the Highest, of which both Brahma and Kṣatra are said to be the *odana*. Now *odana* is a term from the sacrificial context, which denotes the cooked rice, to be ritually partaken of by the priest. In the same context, Death is said to be the *upasecana* of the Highest Principle. *Upasecana* refers to the sprinkling of the clarified butter on the cooked rice (*Kaṭha Up.* I.2.24), thus again a term taken from the sacrificial context.

The *Śvetā. Up.* instructs that imagining one's own body to be the lower kindling wooden slab (for the production of fire) and the syllable *Om* the upper wooden rod (i.e., *araṇi* and *manthā* resp.) one should visualise the Highest Principle by the repeated practice of meditation. Thus meditation is seen as a ritual of kindling the fire and the whole body is imagined to be the apparatus for it (*Śvetā. Up.* I.14; also *Kaivalya Up.* I.11, here also the body is the lower *araṇi* and the syllable *Om* (Praṇava), the upper *araṇi* i.e. *manthā*, also called *uttara-araṇi*).

In the *Chānd. Up.* we have the five householders going to Uddālaka Āruṇi for the gain of the knowledge of Ātman. The latter however directs them to King Aśvapati Kekaya, himself accompanying them to Aśvapati. The doctrine of the Vaiśvānara Ātman is expounded by Aśvapati Kekaya as—The Vaiśvānara Ātman has the altar (*vedi*) for the chest, the sacrificial grass (*barhis*) for his hair, the Gārhapatya fire for his heart, the Anvāhāryapacana (*Dakṣiṇa*) fire for his mind and the Āhavanīya fire for his mouth (*Chānd. Up.* V.11). Here the Vaiśvānara Ātman (Vaiśvānara Fire on both the microcosmic and macrocosmic levels) with the help of metaphorical expression, is said to be not beyond the traditional sacrifice. While teaching about the importance of the syllable *Om* (the Udgītha), the *Chānd. Up.* points out that Speech is *ṛc* and the life-breath is the *sāman* and the two form a copulative couple (I.1.5). This concept of formulating a couple (*mithuna*) has primarily come from the ritual context. The belief underlying the utterance of the word *mithuna* is a clear charm for the gain of progeny and prosperity.[144] The *Chānd. Up.* has the same idea and the same belief while mentioning the pair of Vāc and Prāṇa taking them to be that of *ṛc* and *sāman* (I.1.5).

And here are some beautiful metaphors rooted in the sacrificial terminology, used to explain the knowledge about the Highest Principle. The *Praśna Up.* in its fourth Praśna poses five questions. In reply to Gārgya's question as to who keeps awake in the 'town' (*pure* i.e. Body), Pippalāda points out that fires in the form of vital breaths keep awake in this 'town'. Here the vital breath Apāna is said to be the Gārhapatya fire, Vyāna the Anvāhāryapacana (i.e. Dakṣiṇa) fire and Prāṇa the Āhavanīya fire. The in-breath and the out-breath are the offerings which the vital breath Samāna carries in equal measure (*samam*). Mind is the lord or master (of this 'town') and Udāna the vital breath is the fruit desired by the master of this 'town', which is said to lead him to the Brahman daily (*Praśna Up.* IV.3-4). Thus, the process of controlling the life-breaths and concentrating the mind on Brahman is explained through sacrificial metaphors.

The *Chānd. Up.* (III.16) says that the very Puruṣa i.e. man, is the sacrifice. The first twenty-four years of man's life amount to the morning Soma-pressing (*prātaḥsavana*), which is associated with the metre Gāyatrī having twenty-four syllables (three feet with eight syllables in each foot). The next forty-four years of man's life amount to the mid-day Soma-pressing, associated with the metre Triṣṭubh having forty-four syllables (4x11). The last forty-eight years of man's life stand for the evening Soma-pressing, associated with the Jagatī metre having forty-eight syllables (4x12). In the same Upaniṣad (*Chānd. Up.* III.17.1-15), the whole span of life is said to be a sacrificial session. Thus, whatever one desires to eat and drink but does not enjoy (as he does not get it and thus has to abstain from it) stands for his initiation (*dīkṣā*). Whatever one eats, drinks and enjoys stands for his *upasad*- rites, lasting for several days. As he laughs, eats and enjoys sexual union, all these amount to the *mantra*s chanted in the sacrifice. One's patience, gifts, simplicity, non-injury, truthfulness are the gifts at this sacrifice. Whenever they say that a certain woman has delivered, that is one's re-birth and death is verily one's *avabhṛtha* (the concluding bath indicating the completion of the sacrificial session). The whole span of life is thus nothing but a sacrificial session.

The *Chānd. Up.* (X.2.4-8) and the *Bṛhad. Up.* (VI.3) mention the 'Mantha-vidyā' (the lore called Mantha), which is regarded as the highest lore and has a clear ritual set-up. Mantha initially means a certain kind of drink to be taken for the gain of strength[145] and is referred to in ritual and other literature.[146] The *mantras* in the *Bṛhad. Up.* (VI.3.4) show that the prepared *mantha* stands for the very life-breath of a person. The *mantras* *'tat savitur vareṇyam'* (*RV* III.62.10) and *'madhu vātā ṛtāyate'* (*ibid.* I.90.6) etc. are enjoined to be recited for making the *mantha* perfect for being eaten. The *mantha* is to be taken and eaten by a person with the belief that he would 'become' all this that exists in this universe (*Bṛhad. Up.* VI.3.6). The *Bṛhad. Up.* traces the Mantha-lore from a very long time, starting from Yājñavalkya. (VI.3.8-12). The reformist attitude of Yājñavalkya is seen at several places in the *Śat.Br.* of which the *Bṛhad. Up.* forms the concluding part. This is how the Brāhmaṇas, Āraṇyakas and Upaniṣadas many a time form a unit, connected internally.[147] Yājñavalkya was a ritualist reformer.

The *Chānd. Up.* (V.2.4 ff) says that the *mantha* is to be prepared from certain herbs (they being mentioned here) and is to be mixed with curds and honey. The offering of clarified butter is to be made into the fire with a specific *mantra*, and the remaining of the clarified butter is to be placed into the *mantha*. Taking the *mantha* into the joined up palms, the performer has to recite a *mantra*: "You are by name 'Amaḥ', because, all this, verily, is near (*amā*) you (i.e. included in you); Let me be all this" (*ibid.* V.2.6). The *mantra* is addressed to the *mantha*. The whole idea of this ritual is to attain identity with the universe, the macrocosm; and this, not by meditation, but by partaking of the holy ritual drink, which is believed to have mystic strength.

The *Chānd. Up.* (III.1-11) and the *Bṛhad. Up.* (II.5, 6) mention the lore of Madhu (Madhu-vidyā). The concept of *madhu* like that of *mantha* goes far back to the *RV*, where it stands for the essence of the whole universe (*RV* I.90.6ff; VII.101.1). The *Chānd. Up.* (III.1-5) identifies the sun with *madhu* and with this, several other things are brought in and set up in the context of the lore of *madhu*. Madhu-vidyā is ultimately identified with the lore of the Brahman—Brahmavidyā (*ibid.* III.11).

The *Bṛhad. Up.*, while discussing the lore of *madhu* identifies several concepts with that of *madhu* (II.5) and the Upaniṣad comes to the conclusion that the self (soul) of all beings is the *madhu* (*ibid.* II.5.14, 15). The lore of *madhu* is said to be the lore of Ātman, and lore of *madhu* is said to have been given to the Aśvins (the twin-gods) by Dadhyaṅ Ātharvaṇa (*ibid.* II.5.16-19). Here the Upaniṣad gets connected to the Ṛgvedic account of Dadhyaṅ Ātharvaṇa. The *RV* mentions that the Aśvins gave a horse's head to Atharvan's son Dadhyañc, who then told them the place of mead (*RV* I.116.12; I.117.22).

The *Kauṣ.Br.Up* mentions the lore called Paryaṅka (*paryaṅka-vidyā*), where the life-breath, called here Amitaujas (Limitless Splendour) is said to be the cot, on which Brahman (Brahmā in personification) is said to be seated (I.5).

Thus, we see that the Upaniṣadic philosophy has a strong basis of the sacrificial details. It kept the ritual details, in many cases, as a support. In fact, these sacrificial details serve as *arthavāda* to justify the philosophical thought of the Upaniṣads. This was the need of that society, which was familiar with the ritualistic atmosphere. Hence, any new thing including the philosophical thought had to take the help of the sacrificial matter to explain its stand-point.

Even the *Bhagavadgītā* takes the all-pervading concept of *yajña* (Sacrifice). It speaks of the seven constituents - *akṣara - brahma - karma - yajña - parjanya - anna - bhūtani* (*Bh.G.* III.14-15), and calls this whole world process a *cakra* (*yajña-cakra*)—the Wheel of Sacrifice, which a person has to rotate as per his station in life, by doing his duty (*ibid.* III.16). It speaks of several kinds of sacrifice *viz.* Dravya-yajña (sacrifice in the form of material offering), Tapo-yajña (sacrifice in the form of austerities), Yoga-yajña (sacrifice in the form of yogic practices), Svādhyāya-yajña (sacrifice in the form of daily study of the sacred texts), Japa-yajña (sacrifice in the form of muttering the *mantras*) and Jñānayajña (sacrifice in the form of knowledge of the Highest)—Realisation of God, knowledge is of utmost importance, and it is the true sacrifice. Thus, the *Bh.G.* explains its philosophy with the help of the concept of *yajña*, which was so familiar and convincing to the then society.

We have dealt with—'Sacrifice' from the Vedic tradition as also seen how non-Vedic elements crept up in the Vedic ritual tradition. These sacrificial matters are justified by the device of *arthavāda*, which many a time appears in the form of mythical accounts. We have dealt with the Upaniṣadic philosophy which is given in the ritual setting, the details in the sacrificial tradition and rituals acting as *arthavāda* to glorify that philosophy. The *Bh.G.* forming a part of the *Mbh.* (Bhīṣma. chaps. 25-42), treads on the same path and takes the help of the age-old tradition of sacrifice by propounding the concept of *yajña-cakra*, in its endeavour of giving an all-embracing philosophical thought. This concept of *yajña-cakra* and the various *yajñas*, noted by us act as *arthavāda* to glorify the philosophical thought. The five great sacrifices (Pañca Mahāyajñas) occurring in the *Śat. Br.* and the *Tait. Ār.* (which we have already dealt with) and later on enjoined by the

Smṛtis (*Manu. Sm.* III.69-70; *Yājñ.S.* I.41-46) are really the daily duties of a householder but are glorified by the term *mahāyajña*. This non-ritualistic literature using the term *yajña* or *mahāyajña* as *arthavāda* has its reasoning, which we now intend to see.

We have noted the three constituents of sacrifice *viz. dravya, devatā* and *tyāga*. Out of these three, the first two (*dravya* and *devatā*) underwent change, but the third constituent namely *tyāga* (offering) remained the same; 'Offering'—that too offering in any form—there also 'selfless offering' as 'duty'—is the inherent concept in the term *yajña* in the philosophical context, as well as in the *mahāyajñas*.

When we come to the Epic and Puranic age, as per the need of the then society suiting to the changed times, there emerged a new era in the history of ancient Indian man. As changes in several issues having new dimensions were introduced and were subsequently accepted by the society, the ancient Vedic-brahmanical *dharma* (code of conduct) acquired new face-lift, so as to become all-pervasive and reach the common masses, never losing sight of the 'old'. The statement of Hopkins about the *dharma* of the *Mbh.* can be applied to the *dharma* of the Purāṇas also. According to him, the *dharma* propounded by the *Mbh.* forgets nothing and absorbs everything.[148] In the pages to follow, we will be often reminded of this statement. In this later age, the march of the society, though slow, was in a definite direction, so as to become a norm for the centuries to come and in this the device of *arthavāda* or Arthavādaism unerringly helped the Epics and Purāṇas, when they came forward with their new thoughts.

NOTES AND REFERENCES

1. E.W. Hopkins, *Origin and Evolution of Religion,* Reprint, Bharatiya Vidya Prakashan, Delhi, year not mentioned (place and year of the 1st ed. not given), p. 151.
2. *Kāty.Ś.S* I.2.2.
3. E.B. Tylor, *Primitive Culture,* Vol. II, London, 1891, p. 375.

4. *RV* I.2.1—Vāyu is invoked with the Soma-draughts and prayers; *ibid.* I.5.8—where the prayers are said to have boosted Indra; I.10.5—where the song of praise is said to increase the strength of Indra for vanquishing many enemies; I.31.18—Agni is asked to grow with the *mantra* (*brahman*); I.52.7; I.77.5 etc.; the desire to exclusively possess the god, *ibid.* I.7.10 (Indra); I.13.10 (Tvaṣṭṛ—as per Sāyaṇa, Agni of that name).
5. G. van der Leeuw, *Religion in Essence and Manifestation*, London, 1938, p. 353 f.
6. E.W. Hopkins, *op. cit.*, loc. cit.
7. E.B. Taylor, *op. cit.*, p. 375 f.
   According to Max Müller, science of culture is "Mr. Tylor's culture". Therefore, in the English-speaking world at least, E.B. Tylor (1832-1917) is the "first anthropologist." His single work *Primitive Culture* gave him the name. Vol. I, London, 1871 (further eds. 1873, 1891, 1903, 1913); Vol. II, London, 1891; also see Ivan Strenski, *Thinking about Religion*, Blackwell Publishing Ltd. Malden, MA, USA, 2006, p. 91.
8. The word 'totem' can be compared with the Inca word '*otetman*'; W.R. Smith, "Sacrifice', the long article in *Encyclopedia of Britannica*, 9th ed., 1875-1880; his *Lectures on the Religion of the Semites*, Adam and Charles Black, London, 1923.
9. Ivan Strenski, *op. cit.*, p. 127 f.
10. See Henri Hubert and Marcel Mauss, *Sacrifice: Its Nature and Functions*, tr. by W.D. Halls, Midway Reprint, The University of Chicago Press, 1981, p. 13.
    The Study of Sacrifice by Henri Hubert and Marcel Mauss, was first published in *L'Année sociologique*, Paris, 1898 (pp. 29-138). It was entitled, "Essai sur la Nature et la Fonction du Sacrifice."
11. For the view-point of E. Westermarck, see his *Origin and Development of the Moral Ideas*, London, 1908, Vols. I and II.
12. See J.G. Frazer, *The Golden Bough*, Abridged ed., Vol. I, Macmillan and Co. Ltd., London, 1957, Chap. III "Sympathetic Magic", pp. 14-63.
13. For the view-point of Emile Durkheim, see his *The Elementary Forms of Religious Life*, London, 1915.
14. For Australian *Intichiuma* ceremony (or rite), see E.W. Hopkins, *op.cit.*, p. 166. Totem is regarded as only a clan-spirit or power. While a little of totem is eaten, which implies communion with

the spirit, there is scattering of the totem's blood, and dust and grain to increase the growth of the totem-species. It is certainly not a gift-sacrifice.

15. Kālidāsa, the famous Sanskrit poet, probably refers to this practice prevalent among the Huns, a non-Aryan tribe, when he says that Raghu's victory over the chieftains of the Hūṇa tribe became patent on the pale-red cheeks of their wives (*Raghuvaṁśa* IV.68). This indicates that at the death of their husbands at the hands of Raghu, the Hūṇa women slapped or scratched their cheeks so much as to make these pale-red or pink, which spoke of Raghu's victory.
16. For all this, see *ERE*, Vol. XI, pp. 5a, 6a and 6b.
17. E.W. Hopkins, *op.cit.*, p. 151. He says ".... though all (theories) are correct in their interpretation of certain phenomena, all are deficient in that they are intended to make one interpretation cover all phenomena."
18. K.R. Potdar, *Sacrifice in the Ṛgveda*, Bharatiya Vidya Bhavan, Bombay, 1953.
19. Such a ritual is noted in the *Rām.* Vide *Rām.* Ayodhyā 56.19-30. While in exile, Lakṣmaṇa, for pacifying the place of residence made of leaves, kills a black deer (*aiṇa* or *kṛṣṇamṛga*) on the word of Rāma and throws that whole deer into the fire. The parts of that cooked (roasted) deer are offered by Rāma to the gods. The fact to be noted is that such a ritual of roasting the whole sacrificial victim (animal) is not referred to or mentioned in any ritual in later times. The ritual seems to be lost.
    The practice (in ritual) of burning the whole animal occurs also in *Old Testament,* "Numbers". Chap. 19, 1-10. A red cow after being killed, with its blood sprinkled in the four quarters of the tent, is burnt in fire by (the priest) Eleazar, for its ashes to be dissolved in water to make it purificatory for being used at rituals. Here again there is a reference to burn the whole animal.
20. See Sadashiv A. Dange, *Vedic Sacrifices—Early Nature,* Vol. I, Aryan Books International, New Delhi, 2000, "Ādhāna (Introduction)," pp. xiii-xvi.
21. See note 2 supra.
22. *Śat. Br.* I.2.3.5. Here the sacrificial cake (*puroḍāśa*) is said to be the sacrificial victim (i.e. beast), which is killed. The sacrificial beast is said to be *pāṅkta*-having five constituents. See *ibid.* I.2.3.8.

23. See Sindhu S. Dange, "Animal Alter-Morphs of Agni-Prajāpati", *Journal of the Asiatic Society of Bombay*, Vol. 73 for 1998, Mumbai, 1998, pp. 24-36. Also see by the same author, *Vedic Beliefs and Practices through Arthavāda*, Vol. I, pp. 176-226 (the chap. "Animals and Birds").
24. In later times, only two animals are sacrificially slaughtered—a hornless dark grey (he-goat) for Prajāpati (*Śat. Br.* VI.2.2.1-2) an a white, bearded (he-goat) for Vāyu Niyutvat—Wind, having a group of horses (*ibid.* 6).
    Sāyaṇa in his commentary on the *Tait. Sam.* (II.1.1) and especially on the statement of injunction (*vidhi*)—'He should offer a white (beast) to Vāyu (II.1.1.1) says that wherever there is no specific mention of a particular beast, the 'goat' alone is to be understood as the beast meant, due to the earlier mention of goat (in the statement of *vidhi*) not being refuted.
25. See Sindhu S. Dange, "Animal Alter-Morphs of Agni-Prajāpati," *Journal of the Asiatic Society of Bombay*, Vol. 73 for 1998, Mumbai, 1998, pp. 25-33.
26. The *Tait. Sam.* says that Agni is an animal (V.7.6.1).
27. In the times of the ritual-texts, the procedure followed was of killing the victim by smothering it. This was carried out by Śamitṛ, who could make the victim quiet (fr. √*śam*-causal-'to make quiet or peaceful'). The place for Śamitṛ for this work might be a bit away from the actual sacrificial place.
28. See Sindhu S. Dange, "The Severed Head in Myth and Ritual", *Annals* of BORI, Pune, Vols. LXXII and LXXIII (for the years 1991 and 1992), pub. in 1993, Amṛtamahotsava (1917-1992) Vol., pp. 487-96. Also see by the same author, *Vedic Beliefs and Practices through Arthavāda*, Vol. I, p. 217f.
29. See E.W. Hopkins, *op.cit.*, p. 153.
30. See Sindhu S. Dange, *Vedic Beliefs and Practices through Arthavāda*, Vol. I, p. 249 ff.
31. *Tait. Sam.* V.2.8.4, 5—The sacrificial cake becoming a tortoise crawled after the Aṅgirases when they went to the world of heaven. So, the live tortoise when placed at the lowest level leads the sacrificer straight to the world of heaven.
32. The expression often occurring in the Vedic ritual texts is *vāg vai yajñaḥ* ('Speech verily is Sacrifice'). See *Śat. Br.* I.1.2.2; III.1.3.27; III.4.3.16 etc. For the major role of Speech, with all its

aspects, in the Vedic ritual tradition, see Sindhu S. Dange, *Aspects of Speech in Vedic Ritual.*

33. See *Ait. Br.* I.13=3.2; I.16=3.5; I.19=4.2; I.21=4.4 etc.
34. *Yasht* XIV.48; XV.7-9; 11-13; 15-17; XV. 19-21; XV.25
35. See Sindhu S. Dange, *Aspects of Speech in Vedic Ritual*, pp. 206-30 (the chap. "Songs from Secular Tradition").
36. *Bhār. G.S.* II.21 - *gāthā* enjoined in the Smāvartana ritual; *Pār.G.S.* I.7.2—*gāthā* in the marriage ritual; *Kāṭh. G.S.* 25.23—*gāthās*, in the marriage ritual after the rite of Pāṇigrahaṇa; *Āśv. G.S.* I.14.6-7—*gāthā* in the rite of Sīmantonnayana. etc. Some of these *gāthās* were sung by the lute-players. Thus singing (i.e. vocal) and playing on lute (i.e. instrumental)—both as aspects of Speech, served as *mantras*, supporting the ritual.
37. Sāyaṇa says that a *yajñagāthā* is sung and recited by all the ritualists, with respect to the sacrifice, which is being performed. See Sāyaṇa on the *Ait. Br.* VII.8=32.7; VII.9=32.8; V.6=22.1 etc.
38. Sāyaṇa on *Pañc. Br.* XXIV.18.5-7, where the Brāhmaṇa-passage, containing the *ślokas*, is given for justifying what has been said already. Again, Sāyaṇa on *Śat.Br.* X.5.2.4; XI.5.5.12.
39. See note 36 supra.
40. See P.V. Kane, *HDS*, Vol. II, Pt. I, p. 223.
41. See Sindhu S. Dange, *Aspects of Speech in Vedic Ritual*, pp. 247-56 (the chap. "Vocal and Instrumental Music in the Vedic Ritual").
42. *Ibid.*, p. 252 f.

    Tait. Sam. (VII.5.9.2, 3), in the context of the Gavām-ayana sacrifice, says that the sound of the drum, which is being beaten, is the highest aspect of Speech; also *Śat.Br.* (V.1.5.6, 7 & 10) enjoins placing of seventeen drums in the Vājapeya sacrifice; beating one of them, along with a *mantra*. For 'earth-drum' (*bhūmi-dundubhi*), see P.V. Kane, *HDS*, Vol. II, pt. II, p. 1244.
43. However, there are some exceptions. These are *upāṁśu* (low-voiced) offerings, for which *mantras* are to be offered in a low voice, not to be heard distinctly; *tūṣṇīm* (silent) offerings, for which *mantras* are to be remembered in mind only and not to be uttered and *mantras* in such cases are said to be undefined (*a-nirukta*—i.e. not defined). See, Sindhu S. Dange, *Aspects of Speech in Vedic Ritual*, pp. 231-46 (the chap. "Upāṁśu, Anirukta and Tūṣṇīm Offerings").

44. The Great Cosmic Puruṣa, without any female partner, can create Virāj, for He is to be regarded as a Bi-sexual deity—the Androgene—the Great He-She. Thus, the Creater-gods, such as Prajāpati (in the ritual-texts), Brahmā (in the Purāṇas), Ādibuddha and Avalokiteśvara (in the Mahāyāna Buddhist faith) have to be regarded as the Bi-sexual deities.
45. *RV* X.90.9, 10, 12-14. Also see Norman Brown, "The Sources of and nature of Puruṣa in the Puruṣa-sūkta", *JAOS*, Vol. 51, 1931, pp. 108-18.
46. O' Flaherty, Wendy Doniger, *Hindu Myths*, Penguin Books, New York, 1982 (1975), p. 27.
47. Andrew Lang, *Myth, Ritual and Religion*, London, 1913 (1887), p. 230.
48. *Ibid.*, pp. 236-37.
49. For a detailed information on myths dealing with the problem of 'Creation', with its several 'Knotty' points, see Sadashiv A. Dange, *Towards Understanding Hindu Myths*, Aryan Books International, New Delhi, 1996, pp. 11-30.
50. Ninian Smart, *Dimensions of the Sacred—An Anatomy of the World's Beliefs*, London, 1996, pp. 146-47; also see Ivan Strenski, *op.cit.*, pp. 316-17, where he deals in details, Mercia Eliade's novel method of interpretation proposed for the study of religion namely "Creative Hermeneutics"; also see Mercia Eliade, "Crisis and Renewal", *The Quest*, University of Chicago Press, Chicago 1969, p. 62.
51. See K.F. Geldner, *Der Rig-Veda*, HOS, Vol. 35, Harvard University Press, Cambridge, London, 2nd Print, 1978 (1951), p. 289 (tr. of *RV* X.90.16).
52. A.A. Macdonell, *A Vedic Reader for Students*, Oxford University Press, Madras (Chennai), 14th impression 1988 (first pub. in England 1917, Reprint in India 1951), p. 203, (tr. of *RV* X. 90.16).
53. At the end of the sacrifice, the outward signs of sacrifice such as the *prastara* (bunch of grass) is thrown into the fire (*Śat. Br.* I.8.3.16-17), as also the *paridhis* (enclosing-sticks, kept on the three sides, excepting the eastern side, of the Āhavanīya fireplace) are thrown into the fire (*ibid.* 22). On the eastern side, there is no *paridhi*, for there the sun is the protecting deity.

54. See Sadashiv A. Dange, "*Axis Mundi* and the Vedic *Yūpa*", *Gleanings from Vedic to Puranic Age*, ed. by Sindhu S. Dange, pp. 13-24.
55. For details see Sindhu S. Dange, *Vedic Beliefs and Practices through Arthavāda*, Vol. II, pp. 375-78 (the entry "*Āsandī*")
56. For detailed information on this point, see Sindhu S. Dange, *Aspects of Speech in Vedic Ritual*, pp. 6-13.
57. See Sadashiv A. Dange, *Vedic Sacrifices-Early Nature*, Vol. I, Intrn. p. xlii.
58. *Ibid.*, pp. xlii-xliv.
59. See Sadashiv A. Dange, *Ency. PBP* Vol. V., pp. 1524-77 under the entry 'Vow' (*Vrata*).
60. R.T. Rundle Clark, *Myth and Symbol in Ancient Egypt*, Thames and Hudson, London, 1959, p. 28; for the figure *ibid.*, p. 51.
61. Sadashiv A. Dange, *Vedic Sacrifices—Early Nature,* Vol. I, Intrn. p. xxxix.
62. The word *dharmāṇi* (*RV* X.90.16) denotes 'fixed ordinances', which also are for a particular arrangement for being sustained.
63. Interestingly we have Manu speaking of Daṇḍa (Rod of Punishment) as dark in colour (*śyama*) and having red eyes (*lohitākṣa*)—*Manu S.* VII.25. Can we say from this that an actual rod of black iron with red eyes painted on it was used to be kept in the court of the king? This could be like the sceptre of the king, coming very close to the Mayet of the ancient Egyptian kings. See note 60 supra.
64. See Sadashiv A. Dange, *Vedic Sacrifices—Early Nature,* Vol. I, Intrn. p. xl.
65. Ṛta in the cosmic sphere was restricted to the Ṛgvedic data and Ṛta in the moral sphere, with the name Dharma, developed in the branch—Dharmaśāstra.
66. For details about Indra's status from 'human' to 'divine', see Chap. 2, notes 41 and 42.
67. See Sadashiv A. Dange, *Vedic Sacrifices—Early Nature,* Vols. I and II, through which he has tried to trace the variation and evolution of ritual in the Brāhmaṇa texts. See Vol. I, "Preface", p. viii.
68. The *Śat.Br.* has dealt with the Agnicayana rite in five *kāṇḍas* (VI-X) in details.

69. *Śat. Br.* VI.1.2.12-17.
70. See Sindhu S. Dange, *Vedic Beliefs and Practices through Arthavāda*, Vol. II, pp. 469-71 f.
71. For details, see T.N. Dharmadhikari, "The Philosophy of Vedic Sacrifice", *Oriental Journal*, Vol. XLII, Pts. 1 & 2, 1999, Oriental Research Institute, Sri Venkateswara University, Tirupati, pp. 121-51.
72. See Sadashiv A. Dange, *Sexual Symbolism from the Vedic Ritual*, Ajanta Publications, Delhi, 1979.
73. For the new term "Cosmosexualism" coined by him and its sphere in the Vedic ritual, see *Ibid.*, pp. 19-49.
74. For the detailed information about the *yajñapātras*, see T.N. Dharmadhikari (ed.), *Yajñāyudhāni*, Vaidika Saṁśodhana Maṇḍala, Pune, 1989. (The book containing the Album of pictures of Sacrificial Utensils).
75. *RV* X.14.16—
trikadrukebhiḥ patati ṣaḍ urvīr ekam id bṛhat ǀ
triṣṭub gāyatrī chandāṁsi sarvā tā yama āhitāḥ ǀ
76. A.A. Macdonell, *A Vedic Reader for Students*, p. 175 (tr. of *RV* X.14.16).
77. See K.F. Geldner, *op. cit.*, p. 144.
78. *Ibid.*
79. W. Caland, *Pañcaviṁśa Brāhmaṇa*, Sri Satguru Publications, Delhi, 1982 (Calcutta, 1931), p. 430 (tr. of XVI. 3.8).
80. For detailed discussion, see Sindhu S. Dange, *"Trikadrukebhiḥ Patati* (RV X.14.16): An Interpretation," *Proceedings* of the All India Oriental Conference, XVII Session, Kurukshetra, BORI, 1974, pp. 221-23; also *Vishveshvaranand Indological Journal*, XIII (1975) (*Acharya Dr. Vishva Bandhu Comm. Vol.*), Part II, ed. by K.V. Sarma, Vishveshvaranand Vishva Bandhu Institute of Sanskrit and Indological Studies, Panjab University, Hoshiarpur, 1975, pp. 82-87.
81. See W. Caland, *op. cit.*, p. 634, note 1 on *Pañc. Br.* XXV.9.4.
82. See Sindhu S. Dange, *Vedic Beliefs and Practices through Arthavāda*, Vol. I, pp. 227-58 (The chap. "Complementary Numbers").
83. In fact 'Infinity' ('infinite number' shown with the sign ∞) is a concept from the sphere of Mathematics, e.g. Number 1 when divided by zero (0), will lead to the result of 'Infinite'.

84. See R.N. Dandekar, "Comparative Religion and Mythology", *Dialogue'* 72/'73 for F. Max Mueller 150th Birth Anniversary, ed. by Heimo Rau, published by the Branches of Max Mueller Bhavan (in India), 1972-73, p. 26 f; also see Max Müller's *Hibbert Lectures*, p. 207-08.
85. See Sadashiv A. Dange, *Towards Understanding Hindu Myths*, Intrn. p. lxi note 4, where are given the opinions of anthropologists and ethnologists. Max Müller himself admits that he was called 'Sun' as also 'solarist' by others *Ibid.*
86. See R.N. Dandekar, "Comparative Religion and Mythology", *Dialogue* 72/'73, p. 27.
87. Agnihotra rite is laid down for both—*āhitāgni* and *anāhitāgni*. See *Śāṅkh Ś.S.* III.7-12; *Āpa. Ś.S.* VI; *Baudh. Ś.S.* III. 4-9; *Mān. Ś.S.* I.6; *Kāty. Ś.S.* IV.12-15; *Āśv. Ś.S.* II.2-5.
88. For details see, Sadashiv A. Dange, *Ency. PBP*, Vol. II, p. 412f.
89. See Sindhu S. Dange, "the Disappearing Sun-from Myth to Ritual", *Nyāya-Vasiṣṭha* (*Fel. Vol. of Prof. V.N. Jha*), ed. by Manabendu Banerjee and others, Sanskrit Pustak Bhandar, Kolkata, 2006, pp. 18-24.
90. See G.S. Kirk, *The Nature of Greek Myths*, Reprint, Penguin Books Ltd., Harmondsworth, Middlesex, England, 1976 (1974), p. 66.
91. See Joseph Campbell, *The Hero with A Thousand Faces*, Bollingen Series XVII, Princeton University Press, Princeton, New Jersy, Third Printing, 1973 (1949), p. 30.
    Campbell uses the word 'monomyth'. He notes that this word ('monomyth') is taken by him from James Joyce, *Finnegans Wake*, New York, Viking Press, Inc., 1939, p. 581.
92. The word 'embroidery' is used by Peter Munz, for the mythological layers, which are added to the original proto-myth or myth, which can make the latter meta-myth. See Sadashiv A. Dange, *Towards Understanding Hindu Myths*, p. 189.
93. See notes 35 and 36 supra.
94. In ancient Indian tradition, the concept of an *'atithi* (guest) was always of a person who was a stranger to the householder and to be felt awe of, for if displeased, the guest could take away (i.e. destroy) all the 'merit' accumulated by the householder. See Sindhu S. Dange, "Atithi": A Probe in concept", *Studies in Indology* (Prof. *Mukund Madhav Sharma Fel. Vol.*), Sri Satguru Publications, Delhi, 1996, pp. 119-22.

95. See Sindhu S. Dange, "The Disappearing Sun-From Myth to Ritual", *Nyāya-Vasiṣṭha*, p. 24 note 14.
96. For code of conduct in ritual, see Sadashiv A. Dange, *Vedic Sacrifices—Early Nature,* Vol. I, "Ādhāna—(Introduction), pp. xxxix-xliv.
97. See J. Eggeling, *The Śatapatha Brāhmaṇa*, pt. II, SBE, Vol. 26, Reprint, Motilal Banarsidass, Delhi, 1988 (1885), pp. 97, 98 for the word *tapas* as 'fervour' (*Śat.Br.* III.4.3.2, 3), p. 100 as 'heat' (*ibid.* 10) and p. 111 as 'devotion', also 'austere devotion' (*ibid.* III.4.4.27).
98. See Sindhu S. Dange, *Vedic Beliefs and Practices through Arthavāda*, Vol. I, pp. 340-73, the chapter-"Sacrificer's Code and His Immortality (!)"
99. See A. Lang, *Myth, Ritual and Religion*, Vol. I, Longman's Green and Company, London, 1913 (1887), p. 35.
100. Lang says that myths are not evolved in clear civilised thought. *Ibid.*, p. 6.
101. Sadashiv A. Dange, "The Riddle of the Black Antelope", *Abhinandana-Bhāratī* (*Prof. Krishna Kanta Handique Fel. Vol.*), Kāmarūpa Anusandhāna Samiti (Assam Research Society), Gauhati, 1982, pp. 27-33.
102. For *yajñāyudhāni*, see note 74 supra.
103. For more details, see Sadashiv A. Dange, *Vedic Sacrifices—Early Nature*, Vol. I, p. 81 f.
104. *Pūrvamīmāṁsā Sūtra* VI.1.25.
105. Malati J. Shendge, *The Civilised Demons—The Harappans in the Ṛgveda*, Abhinava Publications, New Delhi, 1977, pp. 91-92.
106. See Veena A. Londhe, *The Cult and Lore of the Vedic Agni,* Thesis, University of Bombay (Mumbai), 1977.
107. H. Converse, "The Agnicayana Rite: Indigenous Origins?" *History of Religions*, Vol. XIV, 2, 1974-75, p. 81.
108. Nama Drury, *The Sacrificial Ritual in the Śatapatha Brāhmaṇa*, Motilal Banarsidass, Delhi, 1981, p. 95.
109. For more details, see *Śat.Br.* I.2.5.16, where the exact description of the altar resembling a woman is given.
110. As Viṣṇu (sacrifice) concealed himself below the surface of the earth, among the roots of the herbs that lie three *aṅgulas* deep, the place for the altar should be dug as far as three *aṅgulas*. *Śat. Br.* I.2.5.1ff, 9.

111. See J.G. Frazer, *Folk-lore in the Old Testament,* Vol. I, Macmillan and Co. London, 1918, p. 362.
112. *Ibid.*, p. 364.
113. *Ibid.*, p. 377.
114. *Ibid.*, p. 378.
115. See *A Zoroastrian Tapestry* (Art, Religion & Culture), ed. by Pheroza J. Godrej and Firoza Punthakey Mistree, Mapin Publishing Pvt. Ltd., Ahmedabad, 2002, p.44, photographs no. 5a and 5b, by Khojeste Mistree. Even Nama Drury, *op.cit.*, p. 94, has given a drawing from the photograph which occurs elsewhere. See Robert Graves, *New Larousse Encyclopedia of Mythology,* London, Paul Hamlin, 1968, p. 310.
The photographs (no. 5a & 5b) of Khojeste Mistree, give the exact idea of the raised fire-altar.
116. *RV* I. 103.2; II.12.12; *AV* XX.128.13.
117. Soma-vat is said to be the head of the *asura* Vṛtra-*Śat. Br.* V.5.1.3; *Mait. Sam.* IV.7.4; a round piece of lead is tossed away as the head of Namuci in a rite in the Rājasūya sacrifice—*Śat. Br.* X.4.1.9-10.
118. The idea seems to be that the ordinary fire itself gains the status of the fire that was lost. The fire given earlier was, obviously, the household fire of the *gandharvas,* who, like all other tribes including the Vedic Aryans, constantly maintained it, the difference lying only in the ritual and the fire-sticks.
119. *Vāyu P.* Pūrva, *2.15-21; Brahmāṇḍa P.* I.2.15-23.
120. Dange says that Purūravas was a neo-ritualist. See Sadashiv A. Dange, "Purūravas—A Research for Identity", *A Corpus of Indian Studies (Gaurinath Shastri Fel. Vol.)*, Sanskrit Pustak Bhandar, Calcutta, 1980, pp. 52-60.
121. The mythical account of Purūravas and Urvaśī has been studied by many. J.C. Wright, "Purūravas and Urvaśī", BSOAS, Vol. XXX, 1967, pp. 526-47; D.D. Kosambi, *Myth and Reality,* Popular Prakashan, Mumbai, 1962, pp. 42-81; R.P. Goldman, "Mortal Man and Immortal Woman", *Journal of the Oriental Institute,* Baroda, Vol. XVIII, No. 4, June 1969, pp. 273-303; earlier L.V. Shroeder, *Mysterium and Mimus in Ṛigveda,* Leipzig, 1908; also Sadashiv A. Dange, "Urvaśī—The Water-Belle (A fresh interpretation of *RV* X.95)", *Journal of the Oriental Institute,* M.S.

University of Baroda, Baroda, Vol. XXV-I, Sept. 1975, pp. 17-46; also by the same author, "Uravaśī—The Weaver of the Web of Life", *Śrījagannāthajyotiḥ*, Jagannath University Journal of Indology, Puri, No. 6, pp. 63-67; also see note 120 supra.

122. *RV* I.51.5ab—*tvam māyābhirapa māyino' dhamaḥ* ।
svadhābhirye'dhi śuptāvajuhvata ॥
Here, Sāyaṇa takes the word *adhamaḥ* as *apajigamaḥ* taking the help from Yāska, who says *'dhamatirgati'-karmā*, the root √*dham* as meaning 'to go' and here *apa-adhamaḥ*—'you went against' i.e. 'attacked'.

123. See K.F. Geldner, *op.cit.*, HOS, Vol. 35, p. 62 (tr. of *RV* I.51.5).

124. A. Barth, *Religion of India*, London, 1882, p. 603.

125. *ERE*, Vol. VII, p. 142b.

126. See E.B. Tylor, *Primitive Culture*, Vol. II, London, 1891, p. 143. Centuries ago, the Portuguese in West Africa noticing the veneration paid by the Negroes to certain objects, such as trees, fish, plants, idols, pebbles claws of beasts, sticks and so forth, very fairly compared these objects with their familiar amulets or talismans and called them *feitiso* or 'charm', a word derived from Latin *'factitius'* in the sense of 'magically artful'. In modern French we have the word *fétiche* and in English 'fetish', both languages adopting the word from the Portuguese.

127. L.D. Barnett, *Hindu Gods and Heroes*, London, 1922, p. 28; also see chapter II, notes 41-43.

128. See *Manu Sm.* (III.152, 180), where Manu notes the *devalakas* who serve the temples and idols and images of gods for their livelihood.

129. *ERE*, Vol. VII, p. 143 a & b.

130. *Tait. Sam.* I.3.9.2; *Śat. Br.* I.9.2.34, 35; *Ait. Br.* II,7; *Āpa. Ś.S.* VII.18.14; *Āśv. Ś.S.* III.3.1

131. As per the Vedic ritual tradition, the sacrificial beast was 'silenced' by smothering it and thus immolated, it is skinned and its selected (not all) parts were offered in fire to the gods. There was a person specially given the task of 'silencing' the sacrificial animal and he was called Śamitṛ (fr. √*śam*—'to pacify, to silence') and the place for this task was named *śāmitra*.

132. See Madhavi R. Narsalay, *Epics and Mahāpurāṇas on Vedic Sacrifice*, Aryan Books International, New Delhi, 2015.

133. See Sadashiv A. Dange, "Vāstoṣpati, Rudra and Cyavana", *Gleanings from Vedic to Puranic Age* (collected papers of Dr. Sadashiv A. Dange), ed. by Sindhu S. Dange, Aryan Books International, New Delhi, 2002, pp. 73-81.
134. See Sadashiv A. Dange, "Vāstupuruṣa", *Purāṇa-Itihāsa-Vimarśaḥ* (Prof. S.G. Kantawala Fel. Vol.), Bhartiya Vidya Prakashan, Delhi, 1998, p.41f.
135. *RV* X.27.2—"O Indra! I shall cook a bull for you" again *ibid.*17—"They cooked the fat ram." Here the cooking of the animal is mentioned, but whether it is for offering the whole animal in fire is not made clear, as the word for sacrifice is not used.
136. Sadashiv A. Dange, "The Riddle of the Black Antelope", *Abhinandana-Bhāratī (Prof. Krishna Kanta Handiqui Fel. Vol.)*, Kāmarūpa Anusandhana Samiti (Assam Research Society), Gauhati, 1982, p.31.
137. See note 99 supra.
138. Sindhu S. Dange, "Āraṇyakas—A Search for their Identity" (Key-note Address), *The Studies in the Āraṇyakas*, ed. by Bhagyalata Pataskar, Adarsha Sanskrit Shodha Samstha, Vaidika Samshodhana Mandala, Pune, 2010, pp. 74-76.
139. See *Śaṅkhāyana Āraṇyaka* (*Kauṣ. Ār.*), ed. by V.G. Apte, Anandasharam Sanskrit Series, No. 9, Poona 1922, p.3 (Introduction in Sanskrit, where the list of chapters is given, containing the name 'Saṁhitopaniṣad').
140. For the Pañcamahāyajñas, see P.V. Kane, *HDS*, Vol. II, pt. I, pp. 696-704.
141. See Ram Gopal, *India of Vedic Kalpasūtras*, National Publishing House, Delhi, 1959, p. 345.
142. The word *śastra* (fr. √*śaṁs*—'to praise') as also *stotra* (fr. √*stu*—'to praise') mean 'praise' or 'laud'. *Stotra* is a *sāman* sung by the Udgātṛ priest, while *śastra* is a praise-formula recited by the Hotṛ priest. A *śastra* always belongs to and follows a *stotra*. See Śabara's comm. on *Pūrva. Sūtras* (VII.2.17). Also P.V. Kane, *HDS*, Vol. II, Pt. II, p. 1181.
143. See note 33 supra.
144. For the detailed information on this point, see Sadashiv A. Dange, *Sexual Symbolism from the Vedic Ritual*, pp. 51 ff.

145. RV X.86.15, where the *mantha* is said to have been prepared for Indra to rejuvenate him. Also *AV* II.29.6; V.29.7; *Tait. Sam.* I.8.5.1 etc.

146. *Śat. Br.* IV.2.1.2; *Śaṅkh. Ār.* XII.8 for several kinds of *mantha; Suśruta Sam.* I.233.12, where *mantha* is said to signify the mixture of several choicest things to be pounded with barley and milk.

147. See note 138 supra.

148. E.W. Hopkins, *The Religions of India*, Delhi, 1970 (1896), p. 376.

CHAPTER 4

Code of Conduct—Epic-Puranic Approach

Here we come to the Epic and the Puranic age, in which are seen the changes in the norms of conduct justified and upheld by the device of *arthavāda*.

As compared to the *Rām*, the *Mbh.* has made a wider use of this device. The reason of this lies in the very structure of these two epics. *Rām.* is the story of Rāma and is regarded as an *ādikāvya*, which unknowingly has laid down the tenets to be followed in later times, while composing an Epic. On the other hand, the *Mbh.* is an *itihāsa* (*iti-ha-āsa*—'This happened so')—a cluster of olden accounts of the age-old ancient society of India and according to the orthodox and practically unanimous opinion of later thinkers, is a composition of three editors—Vyāsa, Vaiśampāyana and Sauti (Ugraśravas—the son of Lomaharṣaṇa). It was in the days of the last editor that the *Mbh.* grew so enormous as to attain the present day vast bulky size, containing one lac verses (*śatasāhasrī saṁhitā*) and become a compendium of all knowledge.

The *Mbh.* mentions various kinds of sacrifices, for sacrifices are said to surpass all rites (*Mbh.* Śānti 60.53-54). They nourish the mortals, *pitṛs* and gods (*ibid.* 72.21). Apart from giving worldly and heavenly rewards and satisfying gods and manes, the sacrifice could act as an atonement for a sin. Viṣṇu thinks that performing an Aśvamedha sacrifice could relieve Indra from the sin of *brahmahatyā* (*ibid.* Udyoga 13.15).

The age-old practice of offering a sacrificial victim (animal) still persisted in the times of the *Mbh.* But the *Mbh.* is seen trying hard to show its dislike for this ancient practice. The various accounts which figure in the *Mbh.* as *arthavādas* not only bring out the aversion of the *Mbh.* to the practice of animal-sacrifice but also shows the utter condemnation of it. Here we take a note of the dialogue between a *yati* (*sannyāsin*) and the Adhvaryu priest. The Adhvaryu says that the animal sacrificed as oblation in the sacrifice acquires great good (*śreyas*) as per Vedic injunctions. All parts of the animal merge with the Five Great Elements (Earth, Water, Lustre, Wind and Ether), from where they came. *Yati,* while replying, says that if such a good thing happens to that animal, which is sacrificed, then the sacrifice is for the animal and not for the sacrificer. He further says that the sacrificial fuel itself can act as an animal and there is no need to kill an animal. Whatever act can be performed without *hiṁsā* (injury to any being), that is to be undertaken. The attitude of *ahiṁsā* (non-injury) towards all beings is the ideal one, propounded by the elderly people (of yore) also (*ibid.* Āśva. 28.6-18). This account is called the ancient *itihāsa* (*ibid.* 28.6), which obviously is used for the sake of readers or listeners.

Vaiśampāyana narrates an incident to Janamejaya to show that sacrifices were performed only with grains. Formerly when Indra wanted to perform a sacrifice, he seized many animals (for being sacrificed). Having felt compassion for the animals, the sages present there advised Indra to perform the sacrifice according to the true import of the ordinance *viz.* to perform sacrifices with the seeds of grain that have been kept for three years. When Indra did not agree with them, the sages went to King Vasu and asked him to clear the doubt. The king, without considering properly both the views gave a verdict. He said that one should perform sacrifice with whatever is brought (at that particular time) indicating grains or animals. But because of this wrong verdict, king Vasu fell from the heaven to the nether region (*ibid.* Āśva. 91.8-23). The same story occurs in the Śānti *parvan* also, where it is said that King Vasu supported Indra and the deities due to partiality, inspite of knowing the truth that *aja* which is stated in Vedic sacrifices is not 'goat', but 'vegetable seeds' (*ajasaṁjñāni bījāni*). For this partiality, he was cursed by the sages to fall down from heaven (*ibid.* Śānti 337.2-40). This story is also called the ancient *itihāsa* (*ibid.* 337.2), and is pressed into service as *arthavāda*, justifying the disappearance of animal sacrifice, though with a slow pace, in the times of the *Mbh.*

In this respect, mention has to be made of the account of thc proud *brāhmaṇa* Jājali, who has to get the knowledge of 'true' sacrifice from Tulādhāra a merchant (really speaking a trader or grocer, who earns his livelihood with the help of balance used for weighing i.e. *tulā*). The account—again an old *itihāsa*—occurs in the Śānti *parvan* of the *Mbh.* and runs into four chapters (*ibid.* chaps. 261-64). For our purpose, the chapter no. 263 is important, for here we find the real import of 'sacrifice' as known by Tulādhāra and told by him to Jājali. Tulādhāra states that in olden times, people practised truth and self-restraint as the sacrifice and aspired to get the highest object of life (*artha*—here 'emancipation) not having any greed for worldly wealth (*artha* here 'wealth'), discarded all provisions (stored for the future) and were free from jealousy (*ibid.* Śānti 263.18-19). They did not covet for heaven nor did they perform costly sacrifices for fame and wealth. They knew trees, herbs, fruits and roots as the only sacrificial offerings. The *brāhmaṇas* (*dvijāḥ*) performed mental sacrifice, offering oneself as the offering, for the well-being of the people at large (*ibid.* 25-28). This is obviously the *mānasa yajña*, performed through meditation, with a feeling of empathy for the whole world. This account coming as *arthavāda* is important for supporting the thought of *ahiṁsā* (non-injury) in sacrifice, as deviating from the older thought of animal sacrifice. It is significant that this knowledge of the changed face of older sacrifice comes from Tulādhāra—a *vaiśya* trader and it is given to and accepted by a *brāhmaṇa* steeped in the ideology of the Vedic sacrifice. This account is immediately followed by chap. no. 265, which condemns, in clear cut terms the *hiṁsa* in sacrifice and propounds the principle of *ahiṁsā* (*ibid.* Śānti 265.2-12).

The age-old concept of sacrifice does occur in the Epic and Puranic age but in a changed form, giving stress on *ahiṁsā* (non-injury to any being). We have noted in the earlier chapter, the story of *brāhmaṇa* named Satya, coming from the Śānti *parvan* of the *Mbh.* where also the principle of *ahiṁsā* is stressed. Together with the principle of *ahiṁsā* the *Mbh.* lays stress on faith (*śraddhā*), which is regarded as an important part of sacrifice. In the Śānti *parvan*, a full chapter brings out the importance of faith in sacrifice (*ibid.* 264.6-19) especially while giving gifts (as *dāna*), which we shall see further. In the Puranic age, small or big sacrifices might have been in vogue, as per the need of the social structure. But as women and *śūdras* were denied the right to study the Vedas, the Purāṇas evolved a new set of norms in order to reach the common masses. In fact, this movement had already started from the times of the *Mbh.*, only to be prominently seen in the times of the Purāṇas.

Here, we have the concepts of *Dāna* (giving gifts), *Vratas* (observing vows), *Upavāsa* (observing fast) and *Tīrthayātrā* (going on pilgrimage), which could be regarded as the four pillars of the edifice of this new thought. But, as we have noted at the beginning of this book, every new idea in Indian tradition is in continuity with the old idea, always keeping in view the principles of 'change' and 'continuity'. This is also observed with respect to these four concepts (*dāna, vrata, upavāsa* and *tīrthayātrā*).

Scholars like Kane, Dange etc. have given a detailed treatment to the topics—*dāna, vrata, upavāsa* and *tīrthayātrā.*[1]

Hence, only such details from these topics will be taken here, which have taken recourse to *arthavāda* to make themselves convincing.

The concepts of *dāna* etc. can be traced to the *RV* or to the ritualistic tradition, at times not fully developed in those texts. The study of knowing their origin and later development proves rewarding.

A. DĀNA

With the word *dāna* (giving gifts), we are reminded of the hymns from the *RV*, which are related to and deal with the eulogy of *dāna*. These are known in the tradition as 'Dānastutis'.[2] Though some of them praise Indra as a warrior-god, some have the eulogy of the king or the generous person, who gave helping hand to the seer-poet. Normally, such an eulogy of *dāna* comes in the ending *mantras* of the hymn, which thereby gets the designation 'Dānastuti'. The same concept of *dāna* is seen developed into that of *dakṣiṇā* in the Brāhmaṇa-texts (or the same as the ritual-texts). The *dakṣiṇā* (gift) is given in sacrifice, in order to invigorate it. The sacrifice is slain, when they press the Soma-shoots; when they 'quiet' the sacrificial victim at the hands of Śamitṛ[3]; when they 'slay' the *havis* (corn offering) with mortar and pestle, with the upper and lower millstones. When thus 'slain', the sacrifice in ancient times was no longer vigorous. By means of *dakṣiṇās* (i.e. by giving away *dakṣiṇās*), the gods invigorated it. So, the name *dakṣiṇā* (fr. the root √*dakṣay*). Thus, the sacrifice becomes successful (*Śat.Br.* IV.3.4.1, 2; also *ibid.* II.2.2.1, 2). The *Pañc. Br.* in the context of the Jyotiṣṭoma sacrifice says that the *dakṣiṇās* are the internal fastenings of the sacrifice. They are the adornments of the sacrifice. When the sacrificer performs a sacrifice accompanied with *dakṣiṇās*, he brings beauty to that sacrifice (*Pañc. Br.* XVI.1.13, 14). The *dānas* prescribed in the Purāṇas for having some gains or for averting some evils can be conceptually traced to the *dakṣiṇās* which are enjoined in the sacrifices dating from the Vedic age.

B. VRATA (VOW)

Kane has given a detailed treatment to the concept of *vrata*, meaning of the word *vrata*, its definition etc.[4] Starting from the meaning of the word *vrata* as 'divine ordinances' or 'ethical patterns of conduct', Kane directs us to the two meanings of the word *vrata* given by Yāska *viz.* (i) observance or vow, coupled with restrictions on food and behaviour; (ii) the special food prescribed (*Nir.* II. 14).[5] In the chapter dealing with 'Sacrifice', we have noted the restrictions laid down for a consecrated sacrificer regarding his food, sleep and even the speech, which he utters. He is required to imbibe in him such qualities as *tapas* (toiling fr. the root √*tap*— 'to heat oneself'), *śraddhā* (faith), gratitude, humility, truth etc.[6] Interestingly, the word *vrata* and *vratadughā* occur in the ritual-texts but with a different meaning. The word *vrata* denotes the 'fast-milk', which the sacrificer consecrated for the Agniṣṭoma sacrifice has to drink and not offer in fire as oblation, while performing the Agnihotra rite. Normally, in the Agnihotra rite, the offerings of heated milk are given in fire by the *agnihotrin*, who maintains the three fires (Gārhapatya, Āhavanīya and Dakṣiṇa) and these are given at the time of sun-rise and also at the evening time. But it is not so, as we have noted above in the Agniṣṭoma sacrifice. The cow from which the 'fast-milk' (*vrata*) is taken is called *vratadughā*. Thus the words *vrata* and *vratadughā* have specific meanings in the ritual context denoting fixed food, the vow undertaken of the rules of consecration not lost sight of.

It is interesting to note the changes in the meaning of the word '*vrata*. In the *RV* it denotes 'ordinance' or 'laws', Varuṇa being pre-eminently called *dhṛtavrata*—whose laws are fixed, for he is the upholder of the cosmic and moral Order (Ṛta). In the ritual-texts, the meanings centre round the consecrated sacrificer, which are stated by Yāska and which we have noted above. These same meanings are carried over to later ages, especially the Puranic age, when the concept of vow (*vrata*) acquired a large canvas. Here we find the *tithivratas* (to be performed on the particular days in a month), *māsavratas (to* be performed in a particular month), *grahavratas* and *nakṣatravratas* (in honour of planets and constellations), *vratas* specially with respect to the sun, *vratas* to last for specific duration of time. Kane notes several items such as bath, morning prayer, mental resolve, *upavāsa* (fast) etc. featuring with *vrata.*[7] The concept of *vrata* is in many cases associated with that of *upavāsa* (observing a fast).

C. UPAVĀSA

The concept of *upavāsa* also has originated from the ritual context. In the context of the New-moon and Full-moon sacrifices, we have a reference to the 'Upavasatha' day, which is a preparatory day on which 'fast' is to be observed. Āṣāḍha Sāvayasa explains the word *upavasatha* as the day when the gods come to the sacrificer's house and abide by him or the fires (*upavasatha* fr. the rood *upa+√vas*—'to stay near') in his house. He states that the gods see through the mind of man and know that when the sacrificer enters on the vow of consecration, he has already decided to offer to them oblations (in the sacrifice) next morning. Now, it would be improper on the part of the sacrificer to take food before the gods, who are staying with him and would partake of the oblations (i.e. food) next morning. So the sacrificer should not take any food on this preparatory day i.e. the Upavasatha day. But according to Yājñavalkya, if the sacrificer does not eat, he becomes a sacrificer to the manes (i.e. It becomes a *pitṛkarma*) and if he eats on that day, he eats before the gods have eaten (as we have noted above). Hence, he should eat that, which when eaten, is regarded as not eaten. He should eat only what grows in the forest, be it forest-plants or the fruits of trees, which forest-produce he does not eat daily (*Śat.Br.* I.1.1.7-10). However, in the context of the Agnicayana rite, in the *Śat. Br.* itself, there is enjoined, total abstention from food on the

Upavasatha day. When the Great Fire-altar is ready, on the preparatory (i.e. earlier) day—the Upavasatha day—of the rite of bestowing immortality upon Agni by offering Soma in the fire or on the Fire-altar, only milk is laid down as the fast-food for the consecrated sacrificer. The *arthavāda* which figures in this connection states that when the drink of immortality went away from the gods, they decided to seek for it by toil and penance. Having become consecrated they were living on fast-milk (*vrata*). For this fast-milk, they first resorted to three teats of the cow, then to two teats and lastly to one teat. On the day of preparation, they completely abstained from food. The perfection in the practice of penance requires total abstention from food (*ibid.* IX.5.1.1-9). However, a moderate view occurs in the context of the Agnyādhāna rite (i.e. the rite of establishing the three fires—Gārhapatya, Āhavanīya and Dakṣiṇa). On the Upavasatha day, the sacrificer can take his food in the daytime and he may also take food at night (as per his wish), for the observance of the vow is not necessary for him, as he has not as yet performed the Agnyādhāna (or Agnyādheya). As long as he has not set up a sacrificial fire of his own, he is merely a man (not a sacrificer!) and so he can take food at night (*ibid.* II.1.4.2).

D. TĪRTHAYĀTRĀ

Pilgrimage to places, of which most of them are on the banks of the rivers. Here we come to the place of honour given to Apāḥ—'Waters' right from the Ṛgvedic times. They are eulogised in the *RV* in four hymns as well as in a few scattered verses. They are regarded as mothers, young wives and goddesses, who bestow remedies, health, wealth, strength, long life and immortality. In the ritual-texts they become one of the requisites of Vedic sacrifice, having several qualities. They are purifying, healing and soothing and also figuring as an elixir of immortality[8]. They serve as a means of expiation (*Śat.Br.* I.2.2.11). In spite of the fact that the waters were regarded as holy right from the Ṛgvedic times, the concept of pilgrimage to places on river-banks, evolved in the time of the *Mbh.* and the Purāṇas, in which age the river-mythology is seen having enormous growth.

Thus the concepts of *dāna, vrata, upavāsa* (at times to be included in *vrata*) and *tīrthayātrā* seen in the Epic and Puranic age, are not totally new and can be traced to olden tradition. But they are seen fully developed in the *Mbh.* and the Purāṇas, for it was the need of those times. Though the sacrifices were performed in the Epic and Puranic times, the people at large did not have that age-old fervour for ritualism. The new pattern of observances (*dāna* etc.), coming to the fore-front, envisaged 'fruits' (or merit) which were the same as those promised by the sacrificial institution of yore. Easy to follow, devoid of the priestly encumbrancc, involving less expenditure, this new pattern introduced in the code of conduct could reach the common masses, having direct appeal to their head and heart. Moreover, it could wean away these masses as well as the 'elite' class, from the two rival faiths namely Jainism and Buddhism. Kane has noted this fact[9] and Dange has dealt with this in details under the title *Lokadharma* and its journey as seen in the *Mbh.* and the Purāṇas[10]. In the endeavour to propound the new pattern of observances and to convince the listeners of these, the Epics (really the *Mbh.*) and the Purāṇas unreservedly employed the device of *arthavāda.* Here we intend to take a detailed note of it in the present chapter.

A. DĀNA (GIFT)

We have already noted that the concept and practice of bestowing gifts can be traced to the Dānastutis in the *RV* and the *dakṣiṇās* (śacrificial fees', though this cannot be an exact translation of the word *dakṣiṇā,* which apart from being mere gift involves in it the respect for and the honour shown to the sacrificial priest). The famous Bhikṣu-*sūkta* (*RV* X.117.1-9) has *'dāna'* (charity of wealth and food) as the main theme and according to Sāyaṇa, *'dāna'* verily is the deity of the hymn. The opening words of the first *mantra* of the hymn have become almost proverbial. It says—"Indeed it is not Hunger (*kṣudh*) that the gods have created, but it is really the Death (*vadha*), which they have given to all (the living beings)." The hymn goes further condemning a selfish and stingy person but praising and blessing a generous one (*ibid.* X.117.2-4). The hymn notes the eternal fact of life that 'the riches revolve like the wheels of a chariot (leaving one person and resorting to another, the other day). Hence (knowing this transitory nature of wealth), a rich person should be generous in giving his helping hand to the poor and needy (*ibid.* 5). In vain he earns food (or wealth), who is bereft of any soft feelings (and does not 'give'); he neither pleases the gods nor his friends (also 'guests'—*atithis*). One who himself eats alone i.e. without giving to others (*kevalādī*), is 'Sin' incarnate (*kevalāghaḥ*). This *ṛc*, especially the last part (*ibid.* 6 d), which we have noted above, speaks volumes for the concept of *dāna*, nurtured by the ancient Indian mind, spreading over centuries after centuries.

The Saṁhitās (*Tait.Sam.* in particular) and the Brāhmaṇa-texts speak highly of the concept of *dakṣiṇā*. When a man makes a gift of what he owns, it is indeed his *tapas* (his 'exerting', 'toiling', later on leading to the concept of penance, fr. the root √*tap*) says the *Tait.Sam* (VI.1.6.3). Of the sacrifice, which is allegorically described by the *Chānd.Up.* (III.17.4), penance, (generosity in) giving (*dāna*), righteousness, non-injury (kindness) and truthfulness are the *dakṣiṇās*. Noteworthy instructions to a person, who gives *dāna*, occurs in the *Taitt.Up.* in its Śikṣāvallī. The student, when his stay in the preceptor's house for study is about to end, is instructed by the preceptor and this *upadeśa* ('lesson of instructions') has stood the test of time (Śikṣāvallī 11). With respect to 'giving' (i.e. *dāna*), each and every instruction of the preceptor is significant. He says—"Giving (*dāna*) should be with faith; nothing is to be given without faith "(i.e. the action of giving should be from the bottom of heart and not just formality). "Giving should be with glory (*śriyā*)" i.e. not with a stingy outlook, if one can afford. "Giving should be with a feeling of shyness" i.e. One should not give with an attitude of superiority, but with shyness or modesty that he is giving so less. "Giving should be with fear" (that he is not harming the self-respect of the other person). "Giving should be with perfect and proper knowledge" (naturally 'of the cause' for which he is giving, avoiding giving blindly)[11] Though these instructions are meant for the *snātaka* (one who has taken bath, to mark the end of his studentship), they are of use to any donor, who wants to give any gift or donation, the Upaniṣadic advice thus transcending the limits of Time and Space.

Dāna occupies an important place among the duties of the householder, for the other three *āśramas* (Brahmacarya, Vānaprastha and Sannyāsa) depend upon the householder for support, for their maintenance and survival. Manu eulogies the stage of a householder (*Manu S.* III.77-80), for its unique and towering place. Devala has dealt with the topic of *dāna* in 165 verses, explaining all the details of the various types of *dāna* (vv. 885-1050).[12] Devala defines *dāna* as that 'when wealth is given with faith to a receiver who is a fit recipient" (Devalasmṛti v. 891). The six constituent elements in *dāna* are — a donor, a receiver, faith, gift (that is to be given), which must have been acquired by the donor in a proper way, (proper) place and (proper) time (v.901). *Manu S.* also indicates the first four of the constituents of *dāna* we have noted above from Devala (IV.226, 227), and speaks of the fruits of *dāna* (IV. 224-35). The *Mbh.* (Śānti 232.28) and *Manu Sm.* (I.86) both agree that the principal features, which are prominently seen and followed in the four ages (*yugas*) are *tapas* (in Kṛta *yuga*), knowledge (in Tretā *yuga*), sacrifices (in Dvāpara *yuga*) and *dāna* (in Kali *yuga*). The *Mbh.* is bold to condemn a rich man, who does not give (*dāna*). It says that two persons should be drowned in water after tying round their neck a large stone, *viz.* a rich person who does not give (*dāna*) and a poor person who is not restrained (*Mbh.* Udyoga 33.60).

That the *Mbh.* knows the human mind and its inclination perfectly, can be seen from Vyāsa's reply to Yudhiṣṭhira's query. When Yudhiṣṭhira asks Vyāsa which among the two *viz. dāna* and *tapas* (penance), is difficult to perform and is greater of the two, Vyāsa's reply is very pointed, based on the worldly experience. He says that nothing is more difficult than giving *dāna*. A person obtains wealth with great difficulty and hence it is difficult for him to part with it (*Mbh.* Vana 259. 28-31; 260.26). In order to convince the listeners (or readers), the *Mbh.* gives the account of Mudgala, who resorting to the mode of living like a pigeon (*kāpotī vṛtti*) gathered only a *droṇa* (a wooden vessel or a particular measure) of rice. This rice he every time offered to the sage Durvāsa, himself remaining without food. In the end the angry sage Durvāsa is pleased to bless Mudgala. It has to be noted that this account (*purātana itihāsa*—'old account') comes (chap. 260) immediately after chap. 259 in the Vana *parvan*, where *dāna* is said to be the most difficult of the acts.

The *Mbh.* mentions various articles which can be given as *dāna*. But it is very firm in pointing out that the merit gained by *dāna* depends upon the mental attitude (of the donor), donor's capacity and the way by which he has acquired the wealth. Again, greater or lesser merit of *dāna* is not dependent upon the quantity and the category of *dāna*. *Dāna* of wealth (may be of the whole earth) acquired by unjust means, or that given without faith (*śraddhā*) or that given to an unworthy person, would never give the donor prosperity or religious merit. On the other hand, by making *dāna* (a gift) of even a handful of vegetables or even water, with faith to a worthy person, the donor can get all prosperity. The *Mbh.* here refers to olden accounts in order to convince us of its stand. King Rantideva did not have anything to give. So he offered only water with a pure heart, due to which merit he attained heavenly abode. King Nṛga made gifts of thousands of cows but by giving only one cow that did not belong to him, he fell into hell. King Śibi by giving the flesh of his body to the hawk for the sake of pigeon attained heaven (Āśva. 90.96-100). As the accounts of these three kings of olden times are referred to here for glorifying the concept of *dāna* and its practice, let us have more information about these kings as recorded by the *Mbh.* King Rantideva, the son of King Samkṛti, was famous for his hospitality and generosity to the *brāhmaṇas*, guests and to all those who came as needy and supplicants. The *Mbh.* waxes eloquent on his entertaining these persons with delicious food and gold-*'niṣka'* (Droṇa 67.1-19; Śānti 29.120-29). It is just possible that he might not be having anything left with him and then he had to entertain Vasiṣṭha by offering him only water, by which act he attained the heavenly world (Śanti 234.17; Anu. 137.6). By his generosity his name is included among those, which are worthy of being remembered and uttered in the morning and evening (Anu. 150.51).

In the case of King Nṛga, the Anu. *parvan* of the *Mbh.* devotes one full chapter (chap. 70.1-33). To give it in short—Nṛga the king gave the *dāna* (gift) of cows in hundreds, lacs and crores. But once it so happened that a wayward cow belonging to an *agnihotrin brāhamaṇa* who had gone on journey, somehow entered the herd of cows of the king and was counted by the royal cowherds among the thousand cows and was given as gift to a *brāhmaṇa*. When the *agnihotrin brāhmaṇa* (the owner of the cow) came back, he spotted his cow in the house of that *brāhamaṇa* and there ensued a wordy battle between the two *brāhmaṇas*. The king tried to pacify them, but each one was having his own genuine right over the cow—the *agnihotrin* was the original owner, while the other *brāhmaṇa* also was the (new) owner, because of the gift of the cow made to him. The king was prepared to give the former ten thousand cows, but he wanted to have his cow back to him. The (new) owner was promised gold, horses etc. but he also was not prepared to leave off his right over the cow. When the king Nṛga died, he went to the world of Yama. Yama honoured him for the merit he had gathered in his life, but said that the king had committed a sin though through ignorance. He had committed a double sin in that even though being sworn in as a 'protector', he could not protect the *agnihotrin's* cow and moreover he took that cow as his own and counted her among the thousand cows, which were given as *dāna*. As a result, Nṛga should undergo suffering, was Yama's verdict and Nṛga became a chameleon resorting to a hollow near a well. And as Yama himself had foretold, Vāsudeva (Kṛṣṇa) released King Nṛga (the chameleon) from that wretched state, at the end of thousand years. This account of King Nṛga occurs in the Anu. *parvan* as we have noted above. But it is again referred to (though in short) in the Āśva. *parvan* (90.99-100) in the context of *dāna*, obviously to glorify that concept. In the *Rām.* the state of being a chameleon for Nṛga is stated to be the outcome of curse given to him by both the *brāhmaṇas* (whom we have noted above) for failing in his royal duty (*Rām.* Uttara chap. 53) and it will be discussed in the chapter dealing with Curses and Boons.

The name of King Śibi, as we have noted, also figures in the context of *dāna* as given in the *Mbh.* (Āśva. *parvan* 90.100-101). The account occurs fully in the Vana *parvan* (131.1-34), prior to this starting from chap. 130 (21-24). Just for testing King Śibi, the gods Indra and Agni, come to King Śibi in his sacrifice, in the form of a hawk and a pigeon resp. As the king is sitting in the sacrificial chamber, the pigeon (Agni) perches on the lap of the king feigning fear from the hawk (Indra) pursuing him. The hawk following the pigeon demands his prey (i.e. the pigeon), to which king is not ready, for he has given protection to the bird, which has approached him. The king offers the hawk any other creature far fleshy than the pigeon. But the hawk is not ready to accept anything in lieu of his prey (i.e. the pigeon), ultimately suggesting that the king can offer his own flesh equal to the weight of the pigeon. The king agrees and cuts off chunks of flesh from his body only to find that every time they are outweighed by the pigeon in the balance. Ultimately the king, with whatever body-flesh is remaining on his person, sits in the balance. Seeing the climax of the king's generosity, the hawk discloses his identity as Indra and that of the pigeon as Agni. The gods assure King Śibi that his fame would go beyond the worlds and the king's body is restored to its original form and lustre.

It seems that king Śibi's name was famous for his generosity and self-sacrifice. Among the Jātakas, we have the *Sivi Jātaka*[13] in which king Sivi (Śibi) is seen parting with his eyes to help a blind person. The question of borrowal from the *Mbh.* by the Jātakas in the Buddhist tradition or vice-versa need not arise, for the tales of Śibi's self-sacrifice must have gathered in the floating mass of literature, which could be the common source for both the traditions.

It is very clear that the accounts passingly referred to of Rantideva, Nṛga and Śibi in the context of *dāna* are given to glorify the concept of *dāna* (*Mbh.* Āśva. 90.96-100). Here, we come to an interesting tale of a mongoose in the Āśva. *parvan* in the *Mbh.*, which is given as an *arthavāda* to point out that sacrificing food for the sake of other person with devotion is more meritorious than the fruits attained by Aśvamedha and Rājasūya sacrifices performed with largesse. The account runs thus—when Yudhiṣṭhira completed his Horse-sacrifice (Aśvamedha), gratifying all kinsmen, a blue-eyed mongoose with one side of his body changed into gold came there. He told that the sacrifice performed by Yudhiṣṭhra was in no way equal to the merit of *dāna* earned by a poor but generous *brāhmaṇa* of Kurukṣetra. The *brāhmaṇa* together with his family-members, even being hungry, offered food to a hungry guest, with nothing left for them. The mongoose stated that the power of *brāhmaṇa's* penance and his generosity and the aroma of the barley-grains (which while being offered to the guests were fallen) turned half of his body golden. Thinking to make the other part of his body golden (made of gold), he came to attend the Horse-sacrifice of Yudhiṣṭhira. But no change took place in his body (i.e. in the other half of his body). The mongoose concludes that the *dāna* made by the poor *brāhmaṇa* is higher than the Horse-sacrifice performed by Yudhiṣṭhira (*Āśva* chap. 90). This story is one of the apt examples, which shows how a narrative can carry home an ethical teaching, here the stress being on the concept of *dāna*. The story mentions the gift of food (*annadāna*) and that too to a hungry person, at the cost of one's own want of food. The *dāna of* food is highly praised by the sage Parāśara (*Anu.* 66.56-65). King Janaka's wife, distressed due to his decision of taking *sannyāsa* (renunciation from his stage of a householder and the responsibility of a king), says that in that case, the giving of food (to the needy, and even to the mendicants) will be difficult. We have already noted that on the householder depend the remaining three *āśramas* (*brahmacarya, vānaprastha* and *sannyāsa*). Janaka's wife praises highly the *annadāna* saying that as life flows from food, the giver of food is giver of life (Śānti 18.27-28). A full chapter (chap. 63) occurs in the Anu. *parvan* of the *Mbh.* highly praising the giving (*dāna*) of food (63.5-52), which reminds us of the Bhikṣusūkta (*RV* X.117) necessitating the act of giving.

The *Mbh.* lays stress on giving land (i.e. *bhūmidāna*), which is said to be the highest *dāna* (Anu. chap. 62 and especially vv.4, 19-20, 89-92). No *dāna* can surpass giving of land (*bhūmidāna*) in merit. It has to be pointed out that giving of cow is brought on par with the *bhūmidāna*. The *Mbh.* points out that by giving a cow, a person obtains the merit equal to giving the earth with its ocean, caves, mountains and forests. When he gives a cow, he makes the gift of what is the resort of all (Anu. 66.50). Here, we are reminded of the belief firmly rooted in the Epic and Puranic age that cow stands for the

Earth. We have noted the cow Nandinī, from whom various tribes are said to be born. Again, on several occasions the Earth takes the form of a cow and approaches either Brahmā or Viṣṇu (more often Brahmā) entreating upon him to save her from the burden of sin, heaped on her by the sinners.

The giving of land (*bhūmidāna*) and its eulogy seem to be a later development, for the ritual-texts present a different picture of this issue. This issue is concerning the gift (*dakṣiṇā*) of earth to be made in the Viśvajit sacrifice. It is said that in the Sarvamedha (Soma-sacrifice performed for getting all types of food) the tenth day is of the Viśvajit Atirātra sacrifice (*Śat.Br.* XIII.7.1.2, 12). It is said that not laying hand on the wealth of a *brāhmaṇa*, of the wealth (including land and men), the eastern part is to be given to the Hotṛ priest, southern to the Brahman priest, western to the Adhvaryu priest, northern to the Udgātṛ priest and the Hotrakas (mainly the assistants of the Hotṛ priest, but in a wider sense the assistants of all the priests) to share with all these (*ibid.* 13). In this connection, the *Śat.Br.* relates a mythical account, coming as *arthavāda,* which runs quite contrary to what we have mentioned above. It so happened that when Bhuvana's son Viśvakarman performed the Viśvajit sacrifice and was to give the gift (*dakṣiṇā*) of the Earth to his priest Kaśyapa, the very Earth is shown as uttering a *śloka*. The Earth says that nobody should give her as a *dakṣiṇā* to anybody. If this happens, she would plunge in waters and then the promise of Viśvakarman to his priest would prove false (*ibid.* 14, 15). The same verse from the 'mouth' of the Earth occurs in the *Ait.Br.* in the context of the Great Anointing of Indra (*Ait.Br.* III.21=39.7). Sāyaṇa in his commentary on this passage calls this verse *gāthā*. It was difficult, it seems, for the commentators to mark the difference between a *gāthā* and a *śloka*.[14]

The *arthavāda* passage regarding Bhuvana's son Viśvakarman with the words from the 'mouth' of the Earth is important for the clear instruction stated in it that one should never make a gift of land (*Śat.Br.* XIII.7.1 14, 15). But it is in the *Śat.Br.* itself in the earlier passage (*ibid.* 13) that the gift of land (Earth) is enjoined in the Viśvajit sacrifice. The *Śat.Br.* elsewhere (XIII.6.2.18) prohibits the land-*dakṣiṇā,* as we have seen above (*ibid.* XIII.7.1.14, 15), both stated in the context of the Viśvajit sacrifice. The *Ait.Br.* (VIII.21=39.7) also prohibits the land-*dakṣiṇā*, though the context is of the Great Anointing of Indra.

The same trend of prohibition of giving the *dakṣiṇā* of land continues in the Sūtra period. Jaimini clearly states that the king should not give the entire earth (or land) as *dakṣiṇā* in the Viśvajit sacrifice, for the earth belongs to all (*Jai. Sū.* VI.7.3). In the Viśvajit sacrifice, the sacrificer has to give away everything that belongs to him. But as per Jaimini's instruction, noted above, even an emperor cannot make a gift of the whole earth (in the Viśvajit sacrifice), even though he rules the earth. Śabarasvāmin while explaining this *sūtra* of Jaimini adds a vital point. He says that there is no difference between the emperor and other persons as to the right over the earth, for other persons also walk on the earth, produce crops on it and get their sustenance from it and hence they also have a right over the earth. Hence, the emperor (even though he rules over the earth) is entitled to a share of crops produced from the earth as his, since he protects the people.[15] Nīlakaṇṭha, the author of the 'Nibandha' (Digest) work—*Vyavahāramayūkha*—respecting the view of Jaimini noted above, states that therefore it is said in the sixth chapter of Jaimini that the whole earth cannot be given away by the emperor and a province by a feudatory chief.[16] When kings make what is technically called gifts of fields, no gift of land is effected thereby, but only provision is made for the maintenance of the donee (from the taxes which are alienated by the king).[17]

These instructions regarding the giving away of earth or land seem to be of the later times. But the *Mbh.* being an *itihāsa,* takes us to the olden times. It speaks of Paraśurāma giving away the whole earth to the sage Kaśyapa (*Mbh.* Ādi 129.62;

Śānti 49.63-64; Anu.137.12 speaks of the *dāna* of the earth given by Paraśurāma to a *brāhmaṇa*). The Śānti *parvan* mentions the giving of kingdom by Nimi, the king of the Videhas; the giving of the earth by Paraśurāma as well as by the king Gaya—all these *dānas* to a *brāhmaṇa* (Śānti 234.26). Here in all these *dānas* there is no mention of the specific sacrifice or at some places no mention of any sacrifice, as we have in the Brāhmaṇa-texts, mention of the Viśvajit or the Aindra Mahābhiṣeka (Great Anointing of Indra) sacrifice. The ritual-texts are required to give specific instructions with exactitude, while the *Mbh.* being an *itihāsa* has the records of olden accounts, which are carried to us, through the layers of innumerable past generations. Hence we need not stress the point of chronology regarding the two view-points concerning *bhūmidāna* (giving away of the earth or land)—one prohibiting this *dāna* (as the verse—*śloka* or *gāthā*—put in the 'mouth' of the Earth states, which we have noted earlier) and the other praising it (as we have in one passage of the *Śat.Br.* and several verses in the *Mbh.*). However, the exact implication of the *bhūmidāna* explained by Jaimini, Śabarasvāmin and Nīlakaṇṭha is a phenomenon of later times, when there might have arisen the need for a systematic treatment of this issue.

It has to be pointed out here that the Dharmaśāstra-texts have praised the gift of land. Manu says that one who gives land (as *dāna*) acquires land (*Manu Sm.* IV.230 a). Yājñavalkya includes in the articles to be given in *dāna*, land and says that by giving these a person (i.e. donor) is extolled in the heaven (*Yājñ. Sm.* I.210a). According to Kātyāyana, the gift of land is the best, for he who gives away land (as though) gives away gold, silver, clothing, diamonds and precious stones i.e. attains the merit of giving these (*Kāty. S.* 4, 5), and the gifts of cows, land and (imparting) learning are the supreme gifts, that rescue the giver from all sins (*ibid.* 18). The *Viṣṇu Dh.S.* says that by giving protection and land, the giver attains the region which he wishes to get (92.2, 3).

Here we take a note of an interesting detail, which brings in clear terms, the identification between a cow and the earth. Yājñavalkya, while praising the concept and practice of *dāna* (which in details we will see subsequently), says that a person who makes a gift of a cow, who is *ubhayatomukhī,* enjoys the heavenly region for years equalling the number of hair existing on the body of the cow as well as that on the body of her calf (*Yājñ. Sm.* I.206). The *Yājñ. Sm.* in the very next verse explains that while delivering the calf, as long as (that time may be short!) only the two feet and the face of the calf are seen from the womb of the cow, till that time the cow is regarded as the Earth (when the cow has not as yet delivered the calf). The comm. Mitākṣarā explains the concept of *ubhayatomukhī* by saying that at this hour, the cow is seen having two faces—her own face and that of the calf (Comm. on *ibid.* 207).

When the Purāṇas speak about the various *dānas,* they already know what the Dharmaśāstra-texts have stated in this respect, the difference being that of the wider sphere chosen by the Purāṇas with respect to the donor, donee and various articles to be gifted together with the fruits achieved by giving these gifts (*dānas*). The Dharmaśāstra-texts also speak about the fruits to be obtained by making the gifts. A point to be noted with respect to the fruits of the *dānas* is that the fruits are related to the *dānas* on the basis of sympathetic magic or as Frazer has called 'homeopathic' magic and to elucidate it in simple way, 'Like produces like'.

It was J.G. Frazer who made a scientific study of the concept of magic[18], though the practice of magic has been an age-old phenomenon. In magic as he has pointed out, the 'Law of Similarity' works and has two aspects *viz.*

(i) Imitative or mimetic magic, Frazer himself coining for this the word 'Homeopathic' magic, which works on the principle—'Like produces like'. e.g. from Indian context—'A giver of lamp gets excellent eye-sight' (*Manu Sm.* IV.229), for a lamp and an eye have the same common factor i.e. light or lustre.

(ii) Contagious magic, based on the Law of Contact or Contagion, the principle being—'A part stands for the whole' or 'Once in contact (remains) always in contact', e.g. the belief all the world over regarding the cutting of hair and nails and their disposal at a safe place (mostly at the water place as in India), to avoid anybody taking hold of these and carrying out black magic on them to harm the person, to whom they once belonged.

These principles of magic can solve the incongruity which may appear in the texts as regards the 'fruits' prescribed for certain religious actions and can provide a basis for justifying the rites and rituals with the help of *arthavādas*. Like other faiths, the Vedic-brahmanical Hindu faith does contain a 'magico-religious' element.

Manu speaks highly about giving various gifts (*dānas*) and mentions the fruits thereof (*Manu Sm.* IV.229-232). To note some of them with the fruits obtained—A giver of water gets satisfaction (with his thirst quenched); a giver of lamp, excellent eyesight (*ibid.* 229); a giver of land gets land; a giver of gold gets long life (right from the Vedic times, gold being associated with immortality, solar lustre etc.); a giver of house gets excellent mansions; a giver of silver (*rūpya*), charming beauty (*rūpa*) (*ibid.* 230—similarity between the two words *rūpya* and *rūpa*, not to be unheeded); a giver of carriage or bed, gets a wife (*ibid.* 232); a giver of Brahman (one who imparts the knowledge of Veda) gets near to Brahman (the Highest), Manu stating that this *dāna* is the best among all the *dānas* (*ibid.* 232, 233). Yājñavalkya mentions several articles such as land, lamp, food, clothing, water, sesame, ghee, resort (to the travellers), a girl given in marriage, gold, bull, house, corn, foot-wear, umbrella, unguent, carriage, tree, bed, etc., which can be given as *dāna* (*Yājñ. Sm.* I.210-11). Like Manu, Yājñavalkya also regards imparting Brahman to be the best—nay surpassing—all the *dānas* (*ibid.* 212).

The composers of the Purāṇas had before them the Dharmaśāstra-texts, the oldest of these being the *Manu Sm.* and the *Yājñ. Sm.* in recognition and general application and prior to these the *Mbh.*, especially its Anuśāsana *parvan*, which is also known as Dānadharma *parvan*. Hence to make themselves appealing to common masses, including women and *śūdras*, the Purāṇas while prescribing the gifts (*dānas*), have taken recourse to *arthavāda* and thus we have various narratives glorifying a particular gift. Again, for each gift (*dāna*) its 'fruit' is spoken of at times on the basis of sympathetic magic, and several times bringing that 'fruit' on par with the 'merit' acquired by performing a Vājpeya or Aśvamedha sacrifice. These two sacrifices are often referred to in this context.

Let us have some glimpses of the Puranic appeal with respect to *dāna*.

A very simple word of convincing is stated by the *Gar. P.*, which maintains that whichever gifts are given away by men in this world attend on them arriving prior in the yonder world (II.23.12). Here, we are reminded of the etymology of the word *āhuti*—'offering', which is stated in the *Śat.Br.* (XI.2.2.6) and which we have noted in one of the earlier chapters. The offering given by the sacrificer becomes his body in the yonder world and waits for his arrival there (after his passing away from this world), to welcome him with the words, 'Come here, I am here your body.' So the word *āhuti* fr. the root *ā*+ √*hve*—'to call out'. The concept of 'giving' either *āhuti* or as in the Purāṇas 'gift' is obviously based on the doctrine of *karman*. The *Sk.P.* while eulogising gift (*dāna*) says that in the horrid ocean of the transmigratory existence, turned turbid due to the waves of *dharma* and *adharma* (righteous and unrighteous dealings), one should resort to giving gift (*dāna*), which is like a boat made, obviously to cross this ocean (*Sk.P.* I.2.2.84). This again is an echo of the Vedic thought, which maintains that sacrifice (where 'offering' figures prominently) is a divine boat, which both the father and the son steer and which does not sink (*Jaim. Br.* I.166).

The concept of *dāna* and in practice its various types, the things comprising the *dānas*, its division into two broad heads—*iṣṭa* and *pūrta*—have been dealt with in details by Kane and Dange, by the former from the point of view of Dharmaśāstra and historical records of ancient India[19] and by the latter from that of the Puranic practices and the beliefs related to them.[20] Kala Acharya has discussed in details the Puranic records of gifts.[21] Hence, here we shall take into account only those *dānas*, which are somewhat unique in nature or are stated with *arthavādas* based on age-old beliefs or are woven with some legendary accounts, the aim being to make the concept and practice of *dāna* convincing.

The *Sk.P.* lays down the gift of a black antelope skin, which is said to be equal to all gifts (*Sk.P.* VI.214.93, 101). The *Kūrma P.* states that a person, who places sesame, gold, honey and clarified butter on a black-antelope skin and gives this as a gift (*dāna*) to a *brāhmaṇa* crosses all calamities. This is to be given at the change of the solar course, at the day of the solstice, at the solar and lunar eclipse and at the Saṅkrānti day i.e. in Māgha month as per the Hindu almanac (*Kūrma P.* II.26.22 and 54). This is a *namittika dāna* (giving gift on a certain occasion), to surmount all calamities, as it is in the present case. At other places, reasons for giving the occasional (*naimittika*) gifts may be different. While stating this *dāna* of sesame, gold etc. to be given on a black-antelope skin, the *Kūrma P.* has followed the *Viṣṇu Dh.S* (87.1.8-10), where it is pointed out that the merit acquired by this gift is the same as that of giving away (as *dāna*) the entire earth with all its forests and mountains. We have dealt with the use of the black-antelope skin in sacrifice in the chapter dealing with the concept of 'Sacrifice' and its various facets when brought into practice. Sacrifice is said to have taken the form of a black antelope (*Śat.Br.* I.1.4.1; *Tait.Br.* III.2.6.1,2). The skin or hide of an animal stands for that animal[22] and so here the black-antelope skin has the sanctity and it stands for sacrifice, which is said to be the birthplace of Ṛta (Order). This may appear allegorical in the sacrificial context. But on the physical level, the sacrifice has been regarded as a 'desire-fulfilling' device. So when the *Kūrma P.* states that by giving a gift of black-antelope skin, with the things such as sesame, gold etc. (placed on it), a person crosses all calamities, it is quite convincing, for it has the basis of the belief about the black-antelope skin (=black antelope=sacrifice). It is on the basis of contagious magic, which maintains—'A part stands for the whole.'

One of the *dānas* to be specifically mentioned is 'the gift of land', and according to the *Sk.P.*, the land should be of ten cubits (*Sk.P.* II.1.20.41) and with standing crops of sugar-cane, wheat, beetle-nut etc. (*ibid.* 45). Even a small piece of land could be given as a gift (*ibid.* 46; also *ibid.* VI.268.7-28). The *Sk.P.* eulogies the gift of land by saying that one who gives the land rich with the crops of sugarcane etc. is no doubt Viṣṇu himself (*Sk.P.* II.1.20.45), and even giving a small piece of land he attains intimate union with or absorption in Viṣṇu (*ibid.* 46). The gift of land is equal to donating the entire earth (*ibid.* 45). The *Sk.P.* does not forget to make a mention of two *brāhmaṇas* named Sughoṣa and Bhadramālī, who attained the heavenly world after giving the gift of land on the mountain Veṅkaṭa (*ibid.* 56-93).

Another gift to be mentioned is that of a lamp, which, on the basis of 'sympathetic magic' is linked with sharp eyesight (*Agni P.* 200.3), both—lamp, and eye—having the common factor namely 'lustre' (*Sk.P.* III.7.50 cd; also *Var. P.* 307.53 cd). The same principle of 'sympathetic magic' is seen working, when the *Brahma P.* says that a person worshipping the sun with a lamp, lighted in ghee or sesame-oil does not become blind, becomes a learned person and gets faultless eyesight (*Br.P.* 29.35-36). *Agni P.* has an interesting account to relate regarding the gift of a lamp. Lalitā, the daughter of the king of Vidarbha offered a lamp to Viṣṇu. Once that lamp was about to get extinguished, but burnt more brightly due to the contact of a she-rat that was chased by a cat. When Lalitā died and was reborn, she became the favourite wife of a king, beloved of him among a hundred others. And this was due to the merit she acquired by offering a lamp to Viṣṇu and its flaring up by chance (*Agni P.* 200.6-18). Hence, the *Agni P.* warns (by way of *arthavāda*) that a person who steals a lamp becomes dumb or a dunce and after death goes to hell, full of blinding darkness (*ibid.* 200.11). Theft of lamp, making that area dark, hence leading the thief to dark hell is an *arthavāda* based on reason, giving an ethical note. The *Padma P.* says that the gift of a lamp leads to the upliftment of hundred families (VI.121.14). Here we are reminded of a common proverbial expression in India, which speaks of a son in the family as its 'lamp', which illumines the family by carrying its name.

A *dāna* unique in concept and practice is given by the *Sk.P.* It is the *pāpapuruṣa-dāna,* to be made on the 15th bright of the month of Kārttika and forms a part of the vow called Bhīṣma-pañcaka-vrata. By this *dāna,* the donor is said to get a son within a year (*Sk.P.* II.4.32.12). The word *pāpapuruṣa,* indicates a (small) image of a man, possibly given 'to evil', which is believed to hinder the path of progeny in the family. The image is a scapegoat. This *dāna* has a basis of belief, comprising an unusual practice, bringing with it the fruit also.

The Purāṇas adore the (milch) cow and hence the gift of a cow is regarded as the best of all the gifts. The cow to be given as a gift should have golden (i.e. covered with gold) horns and the hoofs covered with silver and the fruit is—the donor of such a cow is said to rest in heaven for years equal to the number of her hair (*Agni P.* 210.30ff). The cows are said to be the offsprings of the Sun, gold that of Fire and land that of Viṣṇu (*Garuḍa P.* II.31.4). The gifts of land (earth), cows and Sarasvatī (learning) are the 'excellent gifts', (*ati-dānāni*) says the *Garuḍa P.* (*ibid.* 5).

The Purāṇas take a step further and enjoin gifts of 'cows' made of various materials. *Agni P.* enumerates these cows 10 in all as follows:

(i) *guḍa-dhenu* — *dhenu* (cow) of jaggery;
(ii) *ghṛta-dhenu* — *dhenu* of ghee;
(iii) *tila-dhenu* — *dhenu* of sesame;
(iv) *jala-dhenu*—*dhenu* of water;
(v) *kṣīra-dhenu*—*dhenu* of milk;
(vi) *madhu-dhenu*—*dhenu* of honey;
(vii) *śarkarā-dhenu*—*dhenu* of sugar;
(viii) *dadhi-dhenu*—*dhenu* of curds;
(ix) *rasa-dhenu*—*dhenu* of juice

and (x) a real cow (*Agni P.* 210.10cd-12; also *Matsya P.* 82.18-19).

The *Agni P.*, with regards to the nine symbolic cows(i-ix) gives instructions for the preparation of the cows. For making the cows containing liquids, jars should be used, while for forming the cows containing solid matter like sesame etc., heaps are to be formed (*Agni P.* 210.13ab; also *Matsya P.* 82.20). The *Agni P.* clearly says that the cow should be formed facing the east with its legs towards the north. Again, it should be formed always with a calf (*Agni P.* 210.15ab). Here the quarters mentioned—east and north—are significant. East is the quarter of the rising sun and the repository of solar light and hence connected with the world of heaven and is the abode of gods. Next in importance comes the north, which is associated with men and is famous for cultured speech-habits[23]. Here also is mentioned the black-antelope skin, which is to be spread out on the earth in the process of forming the symbolic cows (*ibid.* 210.14). The details of the measures to be used for the cow and the calf, such as *bhāra, māṣa, suvarṇa, pala, tulā, droṇa* and *āḍhaka*, are given by the *Agni P.* (210.17cd-18). The *Bhaviṣya P.* (Uttaraparva chapters 152-156) and the *Varāha P.* (chapters 99-110) give all the minute details about the making of these cows.[24] The merit of performing all sacrifices and release from all sins accrue to the giver of these cows. A person about to die, if in his last moments makes a gift of cow along with a calf, will not be required to cross the river Vaitaraṇī on his way to the other world (*Agni P.* 210.31-34). The *Bhaviṣya P.* (Uttaraparva 152.3) says that the gift (here of cow) should be accompanied with *dakṣiṇā* and should be given with the proper ritual. The rewards promised for the gifts of these cows in the form of worldly and heavenly bliss to the extent of freedom from the blemish of the *mahāpātakas* and the *upapātakas* (Great Sins and the Minor Sins) are for the glorification of the gifts of these cows. Mention of different symbolic cows, their minute descriptions, together with the incredibly great rewards promised for gifting these cows in *dāna*, display the highest reverence shown to 'cow' in the Vedic-brahmanical Hindu tradition as seen in the Purāṇas, which has continued even upto the present times.

Another important *dāna* to be mentioned is of symbolic mountains, which are to be given as gifts. The things, which are needed in daily life regularly, such as corn, salt, jaggery, sesame, sugar etc. are given in a mountain-form along with a ritual. The *Agni P.* speaks of ten mountains (*Agni P.* 210.5cd-10ab; also *Matsya P.* 83.2-6). The same (*Agni*) Purāṇa states twelve mountains under the title *Merudānāni* (Agni P. 212.9cd-32). It has to be mentioned that these mountains are denoted by the words—*meru, acala, adri, parvata, giri* and *śaila*, prefixed with a word denoting one thing or the other. Thus we have mountain of corn (*dhānyameru*), mountain of salt (*lavaṇācala*), mountains of jaggery (*guḍādri*), mountain of cotton (*kārpāsaparvata*), mountain of ghee (*ghṛtācala*), mountains of silver (*rajatācala*) and such others (*ibid.* 210.5cd-10ab). Then under 'Merudānāni', we have such costly mountains as jewel-mountain (*ratnameru*), gold-mountain (*hemameru*), silver-mountain (*raupyameru*), elephant-mountain (*hastimeru*), horse-mountain (*aśvameru*), cow-mountain (*gomeru*), garment-mountain (*vastrameru*) and others (*ibid.* 212.9cd-32). *Bhaviṣya*

P. also mentions corn-mountain (*dhānyaśaila*), sesame-mountain (*tilaśaila*), juice-mountain (*rasaśaila*) and seven others (*Bhaviṣya P.* Uttaraparva 195.5cd-7). The *Bhaviṣya P.* has given detailed information about ten mountains.[25] In order to stress the importance of giving these mountains, the *Bhaviṣya P.* gives a mythical account, which obviously is an *arthavāda*, and runs as follows. A king by name Dharmamūrti was unparalleled in valour and lustre. His wife Bhānumatī was the most beautiful woman in the three worlds. Once the king asked Vasiṣṭha the cause of his own lustre and that of his wife's beauty. Vasiṣṭha told the king about their previous births. A prostitute named Līlāvatī, a devotee of Lord Śiva, gave according to the ritual a salt-mountain (*lavaṇācala*) to the preceptor. It was given with the (replicas) of trees and images of gods made of gold. These golden trees and golden gods were made by the prostitute's (Līlāvatī's) goldsmith Śauṇḍa, who was her servant. His wife helped him in this by heating and melting the gold for making the trees and images of gods in gold. The goldsmith (Śauṇḍa) did not take any remuneration for this work, and he with his wife served the *brāhmaṇas* in Līlāvatī's house. Līlāvatī due to her merit acquired by gifting the salt-mountain went to the abode of Śiva. The goldsmith (Śauṇḍa) and his wife doing their work selflessly for Līlāvatī were born (in the next i.e. present birth) as King Dharmamūrti and his wife Bhānumatī. Due to their help given to Līlāvatī with regards to the ritual of giving the salt-mountain (with the trees and images of gods in gold), King Dharmamūrti became invincible and lustrous and his wife Bhānumatī a paragon of beauty. Here the priest of the king (Vasiṣṭha as we have noted above) advised the king to give ten types of mountains in his lifetime.

The composer of the *Bhaviṣya P.* is aware of the fact that giving such costly mountains as gifts is beyond the reach of common man, and to reach the common masses including women and *śūdras* has been the mission of the Purāṇas. Hence the *Bhaviṣya P.* in a convincing tone says that even a poor person can go to heaven by observing the ritual and listening to its importance with devotion. Even reading the verses about the gift of mountains will nullify the effect of evil dreams and fear of the mundane existence (*Bhaviṣya P.* Uttaraparva 204.17cd-38; also *Matsya P.* 92.17-34).

In the case of the symbolic cows we have to say that as the 'cow' from the Ṛgvedic times was regarded as the mainstay of the pastoro-agricultural life of the Vedic Aryans and in the Epic and the Puranic age was identified with the earth, the gift of a symbolic *dhenu* ('milch cow', fr. the root √*dhe*—'to suck'; causal— 'to suckle')[26] is certainly reasonable, especially when it is mentioned as accompanied by a symbolic calf.

And now about the gift (*dāna*) of a symbolic mountain, of so many types (*merudāna*)—Right from the Ṛgvedic times, the mountains have their own significance. In the dual deity (*dvandva-devatā*), 'Indrāparvatā', we have mountain as a deity together with Indra. In the *Kāṭh. Sam.* (XXXVI.9) and the *Mait.Sam.* (I.10.13), they are said to be the 'sons of Prajāpati'. The hugeness of mountains and their nature of being the first recipient of the divine drops of rain might have caused a feeling of awe in the ancient people.[27] The hugeness of mountains and their power of giving rain and other things[28], is apt to create reverence for them. By the time of the *Mbh.*, every mountain has become a potential divinity as well as a resort of gods, *gandharvas* etc. Legends abound in regard to the mountains as holy beings as well as holy places.[29] The mountains are said to be the 'earrings' of the earth (*Mbh.* Vana.142.45). The mountain holds the earth (*ibid.* Ādi 175.46). Here we are reminded of words denoting a mountain which are in common use as *dharaṇīdhara, bhūdhara, mahīdhara* etc., which show that it is the mountain which supports the earth. The Govardhana episode occurring in the *Bhāg. P.* (X.chaps 24 and 25) has to be noted in this connection. When Kṛṣṇa suggested to Nanda and other cowherds to worship the mountain Govardhana instead of Indra in Indrayajña as they were doing it till that time, he as a hero of the folks upheld the mountain-deity and preserved for it a place in public life.[30] The concept of the symbolic mountains and their gifts (*dāna*), spoken of in the Purāṇas has this hoary tradition at its basis. Hence even merely observing the ritual of the *dāna* and listening to its importance or reading the verses (from the Purāṇas) about it prove greatly beneficial to common man—though an *arthavāda*, nevertheless quite convincing for a person of meagre means of livelihood or having paucity of manpower, for the arrangement of this gift.

Here we take a note of two *dānas*, which are somewhat unique but which point out the Puranic approach. One is the gift of a boar, symbolic one, made by four *droṇas* of sesame. A detailed description of the preparation of the symbolic boar occurs in the *Bhaviṣya P.* (Uttaraparva 194.7-12). A particular feature of this *dāna* is that it can be given by all the four *varṇas*, including the *śūdras* and even by women. Again it can be given by both the Vaiṣṇavas and the Śaivas (*ibid.* 21). Actually the gift of a symbolic boar is for eulogising the boar-incarnation of Viṣṇu and is expected to be meant for the Vaiṣṇavites. But as the Purāṇas aim at the spirit of assimilation, this *dāna* can be given by the Śaivites also. The *Bhaviṣya P.* here equates this *dāna* with all the gifts, promises the reward (or merit) of having performed all sacrifices and assures a stay in the 'Viṣṇuloka'.

Another gift to be mentioned is again from the *Bhaviṣya P.* and it is that of a sheep, symbolic or a living sheep. It is to wipe off and destroy the sin committed by a person (who is the giver of the *dāna*) with his action, words or thought (*Bhaviṣya P.* Uttaraparva 163.12 and 13). The Purāṇa convinces us of the efficacy of this gift by giving the examples of Gaurī getting Śaṅkara for her husband; Indraṇī, Indra; Rukmiṇī, Kṛṣṇa. Even Nala gave this gift (*ibid.* 17-19). The rewards of the gift promised are sons, bodily lustre and wealth (*ibid.* 20).[31] A detail regarding this gift, which appears somewhat strange, has to be considered. The gift of sheep, has to be given to a *brāhamaṇa* householder. But as the acceptance of the gift is taken to be sinful, the giver, after giving the gift of sheep, should not talk with the receiver, nor should he see the face of the receiver (*Bhaviṣya P.* Uttaraparva 163.14-15). The reason for this taboo most probably lies in the very gift of sheep, which is believed to wipe off sins. Now when this gift is received by the receiver, all the sins wiped off of the giver are transferred to the receiver. So the giver becomes free of sins and bound by these sins is the receiver. Hence probably is the instruction that the giver (now free from sins) should not look at the face of the receiver and should not talk to him to avoid the contamination freshly coming to him. A possible faint evidence for this may be seen in the *Ait.Br.* (VI.35=30.9), in a mythical account, which runs as follows. The Aṅgirases officiated as priests for the sacrifice performed by the Ādityas. The Ādityas gave them this earth as *dakṣiṇā*. But the Aṅgirases cast her away as the earth caused them to burn. It is said that a person shall not accept a gift cast away. If he wants to accept it, he should give it to a hated rival, who then is ruined.

Of all the gifts (*dānas*), that of food and water is the best. A mythical account occurs in the *Varāha P.* of King Vinītāśva, who is said to have given many gifts to *brāhmaṇas*, except food and water. After death, he suffered from hunger and thirst in the other world. In that world he saw his preceptor, whom he asked the reason and cure for his diseased body. The preceptor told him that if he gave *tila-dhenu, jala-dhenu, ghṛta-dhenu* and *rasa-dhenu* he would be free form the constant thirst and hunger (*Varāha P.* 99.75-82). The king did as directed. In the same tune is the account of King Hemāṅga of the Ikṣvāku dynasty, who gave everything in the Vaiśākha month (summer month) except water. After death, he was born as a lizard (*godhā*) in the house of the king of Mithilā. Once this lizard accidentally got sprinkled over with the water as a distinguished *brāhmaṇa* washed his feet. The lizard remembered its past life and was released from that horrible state, when that *brāhmaṇa* gave his own merit to the lizard i.e. the king (*Sk.P.* II.7.6.3 ff). Even the *Vāmana P.* has given a story in this regard. A *brāhmaṇa* named Somaśarmā gave gifts only once in lifetime on the twelfth day in the Śrāvaṇa month in the form of a water-jar, an earthen jar full of rice and curds, an umbrella and a pair of shoes to a *brāhmaṇa.* After death, every day at noon a jar of water and that of curd-rice appeared before him. The umbrella appeared as the Śamī tree and as he had given shoes, the other ghosts carried him (*Vāmana P.* 53.52 ff). Here we are reminded of the hymn from the *RV* (X.117), which we have taken note of while discussing the concept and practice of *dāna* in the *Mbh.* The hymn in its very first *mantra* has stated that 'it is not Hunger (*kṣudh*) but the very Death (*vadha*) which the gods have given' to the living beings. The Purāṇas have carried the same note of considering Hunger and Thirst as the main enemies of the living beings, have stressed the importance of *dāna* in this respect and to be more convincing, have woven the stories about it in the effort of reaching the 'conscience' of the common masses.

At the end of this discussion about *dāna*, here we take a note of one unique *dāna* and it is of Sarasvatī, also called the *vidyādāna*. The *dāna* of Sarasvatī is that of knowledge. The *Agni P.* says that if Sarasvatī is given, one attains the region of Brahmā after death and when alive, he attains the merit of performing a thousand Vājapeya sacrifices (*Agni. P.* 211.52-56). The gift of Sarasvatī (*vidyā*) comprises the donation of hand-written copies of the various Purāṇa-texts, accompanied with a special gift. The *Matsya P.* devotes a full chapter (chap. 53) for this and gives a detailed information about (i) Purāṇa-text to be donated; (ii) accompanying gift; (iii) the particular month; (iv) the particular day (month and day—when the Purāṇa-text is to be donated) and; (V) the gain for giving the Purāṇa-text as *dāna*. This comprises-obtaining 'a stay in the abode of a particular deity' or 'merit (*puṇya*) of performing a particular sacrifice'. The *Matsya P.* gives the information on these five points in the case of all the eighteen Mahāpurāṇas (It mentions *Vāyu P.* and not *Śiva P.*, since there is a controversy between these two Purāṇas) and mentions three Upa-Purāṇas *viz.* Nārasiṁha, Nandī and Sāmba (*Matsya P.* 53.60-62). We take only a couple of examples from the *Matsya P.* (chap. 53). The *Brahma P.* (i.e. its written copy) is to be donated to a *brāhmaṇa* along with the *jala-dhenu* on the full-moon day of the Vaiśākha month and the fruit is (after death) a stay in the region of Brahmā (*ibid.* 53.13). The *Padma P.* is to be donated with a golden lotus and sesame, on the full-moon day of the Jyeṣṭha month and the fruit is (while living) the merit of performing Horse-sacrifice i.e. Aśvamedha (*ibid.* 14-15). Thus the information about the gifts of all the Purāṇas with all the details occurs in the *Matsya P.* (chap. 53),[32] when the manuscripts of these Purāṇas are enjoined to be given as gift (*dāna*) of Sarasvatī.

This gave impetus to the propagation of the Puranic religious thought, which further was co-mingled with several other trends, to get a wider designation namely 'Hindu'. From another point of view when several manuscripts of one and the same Purāṇa are found, it has been a difficult task to make the authentic edition of a Purāṇa, when it has to take the print form.

B. VRATA (VOW)

We have noted earlier that the word *vrata* can be traced to the *RV* and the ritualistic *tradition*. Manu says that the *vratas* (vows) are born out of mental resolve (*Manu S.* II.3cd). Kullūkabhaṭṭa on the verse from the *Manu S.* (IV.13) explains that *vrata* is a specific mental resolve (*saṅkalpa*) in the form 'This should be done by me, and this should not be done by me.' Śabara on *Jaim.Sū.* (VI.2.20) says that *vrata* is a mental resolve. The Dharmaśāstra-texts lay down several vows (*vratas*) which are expiatory in nature, such as Prājapatya, Cāndrāyaṇa, Kṛcchra, Parāka, Atikṛcchra etc. (*Yājñ. Sm.* II.260, 264, 265). The aim of these is obviously to nullify the sins (*Śaṅkha Sm.* XVIII.14; *Atri Sm.* III.14). Manu has elaborately dealt with expiatory rites as a means to wipe off the sins (*Manu Sm.*XI. 44-232), mentioning various sins and the expiatory rites (*vratas*) enjoined for them. The reason of calling the expiations (*prāyaścittas*) by the term *vrata* e.g. Cāndrāyaṇa-*vrata*) is due to the observance of several strict rules obligatory in them. In the *Mbh.* the word *vrata* is mainly used in the sense of religious undertaking or vow in which one has to observe certain restrictions about food or one's general behaviour (*Mbh.* Vana 296.3; Udyoga 39.71-72; Śānti 35.39; Anu. 103.34) The *Mbh.* also applies this word in the sense of a course or pattern of conduct or behaviour not necessarily religious (e.g. Sabhā 58.16—Yudhiṣṭhira saying that when challenged he would not refuse the dice-play, has been his constant vow).

To sum up this consideration of the term *vrata* we resort to Kane, who states that the principal meaning (of this term) from at least the first centuries of the Christian era onwards has been that of a religious undertaking or vow, observed on a certain *tithi* (day), week day, month or other period, for securing some desired object by the worship of a deity, usually accompanied by restrictions as to food and behaviour.[33] In the times of the Purāṇas, the concept of vows and their practice was already deep-rooted in the Jaina and Buddhist faiths. For the Jaina *munis*, the five great vows (*mahāvratas*) which are laid down, are—*ahiṁsā*, *satya*, *asteya* or *acaurya* or *adattādāna*, *brahmacarya* and *aparigraha*. For the *munis* or the *śramaṇas* these vows are enjoined for being followed strictly, hence known as the *mahāvratas*. But by a Jaina householder (*śrāvaka* or *upāsaka*), these same vows are to be followed in some restricted form (*aṇuvratas*).[34] In the Buddhist faith, there are laid down ten *śikṣāpadas* or *daśaśīlas* for a Bauddha *bhikṣu*, out of which the first five are to be followed by a Bauddha *upāsaka* (householder).[35] Kane has rightly pointed out that "in order to wean away common people from these two schisms it is very probable that learned followers of the Vedic system hit upon the glorification of vratas and promised heaven and other worldly and spiritual rewards to those who performed vratas that were comparatively easy and within reach of all instead of sacrifices and also adopted some of the practices of common folks as vratas."[36]

In fact it has been an interesting study of the *vratas* falling in different categories (*vratas* for a particular day, those for a particular month etc.) with their salient features.[37] Here we take into account a couple of *vratas*, which speak of unique gains by performing these *vratas*. One is the Ārogyavrata in honour of the Sun-god, which lays down worship of the sun for one year and the gains are—sound health, wealth and grains (crops) in this life and (after death) a place in the yonder world from where there is no return (*Varāha P.* 62.2, 4). The gains of another *vrata* for the Sun-god-Sauryavrata—by fasting on Āśvayujanavamī, are—a timid person becomes valiant; a deposed king gets back his kingdom; the ignorant man gets knowledge and a person struck with fear, valour (*ibid.* 64.1, 2, 6). These gains are no doubt *arthavāda* but it is convincing, for these gains can be acquired with the confidence generated in a person, by following the Sauryavrata with faith and sincerity.

The fabulous gains are spoken of by following the Anaṅgatrayodaśīvrata, to be performed on the bright thirteenth day of a month. The unique gains and other details are as follows—(*Bhaviṣya P.* Uttara chap. 90)

(i) Mārgaśīrṣa month—with fasting and controlling senses—gain of the performance of ten Horse-sacrifices; (*ibid.* 90.12);

(ii) Puṣya (Pauṣa) month—fruit of the performance of Rājasūya sacrifice (*ibid.* 90.15);

(iii) Māgha month—with the worship of Naṭeśvara with lotus—gain of many sons, wealth, fortune and the 'merit' of the performance of thousand Gomedha sacrifices (*ibid.* 90.18);

(iv) Phālguna month—worshipping Hareśvara with Karṇikāra flowers—gain of exquisite physical charm;

(v) Caitra month— gain of good fortune and the merit of Naramedhayajña (*ibid.* 90.22).

As noted above, the *vrata*—Anaṅgatrayodaśī *vrata*—is to be followed on the thirteenth day of these months in their bright half—*śukla pakṣa* (*Bhaviṣya P.* Uttaraparva 90.1-49).

In the gains which occur in the *arthavāda* portion, there is a reference to Gomedha (cow-sacrifice) and also to Naramedhayajña (human-sacrifice). Though *arthavāda*, the veracity of these references is to be examined. In the *RV* there is a mention of 'cooking' of a bull (*RV* X.27.2) but not that of offering in sacrifice. Here we are reminded of the *savas* enumerated in the *Kauśikasūtra* of the *AV* and according to Bloomfield, many of these "centre around an animal".[38] Of the twenty-two *savas* (specific rites), twelve involve the immolation of an animal. Out of these twelve *savas*, those mentioning the immolation of a cow or ox are—Śataudanasava—a barren cow (*vaśā*) is the victim (*Kauśikasūtra* 65.1); Anaḍuhsava—draught-ox (*ibid.* 66.12); Karkīsava—a white calf (*ibid.* 66.13); Pṛṣṇisava and Pṛṣṇigasava—a spotted cow (*ibid.* 66.14); Ṛṣabhasava—a bull (*ibid.* 66.18); the two Vaśāsavas—each of a barren cow (*ibid.* 66.20) and Gosava, in which a cow is killed, its parts being offered to different deities (*ibid.* 66.19).[39] This is the tradition of the *AV*, as made very clear by Bloomfield, by mentioning the exact numbers of the *AV* mantras.[40] The *Tait Sam.* in the context of special sacrifices enjoins offering of several types of *vaśās*.[41] Prior to this, the *RV* mentions offering of a *vaśa* cow in fire for getting food (*RV* VIII.43.11). Sāyaṇa takes the word *vaśā* to mean a barren cow.[42] The *Bhaviṣya P.* mentioning thousand Gomedhas (cow-sacrifices) and their merit in the *arthavāda* portion of the Anaṅgatrayodaśīvrata, reminds us of the Gomedha (cow-sacrifice) of olden times but turned obsolete in the Puranic times. Again it is not clear in the *Bhaviṣya P.* which is the cow-sacrifice intended—whether from the Saṁhitās, (*RV* and *YV*), of a barren cow or a cow in the Savayajñas mentioned in the *Kauśikasūtra* of the *AV*.

The mention of Naramedhayajña and its merit mentioned in the *arthavāda*—portion of the Anaṅgatrayodaśīvrata is all the more puzzling. The earliest reference to human-sacrifice (if we can name it so!) is in the Puruṣasūkta (*RV* X.90), where the replica of the Cosmic Puruṣa i.e. second Puruṣa, is sacrificed. But this sacrifice is taken to be a symbolic sacrifice as per unanimous opinion. Next comes the Śunaḥśepa-ākhyāna in the *Ait. Br.* (VII.13-18=33.1-6), where we find Śunaḥśepa (Rohita, the son of king Hariścandra, thus becoming an escapee), bound to the stake for being sacrificed to Varuṇa, may indicate human-sacrifice. But Śunaḥśepa praised the deities Prajāpati, Agni, Savitṛ, Varuṇa, All gods, Indra, Aśvins and Uṣas and with each verse (in praise of these deities) uttered by Śunaḥśepa, each of the bonds was loosened. Thus Śunaḥśepa became free (*ibid.* VII.16=33.4) and we do not have any clear evidence of human-sacrifice here. In the purificatory bath (Avabhṛtha) in the Horse-sacrifice the last oblation is given on the head of a white-spotted, bald-headed (man) with protruding teeth and reddish brown eyes, with the words—'To Jumbaka *svāhā*!' Jumbaka is Varuṇa and by this offering the sacrificer redeems himself from Varuṇa (*Śat.Br.* XIII.3.6.5). The man (Jumbaka) is driven into the water and then the offering is made on his head and afterwards is allowed to go, apparently being driven away. The *Tait.Br.* (III.9.15.3) mentions this offering in the same context. As the man (Jumbaka) is not offered but released, there is no sacrifice of a human. Keith is right in pointing out that remnants of human sacrifice cannot possibly be seen in this rite, as Weber thought.[43] Hence the reference to the Naramedhayajña made by the *Bhaviṣya P.* in the *arthavāda* of the Anaṅgatrayodaśīvrata is tricky, and such a sacrifice (human sacrifice) cannot be traced to the Vedic-brahmanical tradition. It is just possible that a Tantric influence has crept in here (*Brahmavaivarta P.* Prakṛtikhaṇḍa 64.96-101, laying down human-sacrifice). The two sacrifices—Gomedha and Naramedhayajña-mentioned in the *arthavāda* portion have been examined here, only to show that in the effort to convince masses, the Purāṇas while glorifying the matter in hand sometimes go off the track of reason and give information from hearsay, especially with respect to the sacrifices, coloured with Tantric practices.

Here we come to a unique practice of worshipping a malevolent spirit, which when propitiated becomes the guardian spirit of the children in the house. This practice of worshipping the guardian spirit of children has become a *vrata* (vow) in modern times in the state of Maharashtra (India).

The malevolent spirit in the form of a demoness occupies an important place in the account of Jarāsandha's birth, as mentioned in the *Mbh.* The account runs as follows. Bṛhadratha the king of Magadha country married the twin-daughters of the king of Kāśī. Being issueless for a long time, he approached the sage Caṇḍakauśika, who gave him a mango fruit and wished him well. The king gave the fruit to his two queens, who divided it between themselves and ate the respective half parts of the fruit. Both of them conceived, each giving birth to half of an infant's body. Thus were produced two half parts of an infant. The two queens became so depressed and disturbed that their nurses left those two pieces at a place, where four roads met. A demoness Jarā by name joined those two pieces and out of them stood forth a strong child. Hearing the cry of the child (for milk), the persons from the harem gathered around. Jarā presented the child to the king saying that it was his son protected by her (*Mbh.* Śabhā 17.13-49). While giving information about herself, the demoness told the king that she named 'Gṛhadevī' had been created by the god Brahmā for the destruction of the *dānavas*. She said further that whosoever drew with devotion her picture on a wall, showing her to be young and accompanied with sons (boys), would get prosperity, otherwise would perish. As her picture was drawn on the walls of the king's palace (There might have been many pictures!) and was worshipped with incense, flowers, offering of eatables, thus ceremoniously, she was pleased with the king. The king named the child Jarāsandha i.e. 'joined' (from *sam* + √*dhā*—to put together, join) by Jarā (*ibid.* Sabhā=18.1-12), for the two (half-) parts of the child were joined by Jarā. It has to be noted that here Jarā, the demoness, is 'Gṛhadevī', protectress of children, for she, in her picture, as specifically mentioned, is accompanied by sons (boys—from infants to toddlers).

The supernatural element in the birth-account of Jarāsandha is in line with the accounts of other mythological or even at times historical heroes. In the case of Jarāsandha it was all the more needed, for he was a powerful warrior, who could not be killed by treacherous means (*ibid.* Sabhā24.1-8).

But the point of Jarā is to be probed further. In the Droṇa *parvan* of the *Mbh.* we note that Jarā initially was a malevolent spirit and was to be killed. It is said that in order to kill the heroes from the Pāṇḍava side, Jarāsandha threw his mace towards them. But when the mace was thwarted in its speed by a missile let loose by Śrikṛṣṇa, the demoness Jarā together with her sons and relatives was then killed by the very same mace. Had the mace remained with Jarāsandha, he would have subdued everybody from the Pāṇḍava side. As he was made devoid of his mace, Bhimasena could kill him (*Mbh.* Droṇa 181.8-16). Jarā in her ferocious form is said to be a demoness (*ibid.* Sabhā 17.39, 40, 42), but in her mild form, she is the Gṛhadevī, who when propitiated protects the children of the house (*ibid.* Sabhā 18.2-7).

The concept of Jarā—ferocious as well as mild—comes very close to that of the goddess Bhūtamātṛkā, who is said to stay at the place Prabhāsa. She is also named Bhrātṛbhaṇḍā, Bhūtamātā and Udakasevitā and is said to come out from the water of a lake, when Pārvatī dissatisfied with Śiva in the act of union left the bed and went away. The goddess Bhūtamātṛkā is fearful and her worship is to begin from the first day of the dark half in the month of Vaiśākha and lasts till the fourteenth day. It is enjoined that women should worship her on the occasion of this festival and if she is not so worshipped, she enters their house to harm them. In her festival (on the 9th and the 11th day), replicas of faces of various mother-goddesses, Caṇḍikā, ghosts, demons and some others may be exhibited and worshipped.[44] In spite of her terrible nature, she is said to do good to children everywhere (*Skanda P.* VII.1.167.71ab). The evil spirits, goblins and demons will not trouble that person, who worships her and the children in his house prosper with sound health (*ibid.* 77).

The concept of a guardian spirit of children is found elsewhere also and can be traced even to modern times. It is interesting to note that in the state of Maharashtra, in the month of Śrāvaṇa (month in the Hindu almanac), there is a custom of worshipping the goddess Jīvatī, who is drawn in a picture as surrounded by small children. The small board on which this picture is drawn is called Jīvatī-paṭa. The worship of Jīvatīdevī is performed on every Friday in the Śrāvaṇa month. The concept of Jīvatīdevī and that of Gṛhadevī (originally Jarā) come very close to each other. For protection, there is also a custom in the state of Maharasthra of making a pendant for the child, containing a small figure of the goddess Jīvatī. Such a pendant is woven in a black thread, either silken or cotton, and is put round the neck of the child. The black colour of the thread is obviously to ward of the black evil 'eye', whose possible attack is thwarted by the black colour. It is interesting to note a belief (in the living tradition) about this goddess. When infants smile or cry without any reason, it is believed that they are made to do so by the goddess Jīvatī, who is their protectress.

The account of Jarāsandha's birth is shrouded in mystery. He might have been an adopted son of the king Bṛhadratha, and the account of Jarā's joining the two (half-)parts of his body is brought in to cover this fact. Or this supernatural element is brought in to make the powerful Jarāsandha fall in line with the other heroes, in whose cases also such accounts do occur, just to show their greatness,[45] and to convince others of it. The birth-account here is no doubt *arthavāda*, based on the belief about a child-protectress, having two aspects malevolent and benevolent the latter aspect turning into a *vrata* (vow) in the living tradition, as we have noted.

Here we deal with a well-known vow (*vrata*), which the women whose husbands are living, perform in many parts of India. It is the Sāvitrīvrata or Vaṭasāvitrīvrata, which is still a living tradition in India. The image of Sāvitrī stands as an ideal of a wife, so devoted to her husband as to bring him back from the clutches of Yama. This mythical story occurs at great length in the *Mbh.* (Vana chaps. 293-299) and later in the Purāṇas such as *Matsya P.* (chaps 208-214), *Sk.P.* (Prabhāsa-khaṇḍa chap. 166) and *Viṣṇudharmottara P.* (II.chaps 36-41). Here we are taking into account for discussion the *vrata* (vow) and the story thereof, as they occur in the works noted above. There is mentioned another Sāvitrī-vrata in the *Brahmavaivarta P.* (Prakṛtikhaṇḍa 23.42-54) and the *Bhaviṣya P.* (Uttaraparva 102.66-72), but it is to be performed by a male.[46] The *Bhaviṣya P.* in addition lays down a worship of Sāvitrī by a woman, which is to be performed at the Vaṭa tree (*Bhaviṣya P.* Uttaraparva 102.86) called Bodhi Nyagrodha, at Avanti.[47]

Here we take into account the Vaṭasāvitrīvrata which is practised today in India (and not the ones noted above), with the mythical tale of Sāvitrī becoming an integral part of it. To see this tale of Sāvitrī in brief as narrated by the *Mbh.* (Vana chaps. 293-297). Aśvapati, the king of Madradeśa had no issue. He used to mutter the holy Gāyatrī (*mantra,* which in reality is a Savitṛ-mantra) a lac of times with oblations offered to the fire daily and give alms thereafter. After eighteen years, he was blessed by the goddess Sāvitrī and he got a beautiful daughter, who was named by him 'Sāvitrī'. When she reached the marriageable age, the king (i.e. her father) asked her to find a husband for herself. After many days she came back with determination to marry Satyavān, the son of Dyumatsena, the deposed blind king of the Śālva country, who was living with his family in the forest. Nārada, who was present with her father predicted the death of Satyavān before the end of one year thence. In spite of this, Sāvitrī with undaunted courage married Satyavān. And then came the fatal day. Sāvitrī went with Satyavān, who, as usual, went to the forest to collect wood (fire-sticks). In a short time, Satyavān began to perspire and got a severe headache. Sāvitrī knowing the cause of husband's sudden agony took his head on her lap and sat on the ground. And then came Yama and began to depart taking the life of Satyavān. Sāvitrī kept the body of her husband on the ground and followed him. She had an argument with Yama, who became so pleased with her sagaciousness that he gave her boons and released Satyavān from his fetters and Satyavān stood alive.

The *Matsya P.*, as noted earlier, deals with this episode in seven chapters (208-214), on the same lines as the *Mbh.*, the only difference being the mention of the three-day fast observed by Sāvitrī prior to the fatal day (*Matsya P.* 208.17-18).

In both these works (*Mbh.* and the *Matsya P.*) there is no mention at all of the banyan tree. In the *Brahmavaivarta P.* (Prakṛtikhaṇḍa 24.11) there is a mention of a tree, after falling from which Satyavān died. But there is not mentioned any specific tree such as Vaṭa or any other tree. Kane directs us to a reference from the *Bhaviṣyottara P.* quoted by Hemādri, that when the moment of death approached, Satyavān took shelter under the shade of the Vaṭa tree and taking the support of the branch of it, spoke in a choked voice to Sāvitrī that he had pain in the head.[48] In the *Sk. P.*, which is a Mahāpurāṇa (and of the older stock), we have a clear mention of the banyan (Vaṭa) tree. Satyavān cuts the wood and hangs it on the Vaṭa tree. Sāvitrī also takes her seat at the trunk of the banyan tree. During the time Sāvitrī argues with Yama, Satyavān is lying (dead!) under the banyan tree and after getting the boons from Yama, Sāvitrī comes back again to the same banyan tree to see her husband (Satyavān) gradually gaining life (*Sk.P.* Prabhāsa 166.78). It has to be marked that there is no mention of the worship of the banyan tree in all these works.

The *Agni P.* mentions some details of the Vaṭasāvitrīvrata, in which figures prominently the worship at the root of the Vaṭa (banyan) tree. On the full-moon day in the Jyeṣṭha month, a woman, who has observed a three-day fast, should offer worship at the root of the Vaṭa tree, to Mahāsatī with seven types of sprouted corn. Having tied the cotton threads with saffron etc. round the banyan tree, at the night time she should take resort to that tree accompanied by dancing and singing and in the morning bowing down to Sāvitrī and Satyavān, should offer food (*naivedya*) to a *brāhmaṇa*. After going home, having offered food to the *brāhmaṇas*, she should partake of food and thus complete her vow (*vrata*), with a prayer to Sāvitrī. Thus she would get good fortune etc. (*śaubhāgya*—having her husband with her until death i.e. freedom from widowhood). Though in short, the *Agni P.* has mentioned the important features of this vow (*Agni P.* 194.5-8).

Kane has stated the procedure of this vow, as given in the work *Vratārka* and other medieval works, where we have, together with the worship of the banyan (Vaṭa) tree, offering of worship to Sāvitrī, Yama and Nārada.[49] Kane notes that in Bengal the mode of performing this *vrata* is different. On the Sāvitrīcaturdaśī on the 14th day of the dark half of the Jyeṣṭha month the *vrata* is followed to secure blessed wifehood in later lives. It is continued for fourteen years.[50] The procedure of following Vaṭasāvitrīvrata, prevalent in many parts of India to this day, is practically the same as given in the works *Agni P.*, *Vratārka* etc., with negligible difference in details, the banyan tree getting the place of prime importance.

After the 'three-day' fast (In modern times, every married lady may not be observing it!), on the fourth day i.e. the Full-moon day, the main feature of the *vrata* is the worship of the banyan tree. After this worship, hearing of the long tale of Satyavān-Sāvitrī (really speaking of Sāvitrī) forms the integral part of the *vrata*.[51] It is very clear that originally the tale of Sāvitrī and the worship of the banyan tree were quite different. The image of Sāvitrī in the *Mbh.* tale as an emblem of a 'devoted loving wife' is known to the *Ram.* also, for Sītā says to Rāma that she would follow him as did Sāvitrī her husband Satyavān (*Rām.* Ayodhyā 30.6). This shows that the tale was well-known in the ancient world and was passed on from one generation to the other. Dange points out that the main purpose of this tale is to glorify Sāvitrī who is the solar energy and the very principle of procreation or rebirth (fr. the root √*sū*—'to procreate or give birth to'). Satyavān dying and again coming to life is the sacrificer in the Vedic rites, on whom the Gāyatrī (=Sāvitrī, the *mantra* in the Gāyatrī metre being of the god Savitṛ) bestows immortality by bringing 'Soma', or he is the initiate in the Upanayana (initiation ceremony), who gets a new life after being symbolically killed by the preceptor who is the very Death.[52]

The entry of the banyan tree in the tale of Sāvitrī is the gift of the Purāṇa period. Though not mentioned in the *RV*, the *AV* (IV.37.4) knows the banyan (Nyagrodha) tree as a haunt of the *apsarases* (nymphs). The *Ait.Br.* mentions fruits of Nyagrodha together with those of certain other trees for the great anointing of the king (Mahābhiṣeka) and calls Nyagrodha as the lordly power (*kṣatram*) of the trees (*Ait. Br.* VIII.16=39.2). The *Ait.Br.* lays down that a *kṣatriya* when consecrated for sacrifice, should press together the descending shoots (*avarodhāḥ*) as well as the fruits of the Nyagrodha tree and those of Udumbara, Aśvattha and Plakṣa trees and partake of them (*ibid.* VII.30=35.4).[53] In the *Rām.*, when Rāma with Lakṣmaṇa and Sītā starts from the hermitage of Bharadvāja for Citrakūṭa, as already told by Bharadvāja, the three see a banyan tree (Nyagrodha). To this tree, Sītā bows down with a wish that the vow of her husband (of fourteen years of exile) be fulfilled. But there is no indication of Sītā asking for the immortality of her husband. Then she circumambulates the tree (*Rām.* Ayodhya 55.6-24ff). The mention of the Nyagrodha tree again comes in the *Rām.*, when the thumbkin sages (Vālakhilyas) are said to be hanging down from the branch of the Nyagrodha tree (*ibid.* Araṇya 35.27-32).[54] In the *Mbh.* this same tree is mentioned as Rauhiṇa (fr. the root √*ruh*—'to grow'). When Garuḍa is seen seeking a place to alight taking the elephant and the tortoise in his clutches, the Rauhiṇa tree itself tells Garuḍa to make use of its branch and enjoy the food brought (*Mbh.* Ādi 29.42, 43), and Garuḍa breaks the branch only to see the thumbkin sages Vālakhilyas—hanging from it (*ibid.* Ādi 30.1-3).

By the time we come to the Purāṇas, we see that the same tree Nyagrodha or Rauhiṇa—the Indian Fig.-tree—(*Ficus indica*)—banyan tree—gets the name 'Vaṭa', which is with some exceptions, unfailingly used by the Purāṇas, to denote a banyan tree, which they hold in high reverence. There are mentioned several deities (gods and goddesses), which are believed to stay at the root or the foot of the banyan tree *viz.* the goddess Caṇḍī (*Brahmavaivarta P.* Śrīkṛṣṇakhaṇḍa 16.177); the goddess Mātaṅgī (*Sk.P.* III i.e. Brāhma 2.18.59); at the Jagannātha region, the goddess Maṅgalā and at the west of the tree, Vimalā (*ibid.* II i.e. Vaiṣṇava 2.4.42); the goddess Mahāsatī (*Agni P.* 194.5); Śiva with Kālī and the son Gaṇeśa (*Śiva P.* Yuddhakhaṇḍa 35.2; 36.18). Even the gods Śiva and Viṣṇu are said to be staying in the tree—the 'Akṣaya' (non-decaying') Vaṭa (banyan tree).[55] It is interesting to see a detail with regards to the 'Akṣaya' Vaṭa, which points out how the Vaṭa tree (formerly known as Nyagrodha or Rauhiṇa)—'a new arrival'(?) is not entirely new, but carries with it the memory of the old Vedic sacrificial tradition. It is said by the *Brahma P.* (161.66) that after performing the sacrifice, god Brahmā released the various things used therein. The sacrificial post (*yūpa*) was placed by him to the north of the Vindhya at the river Gaṇgā, which came to be named 'Akṣaya'. The *arthavāda* account is for glorifying the Vaṭa tree—here the Akṣaya Vaṭa.

We have noted above that gods and goddesses are believed to stay at the root or the foot of the Vaṭa tree. But the tree is believed to have importance on another account and it is to bless a person with the gain of a son. The sage Gālava propitiated the sun-god at the Vaṭa tree for getting a son. When Gālava got a son, he named him Vaṭeśvara, as the son was given to him by the sun staying at the Vaṭa tree (*Agni P.* 115.71). In popular faith, the banyan tree together with its sister-tree Peepal are worshipped by women for progeny. Generally snake-worship is associated with these two trees. Snakes carved in stones (called *nāgakals*) are placed at the foot of these trees and such stones generally face the sun.[56] The spirit of the banyan tree is called 'Nāga-rājā, and his soldiers are the Nāgas.[57] Dange says that it is difficult to say exactly whether the worship of this tree for this purpose was not a gift of the non-Aryans. But this tree appears very prominently in some very famous tales about the serpents.[58]

From the medicinal point of view also the banyan tree has been taken to be important. The *Agni P.* states that a woman desirous of son should drink milk in which the root of the Śrīvṛkṣa (=Bilva tree) and a sprout of the Vaṭa tree is placed and she should also drink the juice of these two trees through her nose (*Agni P.* 302.19-20). The Purāṇas display thorough knowledge of the medicinal properties of the trees and plants, and their produce-Sahadevā, Apāmārga, Dūrvā, corn sprouts, castor seeds, citron seeds, turmeric, Triphalā etc. [59] The banyan tree has been of use from the medicinal point of view also.[60] Steeped in faith and tradition as a giver of progeny and life and useful for medicines, a separate vow (*vrata*) got evolved for the Vaṭa tree and the vow got glorified by the tale of

Sāvitrī, whose name figures with the name Vaṭa, finally making it Vaṭasāvitrīvrata, the most important vow (*vrata*) for a married lady in India.

Here we take into consideration a somewhat not much known but a unique vow (*vrata*) and it is the Kokilāvrata, which lays down the worship of a cuckoo, as stated in the *Bhaviṣya P.* and the *Sk.P.* The *Sk.P.* supports the vow by a story given in its Kanakādrikhaṇḍa. It is also published under the title *Kokilāvratamāhātmya*[61], which originally forms part of the Kanakādrikhaṇḍa of the *Sk.P.* and lays down the worship of a 'cuckoo-goddess', explaining its importance.

It is in the Purāṇas that we find the concept of 'Mother-goddess' in various forms. The concept was not unknown to the Vedic period, in which we find the mention of Varuṇānī, Indrāṇī etc. ('the wife of Varuṇa', 'the wife of Indra'). But the goddesses, which are mentioned by a general term *mātaraḥ* date from the Puranic times.[62] All these (coming under a common title 'Mother-goddess') are worshipped for general weal and are established at various quarters of a habitat.[63] As there are several goddesses, there could be modes of worship and vows (*vratas*) in their respect, the information about which however is scanty or at times not found.

And now to turn to the vow which centres round a female cuckoo, regarded as a goddess. The information of this vow (Kokilāvrata) is given in detail in the *Bhaviṣya P.* Though this Purāṇa at one place (Uttara 11.8) states *'puruṣo nārī vā'* (man or woman), from the reference preceding to this (*ibid.* 7), it is clear that the vow is to be undertaken by a married woman. The woman who wants to follow the vow, has to make a *śaṅkalpa* (mental resolve) before a *brāhmaṇa* on the eve of the full-moon day in the Āṣāḍha month, in the evening, that she will follow this vow for a month (i.e. upto the full-moon day in the Śrāvaṇa month). The vow compels the woman to sleep on the floor and observe celibacy. During the first eight days, she has to take bath going to a river, well or a lake. Meditating on the sun, respectfully remembering the ancestors, bowing down to the elderly persons, she has to worship the image of a cuckoo with green foliage, Dūrvas (*Panicum dactylon*), sesame and rice grains etc., for blessedness in married life, prosperity and progeny (*ibid.*14-15). Having performed this worship outside, she would then enter the house. At the end of the vow, observing it in the above manner for a month, as a mark of completion (*udyāpana*), an image of cuckoo is to be offered to a *brāhmaṇa.* The image is made of sesame and flour, with golden wings, and rubies fixed for the eyes of the image (*ibid.* 16). *Nirṇayasindhu*, the work of Kamalākarabhaṭṭa has given some information about this vow based on Hemādri's work *Caturvargacintāmaṇi* and the *Bhaviṣya P.* There also the important features of the vow are stated as—observing celibacy, sleeping on the floor, *nakta* for the whole month taking meals only at the night time (and not at all in the day-time) and compassion for the creatures.[64] Kane has mentioned this *vrata* in the list of the *vratas* given by him. Together with the features constituting the vow and the instructions for making the image of a cuckoo, Kane gives some more information from the work *Vratārka* (folios 329-34). The work states that in the Gurjar country (i.e. modern Gujarat State in India) the *vrata* is enjoined in the Aṣāḍha month, when it comes as the intercalary i.e. thirteenth month, thus when there are two Āṣāḍha months—one regular called *nija* and the other additional called *adhika*. Kane has questioned the authenticity of this, as there is not given the name of any authoritative work by the *Vratārka*. The image of cuckoo to be given to the *brāhmaṇa*, having first worshipped the image with sixteen *upacāras* (sixteen ways of doing homage to a deity), should be very costly according to the *Vratārka.*[65]

The composition *Kokilāvratamāhātmya*, which we have already referred to, gives a tale which serves as an *arthavāda* for the *vrata.* The mythical tale runs as follows—when Satī (Gaurī) married Śiva, it was against the wishes of her father Dakṣa Prajāpati. In the sacrifice of Dakṣa Prajāpati, Śiva was not invited. But Satī thought of going to her father's place even though Śiva was unwilling. Satī went there only to hear condemnation of her husband (Śiva) in strong words from Dakṣa Prajāpati. As a person who hears and a person who utters bad words abut Śiva—both are regarded as sinners, Satī immolated herself in the sacrificial fire. And then the destruction of Dakṣa's sacrifice by Śiva at the hands of Vīrabhadra and the Śivagaṇas—attendants of Śiva (*Kokilāvratamāhātmya* chap. 8). The real reason for this destruction was Satī's going to her father's place, for Śiva had objected to it. When Dakṣa Prajāpati appealed to Śiva for fogiveness, Śiva felt sorry for the destruction of the sacrifice. And Satī (Gaurī) got a curse to become a 'cuckoo' for thousand years of gods i.e. innumerable years of humans. Those who make obstacles in penance, sacrifice and gift (*dāna*) are born in the lowest strata i.e. *tiryagyoni* (beasts, birds, insects etc.) for thousand years (*ibid.* 8.47-48). When god Brahmā intervened, Śiva told that Satī's curse would come to an end after gods' thousand years (*ibid.* 9.2-14).

It is very clear that together with various goddesses from the categories of beasts, birds, trees, etc., the bird 'cuckoo' was regarded as a form of Gaurī (Pārvatī) and the Puranic period thought of a vow in this respect. The *Kokilāvratamāhātmya* from the *Sk.P.* gives a detailed information about the vow. In a year in which there occur two Āṣāḍha months—one, as the intercalary month, commonly known as *adhika māsa* and the other, the regular month known as *nija māsa*—after the end of the *adhika* Aṣāḍha month, the vow starts from the full-moon day of the *nija* i.e. regular Āṣāḍha month and spreads over upto the full-moon day of the Śrāvaṇa month. The other details *viz.* the image of a cuckoo, its worship etc. are the same (*Kokilā*.9.18-25). The mantra, which indicates that originally the image of the cuckoo must have been made of sesame,[66] points out that the cuckoo-goddess (a form of Gaurī—the Mother-goddess) is prayed for blessedness in married life, wealth and issues, especially male issues (*ibid.* 9.25). In the *Bhaviṣya P.*, which also gives this vow, practically the same *mantra* occurs (Uttara.11.14). The *Kokilāvratamāhātmya* describes the gains acquired by Arundhatī, Rukmiṇī and Damayantī, by observing this vow (*ibid.* chaps. 17-28).

The sweet notes of (male) cuckoo are heard right from the advent of the spring time (in Caitra and Vaiśākha months i.e. April & May roughly). But even upto Āṣāḍha (roughly June and July) the notes of cuckoo are heard though not regularly. The living tradition in India is that a woman who observes this vow (for a month) should hear the note of the cuckoo's sound at least once in the whole day and then she can end her fast and take food at the night time (*nakta*—taking food only at the night time). But if she does not hear a cuckoo's note in the whole of the day her fast continues upto the next night.[67] The word *nakta* is explained above as it is generally understood, as per the Dictionary meaning. But it has different connotations also.[68] Another idea about this vow in the living tradition of India is that the vow comes nearly after (each) eighteen years. It seems reasonable for the year in which there occur two Āṣāḍha months (one *adhika* and another *nija*) is a rare phenomenon.

The goddess of this rare phenomenon is cuckoo. Sweet notes, advent in the spring season, doe-musk dark colour, but actually rarely seen in the open, and the sudden exit in the early phase of the rainy season—all these of a cuckoo are as attractive as they are difficult to understand. The tale in the *Kokilāvratamāhātmya* of the *Sk.P.* brings in the curse given by Śiva to Satī (or Gaurī) to become a cuckoo for thousand years. In fact, curse, reducing its severity by amending it and boon are all mythological strategies and are used as *arthavāda* to justify the matter in hand. Thus cuckoo could make a place for herself in the Puranic goddesses and in propitiating the Kokilā-goddess (Devī), the idea is to have the seasons at the regular time so as to bless all with happiness, prosperity and progeny. The work *Nirṇayasindhu* states that the vow be observed every year and it is a welcome idea.

The class of the bird cuckoo (*'kokila'*) (CUCULIFORMES) is spread all the world over. In India it is called *'kokila'* (koel), and the scientific name is *Eudynamys scolopacea*. Really speaking, it is the male bird, which gives the sweet notes at the breeding period and not the female bird. But in the tradition, as the bird has been taken as a 'goddess', it enjoys unrivalled importance in the vow (*vrata*).

C. UPAVĀSA (FAST)

We have seen some noteworthy *vratas* from the Purāṇas. Most of the *vratas* (vows) are accompanied by the observance of fast, some *vratas* not enjoining the fast. On the other hand, observing fast implies some kind of vow, which promises some gain, *arthavāda* occurring there supporting it. Here are some instances.

Ekādaśīvrata is continued even in the modern era. The *Agni P.* says that this *vrata* gives the material as well as the spiritual gains and is in the form of simple mode of fasting for the whole day and the worship of Viṣṇu, the *arthavāda* assuring a successful stay in Viṣṇuloka (*Agni P.* 187.9). Ekādaśīvrata is to be observed on the eleventh day in the bright half of the month. The Akṣatavrata was to be performed with a fast on the third day in the bright half of the Vaiśākha month by worshipping Viṣṇu with whole (*akṣata* i.e. not broken) unhusked rice grains and it was to procure for the person the fruit of performing a Rājasūya sacrifice (*Matsya P.* 65.2, 4, 6). The seventh day in the bright half of the Māgha month was considered holy. (It is still the belief and the day is called 'Rathasaptamī' day). On the preceding two days, the person was to have his meal once a day and on the seventh day (the one noted above), he was to observe fast, followed by the eighth day, when he was to feed the *brāhmaṇas*, by which he could secure the fruit of performing the Rājasūya or Aśvamedha sacrifice (*Bhaviṣya P.* I.197.1, 3, 6, 10).

It has to be pointed out here that observing fast irrespective of vow (*vrata*) is enjoined by the *Mbh.* and it is for expiation, much on the lines of the Dharmaśāstra.[69] Thus a king, who connives at his duty of punishing the offender, has to observe fast for one night and the priest (not giving the king proper advice) should observe fast for three nights. A person who, out of grief, tries to commit suicide by resorting to weapons, should observe fast for three nights (*Mbh.* Śānti 36.17-18). Hence a distinction has to be made between observing a fast as a part of any vow (*vrata*) and that in the form of expiation, our idea being to think of fast as accompanying a vow.

D. *TĪRTHAYĀTRĀ* (VISITING HOLY PLACES)

We have already noted that the concept of going to a holy place (*tīrtha*) evolved in the times of the *Mbh.* and the Purāṇas. In the *Purāṇas*, such holy places are invariably on the banks of the rivers, the latter enhancing the sacredness of the *tīrthas*.

The Vaṇa *parvan* of the *Mbh.* deals with the topic of *tīrthābhigamana* (visiting a holy place) exhaustively (chaps. 82-95), and at all places where the *tīrthas* are mentioned, the device of *arthavāda* is resorted to glorify the greatness of these *tīrthas*. Here are some examples. It is said that the merit (*puṇya*) acquired by going to a *tīrtha* excels even that of the sacrifices (*Mbh.* Vana 82.17). A person is reckoned as wretched, if he does not observe fast for three days, does not visit holy places and does not give gold and cows as *dakṣiṇās* (*ibid.* 18). Visiting a holy place excels the sacrifices like Agniṣṭoma etc. in merit, where fabulous *dakṣiṇās* are given (*ibid.* 19). The Puṣkaratīrtha is spoken of highly. A person who makes an *abhiṣeka* here (i.e. the ritual of offering water), having worshipped ancestors and gods, will get the merit ten times more than that of (performing) the Aśvamedha sacrifice (*ibid.* 20-39). Even going to Puṣkara is difficult and to practise penance there, giving gifts (*dāna*) and a stay there is still difficult (*ibid.* 39). The Prabhāsa *tīrtha* is spoken of as always having Agni (the deity) established there. A person taking bath there, being pure and having his mind controlled (i.e. not carried away by any allurements) acquires the merit of the Agniṣṭoma and Atirātra sacrifices (*ibid.* 58-60). By going to the river Vitastā, a person giving offerings to the ancestors, attains the fruit of the Vājapeya sacrifice (*ibid.* 89). In the Kashmir country itself, there is a place (shrine?) dedicated to (or having the image of) the Takṣaka Nāga, which is called 'Vitasta' and which releases a person from all sins. By taking bath there (the *tīrtha* being on the bank of the river), a person gets the fruit of Vājapeya sacrifice (*ibid.* 90-91). In the region of Kurukṣetra, when he goes to 'Sarpadevī' (having the image of the Serpent-goddess?)[70], which is the excellent holy place (*tīrtha*) of the Nāgas, he acquires the fruit of the Agniṣṭoma sacrifice (*ibid.* Vana 83.14-15). These two references are to be particularly noted, for they clearly point out that the process of acculturation of the Nāga-tribes together with their deities, in the Vedic-brahmanical Aryan fold, had been completed by the time of the *Mbh.* The places of the Nāga deities had become the *tīrthas* (holy places) and even a visit to these places could procure for a person the fruit of the Vedic sacrifices such as Vājapeya and Agniṣṭoma—a fine amalgamation of non-Vedic and Vedic.

We now take into consideration the Saptasārasvata *tīrtha* again from the Kurukṣetra region, in which context we have a mythical account by way of *arthavāda*. It runs as follows. There was a sage by name Maṅkaṇaka, who was famous in the world for being a *siddha* (i.e. a person, who had mastered all the *siddhis*—supernatural or yogic powers). Once this sage pierced his hand with the tip of a Kuśa (grass) blade and there oozed out from his hand the juice of (green) vegetables. Seeing this, the sage, becoming overjoyous began dancing with ecstacy. Being enamoured of his lustre, the movable and the immovable (in this world) started dancing. All the gods-Brahmā and others—and the sages, then approached Mahādeva and requested him to put a stop to the sage's dancing. Mahādeva came to the sage Maṅkaṇaka, when the latter told the god how he was overwhelmed with joy, seeing the juice of vegetables oozing out from his hand. Mahādeva in order to teach him, struck his own thumb with the tip of his finger and from that wound came out white ashes. The sage was ashamed of his pride and behaviour, and prostrated before the god praising him in many words. He requested Mahādeva that his penance (i.e. its merit) should not be destroyed (due to his behaviour). Mahādeva assured the sage that he would reside with the sage in that hermitage, and whosoever taking bath in the Saptasārasvata *tīrtha* offered worship to Mahādeva, for him nothing would be unattainable in this world and the other world (*ibid.* Vana 83.115-134). Even the hermitage of the sage Mataṅga is eulogised as putting an end to the troubles (toils) and grief of a person who enters it. Moreover, the person gets the fruit of the Gavāmayana sacrifice (*ibid.* Vana 84.101-102).

Thus the *Mbh.* in its Vana *parvan* (which is also called Tīrthayātrāparva—the *parvan* of the pilgrimage) names innumerable holy places, giving details about them, though many times scanty. The concept of a *tīrtha* for the *Mbh.* is very exhaustive. Rivers, mountains, and holy resorts (or hermitages) are all the *tīrthas* (*Mbh.* Vana 87.27 cd; 28 cd). Visit to any of these *tīrthas* and a bath there, bestow on a person the merit of a Vedic sacrifice. Together with the *tīrthas*, the Vedic sacrifice *viz.* Aśvamedha=Vājimedha, Vājapeya, Rājasūya, Gavāmayana, Agniṣṭoma, Daśa-aśvamedha (ten Aśvamedhas), and Gosahasraphala i.e. the gift of thousand cows, are mentioned for endless times. This shows that the change needed for the social structure of those times was introduced by the *Mbh.*, by making the *dharma* (code of conduct) prone to people, however not forgetting to catch the finger of the old Vedic sacrificial *dharma*, which though not actually performed showered its 'merit' (*puṇya*) on any devout pilgrim. Hence, it is but natural for the Purāṇas to toe the line of the *Mbh.* in later times.

Here we come to the Puranic thought on pilgrimage—visiting the holy places (*tīrthas*). Dange has dealt with this topic exhaustively.[71] In fact every Purāṇa gives a long list of holy places.[72] As the aim of the Purāṇas was to simplify *dharma* for all classes in the society, as we have noted earlier, visit to holy places (*tīrthayātrā*) was the easiest way of gaining 'merit' (*puṇya*) or even worldly rewards, which were promised by the toil-some Vedic sacrifice, those too also reserved for certain classes in the society.

The holy places are generally situated on the banks of the rivers. The important characteristics to be noted are, as Dange has pointed out.[73]

(i) The *tīrthas* are, as *Vāmana P.* (7.37) says, on the earth (Naimiṣa), in heaven (Puṣkara) and in the nether world (Cakratīrtha). Puṣkara and Cakratīrtha are mentioned elsewhere. But to place these two in the heaven and the nether world resp. is an *arthavāda* to elevate the two, which are really on the earth.

(ii) Apart from the gods of the Vedic-brahmanical tradition, there are some unusual names of gods, which are associated with the *tīrthas*. e.g. holy place—'Daṇḍimuṇḍi', where the goddess is Daṇḍikā and the god is Muṇḍī, which are certainly the local divinities; another e.g. 'Bhārabhūti'—the holy place, where Bhāra is the god and Bhūti is the goddess. The *Sk.P.* gives a long list of such deities (I.3.2.80 ff). These local deities have given, in popular belief, holiness to the places, where these are worshipped.

(iii) Influence of the cult of Mother-goddess and also of the cult of Yoginīs can be marked on *tīrthas*. e.g. in the Saurāṣṭra region, at Hāṭakeśvara, sixty-eight *tīrthas* of the mothers, influenced by the Yoginī-cult (*Sk.P.* VI.108.27ff).

(iv) Holy places clustered at one place i.e. the river Gautamī or Godāvarī, are dealt with in details by the Brahma P. Such *tīrthas* are there on the banks of the rivers Gaṅgā and Narmadā.

(v) Holy places are named after qualities and virtues. Thus starting from Prayāga, we have Satyatīrtha ('Truth'—*tīrtha*), Kṣamātīrtha ('Forbearance'....), Dānatīrtha ('Gifts'.....), Dhṛtitīrtha ('Courage'......). The *Sk.P.* is eloquent about these (IV.6.30ff).

(vi) Sun and Śiva are the two important deities associated with the *tīrthas.*

(vii) Taking bath at the holy place and worship of the god or goddess there, are taken to be very important.

The mythical account figuring as *arthavāda* supports the holiness of the place, thus justifying its claim to be a *tīrtha,* and gives assurance of the reward, which awaits the person, visiting that *tīrtha* and taking a bath there.

Innumerable are the *tīrthas* spoken of by the Purāṇas and so are the *arthavādas* convincing the listners of their greatness. Here we take only few examples from the Puranic lore.

First we take a note of Gayā, which as a holy place (*tīrtha*), has assumed a place of prime importance in the Indian tradition. Kane has dealt with this topic exhaustively.[74] The *Mbh.* gives information about it in two chapters (Vana 84.82-103; 95.9-29). In the Anuśāsanaparvan of the *Mbh.*, we get additional information (Anu. 25.42) about Gayā, which has the three sacred spots *viz. Aśmapṛṣṭha, Niravinda and Krauñcapadī. The Agni P.* (chaps. 114-116) and the *Vāyu P.* (chaps. 105-112) also contain information about these.

It is said that in Śvetavārāhakalpa, Gaya performed a sacrifice and the place Gayā was named after him (*Vāyu P.* 105.7-8; *Agni P.* 114.41). *Vāyu P.* (chap. 106) narrates the story of Gayāsura at great length. To give it in short—we have here the austere penance of the *asura* Gaya; Viṣṇu on the request of all gods, approaching him and granting him the boon asked for; Brahmā on the word of Viṣṇu requesting Gayāsura to give his pure body for the purpose of a sacrifice, to which Gayāsura agreeing; Brahmā performing a sacrifice on Gayāsura's body; Gayāsura's body not being stable moving on; then Viṣṇu with several gods sitting on it and thus making the body of the *asura* very stable. As Gayāsura was made stable by the first Gadā (mace) wielded by Hari, the latter was called Ādigadādhara. Gayāsura asked a boon that the sacred spot (where all this took place) be known by his name; and all the *tīrthas* be centred in the midst of Gayā; the gods should remain there in manifest forms and also unmanifest forms; to whomsoever *śrāddha* with *piṇḍas* would be offered he would go to the world of Brahmā and all the grave sins (*mahāpātakas*) be destroyed at once. The gods granted him the boon. *Vāyu P.* in the next chapter (i.e. chap. 107) deals with the tale of the stone-slab (*śilā*) that was placed on the head of Gayāsura for making it stable. Offering barley-flour balls and rice-balls to the manes at Gayā, is enjoined. The *Agni P.* narrates the story of Viśāla who performed funeral rites at Gayā and could see his (dead) father, grandfather and great grandfather and could know from them that due to his offering of *piṇḍas* to them, they were released from hell and were going across the sky to heaven (*Agni P.* 115.54-59; *Garuḍa P.* I.84.36 f; *Varāh P.* 7.13-25). Gayā is known as Pitṛ-tīrtha (*Matsya P.* 22.4-6).

In the early phase of research, the story of Gayāsura was interpreted variously. Kane's opinion is convincing, to some extent. He says that the legend of Gayāsura is a *post facto* attempt to account for the sanctity of Gayā and its surrounding area[75] which had become a *pitṛ-tīrtha* centuries before Christ. It is very clear that the story of Gayāsura is purely an *arthavāda* to convince the people of the importance of Gayā—an age-old method followed by the ancient texts to glorify a particular matter in hand. The *arthavāda* in the form of the mythical account of Gayāsura is validatory (justificatory) in nature, for it validates the importance of the place Gayā as a sacred place, especially for the *pitṛ-karma*, which involves offering to the ancestors. This ritual at the Gayā no doubt precedes the story of the *asura* Gaya. The story most probably evolved from the floating mass of oral literature, stored by the Sūta tradition and got entry in the Purāṇas Vāyu, Agni etc. through the *Mbh.* In the *Mbh.* there is only a small account of the sacrifice performed by Gaya, in which he gave fabulous *dakṣiṇās* (Vana 95.9-29 for the account of Gaya and his sacrifice). It is said that people praise his generousness seen in his sacrifice through *gāthās* (*ibid.* 95.24), the generousness in the form of *annadāna*—feeding people. Gaya is here a pious king (*rājarṣi*), who gave the best of the *dānas* i.e. food to people. From this slender thread, stored in the *gāthās* ('an oral tradition') and made use of by the *Mbh.* in the context of *Tīrthayātrā* (pilgrimage) and the holy places thereof, the Purāṇas such as Vāyu and Agni, especially Vāyu, have woven the story of the great *asura* Gaya, which displays his austere penance, his readiness to help the gods by giving his large body for being a seat of sacrifice, nevertheless his ambition to make his name immortal, permanently sticking to that sacred spot, to change that spot into a holy place. Thus it is the Purāṇas, which have made use of the device of *arthavāda* and through the story of Gayāsura have tried to imbibe on the minds of the listeners (for in the initial stage, it was the Paurāṇika who spread the message of the Purāṇa by telling it orally) the importance of the holy place Gayā.

We have noted the holy places enshrining Nāga-worship, as seen from the *Mbh.* The *Sk.P.* is replete with the accounts of the Nāga-tīrthas.[76] Here we take an account, in which is seen the perfect assimilation of the Nāga-tribes in the Vedic-brahmanical Aryan fold. The account is of the Nāga-tīrtha in the region of Hāṭakeśvara (the region of Saurāṣṭra in the Gujarat State in India) and it runs as follows. Once Brahmā was practising penance. A child, who was his grandson came there and playfully threw a water-snake in the sacrificial chamber. The serpent coiled itself around the sage Bhṛgu, who sat motionless. Bhṛgu's son Cyavana, afraid of the danger to his father, cursed the child (Brahmā's grandson) to become a serpent. The child pleaded for his innocent fun, saying that it was only a water-snake. The serpent left Bhṛgu, but the child became a serpent and requested Bhṛgu to save him. Bhṛgu asked Cyavana to take the curse back, but he simply refused. Brahmā intervened and consoled his grandson (i.e. the child) that even in that state of serpenthood, he would become the progenitor of the ninth dynasty of the Nāgas. He asked the grandson to go and stay at the holy water-place in Hāṭakeśvara and foretold that he would marry the daughter of Nāga Karkoṭaka, who would give birth to the ninth family of the Nāgas, which will be worshipped by all on the Nāgapañcamī day (*Sk.P.* VI. chap 183). The place where the grandson of Brahmā stayed was later on called Nāga-tīrtha.

The mythical account is unique for it starts from the god Brahmā from the Vedic-brahmanical Hindu tradition with a reference to the sacrificial chamber. There are the two sages—father and the son—again from the same fold. And the grandson of Brahmā (though at that time a child), taking a Nāga girl as wife and through her becoming the progenitor of the ninth family of the Nāgas! With all these details, the mythical account is so tailored as to perfectly serve as an *arthavāda* to glorify the Nāga-tīrtha at Hāṭakeśvara. But the *arthavāda* is important on other accounts. It traces the origin of the ninth Nāga-family to an Aryan father. It points out the Aryan and Nāga marriage—and inter-racial marriage! However this is not unheard of, for such marriages are seen taking place right in the time of the *Mbh.*[77] The important note from the *arthavāda* is of the complete acculturation of the Nāga-tribes in the Vedic-brahmanical Aryan fold. The importance of the Nāga-tīrtha and the mention of the origin of the ninth Nāga-family are again the points to be considered. We have already noted in the chapter on Tribes, Clans etc. the nine Nāga families. The intervention of Brahmā and his prediction about his grandson's marriage and the son's future status as the one who would start a Nāga-family, as stated in the *arthavāda* have all given an elevated status to the Nāga-tīrtha.

Kapālamocana is a name given to a holy place, which is mentioned as associated with various regions.[78] The mythical account widely known is that of releasing the head (i.e. the skull) of the god Brahmā, which got stuck to the hand of Śiva, when the latter cut it. The place where this happened came to be known as Kapālamocana-tīrtha (*kapāla*—'skull'; *mocana*—'releasing'). The *arthavāda* account explaining the name 'Kapālamocana' occurs in the *Vāmana P.* (3.1-51, for the name 'Kapālamocana' *ibid.* v.51). In the *Śiva P.* we see Śiva in the form of Bhairava, to whose hand the sin of Brahmahatyā was sticking in the form of god Brahmā's skull. When Bhairava went to the city of salvation, Varaṇasī, *brahmahatyā* (the sin of killing a *brāhmaṇa*, here Brahmā) felt aggrieved and entered the nether world. The skull of Brahmā suddenly fell on the ground from the hand of Bhairava and the holy place became the Kapālamocana-tīrtha (*Śiva P.* III i.e. Śatarudra-saṁhitā 9.54-56). The *Śiva P.* here eulogises the holy place, as the remover of evil, sin especially that of *brahmahatyā* (*ibid.* 59-61). Here stands the god Bhairava, ready to devour the series of sins of the devotees (*ibid.* 62).

The Purāṇas give various accounts as regards the heads of Brahmā, which formerly are five, out of which Rudra-Siva cuts one. At one place the fifth head of Brahmā is said to be the Ukārāgni (the fire in the form of the letter *U*). At another place it is said to be that of a tiger, in yet another account that of a horse.[79] The *Śiva P.* says that the fifth head of Brahmā was cut by Bhairava (a form of Śiva), as with that head Brahmā blamed Śiva (*Śiva P.* III.8. 7-53). The *Brahma P.* relates the account of the donkey-head of Brahmā (*Brahma P.* 113.3-23). All these accounts verge on one uniform note and it is of Śiva cutting the fifth head of Brahmā and incurring the sin of *brahmahatyā* and in the mythical account the fifth head (i.e. skull) sticking to the hand of Śiva. And so comes the Kapālamocana-tīrtha in picture.

The myth of Śiva or Bhairava cutting the head of Brahmā goes back to the Vedic source, where Prajāpati—the prototype of Brahmā—is shot with an arrow by Rudra, when the former (i.e. Prajāpati) lustily runs after his daughter. Prajāpati takes the form of a deer and his daughter that of a doe.[80] The strife between Rudra (Śiva) and Prajāpati (Brahmā) goes back to the Vedic texts, giving rise to one more myth and it is of *prāśitra*.[81] The myth of Prajāpati and Rudra and their enmity is seen in the *Śiva P.*, when after the self-immolation of Satī in the sacrifice of her father Dakṣa Prajāpati, Vīrabhadra (the chief of the Śivagaṇas) beheads the sacrifice, when it is fleeing up the sky in the form of a deer (*Śiva P.* II i.e. Rudrasaṁhitā (37. 45-46) and striking Dakṣa's head with sword, throws it into the fire-pit (*ibid.* 58-61).

Thus cutting the head of Brahmā by Śiva is only an old myth in new form (in having the names changed). But the Purāṇas added to it the detail of the sin of *brahmahatyā* incurred by Śiva, in the form of the skull of Brahmā sticking to Śiva's hand and Śiva on the run to find out a place for the release of it. And here is the Kapālamocana-tīrtha, justifying its claim to be a *tīrtha* (holy place), nevertheless giving an ethical note to desist from the sin of *brahmahatyā*.

Now we come to a famous region and it is of Kāśī. In fact the *Sk.P.* devotes one whole book (IV, i.e. Kāśīkhaṇḍa), eulogising the various places in this region. The *Śiva P.* while praising Kāśī through etymology says that it is called 'Kāśī' because it pulls out i.e. destroys our actions (*Śiva P.* Koṭi-rudrasaṁhitā 22.24). The *Śiva P.* in the next chapter (Koṭirudrasaṁhitā 23.1-56) narrates the greatness of the two—Varāṇaśī and Viśveśvara—the two 'Avimuktas'. Here we find the simplifying of the religious code in that there is required neither perfect knowledge, nor devotion, nor holy rites, nor charitable gifts, nor meditation, nor repeatedly taking god's names, nor adoration, nor noble nativity, but only stay here at the moment of death that gives the salvation to any living being, human or non-human i.e. the sweat-born—lice, bugs etc.; the egg-born—birds; germinating ones—plants, trees and the embryo-born—mammals (*ibid.* 17-20). People of all castes, of all stages of life, of all ages, of any gender (especially women), if they die here attain salvation (*ibid.* 14-16). The place (Kāśī or Vārāṇasī) is also called 'Avimukta' ('not left off') as it was not 'left' by Śiva even at the doom (*Sk.P.* IV.26.27; also *Vāyu P.* Uttarakhaṇḍa 30.27-53, where through a mythical account we note that after the destruction of Vārāṇasī, Śiva made the place Avimukta, his permanent abode).

Hence, it is but reasonable that various places associated with Kāśī came to be regarded as auspicious. Many of these are situated on the bank of the river Gaṅgā and are called by the term *ghāṭa*, where steps are made to enter the stream of the river. We take into account two such famous *ghāṭas* (sacred places), where the *arthavāda* accounts justify their names. The first one we take for information is the Maṇikarṇikā. It is said that when everywhere there was darkness, Śiva created two things—his *māyā* (his 'magic') and the place Avimukta (i.e. Kāśī). Then he desired to produce somebody else. So he produced Mahāviṣṇu, who dug up the earth here with his disc (*cakra*), making a long narrow trench there. Mahāviṣṇu filled it with his own perspiration, with that (liquid) making the place 'Cakrapuṣkariṇī' (fountain, here rivulet, made by the disc). On its bank Mahāviṣṇu practised penance for a thousand years. On seeing this, Śiva became so joyous that in appreciation of it, Śiva shook his head again and again. And down fell, in this act, one of the earrings of Śiva decked with jewels, to make the place 'Maṇikarṇikā' by name—'having an earring set with jewels'. On Viṣṇu's words the place also came to be called Muktikeśvara, as the earring was having the pearls (*muktās*). Again as the highest light shines here, so the name of the place is 'Kaśī' (*Sk.P.* IV i.e. Kāśīkhaṇḍa chap. 26).

The account of Maṇikarṇikā occurs also in the *Śiva P.* (Koṭirudrasaṁhitā 22.9-16). At the behest of Śiva, Viṣṇu, with a desire for creation (of the world) performed penance for a long time, at the beautiful city (of Kāśī) extending to five *krośas*, created and established by Śiva as a place of penance for Viṣṇu. Due to his exertion in performing penance, various currents of (perspiration) water began to flow from Viṣṇu's body to pervade the whole void. Viṣṇu wonder-struck at this sight, shook his head and a jewel fell in front from the ear-ornament of the lord Viṣṇu, to give the name 'Maṇikarṇikā' to that holy place where this happened. The holy place began to float on water. Viṣṇu (the Puruṣa) slept there itself along with his consort Prakṛti, and at the behest of Śiva, Brahmā was born of Viṣṇu's navel lotus. At the behest of lord Śiva, from Brahmā evolved a wonderful creation (*ibid.* 17).

These two mythical accounts coming as *arthavāda* in the two Purāṇas are given mainly to explain the name 'Maṇikarṇikā', by which the holy place at Kāśī is known. Both the accounts point out that the name 'Maṇikarnikā' is related to or has sprung from the mention of the falling of one of the ear-ornaments, decked with jewels, belonging either to Śiva (*Sk.P.* account) or to Viṣṇu (*Śiva P.* account). The accounts speak of the coming together of the two prominent gods—Śiva and Viṣṇu—the place of prime importance, however, going to Śiva, as both the Purāṇas (*Sk. P.* and *Śiva P.*) are Śaivite in character. Both the accounts, with the mention of Śiva, in the beginning, alone and then creating Viṣṇu, tread on the lines of the accounts of the Creator-god Prajāpati, who is also seen alone in the beginning but desires to be many. The ritual-texts are replete with such references.[82] Viṣṇu's perspiration giving rise to a river, lake etc. is not an unknown phenomenon to the Purāṇas. The flow of a river is many times associated with body-moisture or body-fluid, may it be blood or tears or such other types of body-fluids.[83] The account in the *Sk.P.* gives 'Muktikeśvara' as the alternate name for 'Maṇikarṇikā' as we have noted. There is a pun on the word *muktikā*—meaning both 'pearl' as well as 'release' (*mokṣa*, from the cycle of birth and death).

It is needless to state that long ago the holy place named 'Maṇikarṇikā' was on the bank of the river Gaṅgā (may be, in the times of the Purāṇas, away from the actual stream of the river) and it is even now a *ghāṭa*—the holy place. And so the *arthavāda* to glorify the place is given by the Purāṇas—*Sk.P.* and *Śiva P.* But the *arthavāda* accounts in the Purāṇas are too simple to have any depth, nevertheless carrying out their role, perfectly well. The question posing before us is—has the *arthavāda* here come from the floating mass of literature, which is generally by oral transmission like a folktale or is it skilfully coined by both the Purāṇas by innovating the detail of the falling of the ear-ornament? We opt for the latter, as the trend in the Purāṇas is to resort to Etymology—a simple but skilful device![84] Thus the name 'Maṇikarṇikā'—(A place) with an earring decked with jewels'—(*maṇi*-'jewel'; *karṇikā* 'earring').

We come to another famous holy spot (on the bank of the Gaṅgā in modern times) in Kāśī and it is Daśāśvamedha. The name is self-eloquent and so is the *arthavāda* that god Brahmā and the King Divodāsa together are said to have performed ten (*daśa*) Horse-sacrifices (Aśvamedha-sacrifices) here (*Sk.P.* IV.52.65-67).

Interestingly we have here two *tīrthas*, which have philosophical touch. The *Sk.P.* mentions one as being at Badarī, Catuḥsrota where four streams meet. The eulogy, in the form of *arthavāda*, states that in these four streams stay the four goals of human life (*puruṣārthas*) *viz.* Dharma, Artha, Kāma and Mokṣa (*Sk.P.* II i.e. Vaiṣṇava 3.7.40-41).

Another such *tīrtha* is Jñānoda, from the *Sk.P.* Kāśīkhaṇḍa. In the ages bygone, while wandering in the whole world, when lord Śiva came to this place in the Kāśī region, he saw that the place was completely devoid of water from any source, either from rivers or from the rains. So he established a *liṅga* there and dug up a *kuṇḍa* (a circular pit, not very deep) and propounded his philosophy. This was the knowledge (*jñāna*), which turned into water (*Sk.P.* IV.33.3-41; especially *ibid.* 32).

Hence the place got the name *'Jñānoda'—Jñāna+uda* ("Water of Knowledge").

These two *tīrthas*—Catuḥsrota and Jñānoda—and the *arthavāda* stated in the context of each of them, are such as to appeal to the minds of persons, who want to visit the holy places not only through religious emotion but also with a proper thought of getting some kind of knowledge.

We have discussed the fourfold *dharma* in the Purāṇas and earlier in the *Mbh.*, in the form of Dāna, Vrata, Upavāsa and Tīrthayātrā. Though these can be traced to the Vedic era, as we have noted in the beginning, their heightened effect is felt only in the Puranic age, obviously helped by the *arthavādas*.

NOTES AND REFERENCES

1. P.V. Kane, "Section I Vratas (Religious Vows) and Utsavas (Religious Festivals)", *HDS,* Vol. V, Pt. I, 2nd ed., BORI, Poona, 1974, pp. 1-462; also see by the same author, "Tīrthayātrā (pilgrimages to holy places)', *HDS*, Vol. IV, 2nd ed., BORI, Poona, 1973, pp. 552-727.
   Sadashiv A. Dange, *Ency. PBP,* for "Vows", Vol. V, pp. 1524-1578; for "Holy Places", Vol. III, pp. 761-867.
2. *RV* I.125. 5-7; I.126.1-5; V.61; V.47.22-25; VII.18.22-25; VIII.5.37-39; VIII.6.46-48; VIII.46.21-24; VIII.68.14-19; X.62.8-11 etc.
3. Śamitṛ (from the root √*śam*—causal—'to make quiet', is the one, who makes the sacrificial victim 'quiet' i.e. kills it by smothering it. See *Śat. Br.* III.8.1.15. The idea in this, most probably, is that by closing the mouth and the nostrils of the animal, the breath of the animal remains inside and then the animal remains as a 'live' victim (*paśu*) to be offered to the gods.
4. P.V. Kane, *HDS*, Vol. V, Pt. I, pp. 1-32.
5. *Ibid.*, p. 22f.
6. Sindhu S. Dange, *Vedic Beliefs and Practices through Arthavāda,* Vol. II, pp. 340-373. [The whole chap. "Sacrificer's Code and his Immortality (!)"].
7. P.V. Kane, *HDS*, Vol. V, Pt. I, p. 31.
8. Sindhu S. Dange, *Vedic Beliefs and Practices through Arthavāda,* Vol. I, pp. 120-140 [the chap. "Water"].

9. P.V. Kane, *HDS*, Vol. V, Pt. I, p. 43.
10. Sadashiv A. Dange, *Hindu Dharma āṇi Tattvajñāna* (Marathi), Shri Lekhan Vachan Bhandar, Pune, 1973, pp. 274-308 (the chapter on "The march of Lokadharma—*Mbh.* and the Purāṇas"); also see 2nd edn., Continental Prakashan, Pune, 2016, pp. 303-341.
11. Śaṅkarācārya takes '*saṁvit*' as *mitrakāryam* i.e. taking it to be a friend's work.
12. See M.L. Wadekar, *Devalasmṛti-Reconstruction and Critical Study*, Vol. I (Introduction and The Reconstructed Text), Koshal Book Depot, Delhi, 1996, pp. 110-31; Vol. II (Critical Study), Koshal Book Depot, 1997, pp. 15f. (for the Reconstructed Text-summary of the topic of "*Dānam*".)
13. Jātaka no. 499. See the Pali text of the Jātakas from V. Fausböll, translated under the general editorship of E.B. Cowell.
14. For the detailed information on *gāthā* and *śloka*, see Sindhu S. Dange, "Songs from Secular Tradition", *Aspects of Speech from Vedic Ritual*, Aryan Books International, New Delhi, 1996, pp. 206-30.
15. P.V. Kane, *HDS*, Vol. II, Pt. II, p. 865 f.
16. See P.V. Kane (ed.), *Vyavahāramayūkha*, BORI, Poona, 1926, p. 91.
17. P.V. Kane, *HDS*, Vol. II, Pt. II, p. 866.
18. Sir J.G. Frazer (1854-1941) was the cultural anthropologist, who was the first to make a scientific study of magic, having to his credit such famous works as *The Golden Bough* (total 12 Vols.; 7 main and out of these some having 2 parts, thus making 12), *Folk-lore in the Old Testament*, Vols. I-III. In fact, *The Golden Bough* has a subtitle—'A Study in Magic and Religion', which is self-eloquent of the standpoint taken by Frazer. Strenski says that Frazer moved between the role of being a 'critic' to one being an outright 'undertaker of religion'.
    See Ivan Strenski, *Thinking About Religion*, p. 139.
19. P.V. Kane, *HDS*, Vol. II, Pt. II, pp. 837-88.
20. Sadashiv A. Dange, *Ency. PBP*, Vol. II, pp. 632-58.
21. Kala Acharya, *Purāṇic Concept of Dāna*, Nag Publishers, Delhi, 1993.
22. Sindhu S. Dange, *Hindu Domestic Rituals—A Critical Glance*, (chap. "Animal-Hides"), pp. 82-87.

23. Sindhu S. Dange, *Vedic Beliefs and Practices through Arthavāda*, Vol. I, pp. 89-93.
24. For the detailed information about the nine cows as well that of *Kāñcana-dhenu* (*dhenu* of gold) and *ratna-dhenu* (*dhenu* of jewels), see Kala Acharya, *op. cit.*, pp. 56-84.
25. *Ibid.*, pp. 90-106.
26. For the etymology of the word *dhenu* given by Yāska, See *Nir.* XI.42—*dhenurdhayatervā dhinotervā* ˇ
27. See *ERE*, Vol. VIII, p. 863 a.
28. Soma in the *RV* is 'growing on mountain' (*RV* X.34-1—*maujavata*); 'residing in the mountain' (*ibid.* IX.46.1; 95.4). The wealth in the mountains is mentioned in the *RV* (I.51.4b).
29. E.W. Hopkins, *Epic Mythology*, Motilal Banarsidass, Delhi, 1986 (Strassburg, 1915), pp. 8-11.
30. Sindhu S. Dange, "The Exploits of Kṛṣṇa as a Cowherd-Boy", *The Bhāgavata Purāṇa—Mytho-social Study*, pp. 179-91.
31. *Viṣṇudharmottara P.* (III. 306.59cd) states that one who gives the gift (*dāna*) of sheep is extolled in the Vahniloka—the region belonging to Agni—in the other world. The female goat is said to be Agni's dear form (*Tait. Sam.* V.1.6.2). Milk of a she-goat is offered in the rite of Agnicayana, for the she-goat is connected with Agni (*ibid.* V. 4.3.2). The tradition of the Śrautasūtras prescribes offering of oblation on the right ear of a she-goat (*Bhār. Ś.S.* IX.4.5), or according to some, in its absence, on the ear of a he-goat (*Āpa. Ś.S.* IX.9.3).
32. For this see, Sadashiv A. Dange, *Ency. PBP*, Vol. II, p. 647f, where a chart is given of the information from the *Matsya P.* chap. 53. However the various gains of giving the gifts of (the manuscripts of) the Puraṇas, are left out by Dange, may be because of being hyperbolic expressions of rewards (of these gifts), having the texture of *arthavāda*.
33. P.V. Kane, *HDS*, Vol. V, Pt. I, p. 28.
34. See Sindhu S. Dange, *Jaina Dharma āṇi Tattvajñana*, (Marathi), Continental Prakashan, Pune, 1980, pp. 121-26.
35. See Sindhu S. Dange, *Bauddha Dharma āṇi Tattvajñāna* (Marathi), Continental Prakashan, Pune, 1980, pp. 75-77.
36. P.V. Kane, *HDS*, Vol. V, Pt. I, p. 43.
37. See Alka Bakre, *Religion in Social Flux* (as seen in the Main Puraṇa-s), Eastern Book Linkers, Delhi, 1998, pp. 217-22.

38. See M. Bloomfield, *The Atharvaveda*, Verlag Von Karl J. Trübner, Strassburg, 1899, p. 78.
39. See for details, J. Gonda, *The Savayajñas* (*Kauśikasūtra* 60-68, Translation, Introduction and Commentary), N.V. Noord—Hollandsche Uitgevers Maatschappu—Amsterdam, 1965, pp. 63-66.
40. M. Bloomfield (ed.), *The Kauśika Sūtra of Atharva Veda*, Motilal Banarsidass, Delhi, 1972 (1st ed. 1889, *JAOS*), pp. 177-78.
41. See Sindhu S. Dange, "Animals and Birds", *Vedic Beliefs and Practices through Arthavāda*, Vol. I, pp. 196-97.
42. See Sāyaṇa on *RV* VI.16.47 d; X.91.14 b. He uses clearly the word *vandhyā* (barren).
43. A.B. Keith, *The Veda of the Black Yajus School entitled Taittiriya Sanhita*, Pt. I, HOS, Vol. 18, Motilal Banarsidass, Delhi, 1967 (1914), Intrn. p. cxxxv.
44. For more details see, Sadashiv A. Dange *Ency. PBP*, Vol. II, pp. 702-03 (under the title "Bhūtamātṛkā").
45. For other examples see Sindhu S. Dange, *The Bhāgavata Purāṇa—Mytho-social Study*, pp. 100-107; also see for exhaustive treatment of this motif of 'supernatural' element in the birth-accounts, Sadashiv A. Dange, "Supranormal Birth", *Myths from the Mahābhārata*, Study in Patterns and Symbols, Vol. 2, Aryan Books International, New Delhi, 2001, pp. 140-228.
46. For details, see Sadashiv A. Dange, *Ency. PBP*, Vol. V, p. 1561.
47. *Ibid.*, p. 1561 f; *ibid.* 1575 f footnotes 52 & 53; where Dange points out how Kane has missed the detail about this *vrata*, relying on the secondary sources. Dange states in the footnotes that though mostly followed by women, the *Brahmavaivarta P.* (Prakṛtikhaṇḍa 23.42), *Bhaviṣya P.* (Uttaraparva 102.67 also 11.8) and the *Sk.P.* (V.1.66.34), also mention a male person following it.
48. P.V. Kane, *HDS*, Vol. V, Pt. I, p. 93.
49. *Ibid.*
50. *Ibid.*
51. On this day, a married lady with her husband living reads out the story (Sāvitrī-ākhyāna) and the other ladies being attentive listen to it with devotion. After the completion of this *ākhyāna*, the ladies offer her (in the form of *dakṣiṇā* or *dāna*) coconut and a costly piece of cloth with turmeric and saffron and also some

rice grains. In the state of Maharashtra (India) this has been the living tradition. This is an honour done to her as she narrates the story of Sāvitrī. For that period at least, she is given the status of the 'Paurāṇika Sūta' of the ancient and medieval times. This practice is personally seen by the author of the present book.

52. Sadashiv A. Dange, "Sāvitrī and the Banyan", *Purāṇa*, Vol. V, No. 2, July 1963, All India Kashiraj Trust, Varanasi, pp. 258-66.
53. The *Ait. Br.* gives the etymology of the word 'Nyagrodha' through *arthavāda*. By offering a sacrifice, the gods went to the heavenly world. At that place of sacrifice, the gods tilted over (*nyubjan*) the cups and these cups became the Nyagrodha trees. The Nyagrodha trees are really 'Nyagrodha' (*nyak-roha*), as they grow downwards (fr. *nyak*-'down', √*ruh*-'to grow'). But as the gods like what is abstruse, they call them Nyagrodha (*Ait. Br.* VII.30=35.4; VII.31=35.5).
54. Garuḍa is said to have killed the Niṣādas by a branch of the Nyagrodha tree (*Rām* Araṇya 35.33).
55. For details, see Sadashiv A. Dange, *Ency. PBP*, Vol. V, pp. 1477-78, under the sub-title "Vaṭa" in "Trees".
56. *ERE*, Vol. II, p. 415.
57. *Ibid.*, p. 417.
58. See note 52 supra. Sadashiv A. Dange, "Sāvitrī and the Banyan", p. 265.
59. See for the respective entries, Sadashiv A. Dange, *Ency. PBP*. Vols. I-V.
60. For the medicinal use of Nyagrodha (Vaṭa), see-*Carakasaṁhitā* of the sage Agniveśa, revised by Caraka and later on by Dṛḍhabala, with the comms. of Cakrapāṇidatta—Āyurvedadīpikā and Jalpakalpataru—annotated by M.M. Gangadhar Kaviratna Kaviraj. ed. by and revised by Narendranath Sengupta and Balaichandra Sengupta, Reprint, Rashtriya Sanskrit Sansthan, 2002. For Vaṭa—Caraka. Sūtra; 27.27 p. 1030; Cikitsā, 21.33, p. 3139; Śārīra; 8.14, p. 2082; 8.20, p. 2092. *Suśrutasaṁhitā* of Suśruta (Part I), ed. with Āyurvedatattva-sandīpikā, Hindi comm. by Ambikadatta Shastri, 7th ed., Chawkhamba Sanskrit Sansthan, Varanasi, 1989.

for Vaṭa—*Suśruta,* Sūtra. 40, p. 148; Cikitsā. 11.7, p. 60; 24.11, p. 104; Uttaratantram, 38.48, 49, p. 144; 40.85, p. 223; 44.30, pp. 292-93.

61. This book (*pothi*) in the form of folios was found at the Library of the Prachya Vidya Abhyasa Samstha, Thane (Maharashtra) and was made accessible to the present author, for which she expresses her gratitude. It is published by Balakrishna Lakshmana Pathak from Bombay (Mumbai) in Saka 1834 (1912 AD).
62. See Sadashiv A. Dange, *Ency. PBP,* Vol. II, pp. 685-732 (for the information about the goddesses mentioned and some of these dealt with in detail).
63. *Ibid.*, p. 689, 692.
64. *Nirṇayasindhu* of Kamalākarabhaṭṭa, Tr. in Marathi by Krishnashastri Navare, Rajesha Prakashan, Pune, no year mentioned, pp. 108-09.
65. P.V. Kane, *HDS*, Vol. V, Pt. I, p. 290.
66. *Kokilāmāhātmya* chap. 9.25. The mantra is—
tiladehe tilasnehe tilavarṇe tilapriye/
saubhāgyam dravyaputrānśca dehi me kokile namaḥ//
Here the word *tila* (sesame) used in the first line points out the importance of sesame in making the image of the cuckoo.
67. This information is given to the present author by her (household) family-priest, who officiates at the concluding part of the vow, when a silver image of cuckoo is given as a *dakṣiṇā* (gift) to a *brāhmaṇa.*
68. P.V. Kane, takes the word *naktam*—'eating only after sunset'. See P.V. Kane, *HDS,* Vol. V, Pt. I, p. 56. Dange points out, referring to *Padma P.* Sṛṣṭi 75.93, that it is 'meals in the late afternoon.' Thus meals are to be taken only 'once' in the whole day.
69. The Dharmaśāstra texts enjoin several vows such as Aghamarṣaṇa, Prājāpatya, Taptakṛcchra, Parāka, Kṛcchra, Atikṛcchra, Sāntapana, Mahāsāntapana, Tulāpuruṣa, Cāndrāyaṇa etc. Some of these involve partial foregoing of meals and some total abstinence of food for the stipulated day or days. And these are for the expitation of various sins. See *Yājñ. Sm.* III.314-26, for various vows, which are undertaken for expiation of sins.

70. A mention of Sarpadevī indicates the worship of the serpent-goddess Manasādevī, the cult of which was accepted later in the Vedic-brahmanical Hindu fold and which we have already dealt with in chapter II on Tribes, and their acculturation to the Vedic-brahmanical Hindu fold.
71. See note 1 supra.
72. See Sadashiv A. Dange, *Ency. PBP*, Vol. III, p. 768 note 1.
73. See *Ibid.*, p. 761 ff.
74. P.V. Kane, *HDS*, Vol. IV, 2nd ed., BORI, Pune, 1973, pp. 643-79.
75. *Ibid.*, p. 659. Mitra....... 'nothing appears more absurd or stupid than the story of Gayāsura; "again the same Rajendralal Mitra"—the story of Gayāsura is an allegory of the vanquishing of Buddhism by Brahmanism;" O' Malley—"the Gayāsura legend represents an amalgamation or compromise of Brahmanism with the popular demonolatory which preceded Brahmanism." These opinions are stated by P.V. Kane, see *ibid.* Kane gives his own opinion that the legend of Gayāsura is a *post facto* attempt of account for the sanctity of Gayā, which had become a famous *pitṛ-tīrtha* centuries before Christ. See *ibid.*, p. 660.
76. See Sadashiv A. Dange, *Ency. PBP*, Vol. III, pp. 822-25.
77. The famous example is of the sage Jaratkāru, born in the family of the *brāhmaṇas* named Yāyāvara, who married Jaratkāru, a girl having the same name as his and who was the sister of Nāgarāja Vasuki (*Mbh.* Ādi 14.2-7). The son of this couple was the sage Āstīka, who put a stop to the *sarpa-sattra* of king Janamejaya (*ibid.* Ādi. chaps. 54-58),
78. For more information about the regions associated with this *tīrtha*, see Sadashiv A. Dange, *Ency. PBP* Vol. III, p. 803 f.
79. See Sadashiv A. Dange, *Ency. PBP*, Vol. I, p. 198.
80. See *Ait. Br.* III.33=13.9 makes this a star-myth, for Prajāpati pierced by Bhūtavat (i.e. Rudra) goes to the sky to become the constellation Mṛgaśīrṣa, while his daughter, the constellation Rohiṇī, also see *Śat.Br.* I.7.4.1-10; 13-17.

    The myth can be traced to the *RV* I.71.5, 8; I.164.33, 35; III.31.1, 2; X.61.1, 2, 5-9. But here the pair is named only *pitā* and *duhitā* (*duhitṛ*)—father and daughter. There is mentioned an archer who shoots an arrow at the father. It is not a complete myth, but a proto-myth. See note 81 infra.

81. *Prāśitra* is the wounded or cut off part of the very sacrifice or of Prajāpati, when Rudra shoots an arrow. Being sacred, that part was taken to Savitṛ, Bhaga and Pūṣan, who suffered bodily injury from it. Ultimately Bṛhaspati could eat it. In the ritual, the fore-portion of the sacrificial cake stands for *prāśitra* and it is eaten by the Brahman priest.
For the myth of Prajāpati or Sacrifice and Rudra and that of *prāśitra* see Sindhu S. Dange, "Prāśitra in Myth and Ritual", *Prabhākara-Nārāyaṇa-Śrīḥ-Studies in Indology and Musicology* (Dr. Prabhakar Narayan Kawthekar Fel. Vol.), Pratibha Prakashan, Delhi, 1993, pp. 81-86.
82. See G.H. Godbole, "Later Vedic and Brahmanical Accounts", *Myths of Creation* ed. by Sindhu S. Dange, University of Bombay (Mumbai), Bombay (Mumbai), 1987, pp. 12-17.
83. See Sadashiv A. Dange, *Ency. PBP*, Vol. IV, pp. 1184-87 (under the title "Rivers").
84. See Sindhu S. Dange, *Puranic Etymologies and Flexible Forms*, Viveka Publications, Aligarh, 1989. Here 320 etymologies from the Purāṇas are discussed, which give an idea of the efforts of the Purāṇas to reach the common masses through their own language.

CHAPTER 5

Curse and Boon—Mythological Strategies

Here we come to an interesting and indispensable element in Indian mythology from the Vedic to the Puranic times. This element comprises of curses, boons and oaths, which are strewn in the various accounts in the Vedic literature, the two great epics and the Purāṇas (here Mahāpurāṇas). They are related—nay—they breathe the power of 'word', which is connected with mind and emotions of man.

As a spoken word i.e. Speech, is closely connected with thought i.e. Mind, we have to make clear the mutual relationship between these two and the respective importance of these (Speech and Mind). The Brāhmaṇa-texts (ritual-texts) have often dwelt on this topic, though mainly in the context of sacrifice, nevertheless showing the general trend of thought. The *Śat. Br.* points out that Mind and Speech, when yoked together, convey the sacrifice to the gods (I.4.4.1).[1] The *Śat. Br.* beautifully explains the inseparable connection between Speech and Mind, while enjoining a mantra from the *Vāj.Sam.* (XIII. 35) *viz.* 'May the two Sārasvata wells cheer thee.' This mantra is addressed to the fire-pan (*ukhā*). The *Śat.Br.* says that Sarasvat is Mind and Sarasvatī is Speech and these two are the Sārasvata wells (VII.5.1.31). It is to be remembered here that Sarasvat is the male aspect (and not the husband) of the river Sarasvatī (regarded as a female).[2] The point is, just as Sarasvat and Sarasvatī are inseparably connected, so are Mind and Speech.

In spite of accepting the equal importance of Mind and Speech, a thought often occurs in the ritual-texts that, of the two, Mind is more important than Speech. In order to show the importance of mind, some ritual texts dwell on the relative importance of mind and speech. The *Śat.Br.* (I.4.5.8-12) records the quarrel when each of the two—Mind and Speech—said that he/she was excellent. Mind said that certainly he was better than her, for she did not speak anything that was not understood by him. She was only an imitator of what was done by the Mind and a follower in his wake. Speech said that surely she was better for she made known what he knew and she was the only one who communicated. They went to Prajāpati and Prajāpati decided in favour of Mind saying to Speech that she was only an imitator of Mind's deeds and a follower in his wake. Speech then said to Prajāpati that she would never be his oblation-bearer, as he did not support her. This mythical story (*arthavāda*) is stated to explain why Prajāpati is given offerings in a low voice. But it also shows how Mind is regarded superior to Speech.

Curses, oaths or swearings and boons spring from mind, though they are expressed in speech i.e. word. In Sanskrit, for 'curse' we have the word '*śāpa*', which comes from the root √*śap* 'to utter'. We have also the word '*śabda*' from this root. Phonetically the word '*śapta*' ('cursed', but literally 'uttered', as the past passive participle from the rood '*śap*') and the word '*śabda*' ('word', which we utter) are quite near to each other. Yāska says that the root √*śap* means 'to touch' (*Nir.* III.21 *sāpaḥ śapateḥ spṛśatikarmaṇaḥ*). This brings forth that the meaning of the word *śāpa* has another aspect. The *śāpa* (curse) touches the person cursed as also it has a power over him. In the Irish folklore we find that a curse, once uttered, must find a victim; it can remain suspended for seven years to descend any moment on the party it has been aimed at.[3] Curses in Teutonic mythology operate quickly.[4]

Curses, oaths or swearings and boons display the mind behind them, the words in them serving only as mere instrument needed for expressing the mind. Curse has a strong psychic force; it may affect the one who utters it.[5] It is said to be an emotional force as a factor in the making of both—Magic and Religion.[6] According to Westermarck, it is "a purely magical power, independent of any superhuman will" and ....." it is rooted in the close association between the wish, more particularly the spoken wish and the idea of its fulfilment."[7] At times curses are said to have resulted in epidemics and pestilence as we have the curse of Moses in the Old Testament.

Swearing or oath comes very near to the concept of curse, for when a person takes oath, he is ready to face the ill fate to be inflicted on him, if he proves false. Thus oath in a way is a self-inflicted or self-targeted curse. In the expression of oath, the root which figures is √*śap* (same as in curse—*śāpa*). The person is seen saying 'I swear' (*śape*).

Against the power 'to harm', there is the power 'to bless', which again springs from the mind. This gives rise to 'boons', which are several times mentioned in the ancient texts from Vedic to Puranic texts.

Curses, oaths or swearings and boons springing from 'mind' but expressed in 'word' (i.e. through speech) have been used very often in the ancient texts. In fact they form part of a mythological strategy used for various motifs, the sole aim of which is justifying a matter in hand, thus taking the role of *arthavāda*.

The word *śāpa* and the forms of the root √*śap* occur in the *RV*. At least at one place it has the traditional meaning i.e. the infliction of punishment (*RV* I. 41.8). At other place, the enemies are said to be the *śāpa* of the rivers (*ibid.* VII.18.5). Here also the word carries the sense of evil. The word *śāpam* occurs once more in *RV* (X.28.4b— *pratīpam śāpam nadyo vahanti*). Sāyaṇa renders it as *udaka* (water). Macdonell and Keith (in the *Vedic Index*) say that it is a 'substance', flowing along or floating in the rivers. This occurs in the dialogue between Vasukra and Indra and is put in the mouth of Vasukra and the word *śāpa* here is somewhat enigmatic. In *RV* (X.87.13) we have the word *śapātaḥ* in the context of a couple and it means, according to Sāyaṇa, 'taunting each other'—again with some evil thought. In the *AV*, we have a clear mention of curse (*śapathaḥ*) and the curse-effacing plant (*vīrut śapathayopanī*). The seer says that the curse-effacing plant has washed away from him all curses, as waters do filth (*AV* II.7.1), and expresses a desire that the curse should go back to the curser (*ibid.* 5a— *śaptāram etu śapathaḥ*).

The *Tait. Sam.* mentions the curse given to the fish by Agni. It occurs in a mythical account (*arthavāda*) in the context of placing the enclosing-sticks (*paridhis*) round the Āhavanīya fire.[8] The *arthavāda* runs as follows. Agni had three brothers. They perished while carrying the offering to the gods. Agni was afraid of the same misfortune falling on him. He ran away and entered the waters. The gods came to search for him (as they needed him for sacrifice). The fish told the gods about Agni (being there in the waters). So Agni cursed the fish, as they betrayed him. Agni said that for pleasure (for taste) men would slay the fish (*Tait. Sam.* II.6.6.1). Agni, prior to carrying the offering for the gods, asked from them a boon that whatever of the offering fell outside the enclosing-sticks, that was to be the share of his brothers (*ibid.* II.6.6.2). Here the boon supports the placing of the enclosing-sticks in the name of the three brothers of Agni.

The *Pañc. Br.* gives a mythical account which mentions the curse given to the trees by the gods. Once Speech passed away from the gods and entered the waters. On the words of gods, the water restored her on the condition that they may not be mixed up with any unclean substance. Speech then entered trees, but they did not restore her. So the gods cursed the trees that by means of the handle made from the trees themselves, men will hew them. (*Pañch. Br.* VI.5.10-12).

The curse to the fish and that to the trees explain the facts that are already established in the society. Here the curse comes as a make-belief. In addition, the curse here gives a moral. Causing harm to gods is bad. For this the trees have to be punished. So is the curse. The fish betrayed Agni. Hence, the curse to them. Both the instances carry a moral.

Sometimes curse invites counter-curse. We can see several such instances in the Epic and the Puranic texts. But prior to that let us note what the *Śat. Br.* has to say about it. In this respect we have an *arthavāda* in the *Śat. Br.* (I.6.1.14-18). In the New-moon and Full-moon sacrifices, he, uttering the offering-prayer over Agni's butter-portion, places Agni in front. With the sacrificial cake to Agni, Agni is placed in the middle. With the offering prayer to Agni Sviṣṭakṛt, he places Agni in the rear. At all these stages of sacrifice, Agni serves as a killer and repeller of *rakṣases* (*ibid.* 14). If any one were to curse evil on the sacrificer, at the face i.e. beginning of the sacrifice, one should counter-curse him by saying that the person cursing would suffer from some disease of the face either becoming blind or deaf (*ibid.* 16). If the sacrificer is cursed in the middle of the sacrifice, the person uttering the curse should be counter-cursed as to be the one without offspring and cattle (*ibid.* 17). If the curse is uttered after the completion of the sacrifice, the counter-curse should be that the person cursing, becoming unstable and poor, should immediately depart from this world i.e. should die. The *Śat. Br.* though states the counter-curses as a remedial reaction for the curses uttered first, here strikes a note of warning that a person should not utter any curses (*ibid.* 18). This is to put a stop to the chain of curses and counter-curses. The *Śat. Br.* through this *arthavāda* gives a good piece of moral teaching.

The Vedic texts mention curses but the occasions are few, for they have other means of glorifying or justifying a particular rite or ritual.[9] But the Epics and the Purāṇas have used the strategy of curse on various accounts, their sole aim being justifying the matter in hand. Through curses, boons and oaths—especially curses—the Epics and the Purāṇas have made use of the device of Arthavādaism to the largest extent. Sometimes the curse is employed to establish a particular order of the society. Occasionally, it is used to elevate a particular person. At times it is given to stress the importance of various codes of morality and conduct. In rare cases, it takes us near to a historical fact, by trying to unearth it. There are several such motifs for which the strategy of curse is resorted to.

Here we take into account some of the important curses, boons, oaths which occur in the Epics and the Purāṇas.

RĀMĀYAṆA

The *śloka* form of the *Rām.* is explained by the account of the curse given by Vālmīki to a Niṣāda (hunter) for killing a male bird with an arrow. We note this curse in the second chapter of the Bālakāṇḍa of the *Rām.* from the sage Vālmīki after hearing the wailings of a female *krauñca* bird, when her male partner falls a prey to the arrow of the Niṣāda (*Rām.* Bāla 2.15). As extremely grief-stricken is the mind of the sage, the curse comes out of his mouth in the form of a verse of four feet i.e. lines (*pādas*), each one having equal number of syllables (*ibid.* 2.18, 40). Thus the very *śoka* (grief) attained the form of *śloka* (verse),[10] and the sage decided to compose the story of Rāma in the form of the verse alone i.e. in the metrical form (*ibid.* 41).

The story could be regarded as true, for it is a common scene in any forest, where the animals and the birds fall prey to the hunters. However the curse gives an aetiological (or etiological) explanation of the *śloka* form of the *Rāmāyaṇa*. Vālmīki is the first classical Sanskrit poet to compose a work in the metrical form, he thus is an 'Ādikavi' and the *Rāmāyaṇa* an 'Ādikāvya.

In the Bālakāṇḍa of the *Rām.*, we find that a boon is given to Rāvaṇa by the god Brahmā that the former would not be killed by anybody except a human being i.e. *mānuṣa* (*ibid.* Bāla 16.4, 5). This boon to Rāvaṇa is the very foundation-stone of the whole edifice of the *Rām.* In the earlier chapter of the Bālakāṇḍa we have Viṣṇu coming down to the terrestrial world in the form of Rāma (*ibid.* Bāla chap. 15) and also that Rāma is Viṣṇu himself (*ibid.* 16.1-8). Thus the god Viṣṇu has to assume human form, and through Rāma only, he can kill Rāvaṇa, because of the boon acquired by Rāvaṇa.

Here we come to an important episode and it is of killing the Rākṣasī Tāṭakā, by Rāma. Rāma has been made a target of criticism on this account, for a woman is never to be killed. In the play *Uttararāmacaritam* (V.34), Lava with satire in his words teases Candraketu by pointing out the glaring falls in the life of Rāma. He refers here to the killing of Sunda's wife i.e. Mantharā (=Tāṭakā) by Rāma (*sundastrīmathana*). In fact, killing a woman is regarded as a sin (*pātaka*, though an *upapātaka*—minor sin) by the *Yājñ. Sm.* (III.236), though the comm. Mitākṣarā on this passage takes the word '*strī*' (woman) in a limited sense as 'of Atri *gotra* (Atri family), pregnant or in menstruation or married in the Atri family' etc. Even the great warrior Bhīṣma declined to fight Śikhaṇḍī and obviously to kill him (her) which he could have (*Mbh.* Bhīṣma 108.43). Śikhaṇḍī initially was a woman, turned into man, by the boon given by the Yakṣa Sthūṇākarṇa (*ibid.* Ādi 63.125; Udyoga chap. 191; 192.1-57, 65-69). Whether the *Mbh.* precedes the *Rām.* or *vice versa*, the fact remains that a woman is not to be killed.

This has been the trend of thought in ancient India. Prajāpati is seen telling the gods not to kill Śrī (Splendour or Glory) born from him, though she has been overpowering everything, even them (i.e. the gods), with her lustre, for people do not kill a woman (*Śat. Br.* XI.4.3.1,2).

On this background, when Viśvāmitra tells Rāma to kill the Rākṣasī Tāṭakā (*Rām.* Bāla 25.22), it requires some justification and it is provided by Viśvāmitra himself by narrating the account of curse (*ibid.* chap. 25). Tāṭakā formerly was the beautiful daughter of the great Yakṣa Suketu and was given in marriage to Sunda and gave birth to Mārīca (who later on became a Rākṣasa). After the death of Sunda, once Tāṭakā with Mārīca came upon Agastya to attack him. Hence there was the curse by Agastya to both of them to become Rākṣasī and Rākṣasa resp. (*ibid.* 25.9, 12 & 13). The curse thus provides an aetiological explanation for the killing of Tāṭakā and later on Mārīca by Rāma. Tāṭakā was *śāpasaṁspṛṣṭā*—'sullied by curse' (*ibid.* 16); was *adharmyā*—'sinful' (*ibid.* 19). Hence no sin or blemish for killing a woman be attached to Rāma! Here are given by Viśvāmitra some instances when women are killed by men. Thus Śakra (Indra) killed the daughter of Virocana, Mantharā by name (*ibid.* 20), and Viṣṇu killed the wife of Bhṛgu, the mother of Kāvya Uśanas (*ibid.* 21) and there were other women, steeped in *adharma* (sin) killed by human heroes (*ibid.* 22).

The killing of the wife of Bhṛgu is mentioned in the Uttarakāṇḍa of the *Rām.* and it drives Bhṛgu to give a curse to Viṣṇu. The account runs as follows. Lakṣmaṇa was feeling guilt for taking the pregnant Sītā to the forest on the words of Rāma. In order to console him, the charioteer Sumantra told him what Durvāsa, the sage, had foretold long back. Thus on the request of Daśaratha for knowing the 'future' (life and life-span) of Rāma and other sons, Durvāsa told him about the curse given to Viṣṇu by the sage Bhṛgu. It so happened that in the battle between the gods and the *asuras*, the *asuras* resorted to the wife of Bhṛgu for protection. So Viṣṇu cut off her head with his sharp-edged disc. Bhṛgu lamented that the wife was *avadhyā*— i.e. not to be killed, but as she was killed by Viṣṇu, Bhṛgu cursed him that he (i.e. Viṣṇu) would be born on the earth and would suffer separation from wife for many years (*Rām.* Uttara 51.11-21). The curse of Bhṛgu justifies the hardships in Rāma's life and his separation from Sītā.

In the Bālakāṇḍa of the *Rām.* (chap. 64) occurs the account of the curse given to the nymph Rambhā by the sage Viśvāmitra, when she comes to allure his mind and put an obstruction in his penance. Viśvāmitra already had his penance destroyed, when the nymph Menakā, on the word of Indra, came to attract his mind and he being enamoured of her, spent ten years with her (*ibid.* Bāla 63.4-13), but feeling repentance went away to the northern mountain to practise austere penance. Then came the nymph Rambhā, on the word of Śakra (Indra) again on the same errand, accompanied by Indra, disguised as a cuckoo (*ibid.* 64.6). But this time, Viśvāmitra had become wiser to see through the plan of the gods. Hence to nip the efforts of Rambhā in the bud, Viśvāmitra uttered a curse that Rambhā thereafter would remain a rock for 10000 years (*ibid.* 64.1-13).

The curse here is to show that Viśvāmitra could not be deceived second time by the gods, and thereafter practised such severe a penance, as to become a *brahmarṣi* (*ibid.* 64.1-29). Viśvāmitra though a *kṣatriya* by birth, thus attained the status of a *brāhmaṇa* (the state of brahminhood).

We turn to the curse given to Virādha, the Rākṣasa. When Rāma in his fourteen years' exile with Lakṣmaṇa and Sītā came to the Daṇḍaka forest, Virādha the Rākṣasa spotted them. Having caught hold of Rāma and Lakṣmaṇa, when Virādha was carrying them on shoulders, Sītā pleaded that he should leave them and in lieu of them could take her away. Hearing this lamentation of Sītā, Rāma and Lakṣmaṇa cut off the arms of Virādha. When Virādha was pounded by them, he, at the moment of death, told Rāma that he had recognised them already and had waited for his release from the state (or birth) of a Rākṣasa. He was formerly the *gandharva* by name Tumburu, who was cursed for his mistake by Vaiśravaṇa to resort to the form of a Rākṣasa. When Virādha pleaded for mercy, he was told that only after being killed by Rāma, he getting back his own form (of a *gandharva*) would proceed to the heavenly world (*Rām.* Araṇya 4.1-19).

In the chap. dealing with the acculturation of various tribes in the Vedic Aryan fold, we have taken in details the Rākṣasa tribe with its branches and that of Virādha being one of them. We have also noted that this branch of the Rākṣasas later on was assimilated in the Aryan fold. Hence the efforts to show through the curse that Virādha was formerly a *gandharva* and not a Rākṣasa in the true sense of the term!

Here we come to the curse given to Rāvaṇa, because of which Sītā could remain 'untouched', even when carried away by Rāvaṇa and kept though not in his harem (but) in the Aśokavanikā. At two places the curse is clear and at one place it is near to curse, but equally threatening. There are thus three accounts of curse targeted at Rāvaṇa. The first mention comes in the Yuddhakāṇḍa of the *Rām.*, when Mahāpārśva advises Rāvaṇa 'to enjoy' Sīta. But Rāvaṇa speaks out his fear that formerly for his sin of raping the nymph Puñjikasthalā, the god Brahmā has cursed him that for such a sin committed again, Rāvaṇa's head will fall down into 100 pieces (*Rām.* Yuddha 13.14).

In the Uttarakāṇḍa we have the account of the curse given to Rāvaṇa by Nalakūbara. Nalakūbara was the son of Vaiśravaṇa, the brother of Rāvaṇa. Rambhā the wife of Nalakūbara was forcibly raped by Rāvaṇa. When Rambhā reported this to Nalakūbara he gave the curse (that)—"If Rāvaṇa infatuated with passion forcibly rapes a woman against her wish, his head will break into seven pieces" (*ibid.* Uttara 26.55-56).

In the Uttarakāṇḍa again (chap. 17), we have the account of Vedavatī. Here there is no mention of curse but Vedavatī's molestation at Rāvaṇa's hands sows the seed of his destruction. The account runs as follows. Brahmarṣi Kuśadhvaja, the son of Bṛhaspati, was given to Vedic studies only. Hence Vedavatī born of him was his *vaṅmayī kanyā* ('born as though from his speech'). He desired to give Vedavatī in marriage to Viṣṇu, but the demon Dambhu on hearing this killed Kuśadhvaja when he was asleep. The mother of Vedavatī (i.e. Kuśadhvaja's wife) immolated herself on the husband's funeral pyre. To fulfil her father's wish, Vedavatī was practising penance on the Himalayan peak, where came Rāvaṇa. Hearing the praise of Viṣṇu from Vedavatī's mouth, Rāvaṇa got enraged and pulled her by her hair. Vedavatī feeling insulted cut off her hair by her own hand. She did not curse Rāvaṇa, for that would have nullified the merit of her penance (*Rām.* Uttara 17.33). She says here, "If I have some merit due to good actions (*kṛta*), giving gifts (*datta*) and giving offerings to gods (*huta*), I will be born a righteous woman (but) not from any human womb" (*ibid.* 34) for killing you (*ibid.* 32). Hence, she was born from a *sītā* i.e. furrow (*ibid.* 39, 40). King Janaka got her there and named her Sītā, who ultimately could be the cause of Rāvaṇa's death and total destruction. Vedavatī's words prove fatal for Rāvaṇa as though through a curse.

These three accounts point out the insolence and immodesty of Rāvaṇa, who as though invites curse on himself, according to the doctrine of *karman* ('Reap as you sow'). Nevertheless these accounts also are given to convince that Sīta remained 'untouched' by Rāvaṇa and thus chaste, even though staying in Rāvaṇa's kingdom, away from Rāma. These curse-accounts are thus validatory (justificatory). In Vedavatī's account, Vedavatī was to be married to Viṣṇu, which could not take place. But in the next birth, she was born as Sītā and married Rāma, who was Viṣṇu himself. We have already noted this from the Bālakāṇḍa (chap. 15; also chap. 16.1-8).

In the earlier chapter we have taken a note of the punishment given to King Nṛga, from the *Mbh.* (Anu. 70.7-29). But that occurs in the context of *dāna*, pointing out that Nṛga failed in his duty on two accounts and so he got punishment from Yama to become a chameleon. In the *Rām.*

the wretched state of being a chameleon comes to the lot of King Nṛga due to the curse of the *brāhmaṇas.* The account occurs in the Uttarakāṇḍa, giving stress on the duties of a king. When Lakṣmaṇa comes back after leaving Sītā in Vālmīki's hermitage on the banks of Gaṅgā, Rāma feels dejected (*ibid.* Uttara chap. 52). But he is consoled by Lakṣmaṇa and he becomes conscious of his royal duties, which he has missed for four days (*ibid.* 53.4) and says that a king who does not carry out his duties, goes to terrible hell (*ibid.* 6). Here occurs the account of King Nṛga, who was given a curse by two *brāhmaṇas.* It so happened that when Nṛga gave crores of cows as *dāna* (gift) to the *brāhmaṇas,* a cow of an *āhitāgni* (one who maintains the three fires—Gārhapatya, Āhavanīya and Dakṣiṇa) *brāhmaṇa,* who was poor (an *uñchavṛtti* i.e. who maintains himself on the grains fallen in the field), was given away by the King Nṛga, along with her calf. The *brāhmaṇa* was desperate in searching her and ultimately at the place Kanakhala he could locate her in a *brāhmaṇa's* house. He called out to her addressing the cow by her name 'Śabalā' and she recognised him (for originally she belonged to him). There ensued a quarrel between the two *brāhmaṇas* on the ownership of the cow. Both came to King Nṛga to get the issue settled. Days and months passed by, but the King Nṛga did not see them, avoiding his royal duty and responsibility. Hence, both the *brāhmaṇas* cursed him that he would be a *kṛkalāsa* (a big lizard or chameleon) and would stay in a hole or chasm for many years, till his release by Vāsudeva, who would come in human form (*ibid.* 53.7-21).

We have already pointed out that this account appears in both the Epics. This shows that the account must have been very old, depicting a certain king Nṛga. While the *Mbh.* showed the king Nṛga as a great donor, giving gifts (those too of cows), but suffering a pitfall and hence getting punishment from Yama for his sin(!) committed inadvertently, the *Rām.* paints him in dark colours as a 'failed' king shunning from his royal duties and responsibilities, and so cursed by the *brāhmaṇas*. The curse in the *Rām.* is for ethical purpose, pointing out the importance of the duties of a king. The account of Nṛga points out how this old material is used by the two Epics as per their need, with the aim of justifying or convincing their cause. This also shows how the tradition of the Sūtas carried through centuries old accounts as that of king Nṛga, thus acting as chronicler of immemorial times, which was the Itihāsa (*iti-ha-āsa*—'It happened so').

In the Uttarakāṇḍa, we see the curse given to Daṇḍa. From Manu was born Ikṣvāku, who got hundred sons. The youngest was named Daṇḍa. He was a wanton boy, but was made by his father Ikṣvāku, the lord of the kingdom falling between the mountains Vindhya and Śaivala, making Madhumat as the capital place (*Rām.* Uttara chap. 79). One feels that the father might have thought that a responsible position of a king would give him the sense of duty. But it did not happen. Daṇḍa once came to the hermitage of Bhārgava, where he saw Arajā, the eldest daughter of the sage Bhārgava. On seeing her, Daṇḍa became so full of passion that he raped her. She waited for her father (*ibid.* chap. 80). When Bhārgava came, he came to know what had happened. Hence he gave a curse to Daṇḍa that thenceforth within seven days, Daṇḍa with all his attendants and his army with all its divisions (horses, elephants etc.) will face total destruction (*ibid.* 81.6-7). The curse came true and Daṇḍa became totally extinct, remaining only in the name 'Daṇḍaka-araṇya' (Daṇḍaka forest) for from that time, the country between Vindhya and Śaivala ruled by Daṇḍa was named after him (*ibid.* 18-19). Here the curse acts as a double-edged device. It brings out to what end an immoral and insolent behaviour can take a person, thus giving an ethical teaching. At the same time, it explains the geographical name 'Daṇḍaka' of the forest.

In the Uttarakāṇḍa we have the curse given to Yayāti the king by his father-in-law Bhārgava (Śukra Uśanas). Devayānī's son was Yadu, while her co-wife's—Śarmiṣṭhā's—son was Pūru.

Yadu often complained to Devayānī that Yayāti his father always loved Pūru more than him. Devayānī approached her father Bhārgava who cursed Yayāti that he would be worn out by old age (*ibid.* 58.8-25). The curse points out the pitfall in Yayāti's nature and elevates the character of Pūru, who alone, accepts the curse of old age upon himself, thus relieving his father from the curse. Yayāti becomes young, performs sacrifices and then after many years takes back his state of old age from Pūru, making Pūru a king even while he is alive (*ibid.* chap. 59).

In the Uttarakāṇḍa of the *Rām.* again, we find a fine instance of curse and counter-curse (chap. 55). It so happened that king Nimi having promised Vasiṣṭha to be an officiating priest for the long session of his sacrifice (*dīrghasattra* i.e. going on beyond twelve days), later on chose Gautama for that errand, as Vasiṣṭha had already told him that he had promised Indra (obviously for being an officiating priest in Indra's sacrifice), after which work he would come to Nimi. Vasiṣṭha came, though late and waited for meeting Nimi, but Nimi was sleeping. Hence, Vasiṣṭha became all the more angry and cursed Nimi that the latter would be without body. Nimi pleaded innocence but to no avail and hence counter-cursed Vasiṣṭha that he also would be without body (*ibid.* 55.21). The next chapter of the Uttarakāṇḍa (i.e. chap. 56) deals with the curse of Vasiṣṭha given by Nimi. Brahmā tells Vasiṣṭha that he would enter the lustre of the gods Mitra and Varuṇa (*ibid.* 56.1-12). It so happened that Varuṇa saw Urvaśī the celestial nymph and became passionate about her. But as she was already chosen by Mitra, Varuṇa avoiding copulation with her released his semen (lustre) in a jar. When she approached Mitra, he was angry that she had chosen another husband and cursed her that she would go to the earth for a temporary stay and would take Purūravas as her husband (*ibid.* 16-26). The account goes further narrating that from the jar was born first the sage Agastya and then Vasiṣṭha. Mitra had already kept his semen there and then there was that of Varuṇa. Thus Vasiṣṭha though first bodiless was born with a lustrous body (*ibid.* 57.1-9). And in this chap. we find that the King Nimi, who was cursed by Vasiṣṭha to be without any body, got a boon from the gods by which he chose to remain in the eyes of men i.e. in the act of winking of eyes (*ibid.* 10-17). The story of Vasiṣṭha as born from a jar is mentioned in the *RV* (VII. 33.13). It is said that the gods Mitra and Varuṇa ejected semen in a jar from which Vasiṣṭha is said to be born along with Agastya and the scene is of a sacrificial place. Dange has discussed this in details and has stated that Vasiṣṭha's birth is said to be twofold.[11] The first is celestial, when Vasiṣṭha left the light of the lightning (*ibid.* 10). The very sight of Mitra and Varuṇa caused the lustre to shoot forth from the lightning. The second birth of Vasiṣṭha is sacrificial. Dange points out that the background of the sacrifice is a motif commonly found to be present in many accounts of divine or supernatural birth.[12] The birth of Vasiṣṭha as also of Agastya is from jar. Dange has stated in details the importance of jar in various rituals and the symbolism connected to jar in these rituals.[13] In the case of Vasiṣṭha's as well as Agastya's birth, the jar stands for the womb and thus has procreative power.

The *Rām.* seized upon this Ṛgvedic myth of the birth of Vasiṣṭha and it was used in the game of "curse and counter curse"—curse by Nimi to Vasiṣṭha and the counter-curse by the latter to Nimi. It brings out how Vasiṣṭha has great prowess and that could be due to some miraculous element in him, that is reflected in his rebirth (due to the curse of Nimi) in a bodiless form, for on Brahmā's words he enters the lustre of Mitra and Varuṇa—the detail we have noted earlier.

The account of 'curse and counter-curse' is significant for another point and it is the status of Mitra vis-a-vis that of Varuṇa. Here Varuṇa admits that Urvaśī is chosen first by Mitra and hence avoids direct copulation with her. On the other hand, Mitra seems to be insistent on having his hold on

Urvaśī and hence curses her. This picture of Mitra is totally different from what we see in the *RV*, where in the dual deity Mitrāvaruṇā, Mitra is always subservient to Varuṇa and has only one hymn (*RV* III.59) addressed to him alone. Ṛgvedic counterpart 'Mithra' in *Avesta* is an important deity, having some of the traits of the Ṛgvedic Varuṇa. The concept of Mitra or Mithra (*Avesta*) goes back to those times, when the ancestors of the ancient Iranians and those of the Vedic Aryans were staying together.[14] That Mitra (*RV*) or Mithra (*Avesta*) was a separate deity can be noted from the *Avesta* itself. This is reflected, though faintly, in the account of counter-curse given by Nimi to Vasiṣṭha, by which Vasiṣṭha is to be born bodiless in the next birth.

This account of 'curse and counter-curse' occurs in the *Bhāg. P.* (IX.13.1-13) and it is interesting to see how the device of *arthavāda* has added different shades to it. Here Vasiṣṭha's wrath knows no bounds when he learns that, in his absence, Nimi's sacrifice has already taken place. Hence the terrible curse from him to Nimi as Nimi has been proud of his learning and has transgressed the order of Vasiṣṭha—his preceptor (*ibid.* IX.13.4). The account says that the sages assembled there for the sacrifice, keep Nimi's body intact in ointments and various balms lest his body should putrefy[15] and at the end of the sacrifice ask the gods to revive Nimi, obviously being afraid of the state becoming kingless. Nimi gets revived. But as he himself does not want the bondage of the mortal frame, the gods confer on him the blessing of being '*videha*' (devoid of bodily form), in the eyes of human beings, where his existence could be marked in the form of the rise and fall of the eyelids (*ibid.* 7-11). The sages then churn the body of Nimi. A son is born, who is named 'Janaka' ('*janmanā janakaḥ*'; fr. the root √*jan*—'to be born'); also 'Videha', as he is born from Videha (bodiless) Nimi and 'Mithila', as he is born as a result of churning[16] (fr. the root √*manth*—'to churn') (*ibid.* 12-13).

In this whole episode, the name of the king as 'Nimi' is significant, for *nimiḥ* means the winking of eyes.[17] Most probably this etymological meaning of the word *nimi* has played the magic. It presupposes the king's being devoid of any bodily form, which is the very crux of the curse, and its very basis. The word *adhyātmasaṁsthitaḥ* (firmly established in the thought of the Highest Principle) used in the case of Nimi (*ibid.* 11) makes us ponder over the matter. The *videhatva* of Nimi is well-rooted in tradition. His indifference to the worldly joys might have created a problem. Such a behaviour of a celibate[18] (literally—'state of being bodiless') has been deemed as impracticable in the case of a king, who has to create a heir to the throne. Hence the curse to Nimi and his extraordinary wish to remain *videha* (by *abhidhā* power of the word—'devoid of bodily form'; and by *lakṣaṇā* power of word—'indifferent towards any worldly enjoyment'—thus 'celibate'), which facilitated the easy entry of Janaka Vaideha Mithila on the scene, who most probably was king Nimi's adopted son. Janaka's birth from Nimi by the process of churning is simply an *arthavāda* to make people believe in his legitimacy to the throne. This is the procedure adopted normally, in order to prove the legacy of the new line with the previous line. So was born king Pṛthu with Arcis after churning Vena's two hands (*Bhāg. P.* IV.15.1). Pṛthu no doubt a great king, with his hundred sacrifices, his milching the earth, the earth yielding for him many jewels, but not connected with Vena, required this birth-account, which is an *arthavāda* to make the people believe in his royal line. The birth of Māndhātā from king Yuvanāśva falls in line with this (*ibid.* IX.6), which is to glorify Māndhāta and to convince the people of his heredity.

About the counter-curse of Nimi to the sage Vasiṣṭha, it has to be pointed out that the birth-account of Vasiṣṭha from Mitrāvaruṇā is as old as the *RV*, as we have noted earlier, while Nimi dates much later. Hence to explain Vasiṣṭha's birth from Mitra and Varuṇa as posterior to Nimi's curse and as caused by it will obviously be incorrect. Nimi's counter-curse to Vasiṣṭha shows how the righteous conduct of Nimi could infuse so much potentiality in him as to fight Vasiṣṭha on the moral level.

MAHĀBHĀRATA AND PURĀṆAS

Now here we come to some of the curses, boons and oaths occurring in the *Mbh.* and the Purāṇas. In many cases, the accounts from the *Mbh.* are taken by the Purāṇas, which have added some more layers to these and at times the Purāṇas have tried their hand independently on age-old matter.

The first curse which we take into account is that of King Parikṣit, which we have already seen in short, when we noted the acculturation of the Nāga tribe in the Vedic Aryan fold. According to the *Mbh.* (Ādi 40.27ff) the king went to the hermitage following the deer, that he had shot with his arrow. He asked the sage about the beast but as the sage was in deep meditation, the king received no reply from him. Hence the childish act of the king of putting a dead serpent round the neck of the sage! Here the name of the sage's son is Śṛṅgin, who gives the curse to Parikṣit. The *Bhāg. P.* (I.18.24ff) says that when the king, exhausted after a hunt, entered the hermitage, the sage was in meditation and the son was out. As there was total silence and lack of hospitality for the king, he was annoyed, and hence placed a dead serpent round the neck of the sage. Having softened the prick of his mind, the king left the hermitage and went to his capital. On hearing from his playmates the insolence shown to his father, the sage's son came home and seeing the dead serpent round the neck of his father, cursed the king to die of the bite from Takṣaka Nāga on the seventh day thence and began to weep. When the sage came to the normal state, he rebuked his son for his rash deed of cursing the king. According to the *Mbh.* when king Parikṣit knew of the curse he made a high one-prop chamber built to escape the serpent but was ultimately bitten to death by Takṣaka (*Mbh.* Ādi 42.23ff). The *Bhāg. P.* gives a different shade to the 'seven days' life' of the king. Having renounced the world, the king goes to the river Gaṅgā to perform penance. The *Bhāg. P.* weaves a net of dialogues that goes on for seven days, between Parikṣit and Śuka in that the former asks questions and the latter answers them. Here we have the basis formed for the exposition of the Bhāgavata Dharma (*ibid.* I.19.37ff). Parikṣit becomes prepared for his death calmly and without any fear, on the advice of the sage Śuka (*ibid.* XII.5). Hence on the fatal day, when Takṣaka comes and kills the king, the latter is already one with the Highest Principle (*ibid.* XII.6.13).

Combining the accounts from the *Mbh.* and the *Bhag.P.*, we note that the insult of the sage is said to have caused the death of the king, which indicates that a sage (in all probability a *brāhmaṇa*) is not be insulted. The *Bhāg.P.* specifically mentions that the Nāga (serpent) Takṣaka that bites Parikṣit goes as a *brāhmaṇa* (*Bhāg.P.* XII.6.12). In the *Mbh.* Takṣaka is said to have sent a band of his serpents disguised as hermits, with flowers and fruits for the king Parikṣit and in one of the fruits Takṣaka himself lay hidden as a tiny worm. As the king took the fruit to eat, he saw the worm suddenly changing into a fierce serpent (*Mbh.* Ādi 43.23 ff). It has to be noted that a snake-charmer, Kaśyapa (a *brāhamaṇa*) is preparing himself to revive the king, should Takṣaka bite the king. Takṣaka meets him on the way and seeing his prowess, alluring him with wealth, induces him to go back (*ibid.* Ādi 42.33-41; 43.1-19). This shows that Takṣaka was persistently trying to kill King Parikṣit. Most probably it was a premeditated plan to kill the king through treachery, by a sect of the Nāgas headed by Takṣaka. T.V. Mahalingam has suggested the probability of an armed attack of the Nāgas, to which we have already referred.[19] A folk-tale, current in the Punjab region, to which Mahalingam has not referred, can be noted in this connection. The folk-tale points out that Parikṣit abducted the daughter of the Nāgarāja Basak (Vāsuki). So the Nāga-king invaded Parikṣit's capital Indraprastha and killed Parikṣit.[20] Though all folk-tales cannot be taken to have at least a grain of truth, at times some of them speak of the *itihāsa* (*iti-ha-āsa*—'this happened or was so')—the living tradition of a particular land or place, where a historical fact buried in deep layers is shrouded in mystery.

It seems that a plan to kill the king and counteraction to save him were in the offing. Though the name of the Nāga Takṣaka figures in the curse uttered by the sage's son (*Mbh.* Ādi 41.13-14; *Bhāg. P.* I.18.36, 37), Takṣaka is not particularly ordered by anybody to bite the king. Still he is taking upon himself the task of fulfilling the curse of the sage's son. Hence the conjecture given by Mahalingam stands correct.

The curse given to Parikṣit to die of the serpent-bite i.e. at the hands of the Nāga Takṣaka (the Nāgas being a totemistic tribe, as we have noted in the earlier chapter), leads us to shape a clear historical account of the following details—

1. In all probability the royal dynasty of the Pāṇḍavas had a feud against a sect of the Nāgas.
2. It is corroborated by the extermination of the Nāgas from the Khāṇḍava-vana (*Mbh.* Ādi chaps. 223-226). Nāgarāja Takṣaka had already left that place and had gone to Kurukṣetra. His son Aśvasena was saved by his mother, who swallowed him to protect him from Arjuna's arrows. However the mother fell a prey to Arjuna's barbed arrow (*ibid.* Ādi 226.4-8).
3. Nāga Aśvasena (mentioned above), escaped from the fire of the Khāṇḍava-forest, entered the nether region and in the Arjuna-Karṇa fight, took his stand on the bow-string of Karṇa without his knowledge. As the arrow of Karṇa hit only the crown of Arjuna, the Nāga Aśvasena wished to be on the string again (*ibid.*, Karṇa 90.23; 43-44). But Karṇa declined his offer (*ibid.* 47-49), though Aśvasena was ready to kill Arjuna.

4. For ages, the feud between the Pāṇḍavas and the Nāgas continued, ultimately making Parikṣit a victim of it.
5. This roused his son Janamejaya to a second extermination of the Nāgas, in the Sarpa-sattra.
6. In the accounts the meaning of the word *nāga* placed a serpent in the place of the human Nāga.[21]
7. When King Parikṣit's death by a Nāga (person) but in the lore by a 'serpent' (*nāga*) was established, the whole account was given a moral tinge and with the idea to glorify 'brāhmaṇahood', a curse was brought in with the balance of Serpent (Nāga)-for-serpent, a dead serpent being used to insult the *brāhmaṇa* sage. The words in the speech of sage Śamīka's son (*Bhāg. P.* I.18.33-35) vouchsafe for this. A *brāhmaṇa* was insulted; Nāga Takṣaka when came to kill the king also was in the disguise of a *brāhmaṇa* (*ibid.* XII.6.12).

The curse given to king Parikṣit to die of serpent-bite brings with it a trail of various incidents and concepts, which can be historically veracious, the curse itself however being a pure *arthavāda*.

Here we come to the account of Nahuṣa's curse, where he is said to have forced the sages to carry his palanquin and with the result was cursed by Bhṛgu to become a serpent (*Mbh.* Udyoga chaps. 109-110). Elsewhere in the *Mbh.* we note that after getting the seat of Indra, Nahuṣa became so insolent that he did not follow even the daily worship of the gods by offering incense and lighting a lamp etc. Hence, for arrogance, he was cursed by Bhṛgu, for he made the sage Agastya to carry his palanquin (*Ibid.* Anu. 100.12-41). Here also the curse is to transform him into a serpent. In the *Mbh.* itself Nahuṣa is seen as a historical personage (*Mbh.* Ādi 35.9; also *ibid.* 75.25). He was one of the five sons of Āyu from the daughter of Svarbhānu, and was the father of King Yayāti. It is said that he caught hold of Bhīma in the forest and told him that he was his ancestor (*ibid.* Vana 180.11). He was a Nāga born of

Kadrū and Kāśyapa (*ibid.* Ādi 35.9). It can be seen that Nahuṣa belonged to the Nāga clan, which might have ruled the land and might have come into conflict with the Vedic Aryans and won victory for a long time. All this appears to be enshrined in the episode of the defeat of the gods, dethronement of Indra and capture of heaven by Nahuṣa (*ibid.* Ādi 75.29-30). When Nahuṣa is cursed to become a serpent, a historical fact is given a mythological layer. Oldham notes that to this day. Nahuṣa is worshipped in the Chinab Valley as Indra-nāga.[22]

Nahus or Nahuṣa appears as the name of a tribe in the *RV*.[23] At *RV* (VII.6.5), Agni is said to have held the people of Nahuṣa and made them pay taxes. Sāyaṇa takes the expression—*nāhuṣīṣu vikṣu*—'among the people of Nahuṣa.' According to Ludwig, the king of the Nahuṣas was Āyavasa (*RV* I.122.15) i.e. son of Āyus. Nahuṣa in our discussion was also the son of Āyu. In an earlier chapter on tribes, we have noted that the Sarpa-tribe was being assimilated in the Vedic Aryan fold in the Ṛgvedic period itself. By the time of the Mbh. the Nāga-clan (same as the Sarpa-tribe, it being a totemistic tribe worshipping serpent as a deity) was acculturated in the Aryan fold. Hence in the *Mbh.*, Nahuṣa is shown so near to the gods as to enjoy the seat of Indra due to his own prowess. But his pitfalls took him to destruction and to make him a 'serpent', for he was a Nāga (a person of the Nāga clan) after all! The curse given to Nahuṣa speaks of this *itihāsa*.

Here we take into account the curse given to Citraketu, the Vidyādhara, which appears in the *Bhāg. P.* (VI.17). Once Citraketu was traversing the expanse of the sky in his divine air-car. He saw on the way that in the assembly of the Siddhas, Lord Śiva was sitting with Pārvatī in close embrace. Amazed at the sight, Citraketu remarked that Śiva, the very preceptor of the whole world in 'Dharma' (code of conduct) was sitting before all in an unbecoming and shameful manner (*ibid.* VI.17.6ff). Enraged at this, Pārvatī cursed him to be an *asura*.

She said that the Vidyādhara thinking himself to be full of restraint, really did not know the principle of 'Dharma'.

The account though short is important for two points. The first and foremost point is of the close embrace of Śiva and Pārvatī which takes us to the concept of *mithuna*. This has been a popular concept of worship of Śiva in the form of 'Ardhanārīśvara' (or 'Ardhanārīnateśvara'). The concept of 'male and female in one' points to the principle of procreation found in many countries.[24] The principle can be traced to the Vedic ritual texts where Prajāpati is seen creating from his own self.[25] This is further marked in the concept of Viṣṇu (a male) giving birth to Brahmā from his own navel.[26] We see Brahmā creating various things and beings from his body.[27] The *mithuna* of Śiva and Pārvatī (the symbolic name being *yava-yuma*) was popularised by the Śaiva-Śāktas, who saw in it Śiva and Pārvatī in close embrace. The curse-episode stresses the importance of this.

Another point of the curse-episode is that of its background. Citraketu, the Vidyādhara, was known to have pleased the gods due to his meeting with Lord Saṅkarṣaṇa. Lord Viṣṇu gave him the air-car (*Bhāg. P.* VI.16; VI.17.4). This shows him to be of the Vaiṣṇava faith and hence his bitter remark on the close embrace of Śiva and Pārvatī, followed by the curse to him by Pārvatī. This shows that the followers of the Vaiṣṇava faith and those of the Śaivite faith did not have cordial relations with each other. This might be an historical fact, to put it precisely. But then there were efforts to have reconciliation between the two faiths as can be seen from Citraketu's earnest request to goddess Pārvatī to forgive him for his unwelcome and indecent words. He however does not plead for his curse to be nullified (*ibid.* VI.17.16-24). The account further proceeds to state that the Vidyādhara Citraketu resorted to the state of a *dānava* i.e. *asura*, and was born from the Dakṣina fire (Agni) of Tvaṣṭṛ in the form of the famous *asura* Vṛtra (*ibid.* 37-38). Here the advice of lord Rudra (Śiva) to Rudrāṇī (Pārvatī) clearly aims at the fusion of the Śaiva and Vaiṣṇava faiths (*ibid.* VI.17.27-35). However the high regard shown for the devotee of Viṣṇu (i.e. for Citraketu) by Śiva has to be specifically mentioned (*ibid.* 27-28, 34-35), the *Bhāg. P.* being a Vaiṣṇavite Purāṇa.

According to the need of the times, the composers of Purāṇas tried to bring the society together, blending the Vedic-brahmanical religion with new faiths, the synthesis of the Vaiṣṇavite and Śaivite faiths being one of the prominent attempts in this direction. It is said that it is only at the bidding of Śiva that a lotus sprang up from the navel of Viṣṇu, whence emerged Brahmā (*Śiva P.* IV.22.11-16; also II.6.39ff). An interesting account occurs in some Purāṇas. It is said that Viṣṇu went to Vārāṇasī on the fourteenth day in the bright half of the month Kārttika, took bath at the holy water-place Maṇikarṇikā and decided to offer one hundred golden lotuses to Śiva. As Śiva wanted to test Viṣṇu, he concealed one lotus. When on counting Viṣṇu found one lotus less, he offered his own lotus-like eye. Śiva, becoming wonder-struck and pleased, gave him the disc (Sudarśana). The day assumed great importance as the 'Vaikuṇṭha Ekādaśī' day. It is laid down that on this day in the night one should worship Viṣṇu, while in the next morning, at the rise of the sun, Śiva (*Sk.P.* II.4.35.2-25; also *Śiva P.* IV.34.12-30; *Liṅga P.* I.98.61.77; *Brahma P.* 109.28-55). Dange has dealt with this topic at a great length.[28]

The account of the curse given to the Vidyādhara Citraketu is thus significant. Citraketu is no doubt a mythical figure, but the *arthavāda* of curse woven around him is a pointer to the historical development of synthesis of religious faiths in the Puranic times.

Here we come to two accounts, not connected to one another, having the motif of 'curse', through which we can get to the social history of the Epic and Puranic times. In these accounts 'curse' serves as a device of *arthavāda*, which sheds light on the society and practices of those times.

The first account is of King Saudāsa who became 'Kalmāṣapāda'—i.e. having black feet, and hence also called by that name. The account appears in the *Rām.* (Uttara 65.10-38). and in the *Mbh.* (Ādi 181). But as the *Bhāg P.* has dealt with this episode at a great length with details, we take it as a base, also referring to other Purāṇas. According to the account in the *Bhāg. P.*, once King Saudāsa went out hunting in the forest. There he killed a demon but left his brother unhurt. The brother who escaped unhurt decided to take revenge upon the king for the fatal hunt of his brother. He cunningly got himself engaged as a royal cook at the palace of Saudāsa. On one occasion he managed to serve a dish of human flesh to the king and his preceptor the sage Vasiṣṭha, who was the (king's) guest. Vasiṣṭha was quick to note the mischief and suspecting the hand of the king in the affair, cursed the latter to get turned into a demon as he performed a demoniac act. But when he realized that it was not the mistake of the king, he modified the curse by limiting the demonhood only to twelve years. The king also got enraged at this lack of reason in his preceptor and took water in his hand to curse back. He would have carried his decision through had not his wife Madayantī pacified him. The potent water which he held in his palm however, could not be thrown anywhere lest it should cause injury. Hence, he dropped it on his own feet whereupon his feet became black, and he was therefore called 'Kalmāṣapāda'.[29] King Saudāsa thus got turned into demon Kalmāṣapāda. The account in the *Bhāg. P.* says further that once this demon Kalmāṣapāda was reaming in the forest and saw a *brāhmaṇa*-couple in sexual union. Kalmāṣapāda, being hungry, caught hold of the *brāhmaṇa* and began to devour him unmindful of the entreaties of his wife, even though she hinted at his noble birth and implored upon him to spare her husband as her desire for a son remained unfulfilled. But the demon did not leave the *brāhmaṇa* and ate him up. Now he incurred another curse, this time from the angry and (for that time turned) revengeful wife of the unfortunate *brāhmaṇa*, according to which he would die the moment he enjoyed sexual union with his wife to procreate a son (*Bhāg. P.* IX.9.26f). Twelve years elapsed and the demon Kalmāṣapāda became free from the first curse (that of Vasiṣṭha), coming to his own form of the king. As he was leading his normal life, he once wanted to have union with his wife. But she forbade him, for she 'knew' the curse of the *brāhmaṇa's* wife given to him in his demon-form. He was, thus, in no position to procreate a son for himself (and a heir to the throne). At his request Vasiṣṭha procreated a son for him from his wife Madayantī (*ibid.* IX.9.37-38).

It can be seen that in this account we have a double curse, the first by the sage Vasiṣṭha and the second by the wife of the *brāhmaṇa*. The first curse is the basis of the second curse. The first curse is incurred in normal life and it is this curse that made him a demon. This curse then justifies the act of devouring the *brāhmaṇa* on the part of Kalmāṣapāda, who thereby incurs the second curse. It has to be noted that the second curse was not directed at the demon but at the king himself. The *brāhmaṇa* woman does not curse the king as a demon. As a matter of fact, she recognises him as the king and does not accept his being a demon. She says that he is the very husband of Madayantī (*Bhāg. P.* IX.9.26-27). The question which naturally arises is—How did the *brāhmaṇa's* wife recognise the husband of Madayantī? Again, how could Madayantī know that her husband was cursed by a *brāhmaṇa*-woman to die at the moment of copulation? (*ibid.* IX.9.37b).

Putting these curses together, it could well be said that the second curse imbibes the truth and it is that the king was sonless and got a son procreated by *niyoga* through Vasiṣṭha. An explanation of this fact was felt necessary, as the practice of *niyoga* pricked the sense of morality of the later generations though it was in vogue in very early times.[30] Manu first enjoins it or rather, we should say, documents it and immediately after, denounces it (Manu Sm. IX.59; 64-68). But even then the fact of such a practice in the past remained, and *niyoga*-born heroes, taken to be legal, dominated the tradition, which had to be accepted and respected. There are many such examples, found in the *Mbh.*[31] These facts had to suit the changed circumstances and new ideals of moral. They had to be explained and the motif of curse was employed, while in certain other cases it was mixed with the concept of divine birth. The case of the Pāṇḍavas born out of *niyoga* invites attention. The *Mbh.* at one place states that they were the five Indras in their former birth and were cursed by Śaṅkara to be born as human beings (*Mbh.* Ādi 196.16-26; especially 35). At another place, they are said to be the five husbands of Draupadī, whom she got by the boon from Śaṅkara (*ibid.* Ādi 168.6-15). Here the curse and boon appear to be the two sides of the same coin. At still another place, the Pāṇḍavas are said to be born from the divine personae.[32] This was actually due to the boon, which Kuntī (the mother of the Pāṇḍavas) got from the sage Durvāsa, while attending upon him, when she was an unmarried girl (*Mbh.* Ādi 67.133-134; 110.6). Such clear cases of *niyoga* are explained in such a way to suit the changed social order. In the case of the Pāṇḍavas, the point yet goes further. If the Pāṇḍavas had divine birth, it is all to the good.[33] The real reason behind this divine birth is obvious. Pāṇḍu is unable to procreate. Hence, the divinities are brought in the picture. Why is Pāṇḍu unable to procreate? He was cursed by the sage Kindama, who having taken the form of a deer was copulating with his wife, who was also in the form of a female deer. According to the curse, Pāṇḍu was to die at the moment of union with his wife, for he had killed the said sage, who was in the same state (of copulation) in the form of a deer.[34]

It can be seen that in the episode of King Saudāsa-Kalmāṣapāda, and in the curse therein, the case of the said king (Saudāsa) is the same as that of Pāṇḍu. The point of *niyoga* is the very crux of this account. This is clear from the fact that the *brāhmaṇa's* wife was also desirous of a child, when Saudāsa

Kalmāṣapāda (the demon) devoured her husband (*Bhāg. P.* IX.9.27b). She curses him likewise (*ibid.* 35b). Once this is understood, it is easy to see why Madayantī is said to ward her husband from copulating with her (*ibid.* 37), like Mādrī warding off Pāṇḍu lest he should be dead (*Mbh.* Ādi 124.8).

In this light, the account of Kalmāṣapāda is to be reversed and the points to be noted are—

1. *Niyoga* was necessary, because the king was not in a position to procreate;
2. He was not in a position to procreate, because he was cursed by a *brāhmaṇa* woman;
3. He was cursed by her, for he devoured the *brāhmaṇa* (her husband) in the act of procreation;
4. He devoured the *brāhmaṇa*. Because—? This must be explained. Human flesh is devoured by demons. Hence—
5. He was (!) a demon, for he was cursed to be such by Vasiṣṭha;
6. He was so cursed as he served human flesh to Vasiṣṭha, knowingly or unknowingly;
7. This in its turn, brought the demon whose brother was killed by Saudāsa and who got entry in the king's kitchen. A curse thus brought a number of devices in its trail and it was itself necessary to accommodate the fact of *niyoga* in a changed society.

There is yet another important point. The fact clearly appears to be that King Saudāsa was suffering from a deadly disease, which showed its signs on his feet. That is exactly why he was called 'Kalmāṣa-pāda.[35] The tradition was in the know of the deadliness of the skin-disease and the texts on Āyurveda have dealt with such a disease under the name 'Kuṣṭha', with all its details,[36] *Carakasaṁhitā* giving its different types also.[37] Now *'kalmāṣa'*[38] means 'variegated' or 'black and white'. Actually the colour of the skin affected by *'kuṣṭha'* is also spoken of in the same way.[39] It might be *kuṣṭha* most probably or any other such disease, which was thought to be ill-fated or harmful. In that case it is quite probable that such a person, much less a king, would be forbidden or himself desist from having sexual union with his wife lest he should contaminate the progeny. This would itself necessitate *niyoga* and would also require a curse to account for the dreadful disease.

There obtains a belief supported by the Sūtras that the image of god should not be mutilated.[40] The king being divine[41] is expected to be of sound health and at least should have no bodily defect. Here we have the instance of Devāpi, who could not be coronated on the throne, as he was suffering from a skin-disease (*Mbh.* Udyoga 149.17, 22-25).[42] Hence Devāpi abdicated his right to the throne in favour of his younger brother Śantanu. This shows that a king, as the very god or the very incarnation of the god, the supreme mortal, could not be tolerated with a defective body, howsoever compassionate the people might be towards him. Unlike Devāpi, Kalmāṣapāda appears to have developed the disease after his installation on the throne and marriage. The disease in a king—the representative of the divinity—is inauspicious. It must be due to a curse or some unfortunate event! Hence, again, the device of the quarrel between Vasiṣṭha and the king. In reality, the king with his diseased feet—black-spotted feet—might have gone away to the wilds in desperation, leaving his royal palace. He could not have direct sexual contact with his wife and had to accept the way of *niyoga* to avoid the eventuality of the state being without a king.

It should also be noted that in the *Mbh.*, it is not Vasiṣṭha who curses the king to be a demon. It is Śakti—the son of Vasiṣṭha. The curse comes, not in the dining chamber of the king, but on a lonely passage in the forest. It is said that the passage was so narrow as to facilitate only one person to pass at a time.[43] The king and the sage came in opposite directions and there was an argument for giving priority in passing. The demon named 'Kiṅkara' now enters the kings' body at the desire of Viśvāmitra (*Mbh.* Ādi 175.21). It should be noted that here in the *Mbh.* the account gets into the setting of the traditional feud of Vasiṣṭha and Viśvāmitra.[44] It is he (i.e. the King Saudāsa, now turned demon) orders the cook to serve human flesh to a *brāhmaṇa* and not to Vasiṣṭha. He devours Śakti himself. He devours also a *brāhmaṇa* in sexual union, whose wife curses him that he would die at the moment of sexual union with his wife and that he would get a son *only through Vasiṣṭha* (*ibid.* Ādi 181.20). This would show that in the *Mbh.* also the whole account boils down to the point of *niyoga.*

According to the *Ram.*, the king kills one of the demons in the previous birth, and is deceived by the other demon as he was performing the Horse-sacrifice (in the next birth). The rest of the account—the curse and the foot-disease of the king—is the same as in the accounts we have noted (*Rām.* Uttara 65.10-38).

Putting all the points together, it appears that the main cause for the account of Saudāsa to become legendary is the fact of the *niyoga* with Vasiṣṭha. The *Bhāg. P.* states that on the word of the king (who was cursed by the *brāhmaṇa's* wife), Vasiṣṭha procreated a son on the king's wife, Madayantī (*Bhāg. P.* IX.9.38). Here the curse of the *brāhmaṇī* only hints at the death of the king, if he would try to approach his wife for laying the seed (*ibid.* IX.9.35), but does not speak of the *niyoga* with Vasiṣṭha, though it was the eventual necessity of the king. But in the account from the *Mbh.* noted above by us, the most significant words, obviously, are those of the wife of the *brāhmaṇa*, killed in sexual union (*Mbh.* Ādi 181.20). The same Vasiṣṭha, whose sons the king killed (*ibid.* Ādi 175.40, 42), would create a son from the wife of Saudāsa—as if in revenge! Irony of 'Fate' indeed!!

Does this indicate that there was disrupture between the king and his family priest-Vasiṣṭha—because of *niyoga*? Though in all the accounts the point of *niyoga* comes subsequent to the '*curse-ful*' disrupture, was it a cause of the latter? The point to be noted is that Vasiṣṭha was the king's preceptor. Could he be the rightful person to be appointed for the *niyoga*? Here we have to pause a little and think. The question is—who could be appointed for *niyoga*? The tradition recorded in the Dharmaśāstra texts states that in the case of a son-less widow or a son-less woman having a sexually impotent husband, the person to be appointed in *niyoga*, could be her younger brother-in-law, a *sapiṇḍa* person, a *sagotra* person[45] or a person having the same *pravara*. In this, the woman and also the person from the above-mentioned categories,[46] had to be permitted by the *gurus* i.e. the elders. This was mandatory.[47] The *gurus*[48], including the family preceptor, were there to appoint a suitable person. In the case of Saudāsa Kalmāṣapāda, the family priest and preceptor Vasiṣṭha is himself appointed. This case thus stands as a unique one.[49] It is not improbable that Vasiṣṭha got appointed in agreement with the queen Madayantī, as the king was diseased. The king, with the awkwardness of the appointment questioned this act of his preceptor. He took revenge by killing Vasiṣṭha's son Śakti and also other sons, the latter at the behest of Viśvāmitra. The curses occurring in Saudāsa Kalmāṣapāda's episode only support this prominent fact of an *awkward niyoga* and the resultant disrupture between the king and his preceptor, who was expected to know the moral tradition—a point clearly suggested in the speech of Arjuna—"Why did King Kalmāṣapāda appoint his wife to his *guru*, who was the very knower of the *brahman*? And why even the great sage Vasiṣṭha, *knowing the proper tradition of law*, committed *the act with a lady that was Forbidden*? (*Mbh.* Ādi 181.1, 2). Howsoever the curses in this episode try to convince us, the questions posed before Arjuna stand as our questions also, with no answers in view!

We now take another curse recorded in the *Bhāg. P.*, *Matsya P.* and the *Mbh.* (critical ed. Ādi 211.27ff), which speaks of a fact of the social order of those times. It is the curse given to Dīrghatamas by Bṛhaspati. The account says that Bṛhaspati and Utathya (in the *Matsya P.* the name is 'Uśija') were brothers. Utathya's (i.e. elder brother's) wife Mamatā was having in her womb a foetus from her husband (Utathya). Once Bṛhaspati had a desire for copulation with Mamatā. While he was having union with Mamatā, the foetus (from Utathya) began to object. But Bṛhaspati without hesitation had his own way cursing the child to be blind from birth and the child was called Dīrghatamas. The account further tells that Mamatā wanted to get rid of Bṛhaspati's seed for fear of her husband. But the gods said that Mamatā should bear the second foetus, as it was of both (*dvāja*) Bṛhaspati and Utathya (*aurasa* son of Bṛhaspati and *kṣetraja* son of Utathya).[50]

Taking into consideration these accounts from the Purāṇas and the *Mbh.*, we note that Mamatā denies Bṛhaspati's demand for copulation, for she is already carrying the seed of her husband Utathya. This would show that she did not think Bṛhaspati's act as immoral, but that she was only concerned with her particular condition at that time.[51] Here we have a case of a younger brother having an easy and normally acceptable union with the wife of the elder brother. Though Manu denounces the union with the elder brother's wife (*Manu Sm.* IX.57), he enjoins such a union in *niyoga*, if the elder brother is impotent or is deceased (*ibid.* 59). But the account under consideration takes us to far earlier times. Bṛhaspati's case is similar to that of the Pāṇḍavas, who had a common wife. A common wife for all the brothers was an order of the day in times far back in the Uttarakurus and in other places in the world.[52] In the case of the Pāṇḍavas, they had equal right to the common wife during their lifetime. Nārada only laid down an arrangement so that there should be no jealousy. But the *Mbh.* does not say here anything about immorality (*Mbh.* Ādi. 211.27ff). This hints at the original concept in marriage that 'the girl was given to the family', all the brothers having legal right over her. Draupadī is seen strictly observing rules in satisfying all the brothers.[53]

When the account of Bṛhaspati and Mamatā traditionally survived, in later times a twist was given to the account by introducing the unwillingness of the former foetus, indicating that at the time of conception from one brother, the other had no right of union.[54] But the account went on with the main point that the wife had no objection. The objection and fear in the mind of Mamatā as seen in the two Purāṇas, especially the *Bhāg. P.* belong to the later times, when the standards of morality are seen to have changed. Hence the objection of Mamatā serves only for making the conscience clear; the conscience not of hers but of the then society. Yet the curse given by Bṛhaspati to the foetus (who later on became 'Dīrghatamas' by name) shows the nature of social order as it was in its earlier stages, far back in the deep layers of history.[55]

Kantawala takes a note of this episode. From Mamatā's words (*Matsya P.* 48.36), it seems that there was nothing repulsive in the sexual intimacy of a younger brother with his elder brother's wife, even when the elder brother was alive. Kantawala's remark that the episode suggests that 'mating need not be confounded with marriage' is very interesting.[56]

Kantawala's remark may be true in the case of the episode considered by him previously. But it appears unconvincing as far as the episode of 'Mamatā-Bṛhaspati' goes. Here a peep into the history and practice of certain customs in a particular social order of bygone times, proves fruitful. The custom of group-marriage based on the principle that 'a girl is given to the family' helps immensely and can unfold many a mystery.

Now we come to the curse given by the sage Māṇḍavya to Dharma, as a result of which the latter was born in the *śūdra varṇa*. The episode of the curse occurs in the *Mbh.* in two (small) chapters. (*Mbh.* Ādi chaps. 106 and 107).[57] The account in short is as follows. The righteous sage Māṇḍavya, observing the vow of *mauna* (not speaking anything, thus having complete restriction on speech) was once practising penance in his hermitage. At that time, some robbers carrying with them the stolen loot entered the hermitage and hid themselves there with the loot. To the guards of the king, who followed the robbers, the sage did not give any reply. But they caught the robbers and also the stolen property. When they reported everything to the king, the king gave death punishment to the robbers and ordered the royal guards to impale the sage on a spike, taking him also as joined with the robbers. (*Mbh.* Ādi chap. 106.2-13). But the sage, not taking any food, practised penance, though impaled on the spike (*ibid.* 14-15). On the report of the guards that the sage was alive in that state even after many days, the king knew his mistake and asked for pardon. He ordered that the sage be released and be brought down from the spike. But the spike pierced in the sage's body could not be extricated and the sage moved with the same spike, getting the title 'Aṇīmaṇḍavya' ('Māṇḍavya with *aṇī*' i.e. a linchpin). After death, when he attained, with his penance, the righteous worlds, he saw the god Dharma ('Yama'—here mentioned as Dharma) and asked him the cause of his severe sufferings on the earth (as he had carried the spike in his body throughout the whole life). Dharma said that Aṇīmāṇḍavya in his childhood (*bālabhāve*), had pricked a thorn in the body of butterflies (actually in their hinder part). Aṇīmāṇḍavya had suffered due to this sin. Aṇīmāṇḍavya replied that whatever sin a child (boy/girl) committed up to twelve years of his age, would not be known to the quarters also. In fact, up to the fourteenth year of his life, no action of the child could be regarded as a sin. Aṇīmāṇḍavya thus sets this age-limit for a child's fault. But he curses Dharma that as the latter has made the *brāhmaṇa* (i.e. Aṇīmāṇḍavya) die, in fact has become the cause of the *brāhmaṇa's* death, which is regarded as the highest sin (one of the five *mahāpātakas*), he i.e. Dharma, would be born as a human being in the *śūdra varṇa.* And thus was born Dharma as Vidura (*ibid.* Ādi 107.2-19), due to the curse given to him by Aṇīmāṇḍavya.

This episode of curse is important on many accounts.

1. Killing of harmless creatures is a sinful act.[58]
2. In spite of such a sin a *brāhmaṇa* is not to be punished, so as to cause his death.[59]
3. This also indicates the mode of punishment even going to the extent of 'Life for life'.
4. The birth of Dharma as Vidura in the *śūdra varṇa*.
5. The age of juvenile mistake (crime or sin) seems to be up to the 'fourteenth' year. After that the boy or girl is regarded as having full understanding of his 'doing', as an adult, and hence liable for punishment due for the adult.

The most important point is the birth of Vidura from a *śūdra* woman, the maidservant of Ambikā (*Mbh.* Ādi 105.23-30). A respectable personality in the well-known Kaurava family, Vidura acquires the position of a law-expounder. He acquires a status next only to Bhīṣma. His sense of justice and adherence to it naturally evoke respect, equating him with Dharma (or Yama—the lord of Dharma). But the influence of the brahmanical religion cannot tolerate a *śūdra* as a wise man. Hence for a person like Vidura, it must have been a curse from the previous life. An unpalatable fact is thus transformed by employing the motif of curse.[60] This episode of Aṇīmāṇḍavya, involving a curse, works on both social and individual levels, the strategy of curse proving to be most beneficial for the *Mbh.*, while explaining the wisdom of Vidura vis-a-vis his *śūdratva*, due to his mother.

Here we now come to a curse, which tries to explain the practice of employing the Gāyatrī metre by various sects to invoke their respective deities. These sects were there (some of these coming down also to the present era) prevalent in the Puranic times in the Vedic-brahmanical Hindu society itself. *Padma P.* (Pātālakhaṇḍa 108.87) mentions Rudra-gāyatrī *mantra*, while the *Liṅga P.* (II.48.5-26) mentions as many as 22 Gāyatrī *mantras* (i.e. *mantras* in the Gāyatrī metre), addressed to and invoking each of the deities—Śiva, Gaurī, Rudra, Dantī (i.e.

lord Gaṇeśa), Skanda, Vṛṣa, Nandī, Viṣṇu, Lakṣmī, Rādhā, Garuḍa, Sraṣṭā (i.e. god Brahmā), Speech (as goddess), Śakra (i.e. Indra), Vahni (i.e. Agni), Yama, Nirṛti (goddess of Death), Varuṇa, Vāyu, Yakṣa, Rudra and Durgā. In this list, some are the names of gods, some others of goddesses, and even the name of the semi-divine being Yakṣa. This shows the practice of invoking these deities in the Puranic times. As the Gāyatrī metre employed in the *mantra* invoking the god Savitṛ was well-known from the *Ṛgveda* (*RV* III.62.10 in the hymn from the Viśvāmitra *maṇḍala*), the same metre was chosen by various sects. So there are seen various Gāyatrīs, each having the name of the deity of that sect. The *Skanda P.* mentions a Gāyatrī name 'Ajapā', which is specially suited for a *yogī* and which destroys the sins of a man simply by meditating on it (*Sk.P.* IV.41.158). There are several such Gāyatrīs which are given with the details thereof.[61] This was the practice of the day that the sacred *mantra* of a sect had to be in the Gāyatrī metre, the original god Savitṛ (the Sun-god) left far off, when it was a Sāvitrī-Gāyatrī *mantra*.

Now to account for this phenomenon in the changed circumstances of the Purāṇas, Sāvitrī (the god Savitṛ taken as a goddess) and Gāyatrī had to be shown as independent separate deities, anthropomorphising them and even showing them as quarrelling with each other. And to account for this, the *Sk.P.* has woven a mythical account and has used the device of curse. The account, obviously an *arthavāda*, runs as follows. Once Brahmā was performing a sacrifice at Hāṭakeśvara. According to the need and tradition of the sacrifice, his wife as *yajamānapatnī* was to be with him. Se he sent Nārada to call Sāvitrī. Nārada suiting to his mischievous nature, wanting to create a quarrel between Sāvitrī and Brahmā, told Sāvitrī to go to the sacrifice at her leisure, taking with her the wives of the gods. As the proper time of the sacrifice was elapsing, Brahmā asked Indra to bring some maiden (in place of his wife). Indra spotted a cowherd girl and calling her, caused her to enter the mouth of a cow and pulled her through the cow's anus. Indra thus purified her and having given her bath, brought her to the place of sacrifice of Brahmā. As the maiden was thus purified, Viṣṇu told Brahmā to marry her. The maiden was named Gāyatrī, as she was caused to enter the mouth of the cow ('*go*') and come out from the cow's anus (*Sk.P.* VI.181.3-75; VI.188.56-83; 189.1ff). As Brahmā's sacrifice was to start at Hāṭakeśvara and the wives of the gods had assembled for the ritual of establishing the Audumbarī[62], Sāvitrī came there, and naturally became furious. She cursed the *brāhmaṇas* (priests) that they would be devoid of a proper dwelling place. She also cursed the goddesses, who took resort to the Audumbarī for protection. According to another account in the *Sk.P.* itself, Sāvitrī, after learning about the marriage of Brahmā and Gāyatrī, came to Brahmā's sacrifice and cursed the pair (Brahmā and Gāyatrī) and all other gods. (*Sk.P.* VI.192.81ff). In this very context, Sāvitrī's curse to Gāyatrī accompanied by indecorous words is to be noted, when we are discussing the strategy of curse as justifying some issue. Sāvitrī here curses Gāyatrī, the *gopakanyā* (as she is said to be originally), censuring her as 'a condemned cowherdess" (*vigarhitā āhīrī*), "having no character like a prostitute" (*veśyeva naṣṭacaritā*) and "having many husbands" (*bahubhartṛkā*) (*Sk.P.* VI.192.54). She also would be termed "one having five husbands" (*ibid.* 62). The account occurs also elsewhere.[63] These words uttered by Sāvitrī while cursing Gāyatrī are to be taken not by the 'Abhidhā' power of the word but by the 'Lakṣaṇā' power. They point out that Gāyatrī (i.e. the Gāyatrī metre and particularly the pattern of words in the Gāyatrī metre addressed to the god Savitṛ) can be taken to invoke any deity and we have noted such 22 deities stated in the *Liṅga P.* The curse given by Sāvitrī is thus for justifying the practice of having so many Gāyatrīs i.e. Gāyatrī *mantras*, in use in the then society, coming down to the modern times.

Here we come to a type of curses, which are for reiterating the established fact. To take the account from the *Sk.P.* Once some of the *brāhmaṇas*, being hungry came to the ocean, as they did not get alms. The ocean gave them food prepared from fish, as there was nothing else to give. After having come to know of this, the *brāhmaṇas* cursed the ocean that its water would be unsuitable for drinking, and it would be undeserving of being touched by the *brāhmaṇas* and other respectable men. Due to the curse the ocean started getting dry and the gods were worried. Brahmā went to the *brāhmaṇas* and pacified them, telling that the ocean would give them gems and the *brāhmaṇas* would be called *'bhūdeva'* ('Gods on the earth'). The *brāhmaṇas* being pleased, blessed the ocean saying that a dip in its water at auspicious periods will be as meritorious as at the confluence of rivers and at holy places (*Sk.P.* VII.1.29.91). The curse here is given to explain the saltiness of the waters of ocean, which is already known to the people.[64] The boon following the curse is to support the practice of having a dip in the sea or ocean at auspicious periods.

Another curse is the one given to the cow Surabhi. The account is given in the *Sk.P.* that once when Brahmā and Viṣṇu were quarrelling, a lustrous fiery *liṅga* (*jyotirliṅga*) emerged in between them. As the *liṅga* fell off, Brahmā and Viṣṇu went in search of its ends. But neither of them could find the ends. However while returning from the heaven, Brahmā was noticed by the celestial cow (Kāmadhenu) as he rested on the top of the mountain Meru. The cow resting near the Ketakī-tree offered herself to be a witness (obviously false) to his having seen the upper end of the *liṅga.* The Ketakī tree also agreed to do the same. Later coming to know Brahmā's fraud, Śiva cursed him and debarred the Ketakī flower from his worship (*Sk.P.* I.1.6.25-50). And the celestial cow Surabhi (here the name is not 'Kāmadhenu') was cursed by the gods and Viṣṇu that as she had told a lie with her mouth, her mouth would be unclean and forbidden in all religious acts (*ibid.* 61-

62). Though not given here, the same curse could be said to be transferred to an ordinary cow, for her mouth is also regarded as unclean and the things licked by her are likewise taken to be impure. Here the curse to Surabhi serves a double purpose. It brings out the fact already known and gives an ethical note that telling a lie takes one to ruin.

The river Sarasvatī is said to be cursed to have the flow of water mixed with blood for a period of one year. As Dange has stated this appears to hint at a geological point.[65] The account of the curse given to the river Sarasvatī by Viśvāmitra occurs in the *Mbh.* Viśvāmitra and Vasiṣṭha, as per their age-old rivalry, were having severe competition, both practising penance. Viśvāmitra being the more fiery one ordered the river Sarasvatī to bring Vasiṣṭha to him, carried in her waters. The river Sarasvatī naturally was in a fix being afraid of a curse from both the sages. However, she carried Vasiṣṭha to Viśvāmitra in her flow. But as she noticed a deadly missile with Viśvāmitra to kill Vasiṣṭha, she carried away Vasiṣṭha in her waters quickly to the eastern quarter, vexed with the fear of committing *brahmahatyā* (though indirectly). And here the curse was flung at her by Viśvāmitra that she should carry or bear blood in the flow of her waters for one year (*Mbh.* Śalya 42.9-40).

As Dange has rightly pointed out, there is indication that the water of the river Sarasvatī turned reddish in some fraction of it. The place Samantapañcaka which is in the vicinity of the river Sarasvatī is said to have been formed from the blood of the *kṣatriyas* killed by Paraśurāma (*Mbh.* Ādi 2.1-5). Again as pointed out in the Śalyaparvan, which reference we have noted above, this stretch of the river Sarasvatī seems to have been through the habitat of the non-Aryan localities, whom the Aryans called *'rakṣas'* (*Mbh.* Śalya 42.39—*rakṣo grāmaṇisammatam*). Due to the defect of the water as having reddish colour (most probably due to the mud it carried) and due to its association with the non-Aryan localities, this stretch was avoided by the Vedic people. Ultimately after hundred years, this stretch was purified by the sages, by bringing the river Aruṇā to confluence with it (*ibid.* 43.2-31).[66] The curse given to the river Sarasvatī thus tries to explain the phenomenon of the reddish colour of its water prevalent in those times. Such a curse occurs in the Rāma story, narrated by the *Padma P.* It is said that Rāma got furious at the river Godāvari for she also could not protect Sītā. He cursed her and the water of the river Godāvarī tuned red. On the request of the sages to purify the river, Rāma said that she would be purified only when Śabarī (the aboriginal ascetic woman) would take bath in her waters (*Padma P.* Uttarakhaṇḍa 269.276-277). Here the curse seems to be simply the blunt expression of Rāma's anger and may not be referring to any natural phenomenon.

That such a change of colour does occur in the waters of a river is prominently seen in the case of the river Nile, on the inundation of which the ancient Egyptions were entirely dependent. During the period of inundation, and prior to the water of the Nile turning green (indicating disease), the ancient Egyptians used to store water in big jars. The river was at the lowest during April through June. From the middle of June, it began to rise, with its water having reddish hue due to the mud it carried. Then for a short period till July end it turned green. By the beginning of August the Nile ran high, when the canals were opened up for irrigation up to September. By the end of September the flood receded, and there started sowing in November.[67]

We now come to an 'occasion' of curse, which is concerned with an established practice of offerings, coming down even to modern times, in India. It is about *'naivedya' (fr. ni +√vid*—causal—'to make or cause to know specifically'), offered to any deity (through which the deity is made to know the devotion of the devotee). The account occurs in the *Brahmavaivarta P.* (Śrīkṛṣṇakhaṇḍa 37.3-32). Once Śiva ate up the whole *naivedya* offered to Viṣṇu, which made Pārvatī very angry. But Śiva pleased her with folded hands, praising her in various words. Pārvatī did not curse Śiva (*ibid.* 14-15), but she reprimanded him for his mistake of eating the whole *naivedya* alone without giving any portion of it to anybody, even to her (*ibid.* 31). The salient feature of *naivedya* is that a portion of it is returned to the offerer for eating, though the whole *naivedya* is presented to the god. Hence she admonished Śiva by saying that from that day onwards all those who ate the *naivedya* offered to Śiva would be turned into dogs for one life (*ibid.* 32). The account runs further stating that Pārvatī became ready to cast off her mortal frame as she was deprived of the *naivedya* offered to Viṣṇu. But Śiva again praises her in noblest words and Pārvatī is calmed down (*ibid.* 36-49). The account is important for it tries to give a convincing explanation for the practice of *naivedya.* And as the *Brahmavaivarta P.* is a Vaiṣṇavite Purāṇa, the account ends in showing Viṣṇu to be a great god, superior even to Śiva. But this is brought out in a very soft way, the trend of reconciliation between the Śaivite and Vaiṣṇavite sects never lost sight of.

Here we come to a series of curses. The curse in this category is flung at a person, when an act of disrespecting the sage or disobeying the preceptor is committed by the person.

The account of Nahuṣa's curse can be seen in this respect. Indra is afraid of the sin of *brahmahatyā*, which he has committed twice by killing Viśvarūpa and later on Vṛtra (both being the sons of Tvaṣṭṛ—*brāhmaṇas*). He, therefore hides himself in a lotus-stem, becoming very small in size. Nahuṣa usurps his throne and longs for Śacī-the wife of Indra. Śacī desperate for protection, avoiding him approaches Indra (her husband) for help. On his advice, Śacī asks Nahuṣa to bring for her a vehicle dragged by the sages. Nahuṣa smitten by passion for her brings it. And here occurs the curse of Agastya, when he sees Nahuṣa humiliating the sages and stamping them under his foot. Agastya says that as Nahuṣa has started on a sinful errand, becoming a serpent he would fall on the earth and would stay there as long as the mountains could be there on the earth. And down falls Nahuṣa due to that curse (*Mbh.* Śānti 342.42-51). This is obviously due to the arrogance of Nahuṣa, which the curse brings to the forefront. Nahuṣa's release from the curse (and incidentally from serpenthood) occurs in the Vanaparvan of the *Mbh.*, when he catches hold of Bhīma, and Yudhiṣṭhira answers all the questions put by Nahuṣa (*ibid.* Vana 180.6-38; 181.1-44).

The *Bhāg. P.* relates the account how Jaya and Vijaya, the doorkeepers of Viṣṇu obstructed the sages Sanaka etc. and made fun of them, when they arrived at the seventh quadrangle of the region of Vaikuṇṭha. The sages Sanaka etc. were great thinkers, though they looked like children of only five years. They could not tolerate the disrespect shown to them and hence cursed the two—Jaya and Vijaya to be born as despicable beings (*pāpayoni*) (*Bhāg. P.* III.15.12-34). Even Viṣṇu felt that the punishment given to them, as a result of curse, was quite appropriate, their fault being grievous (*ibid.* III.16.2-3). The *Bhāg. P.* states that the two doorkeepers (Jaya and Vijaya) entered the womb of Diti, to be born as the two famous *asuras*, Hiraṇyākṣa and Hiraṇyakaśipu (*ibid.* III. chap. 17). The curse evidently arisen from the disrespect shown to the sages serves an important purpose. It shows how even the *asuras* (Hiraṇyākṣa and Hiraṇyakaśipu) were in the former birth attached to Viṣṇu. Temporarily staying as the *asuras*, they ultimately got united with the god, suiting to the peculiar Puranic trait of 'Virodha-bhakti' (enmity turning into devotion), which we have noted earlier in the context of the *asuras*.

The curse given to the six sons of Prajāpati Marīci falls in line with the curse mentioned above. It is said that in the Svāyambhuva Manvantara, Prajāpati Marīci's six sons from his wife Ūrṇā laughed at him when he was enamoured of his own daughter. Due to their disrespect to their father (i.e.

elders), they were cursed to be *asuras* and thus were born as sons to Hiraṇyakaśipu. The goddess Yogamāyā snatched them from their chamber when they were infants and placed them, one after the other, as the six foetuses of Devakī. The moment they were born, Kaṁsa killed them one by one (*Bhāg. P.* X.85.47-55).

The episode of a python who caught hold of Nanda, Śrīkṛṣṇa's father, bears the same moral that disrespect shown to elderly persons leads to curse, resulting into punishment. When Śrīkṛṣṇa freed his father from the clutches of the python, by touching the latter with his feet, the python turned into a handsome Vidyādhara, with his sins washed off by the touch of Śrīkṛṣṇa. Vidyādhara explained that being proud of his handsome form and abundant riches, he once ridiculed the deformed sages of the Aṅgirasa family, who then cursed him to be a python (*Bhāg. P.* X.34.5-18).

The two sons of Kubera-Nalakūbara and Maṇigrīva—also could not escape from curse, when they paid no respect to Nārada. Nalakūbara and Maṇigrīva, intoxicated with wine, were enjoying water-sport with young women. On Nārada's arrival there, the sons of Kubera, neither wore their garments nor showed any respect to him. Hence his curse to them to become two Arjuna-trees for hundred years (*Bhāg. P.* X.10.1-22). Once Kṛṣṇa was bound to the mortar by Yaśoda in order to control his mischievous activities. As Kṛṣṇa dragged the mortar along with him and passed swiftly from these two trees, he gave a quick jerk to the mortar. And down fell the two trees being uprooted and there emerged the two divine persons from the trees. These were Nalakūbara and Maṇigrīva noted above by us (*Bhāg.P.* X.9.12ff). The curse episode is joined to the account of childhood wonderful exploit of Kṛṣṇa, for the emergence of two divine persons from the twin-trees required an explanation. The words of Nārada while giving the curse are important. They point out the futility of the mortal frame of man and his pride for riches. The ethical note is given of showing respect to the elders and the excess of wine is condemned (*Bhāg. P.* X.10.8-20).

We are here reminded of the episode from the *Mbh.* when Kaśyapa intended to perform a sacrifice with a desire for son, he asked Indra and the ascetics for bringing sacrificial faggots. On the way, Indra saw the Vālakhilyas, the thumbkin ascetics, all together carrying a tiny faggot and struggling hard in the 'cow-foot-mark' full of water. At this Indra laughed at them. And then the resolve of the Vālakhilyas, which they fulfilled, of creating (through Kaśyapa and Vinatā), Garuḍa who superseded Indra (*Mbh.* Ādi 31.5-35). It is not a curse flung at Indra. Nevertheless the decision of the Vālakhilyas to create a 'Super Being' (Garuḍa) surpassing Indra's might, has sprung up from Indra's disrespect shown to them, though this ethical note is not patent.

Not giving respect to the sages and harming them leads to one's destruction is stated by the *Varāha P.* The Purāṇa relates an account that once, Śiva in his wanderings burnt the hermitage of the sage Aurva. Aurva got furious and cursed Śiva that the latter will wander being full of sorrow. Śiva approached Nārāyaṇa for help. Viṣṇu showed him the divine cows ("the daughters of the divine cow Surabhi"). With the result Śiva got peace (*Var. P.* 147.16). The *Var.P.* being Vaiśṇavite, it is obvious that Viṣṇu is shown to have the upper hand. However the note struck in the account that even Śiva has to be a target of curse, is worthy of taking note.

We now come to the curses, which are stated simply as Anuvāda. Anuvāda is a type of *arthavāda*, which repeats or reiterates a fact already known in the world or tradition.

We see Jarā, the daughter of Kāla (Time) cursing Nārada, for the latter did not accept her amours, being a *'naiṣṭhika brahmacārin'* (a lifelong celibate). She cursed him to be a constant wanderer (*Bhāg P.* IV.27). At another place in the *Bhāg. P.*, we have the same curse inflicted on Nārada by Dakṣa, for Nārada taught the path of 'Liberation' (*mokṣa*) to Dakṣa's sons (*ibid.*

VI.5). Nārada's image in the Epics and the Purāṇas is of an eternal wanderer in all the regions (heaven, earth etc.). The *Bhāg. P.* at two places, mentioned above, only repeats this mythological fact, through the curse.

Here we have the curse given to the ocean by Āṅgirasa Bṛhaspati, which simply justifies the nature of the waters in the ocean, as we already know. It so happened that in the endeavour of churning the ocean for nectar, in the preparatory (initiatory) rite *puraścaraṇa*—the waters of the ocean were touched by Āṅgirasa Bṛhaspati, when they become turbid. Hence he cursed them to be always like that—muddy and dirty—with the creatures like fish, crocodiles and tortoises residing in them (*Mbh.* Śānti 342.27).

Agni's nature of consuming everything to its flames (*sarvabhakṣī*) has been an outcome of the curse given to Agni by the sage Bhṛgu, as stated by the *Mbh.* (*Mbh.* Ādi chaps 5 & 6). The sage Bhṛgu once had gone away from his hermitage keeping his pregnant wife Pulomā there. The demon Pulomā ('*puloman*' Mas. noun) entered that hermitage and when shown hospitality by Bhṛgu's handsome wife, became full of passion for her. He wanted to take her away with him, for she was formerly chosen by him as a wife. But as he noticed Agni burning in the fireplace in the sacrificial chamber, he entreated upon Agni to tell the truth as to whom belonged Pulomā (Bhṛgu's wife). Agni being afraid of telling falsehood as also curse from Bhṛgu, was in a dilemma. He told in a low tone that though Pulomā (the young girl) was chosen by the demon (Pulomā) formerly for being his bride, it was not accompanied by the sacred *mantras* (of the marriage-ritual). Pulomā was given to Bhṛgu by her father, observing the proper ritual, keeping Agni as a witness. Hence she belonged to Bhṛgu rightfully. Hearing this the demon got wild with rage and tried to kidnap her. But in the scuffle that ensued, from her womb fell down the foetus (fully grown), which (then) was named 'Cyavana' (fr. √*cu*—'to fall down'). The newborn babe was so dazzling with lustre that having a mere glance at it, the demon was burnt to ashes. When Bhṛgu returned to the hermitage, he came to know that it was Agni, who made known to the demon the identity of Bhṛgu's wife. So he cursed Agni to be *sarvabhakṣa* ('consuming everything'). The Ādiparvan has dealt with this episode thus in two chapters (*Mbh.* Ādi chaps. 5 and 6). But it runs further and we see the flared Agni pleading for his act of telling the truth about Pulomā, Bhṛgu's wife. Agni said that he could have given counter-curse to Bhṛgu, but Bhṛgu being a *brāhmaṇa* was to be respected and hence to be spared. Agni then decided to shun from all of his activities of carrying offerings to gods as well as to Pitṛs. The whole world stood benumbed, devoid of any activity. On the insistence of the gods and the sages, lord Brahmā pacified Agni and 'restricted' the scope of the curse given by Bhṛgu. He said that only that aspect (*tanu*-body) of Agni, known as 'kravyāda'—i.e. 'devouring the dead body on the funeral pyre', would be 'all-consuming' in nature (*ibid.* Ādi chap. 7). Then Agni agreed upon his duty of carrying oblations to the gods and the Pitṛs.

The curse-episode is significant for a couple of points. It justifies the 'consuming' nature of Agni, which is an established fact. It brings out the sanctity of the marriage-ritual, when it is accompanied with the *mantras* and performed according to proper procedure, for it is one of the important *samskāras*, in the Vedic-brahmanical Hindu religion. Incidentally, it also indicates the difficulty faced by a person, while telling truth, which could be disagreeable to another person, and reminds us of Manu's words (*Manu Sm.* IV.138b—'*na brūyāt satyamapriyam*'). Nevertheless, it fully supports a person, who is bold to speak out the truth.

In the *Mbh.* in the Anuśāsanaparvan occurs the curse given by Agni to frogs, elephants and parrots (*Mbh.* Anu. chap. 85.28, 36, 40). Prior to this in the earlier chapter we see the curse given by the goddess Umā (Pārvatī) to the gods that they would be issueless, as they had put an hindrance in her union with Śiva and nipped in the bud her desire for having an issue (*ibid.* Anu. 84.73-75). But as Agni was not present there, he was spared from Umā's curse and could carry Śiva's semen fallen on the ground (*ibid.* 76-78). Agni then entered waters in the Rasātala region and the gods came searching for Agni in the waters. A frog came gushing forth from the Rasātala region and divulged to the gods the secret of Agni's hiding place. Agni flared up and cursed the frog to be devoid of knowing the taste. (This was a curse flung at all the class of frogs). But the gods consoled the frogs by saying that even though devoid of the knowledge of taste, they would be able to utter speech of different notes; would be borne by the earth inspite of they becoming of dried up skin, resorting to holes in the ground; and would be able to go everywhere even in the darkest nights (*ibid.* Anu. 85.23-33). Not having any trace of Agni, the gods then asked the elephant and he directed them to the Aśvattha tree, where Agni had taken the resort (after leaving the waters). Agni got furious and cursed all the elephants that their tongue would be inverted (or reversed). Agni then took resort to the Śamī tree. The gods boosted the elephants saying that even with the reversed tongue, they would be able to eat everything and would be able to utter high-pitched sounds (*ibid.* 34-38). Agni's resorting to the tree Śamī was divulged by a parrot and there came the curse of Agni that the parrot (entire class) would be devoid of the ability to speak. But the gods gave the parrot a consoling word that even with the reversed tongue, the parrot's speech though indistinct would be sweet (*ibid.* 39-43). From that time onwards, the Śamī tree is regarded as the seat of Agni (*ibid.* 44). The curse given by Agni to frogs, elephants and parrots is important, for it justifies the characteristic features belonging to them and ultimately states the Śami tree as the permanent seat of Agni.

Incidentally, here we take a note of the two trees —Aśvattha (*Ficus religiosa*) and Śamī (*Prosopis spicigera* or according to some *Mimosa suma*)—mentioned here as the resort of Agni, when he was running, seeking for a hiding-place for himself. In the ritual texts several trees are reckoned as the sacrificial trees. A detail common about them is their greeness, showing their freshness and thus their living element (*Śat.Br.* I.3.4.1). The *Śat. Br.* mentions Palāśa (*Butea frondosa*), Vikaṅkata (*Flacourtia sapida*), Kārṣmarya (*Gmelina arborea*), Bilva (*Aegle marmelos*), Khadira (*Acacia catechu*), and Udumbara (*Ficus glomerata*) as the sacrificial trees and mentions enclosing sticks from them (*ibid.* I.3.3.19, 20).[68] The two trees—Aśvattha and Śamī—mentioned in the account of Agni from the *Mbh.*, figure in the account of Purūravas, which occurs in the *Śat.Br.* When Purūravas wants to be one among the *gandharvas* (as his beloved Urvaśī has gone to their world) and seeks their help, they instruct him to use the three-three fire-sticks of the Aśvattha tree to be offered in the fire. Saying that this method has become recondite, they advise him to make the upper fire-stick (*araṇi*) of Aśvattha and the lower one of Samī and finally both the fire-sticks (*araṇis*) of Aśvattha. Sacrificing with the fire produced by these *araṇis*, Purūravas becomes one of the *gandharvas* (*ibid.* XI.5.1.14-17).

The belief about the Śamī tree deeply rooted in tradition is that it contains fire or is a resort of fire. The *Mbh.* says that Agni when cursed by Bhṛgu disappeared but was found in the Śamī wood (*Mbh.* Śalya 47.14-19). The curse-episode which we discussed also points out the same belief about the Śamī tree.

The plant Tulasī came to assume importance mainly in the Puranic age. The plant is anthropomorphised as the wife of the demon Śaṅkhacūda in one birth and that of Viṣṇu in another birth. The *Brahmavaivarta P.* justifies this mythological detail by the strategy of curse. The goddess Lakṣmī once tried to settle the quarrel between the rivers Gaṅga and Sarasvatī.

Sarasvatī being angry cursed Lakṣmī to be both a tree and a river on the earth. As Lakṣmī became dejected due to the curse, Viṣṇu told her that she should go to the house of Dharmadhvaja and be born as his daughter (not having the normal but the supernatural birth-*ayonisambhavā*), and on the earth itself, she would become the wife of Śaṅkhacūḍa and become a tree (or plant). Then she would become the wife of Viṣṇu and would be famous as Tulasī in the world. As a river she would be known as Padmāvatī (*Brahmav. P.* Prakṛtikhaṇḍa 6.16-47). Even the demonhood of Śaṅkhacūḍa is due to the curse of Rādhā, for he was formerly a cowherd called Sudāman born of Viṣṇu's part (*ibid.* 16.81-82). The curse mainly aims at the deification of the plant Tulasī and tries to save the enigmatic situation of Viṣṇu's seducing the wife of Śaṅkhacūḍa, who was none other than Tulasī.

We have seen several curses from the Epics and the Purāṇas and can now come to the conclusion that the device of curse acts as a mythological strategy used to save many a situation, and mainly to connect two distant and distinct personalities or incidents, thus making us believe the normally unbelievable or problematic in mythology, that too convincingly.

We now come to the Boons which are also used as a mythological strategy. Here the demons, mainly in the Purāṇas, get a boon at the hands of the god Brahmā or Śiva, of averting death in their case. With the result, they become so insolent and belligerent, that they are killed either by Śiva or Viṣṇu.[69] We can mention only names of some demons in this connection and need not dwell on their accounts, they being practically similar. Thus we have Ādi (*Matsya P.* 155.12ff-37; *Sk.P.* I.2.29.1ff-27); Dhundhu (*Vām. P.* 52.13ff); Dūṣaṇa (*Śiva P.* IV.16.14ff); Hiraṇyakaśipu (*Śiva P.* 43.10 ff-39); Kālapṛṣṭha (*Sk.P.* V.3.67.3-76); Mura (*Vām.P.* 34.30-48; 35.74-76); and Namuci (*Vām.P.* 29.4-10 killed by Indra).

We have in the *Sk.P.* a boon asked by Agni, which requires some explanation, the boon being a justification of an age-old concept. It is said that Agni propitiated Śiva on the bank of the river Narmadā and asked him for a boon that sixteen rivers should be his wives. These actually come to seventeen in all because Narmadā and Revā (though one river) are mentioned separately. (*Sk.P.* V.3.22.2ff).[70] The boon asked by Agni and granted to him by Śiva brings out the constant association of Agni with waters. The concept goes back to the Veda. To the Vedic people the cosmos was filled with two main elements—male and female.[71] The male principle was that of Fire, distributed in the three worlds; and corresponding to it was the element of water that gets impregnated by the former.[72] According to Yāska, there are only three deities *viz.* Agni on the terrestrial region; Wind or Indra (as a Rain-god) in the mid-region and Sun in the heavenly region (*Nir.* VII.5). Interestingly in all these three regions, Agni is associated with waters. On the sacrificial plane, Agni is with Vasatīvarī, Ekadhanā, Nigrābhyā and Praṇītā waters. In the mid region, the lightning-fire (indicated by Wind or Indra) is with the cloud-waters; and in the heavenly region, Sun is the collector of all waters from the earth (*Tai. Ār.* I.8.1b *āpaḥ sūrye samāhitāḥ*). A detail regarding the Vasatīvarī waters will elucidate this point still further. The Vasatīvari waters (which are collected on the previous day of sacrifice), which are enjoined to be used in sacrifice are to be brought from the flowing current of waters. The *Tait. Sam.* states that the Vasatīvarī waters are to be taken with radiance or light in them i.e. in daytime, or if the sun sets, they are to be taken having deposited a piece of gold in the jar or they are to be taken from the Vasatīvarī waters kept in a jar of a *brāhmaṇa,* who performs many sacrifices and thus has collected the Vasatīvarī waters (*Tait. Sam.* VI.4.2.2). It has to be noted that the Vasatīvarī waters are connected either with the sun or Agni or gold or a *brāhamaṇa*, all of them having lustre, in the case of a *brāhmaṇa*, the lustre of *brahman*. The *Śat.Br.* also states that if the waters are required to be collected after the sunset, the sacrificer (or the priest) has to hold a firebrand or a piece of gold close above the waters. This is for having the effect of the yonder sun on waters (*Śat. Br.* III.9.2.9). Agni as we have noted earlier is the form of the sun i.e. the principle of 'Heat', and gold is said to be the seed of Agni. When Agni united with waters, his seed became gold, says the *Śat.Br.* (II.1.1.4, 5).

So when Agni asks for a boon to marry sixteen rivers as we have seen from the *Sk.P.* or Agni called Śaṁsya married sixteen rivers, which include many important rivers (practically the same with little variations as given in the *Sk.P.*), as the *Brahmāṇḍa P.* states (I.2.12.13ff), it is an allegorical explanation or justification of the age-old Ṛgvedic concept that Agni rests in all streams (*RV* VIII.39.8). And it is our actual experience that the flowing waters are lukewarm for touch as they contain the heat of the sun and thus are possessed of Agni—the principle of heat.

We have seen how the device of *arthavāda* has made use of curses and boons, by which the matter in hand is explained and stands justified. Here we take two accounts from the *Mbh.*, in which occur swearings and oaths, coming as *arthavāda*.

The practice of taking an oath or swearing can be traced to the *RV*. We see Vasiṣṭha saying that if he is '*anṛtadeva*' ('whose gods prove false') or if he approaches the gods in vain, Agni should injure him (*RV* VII.104.14ab and Sāyaṇa's comm. on it). On this very occasion, Vasiṣṭha swears that he would die on that very day if he is really a sorcerer and he who calls Vasiṣṭha a sorcerer, would be ever separated from his sons i.e. his sons would die. Sāyaṇa here says that this is also in the form of *śapatha* (swearing or taking an oath). In later age, Manu deals with the topic of *śapatha* (*Manu Sm.* VIII.111-116), and mentions swearing taken by the great seers and gods, also by Vasiṣṭha before Sudāsa Paijavana (*ibid.* VIII.110).

As we have noted at the beginning of this chapter, in the word *śabda* as also in the word *śāpa*, the root is √*śap*—'to utter, speak'. The word *śapatha* has the same root. Again as we have marked there, the efficacy of the spoken word was no doubt preceded by the efficacy of the emotion of the inarticulate wish or will. The essence of cursing and swearing was thus in existence before the human speech was developed.[73] The punishing power of a word is particularly conspicuous in the case of an oath and its contagious character resembles that which is attributed to tabooed persons and things, and it acts mechanically.[74] As stated by Westermarck, an oath is essentially a conditional self-imprecation, a curse by which a person calls down upon himself some evil in the event of what he says not being true. The efficacy of the oath is originally entirely magical; it is due to the magic power inherent in the cursing[75] words. Hence we have stated that oath is a self-inflicted or self-targeted curse.

Let us see what purpose is served by the two accounts, which occur in the Anuśāsanaparvan of the *Mbh.* The first account is regarding the theft of lotus-stalks (*bisastainya—'bisa'* the word is taken to mean the 'lotus-stalks', used for eating and not the 'lotus-fibres'). Once in the times of a great drought, the sages *viz.* Kaśyapa, Atri, Vasiṣṭha, Bharadvāja, Gautama, Viśvāmitra, Jamadagni, and Arundhatī, their maid-servant Gaṇḍā and her husband Paśusakha (a *śudra*), being tormented by hunger, while wandering from place to place, come to King Vṛṣādarbhi's kingdom. The king wants to offer them several things in their bad days, which they strongly reject, as for a *brāhmaṇa* accepting anything i.e. *pratigraha*, except *dakṣiṇā* has been regarded a sin. The king feels insulted and gets annoyed for this repudiation of his offer. In order to teach them a lesson, he creates a *kṛtyā*—a female evil spirit—and places her as a guardian of a lake full of lotuses. He asks her to get the 'names' of all of them (even of the servant-couple) known to her and kill all of them by playing black magic on them, when she will know their names.[76] All of them tell the *kṛtyā* their respective names, each of them giving the etymological explanation of his name. She gives permission to all of them to enter the lake. When Śunaḥsakha, who is Indra in disguise and has come there to test the sages, tells his name giving explanation of it, she asks him to tell it again, as she cannot catch the exact import of it. Śunaḥsakha becomes angry and strikes the *kṛtyā* with his staff reducing her to ashes. The sages together with Arundhatī and the servant-couple, enter the lake and give offerings with water. They gather lotus-stalks from that lake and keep them on the bank. But when they come out of the lake, they do not find the lotus-stalks kept on the bank, for they are taken away by somebody. But they firmly believe that the person committing that theft of the lotus-stalks is one of them and so they decide to swear (*Mbh.* Anu. 93.20-112).

Here we have a long list of 'taboos'[77] (prohibited actions or deeds), the sin of committing which, is to befall the person, who has stolen the lotus-stalks. Atri mentions touching a cow with foot; urinating while facing the sun; undertaking the daily Vedic study on the days and occasions, which are forbidden (*ibid.* 113). Vasiṣṭha states studying on the *anadhyāya*—days (prohibited days);[78] dragging a dog; though being a mendicant having licentious behaviour; killing a person who has surrendered[79], subsisting on the income gained through a daughter[80] and desiring money from a niggard (*ibid.* 114-115). Kaśyapa warns of speaking everything at all places; destroying a thing kept as deposit,[81] while standing as a witness, giving false testimony,[82] having flesh which is not intended for gods or manes (*pitṛs*); giving gift which may be revoked or is not made good if promised; 'approaching' a woman (for copulation) at daytime (*ibid.* 116-117). Bharadvāj speaks of discarding one's duties towards women, kinsmen and cows; scoring victory over a *brāhmaṇa*; by repudiating the preceptor, studying *ṛks* and *yajuses* (i.e. *RV* and *YV*); offering oblations in the fire, which is in dry wood or grass (*ibid.* 118-119). Jamadagni points out releasing excreta in waters; killing a cow and hating her; 'approaching' one's wife on the prohibited days; earning one's livelihood through one's wife; becoming a guest of each other[83] (*ibid.* 120-121). Gautama states discarding the Vedas, having first studied them; not maintaining the three fires; selling Soma; residing in a village swept by flood, near a *brāhmaṇa,* who has married a *śūdra* woman[84] (*ibid.* 122-123). Viśvāmitra points out the sin accruing to a person, whose elderly persons and servants are maintained by others in spite of he being alive; that of a person having many sons but not having any means of livelihood[85]; that of a thoroughly learned but impure *brāhmaṇa*, as well as arrogant due to amassing wealth, moreover squeezing (wealth) and jealous by nature, that of a *varṣācara* (According to Monier Williams, this word is of obscure meaning) servant, who is hired; that of the *purohita* (the chief advisory family-priest, irrespective of sacrifice) of a king and that of a person acting as a priest at the place of a person, who is not entitled to perform a sacrifice (*ibid.* 124-126). Arundhatī, Gaṇḍā and Paśusakha point out the sins, which are more on the side of the rules of morality, except the point of *śulka*[86] in the mouth of Gaṇḍā (*ibid.* 127-131).

Then speaks Śunaḥsakha—Indra in disguise—that a person who takes away the lotus-stalks may give his daughter in marriage to an offering priest (Adhvaryu priest)[87] or to a person well-versed in the Vedic studies and has observed the vow of celibacy (*brahmacarya*) or to a person, who having studied the *AV* takes the final bath as a mark of the completion of his studies (*ibid.* 132).

In the Anuśāsanaparvan of the *Mbh.* immediately after this tale (in the 93rd chap.), in the very next chapter (i.e. 94th chap.), there occurs another tale regarding the theft of Agastya's lotus (or lotuses—the word *puṣkara* in Sing. No. can be taken to denote Plu. No. as per the maximum *jātau ekavacanam*). The sages Bhṛgu, Vasiṣṭha etc. and kings Śibi, Dilīpa etc., while visiting various holy places, come to the place where Agastya is living. As his lotus (or lotuses) is not seen, obviously stolen by somebody, he casts aspersions on these great personalities, who in turn swear, each of them pointing out the sin accruing to a person, stealing the lotus of Agastya as equal to that of the various types of wrong doings. Many of these are common to what we have already noted in the context of the tale from the 93rd chap. of the same *parvan* (Anuśāsanaparvan of the *Mbh.*). Dragging a dog for livelihood is tabooed (*Mbh.* Anu. 94.17, 20, 34c). Manu mentions a *śvakrīḍī* (i.e. one who keeps dogs for pleasure) as a *paṅktivigarhita* i.e. a person, in whose company or sitting with whom, meals are not to be partaken of (*Manu Sm.* III.164). The *Bhāg. P.* states that those who are masters of dog or donkey, are pierced by the servants of Yama with arrows (*Bhāg.P.* V.26.24). To treat ailing persons also seems to be a taboo (*Mbh.* Anu. 94.22a). This can be traced to the disrespect maintained about the twin-gods Aśvins, who were not entitled to the share of Soma, as being physicians they moved among the people of any sort.[88] Approaching a woman (for union) by daytime is regarded a taboo (*ibid.* 24b, 27ab). Striking a cow with foot, urinating while facing the sun and abandoning a person who has surrendered, are regarded as serious sins and they are tabooed (*ibid.* 32). Giving a daughter in marriage by taking *śulka* is tabooed (*ibid.* 31c). To entertain a person from the family as a guest is tabooed (*ibid.* 28a). According to the rule of the Dharmaśāstra a guest has always to be an unknown person.[89] Going by a vehicle dragged by a donkey is tabooed for a respectable person (*ibid.* 34 ab). Many of the lapses which a person is said to commit, if he steals Agastya's lotus, fall in the line with the rules of prohibition prescribed in the Dharmaśāstra texts. To mention such lapses—having greed for the deposit kept; giving false testimony while standing as a witness (*ibid.* 18 bc); speaking false, always opposing the righteous persons (*ibid.* 31 ab); knowing the rules of righteous conduct, but not following them (*ibid.* 39c).

At the end of the chapters (*ibid.* Anu. 94th chapter as also the 93rd chap.), there occur three verses, which tell the various types of gain to be obtained by a person, on reciting or studying the two episodes as they occur in the *Mbh.* Thus is brought out the aetiological purpose of the two accounts.

Such taboos (as we have noted above these) are prescribed by the *Śat. Br.* in the context of the Pravargya rite. As he who either teaches or partakes of this Pravargya, enters that life or that light, so the following taboos for him. It is stated that he should not cover himself with a garment, while the sun shines, lest he should be concealed from the sun. He should not spit while the sun shines, lest he should spit on the sun. He should not discharge urine while the sun shines, lest he discharge it upon him (*Śat. Br.* XIV.1.1.33). The area covered here by the taboos is small and limited only to the sun, while the taboos or prohibitions mentioned in the two accounts of the *Mbh.* (Anuśāsanaparvan) are aimed at teaching the moral code. The series of taboos occurring here are customary abstinence or negative rites. Taboo or 'tabu' stands for the whole mass of fear-inspired inhibitions in so far as they proceed directly from the religious emotion, as it regulates the social tradition.[90] The prohibited actions spoken of in the two tales from the Anuśāsanaparvan of the *Mbh.* serve a double purpose. They reflect the fear-inspired beliefs prevalent in the society of that time or those beliefs which might have travelled from a hoary past up to that time and maintained by the then society, thus making it a 'living' tradition. Secondly they present a code of moral conduct, prevalent in the society of those times, with normative (positive) as well as prohibitive rules, both being important.

In respect of these two accounts discussed above, we are reminded of a *gāthā* which occurs in the *Ait. Br.* in the context of the Agnihotra offerings. The *Ait. Br.* deals at great length with the problem of the exact time of the morning Agnihotra, whether the morning offerings are to be given before sunrise or after the sun has actually arisen, and states that the morning offerings are to be given in the fire after the rise of the sun (*Ait. Br.* V.29-31=25.4-6). While enjoining the evening offerings in the fire after the setting of the sun (when the darkness sets in), the *Ait.Br.* quotes a *gāthā*, which is in the form of swearing on the part of a certain (unnamed) person (*ibid.* V.30=25.5). While commenting on the *gāthā*, Sāyaṇa refers to an old account of seven sages, when one of them charged with the theft of lotus-stalks swore before them. The *gāthā* mentions the sins accruing to a person who steals the lotus-stalks and these are- the sin of making a false charge against a sinless person; the sin of denying the blame in the case of a person, who has sinned; the sin of turning away a guest arrived at the evening time. The account preserved in the *gāthā* is certainly of olden time. The *gāthā* itself has come from the secular tradition and is used here by the *Ait. Br.* as an *arthavāda* to support the *vidhi* of giving offerings in the fire at the evening time. These offerings are for the sun and it is the evening Agnihotra. The *Ait.Br.* says that the sun is *eka-atithiḥ*. Like the word *ekavīraḥ* ('unparalleled warrior'), the word '*ekātithiḥ*' can mean 'an excellent guest'. Sāyaṇa takes this word to mean 'one living in a foreign land, without any relatives' (*vaideśikaḥ bandhurahitaḥ*), who resides among the sacrificers, offering oblations. He being a guest is to be given hospitality (of offerings) and is not to be turned away. The *Ait. Br.* here says that 'Hence it is that they (i.e. knowers) state that a guest arrived at the evening time is not to be turned away'. The same thought is maintained in the *Manu Sm.* which says that the guest arrived at the evening time is sent by the sun and therefore is not to be turned away (*Manu Sm.* III.105ab). The *Viṣṇu P.* goes to the extent of saying that the sin committed by a person by turning away a guest, brought by the sun in the evening time, is eight times more than what accrues to him while turning away a guest at the daytime (*Vi.P.* III.11.108). This is perfectly understandable, taking into account the journey (in those times!) undertaken by the guest and his difficulty in finding out a place for his night sojourn. And the 'guest' is 'an unknown person', by rule!

From the *gāthā* which we have noted from the *Ait. Br.*, it seems that in the floating mass of literature, preserved in the secular tradition but made use of by the ritualistic tradition, there was current a mythical tale of a certain unknown person, who by some persons, had been charged of stealing lotus-stalks or lotuses and who in order to prove himself clean of this charge, had resorted to swearing before them. The *Mbh.* known as the unparalleled great repository of the lore of 'Dharma', preserved by the Sūta-tradition[91], which made additions and omissions and at times had its own compositions in it, used this tale of the *gāthā* for imparting moral instructions and laying down various taboos by giving the two mythical tales, woven round the names of sages and personalities, who were illustrious. The two tales of swearing, which we have discussed, thus are used as *arthavāda* to glorify the ancient Indian moral code. As Winternitz has rightly stated that there was an inexhaustible store of prose and verse narratives—Ākhyānas, Itihāsas, Purāṇas and Gāthās—forming as it were 'literary public property', which was drawn upon by the Buddhists and the Jains, as well as by the epic poets.[92]

Curses, boons and oaths are strewn in the narratives from the Veda (especially ritual-texts) to the Purāṇas. Though initially 'formless' and 'unseen' (also 'unpredicted'), being born in mind, they attain a verbal form, when expressed having their target in view, in the case of oath or swearing the target being one's own self. The striking point about them is that they are seen in the narratives for multiple purposes. They come as a bridge between past and present situations or incidents; or present and future situations or incidents; try to explain a particular trait of man's nature and in most cases serve to guard the moral code (*dharma*) in the society. As are the man's emotions multifaceted, so are their verbal outpourings with multiple aims.

NOTES AND REFERENCES

1. Also see *Ait. Br.* (V.33=25.8), where it is said that sacrifice has two paths and they are Speech and Mind, for by these the sacrifice proceeds.
   Kauṣ. Br. (VI.11)—These are two tracks of sacrifice.
   Ṣad. Br. (I.5.4)—With Speech and Mind, the sacrifice can turn to both sides like a chariot.
2. This falls in line with the modern usage e.g. the river Brahmaputrā called Brahmaputra (a male), the river Śoṇa called Śoṇanada (a male), just to show the vastness of the river-bed.
   The river Sarasvatī is said to have a male aspect i.e. Sarasvat, who is sung in three verses of one hymn (*RV* VII.96.4-6), in which the river goddess is praised (*ibid.* 1-3). Even the exuberant breast of Sarasvat is mentioned indicative of his aspect of bestowing fecundity. That way, Sarasvat is a bi-sexual deity—Male and Female combined—a motif found in many a mythology.
3. J. Hastings (ed.), *ERE*, Vol. IV, p. 368a.
4. *Ibid.*
5. *Ibid.*, p. 369a. "Curses like chickens, come home to roost; they turn home as birds to their nests." It may be compared with the Roman notion that certain imprecations were so awful that even the utterer suffered as well as his victim. In Indian context, see *Bhāg. P.* IX.4.49ff. Durvāsas' ill will towards king Ambarīṣa flying back to him.
6. J. Hastings (ed.), *ERE*, Vol. IV, p. 368b.
7. *Ibid.*
8. The *paridhis* are placed round the Āhavanīya fire excepting the eastern quarter, in order to protect Agni. The sun is the protector on the east side, hence excluding the east.
9. See Sindhu S. Dange, *Vedic Beliefs and Practices through Arthavāda*, Vols. I. and II.
10. *Raghuvaṁśa* XIV.70; Dhvanyāloka I.5 also *Rām.* Bāla 2.40, 41—Here the metre of the *śloka* (verse) Anuṣṭubh having four feet, each foot having eight syllables. The curse comes from the sage's mouth in the form of such a verse, in the Anuṣṭubh metre.

11. Sadashiv A. Dange, "The Birth of Vasiṣṭha", *Images from Vedic Hymns and Rituals,* Aryan Books International, New Delhi, 2000, p. 206ff.
12. *Ibid.,* p. 207; also p.213 note 12, where Dange gives instances of 'birth' of illustrious persons (male or female) from the sacrificial fire or the sacrificial altar.
13. Sadashiv A. Dange, "The Jar in Symbolic Rites", *Purāṇic Myth and Culture,* Ajanta Pubns., Delhi, 1987, pp. 49-58.
14. See Sindhu S. Dange, "The Ṛgveda and the Avesta", *Zoroastrianism from Antiquity to the Modern Period,* Vol. VII, Part 8, ed. by Jal Murzban, for the Project of History of Indian Science, Philosophy and Culture (PHISPC), pub. by Centre for Studies in Civilisations (CSC), New Delhi, 2012, pp. 121-23.
15. Cf. *Rām.* Araṇya 66.14 Daśaratha's body was kept in an oil-cauldron till Bharata arrived. The Egyptian method in ancient times of embalming the dead bodies of the kings, with the idea of the soul returning to its dead body, has to be noted here. And hence the 'mummies' in the pyramids in Egypt.
16. Here the etymology of the word *'mithila'* is sought to be given, also suggesting that the city Mithilā was established or founded by him. However it is doubtful how the root √*manth* can give the word *mithila* or *mithilā*. Here the *Bhāg. P.* wears the mantle of Yāska and taking into account the similarity between the two words—*manth* and *mithila* (cf. *Nir.* II.1) gives the etymology. For such Puranic etymologies, see Sindhu S. Dange, *Puranic Etymologies and Flexible Forms,* Viveka Publications, Aligarh, 1989.
17. J. Dowson, *A Classical Dictionary of Hindu Mythology and Religion,* London, 1953, p. 223—"A wink of the eye is called Nimiṣa, and the legend was probably built upon the resemblance of the two words".
18. The instances of Rāmakṛṣṇaparamahaṁsa and King Gopīchanda can be cited here, who though married, could remain celibate.
19. T.V. Mahalingam, "The Nāgas in Indian History and Culture", *Journal of Indian History,* University of Kerala, Trivandrum, Vol. XLIII, Pt. I, April 1965, Serial No. 127, p. 11.
20. See C.F. Oldham, *The Sun and the Serpent,* London, 1905, p.58.

21. The change from the human Nāga to the serpent brought in its trail the "one-prop-chamber' made by Parikṣit for himself in the account from the *Mbh.* In the popular tale, we have a 'craviceless house' constructed to ward off the Serpent-goddess Manasā, who, in spite of this protective measure, could kill the merchant's son, by sending the lord of serpents, as we have Takṣaka. See the *Manasā-maṅgala* (Bengali).
22. See C.F. Oldham, *op. cit.*, p. 72.
23. A.A. Macdonell and A.B. Keith, *Vedic Index of Names and Subjects* under "Nahus".
24. D. Mackenzie, *Myths of Crete and Pre-Hellenic Europe*, London, year not mentioned, pp. 169-70.
25. *Tait. Br. I.* 1.3; II.2.4; *Pañc. Br.* IV.1.7; *Śat. Br.* VII.5.1.5-7; II.5.1.1-4 etc.
26. This is often picturised as Viṣṇu lying on the bed of the serpent Śeṣa and Brahmā sitting in the lotus, the stem of which comes from Viṣṇu's navel.
27. *Bhāg. P.* III.12.3-47; *ibid.* 20.18-48; *Matsya P.* III.2ff—Vedas with the Vedāṅgas from Brahmā's body;
Vām. P. 2.17-37—the mountain Meru and other mountains; ocean and thousands of rivers and a great lake from Brahmā, when he got the form of a cosmic egg;
Śiva P. II.16.4-6—various sages from Brahmā's body.
28. See Sadashiv A. Dange, *Ency. PBP*, Vol. V, pp.. 1518-20.
29. *Bhāg. P.* IX.9.24, 25; also *Viṣṇu P.* IV.4.56 f; *Skanda P.* Brahmottara-khaṇḍa 3.3.2.
30. *Manu Sm.* IX.66 ff; see also Mitākṣarā on *Yajñ. Sm.* II.127, where various views are quoted. Also see P.V. Kane, *HDS*, Vol. II, Pt. I, p. 599ff.
31. Vyāsa procreates children on the *kṣetra* (wife-actually the wives) of Vicitravīrya—see *Mbh.* Ādi 104.24-49 and chap. 105; Bali gets issues likewise by Dīrghatamas, *ibid.* Ādi 104.41-55.
32. Thus we have—the birth of Yudhiṣṭhira from Dharmarāja *Mbh.* Ādi 122.7; the birth of Bhīma from the god of Wind *ibid.*14; the birth of Arjuna from Indra *ibid.*35; the two sons of Mādrī-Nakula and Sahadeva from the two Aśvins *ibid.* Ādi 123.16.
33. That the divine birth of the Pāṇḍavas was looked at with doubt and was mentioned with sarcasm (probably among the people), can be marked through the words of Duryodhana in the first

act of Bhāsa's play *Dūtavākya*. He mentions them as *dharmātmaja, vāyusuta, tridaśendrasūnu* and *aśvisutau* resp. (*Dūtavākya* I.19), and gives a rebuff to Vāsudeva (Kṛṣṇa who has arrived as a messenger) by saying—'How can there be fraternal relations between the 'sons of gods' and the humans?' (*ibid.* 30).

34. *Mbh.* Ādi 117.6-34; for the exact mention of the curse to Pāṇḍu *ibid.* 30-31.
35. See note 29 supra.
36. See *Suśrutasaṁhitā* of Suśruta, Pt. I, ed. with the comm. Āyurvedatattva—sandīpikā by Ambikādatta Shastri, 7th edn., Chaukhamba Sanskrit Sansthan, Varanasi, 1989, p. 251 (V chap. in the Nidānasthāna).
    Also *Carakasaṁhitā*, with the comms. Āyurvedadīpikā and Jalpakalpataru, ed. and revised by Narendranath Sengupta and Balaicandra Sengupta; Reprint by V. Kutumbashastri, Rashtriya Sanskrit Sansthan, New Delhi, 2002, p. 2633 (VII chap., 4th *khaṇḍa*, in the Cikitsāsthāna), verse 7 giving the exact description of the *kuṣṭha*.
    The work *Aṣṭāṅgahṛdayam* of Vāgbhaṭa, with the comms. Sarvāṅgasundarā and Āyurvedarasāyana, ed. by Harishastri Paradkar, Rashtriya Sanskrit Sansthan, 2002, p. 527 (XIV chap. in the Nidānasthāna).
37. *Carakasaṁhitā*, Cikitsā III *khaṇḍa* chap. 7, p. 1570, vv. 21 and 22 mention the different types as Ekakuṣṭha, Carmakuṣṭha, Kiṭima and Vaipādika. These are stated in the *Suśrutasaṁhitā* also.
38. The word *kalmāṣa* is found in the *AV* (III.27.5) joined with the word *grīvā*—neck. Here *kalmāṣagrīva* is a serpent's name. It has to be noted that the word *kuṣṭha* does not occur in the Vedic literature, as the name of a disease. In the *AV* it occurs as the name of a plant and in the *Mait. Saṁ.* it is used for counting numbers. See—A.A. Macdonell, and A.B. Keith, *Vedic Index of Names and Subjects*, the title "*kuṣṭha*". Lord Śiva is called *kalmāṣakaṇṭha*, but here we have the *kalmāṣatva* (blackness) of the neck, due to the drinking of poison. In the case of King Saudāsa, the blackness of the feet was certainly due to some deadly skin-disease.
39. *Carakasaṁhitā* Cikitsā.IV *khaṇḍa*, chap. 7, verse 7, p. 2633, v. 7 says that the affected part of the body has the colour of black or reddish potsherds, and the colour is not uniform on the whole

body. *Suśrutasaṁhitā* pt. I, Nidāna, chap. 5, verse 8, p. 249, v. 8 says that the lesion looks like a piece of black earthen pottery.

40. Ram Gopal, *India of Vedic Kalpasūtras*, National Publishing House, Delhi, 1959, p. 476.
41. *Manu Sm.* VII.4ff; also the famous saying—*nāviṣṇuḥ pṛthivīpatiḥ*—which brings out that an ungodly person cannot (dare to) be the lord of the earth. For the belief in the divinity of the king in various countries, see J.G. Frazer, *The Golden Bough*, abridged ed., Vol. I, Macmillan & Co. Ltd., London 1957, pp. 119-139. also *Mbh.* Udyoga 149.25
42. See *Bṛhaddevatā* VII.148; also A.A. Macdonell and A.B. Keith, *Vedic Index of Names and Subjects*, under "Devāpi".
43. *Mbh.* Ādi 175.6ff. Manu stresses the necessity of allowing passage to a *snātaka* first, obviously to respect his learning imparted to him at the preceptor's place (*Manu Sm.* II.139).
44. For details see, H.L. Hariappa, *Ṛgvedic Legends through the Ages*, Deccan College, Poona, 1953; also U.C. Sharma, *The Viśvāmitras and the Vasiṣṭhas*, Viveka Pubns., Aligarh, 1975.
45. *Gaut. D.S.* XVIII.6.8; also XVIII.2; Vasiṣṭha D.S. XVII.55; *Manu Sm.* IX.59; *Yājñ.Sm.* I.68.
46. The *Arthaśāstra* of Kauṭilya adds three more categories in this respect. It allows a king, who is unable to procreate a son due to old age or disease, to get a son procreated for him on his queen through a *mātṛ-bandhu* (his mother's kinsman), or a member of his own family or a virtuous neighbouring prince. See *Arthaśāstra* I.17.50.
47. *Manu Sm.* IX.59b—*samyaṅniyuktayā* (*striyā*); *Yajñ. Sm.* I.68ac—*gurvanujñātaḥ* (*devaraḥ sapiṇḍo vā, sagotro vā*).
48. *Gautama D.S.* XVIII.4. Here by the word *'guru'* we better understand the elders including the preceptor. Kane, however, takes it to indicate the elderly persons on the husband's side. See P.V. Kane, *HDS*, Vol. II, Pt. I, p.599 note 1408.
    Cf. *Vasiṣṭha D.S.* 17.56-65.
    Kullūka's comment on *Manu Sm.* IX.59 is that for the woman in question person should be appointed by the "elders including the husband."
49. For discussion and other cases of *niyoga*, see Sadashiv A. Dange, "Birth and Marriage of the Pāṇḍavas", *Gleanings from Vedic to*

Puranic Age (Collected Papers of Dr. Sadashiv A. Dange), ed. by Sindhu S. Dange, p. 119-140.

50. *Bhāg. P.* IX.20.35-39; *Matsya P.* 48.32ff; 49.17ff. The same son—Bharadvāja—was given by the Maruts (as he was abandoned by Mamatā and Bṛhaspati) to King Bharata, and became the latter's (i.e. Bhrata's) heir-apparent. Thus Bharadvāja was Bharata's adopted son.
51. It is only in the *Bhāg.P.* (IX.20.37-38) that she is shown to be apprehensive of being abandoned by her husband and that too when the son is actually born, but the gods console her.
52. See J.J. Meyer, *Sexual Life in Ancient India,* Calcutta, 1954, p. 113 ff.
53. The rule underlying the practice of 'Group-marriage' or that of 'Girl given to the family', seems to be 'One brother at a time'. If the girl had conception from one, the other could not go to her, for she was thought to be impure for others during the period of conception. Only when she became purified after her first monthly course after delivery, the other had right over her. This is marked in the Dharmaśāstra texts, where it is said that women become pure after menstruation. See *Manu Sm.* V.66; *Yājñ.Sm.* III.1.20.
54. The history of human marriage has been an interesting subject. See E. Westermarck, *History of Human Marriage,* London, 1901; also by the same author, *A Short History of Human Marriage,* London, 1926. Custom shows that in the demise of his wife, the husband used to choose (it is still prevalent in some places) her younger sister as his (second) wife. It was not mandatory, but it shows that the custom or practice has been to establish relationship between the two families, rather than between the two individuals.
55. According to Patil, the point of 'sexual morality' has to be noted here. The story is all the more important, for Bharadvāja is adopted by Bharata. See D.R. Patil, *Cultural History from the Vāyu Purāṇa,* Deccan College, Poona, 1946, p.159.
56. See S.G. Kantawala, "Matsya Purāṇa and Promiscuity," *Purāṇa,* All India Kashiraj Trust, Varanasi, Vol. III, No. 2, July 1961.
57. The *Bhāg. P.* refers to this curse passingly (*Bhāg. P.* I.13.15), where due to the curse, Yama (who himself decides the fate of

the dead according to his sin or merit) got the state of being a *sūdra* for hundred years.

58. *Manu Sm.* XI.70 speaks of *kṛmikīṭavayohatyā*—killing of small insects and birds—as a minor sin; *Yājñ. Sm.* III.269-275 speaks of the expiatory rites prescribed for such sins.

59. A *brāhmaṇa purohita* (priest) is said to be the very Agni and thus is regarded to have divine power (*Ait.Br.* VIII.24=40.1). Gods are of two types, the gods of the heaven are the gods and the *brāhmaṇas*, who have studied and teach sacred lore are the human gods (*Śat. Br.* II.2.2.6; IV.3.4.4). Also see *Ṣaḍ.Br.* (I.1.29, 30), also *Tait.Br.* (I.4.4.2; II.7.3.1, 2).

    Indra being afraid of the sin of killing a *brāhmaṇa* (Vṛtra) hides himself in waters (*Mbh.* Udyoga 10.46).

    Also *Manu Sm.* VIII.380—A *brāhmaṇa*, even though committing all sins, is not to be killed.

60. The fact of Matsyagandhā being a *śūdra* (fisherman's class) is explained by the episode of King Uparicara, as she is the very source of the royal Kuru family. But even here, though not in the case of Matsyagandhā, the strategy of curse works for Matsyagandhā's mother—an *apsaras* (nymph)—who is cursed by Brahmā (*Mbh.* Ādi chap. 63).

61. See Sadashiv A. Dange, *Ency. PBP*, Vol. II, p. 606 (under the title "Gāyatrī".)

62. At the beginning of the Vedic sacrifice, a branch of the Audumbara tree ('Audumbarī') is to be first planted on the main support of the sacrificial pendal. *Śat. Br.* III.6.1.1 ff. Dange has discussed the concept and importance of Audumbarī from the Veda to the Purāṇas. See Sadashiv A., Dange, "Audumbarī—In Puranic Myths", Appendix C, *Vedic Sacrifices—Early Nature*, Vol. II, Aryan Books International, New Delhi, 2000, pp. 485-493.

63. *Padma P.* Sṛṣṭikhaṇḍa 16.111ff; also *Sk.P.* VII.1.165.15ff.

64. In the context of *arthavāda*, it is called Anuvāda type of *arthavāda*, which repeats (fr. *anu+√vad*—'to speak following the earlier fact'), the matter already known. e.g. *'agnirhimasya bheṣajam'*—'Agni is the medicine for cold', a fact already known. See S.M. Paranjape (ed.), *Arthasaṅgraha*, p. 361 f.

65. Sadashiv A. Dange, *Myths from the Mahābhārata*—Study in Patterns and Symbols, Vol. 2, Aryan Books International, New Delhi, 2001, p. 198 f.

66. *Ibid.*, p. 199; also p. 226 note 72.
67. See Donald Mackenzie, *Egyptian Myth and Legend*, London, year not mentioned, p. 24.
68. For detailed information about the 'green' world, see Sindhu S. Dange, the chap. "Trees, Plants and Varieties of Grass", *Vedic Beliefs and Practices through Arthavāda*, Vol. I, pp. 141-75.
69. See Sadashiv A. Dange, *Ency. PBP*, Vol. II, pp. 391-423.
70. These 16 rivers are—Narmadā, Kāverī, Kṛṣṇaveṇī, Revā, Yamunā, Godāvarī, Vitastā, Candrabhāgā, Irāvatī, Vipāśā, Kauśikī, Sarayū, Śatarudrikā, Śiprā, Sarasvatī, Lhādinī and Pāvanī. Though 17 (as given here), they should be taken 16, for Narmadā and Revā are the names of one and the same river.
71. A. Bergaigne, *Vedic Religion*, Vol. I (Eng. Tr. V.G. Paranjpe), Aryasamskriti Prakashan, Poona, 1969, chaps. II and III.
72. See Sadashiv A. Dange, (the chap. "Cosmosexualism") *Sexual Symbolism from the Vedic Ritual*, p. 29.
73. *ERE* Vol. IX, p. 430a & b.
74. *Ibid.*, p. 431a.
75. *Ibid.*, p. 430a.
76. *Ibid.*, p. 135a.
    The name of a person stands as his very soul—his 'name-soul', which can be brought under control, once the 'name' is known. Hence, in India, there is a practice of keeping the real name secret and giving another name to the boy for daily dealings, to save him from being conjured with magic and thus being harmed. For information from the Vedic texts, see Sindhu S. Dange, *Vedic Beliefs and Practices through Arthavāda*, Vol. II, pp. 455, 457.
77. The word 'Taboo' was introduced into English language by Captain Cook. He first heard this word in 1777 in Tonga. (J. Cook and J. King, *A Voyage to the Pacific Ocean*, London, 1776-1780. Vols. I and II by J. Cook and Vol. III by J. King). In general, the word 'Taboo' signifies that 'a thing is forbidden', and it is applied to all cases, where things are not bo be touched. See *ERE* Vol. XII, p. 181. The word 'Tabu' ('Taboo') stands for the whole mass of fear-inspired inhibitions in so far as they proceed directly from the religious emotion.
    Ibid., p. 183a.

78. For the *anadhyāya* days (when the study of the Vedic texts was not undertaken i.e. a sort of 'off-days') for the students, there were regular holidays (New-moon day, Aṣṭakā etc.) and also casual holidays, when there was the death of a relative, teacher, king etc. and also when there occurred natural phenomena like earth-quake, solar or lunar eclipse, rainbow, fierce gale, rain, thunder etc. See Ram Gopal, *India of Vedic Kalpasūtras*, pp. 344-45.
79. *Manu Sm.* (VII.90-98) states under '*yodhadharma*' (rules to be followed by a *kṣatriya,* when he is fighting on the battlefield), the rule 'not to kill a person, who has surrendered'(*ibid.* 91).
80. *Ibid.* III.52. Manu states that persons subsisting on the wealth of wife, daughter or women in the house, being sinful, go to wretched condition in the other world.
81. *Ibid.* VIII.179-196, for the rules regarding *nikṣepa* (deposit) and *upanidhi* (sealed deposit, the exact idea of its value not being given to the person with whom the deposit is kept).
82. *Ibid.* VIII.118, where Manu says that a statement given by a person, standing as a witness, out of greed, infatuation, fear, friendship, passion, wrath, ignorance, child like behaviour i.e. inadvertence, is regarded as false. He even prescribes punishment (*daṇḍa*) for this. See *ibid.* 120-122.
83. Dharmaśāstra tradition maintains that a person arriving as an *atithi* (guest) has to be a stranger to the householder. A person who belongs to the same village or who is a friend or a fellow-student is not an *atithi*. For details see *Gautama D.S.* V.36; *Manu Sm.* III.103; *Yājñ. Sm.* I.107, 111. Also see Sindhu S. Dange, "Athithi: A Probe in Concept", *Studies in Indology* (*Prof. Mukund Madhav Sharma Fel. Vol.*), Sri Sadguru Publications, Delhi, 1996, pp. 119-122.
84. See *Manu Sm.* IX.178—The son of such a *brāhmaṇa* (from the *śūdra* wife) is called *pāraśava* ('as good as a corpse').
85. Cf. *Nir.* II.8—the interpretation of *RV* I.164. 32d—*bahuprajaḥ nirṛtimāviveśa*/given by the Parivrājakas that a person (obviously a poor person) having many children, goes to wretched condition.
86. *Śulka* is the money, taking which the girl is given to the bridegroom in marriage. Such a girl is said to be *śulkadeyā*. See *Mānava G.S.* 8.1-11; *Kāṭhaka G.S.* 15.1-5; 16.1-5; also *Manu Sm.*

III.31, where Manu calls this practice to be a feature of the 'Āsura' form of marriage; also *ibid.* III.51—The father should not take any *śulka*, for he will be deemed as *apatyavikrayī* i.e. seller of his child, here daughter.

87. *Manu Sm.* III.28. Manu mentions 'Daiva' form of marriage, in which a girl, decked with ornaments etc. is given to the officiating priest at a sacrifice, during the course of its performance.
88. *Jaim.Br.* III.124; for the whole account of their getting that share see *ibid.* III.120-128; also *Śat. Br.* IV.1.5.1-15.
89. See note 83 supra.
90. See note 77 supra.
91. See M. Winternitz, *History of Indian Literature,* Vol. I. (Intrn. Veda, National Epics, Purāṇas and Tantras), Munshiram Manoharlal, New Delhi, 2nd ed., 1972 (University of Calcutta, 1927), p. 315, where Winternitz maintains that the credit of composing the two great epics goes to the tradition of the *sūtas.*
92. *Ibid.,* p. 314.

CHAPTER 6

Epic-Puranic Gods and Goddesses

Some Facets

The efforts, through earlier chapters were to have a look at the facets of the ancient Indian society and incidentally the norms of *dharma* (code of conduct), in the Vedic-brahmanical Hindu religion, through narratives (selected ones!) spread from the Veda to the Purāṇas. These narratives figure as *arthavādas*, trying to justify and convince people of the matter in hand and it has been possible to categorise them in different chapters under specific titles. Nevertheless, some varied narrative details, strewn here and there in the *Mbh.* and the Purāṇas, are being placed in this chapter, for though small in measure, they are certainly of significance, related to the main stand-point of *arthavāda* and its efficacy in narratives.

GODS AND GODDESSES

As it has already been noted in the chap. on Sacrifice, in the Veda, no reference occurs to any idol of a god, excepting that of Indra. At two places in the *RV* there is a mention of the idol or image of Indra (*RV* IV.24.10; VIII.1.5), and these references are duly taken into account in that chapter. The conclusion arrived at is that in the Ṛgvedic times, people might be keeping Indra's idol (made of wood or stone) in the house as 'fetish'.

By the time of the epics, there are references to images or idols. In the Uttarakāṇḍa of the *Rām.*, there is a mention of the 'golden (image of the absent) queen'—Sītā (*Rām.* Uttara 91.25; 99.8), in Rāma's sacrifice, when Sītā, abandoned in the Daṇḍaka forest, is not with Rāma. The *Mbh.* contains references to idols at several places.[1] There can be taken here only one reference from the *Mbh.*, where it is said that 'having seen the image of Śiva (*nandīśvarasya mūrtim dṛṣṭvā*), one is freed from sins' (*Mbh.* Anu 25.61). Purāṇas mention temples in details, also images of gods and even details of the process of worshipping these gods.[2] This phenomenon of the later i.e. Epic and Puranic age, of worshipping the gods in the form of stone-blocks or idols, hitherto unknown, required an explanation. Here comes the mythological strategy of curse for help. The *Sk.P.* states that when Śiva and Pārvatī were having union, the gods, troubled by the demon Tāraka earnestly desired to see Śiva and sent Agni there on their behalf. As there was this hindrance Umā (Pārvatī) became angry and cursed the gods to turn into stones, be issueless and cruel (*Sk.P.* VI.246.22-23). When they pleaded for pardon, she told them that they would go to the mortal world to be changed into images and idols and thus not mere stones (*ibid.* VI.251.11). This *arthavāda* though simple, tries to justify how the gods, upto this time only in the abstract form, have taken a concrete form as images and idols. The idols are made of seven types *viz.* in clay, wood, iron, diamonds, rock; in substance used for unguents and also from flowers (*Agni P.* 43.9). The *Sk.P.* gives an *arthavāda* at another place (there is noted above one from the same Purāṇa) to explain how the idols of gods came to be prepared in stone. Once the goddess Sarasvatī was going along her path, taking the submarine fire (*vaḍavānala*) in her hands. A mountain came in her way and told her that he wanted to marry her. The goddess laid down the condition that he should first hold the fire, which was in her hands. As soon as he did that, the stones therein (on the mountain) got softened due to heat and came to be used for making the idols (*Sk.P.* VII.1.33.54-90). Dange says that this, probably, has a reference to peculiar type of soft stones, the marbles etc., at Prabhāsa.[3]

As we have dealt with the issue of image or idol (and the worship of it), here is taken the case of god Brahmā, whose idols, excepting few places, are not found, nor does he have many temples or worship of his.[4] This is obviously because in the Puranic period, the gods who came to the forefront are Viṣṇu, Śiva and Devī (Umā-Pārvatī), the last one more in the Upapurāṇa (Devībhāgavata). Now this fact that Brahmā lost his position in later age, is brought out in the Purāṇas under the garb of a curse given to god Brahmā. Here the curse, coming as *arthavāda* justifies this fact. The *Sk.P.* narrates an account of the fight for supremacy between Brahmā and Viṣṇu, when as they fight, there emerges a huge column of light in the ocean. There is a contest between these two for the knowledge of the bottom and top of this column. Really speaking it was the *Jyotirliṅga* of Śiva in the form of the column. Brahmā told a lie that he saw the beginning of that column (i.e. bottom of the column). Śiva knowing Brahmā's trick, cursed him that there would not be his (i.e. Brahmā's) worship anywhere. On Brahmā's pleading forgiveness, Śiva softened the severity of the curse that Brahmā would be worshipped in the Vedic sacrificial rites (Śrauta rites) and the household daily rites laid down by the Smṛtis (Smārta rites), but his idols would not be worshipped (*Sk.P.* III.1.14.25-46). The *Sk.P.* at another place, states that when Brahmā was to perform a sacrifice, without waiting for Sāvitrī (his wife, as she was needed for the performance as the *yajamānapatnī*—sacrificer's wife), he married Gāyatrī, the daughter of a cowherd, brought by Indra. Having learnt it, Sāvitrī cursed him for this haste and deceit, that he would not be worshipped, though Gāyatrī softened the edge of the curse (*Sk.P.* VI.181.31ff).[5] In the *Brahmavai. P.* we find Brahmā cursed by his sons that the wise persons would not worship him (*Brahmavai. P.* Brahmakhaṇḍa, 12.6). In the *Śiva*

P., we get the same account of the column (i.e. Śiva himself) standing in between Viṣṇu and Brahmā, as they are fighting. When Brahmā makes the Ketakī-flower a false witness to show that he has seen the end of the column, Śiva gets angry with both—the Ketakī-flower and more with Brahmā and gives him the curse, that no idol of his will be installed at festivals (*Śiva P.* Vidyeśvara-saṁhitā 7.9ff). The curse given to Brahmā and the varied accounts occurring in the Purāṇas thereof, try to give a plausible explanation for Brahmā's heading for downfall though not for oblivion. Thus a fact in the religious history of ancient India is supported by the curse-episode.

To turn to god Śiva, the special feature about him, which attracts our attention is his *gaṇas*, who many times are described as surrounding him or waiting upon him. Certain individuals, appointed by Śiva as his *gaṇas* are specifically mentioned by the Purāṇas, which also give the descriptions of the *gaṇas* of Śiva in a general manner. The importance and the indispensable status of the *gaṇas* in the cult of Śiva in ancient India can be marked when the *Agni P.* enjoins the worship of a *gaṇa*. It states that at the consecration ceremony of a new entrant in the 'Śiva-order', a *gaṇa* is to be worshipped at the north-west corner of the place, where the ceremony is to be performed. Such a *gaṇa* is to be shown as having four arms and as seated on the figure of 'Om' (*Agni P.* 81.41).

Among the *gaṇas*, some individual *gaṇas* are prominent. Prior to a probe in the concept of the *gaṇas* (of Śiva) and a search for its origin, to have a look at some of these.

The *gaṇa* Andhaka[6] is said to have been born from the body of Śiva (*Vām.P.* 40.55ff; also *ibid.* Saromāhātmya 27.3; *Kūrma P.* I.15.90). As he displayed passion for his own mother Pārvatī, he was defeated by Kālabhairava, appointed to guard Pārvatī. Viṣṇu also tried to kill Andhaka by creating hundred goddesses. But at every drop of Andhaka's blood, many other Andhakas would spring. Ultimately Rudra took him on the point of his trident and danced. The *Vām.P.* (44.49ff) states that Śiva purified Andhaka with the fire of his eye, heating him for a thousand years. The *Vām. P.* here states that as Andhaka praised Śiva, he became the *gaṇapati* called Bhṛṅgī. The *Vām.P.* at another place (Saromāhātmya 27.3ff) says that Andhaka was made the *gaṇādhipa* (chief of the *gaṇas*) named Bhṛṅgarīṭi. This name could be explained with the help of the *Sk.P.*, which says that as Andhaka sang in the voice of drone (*bhṛṅga*), he got the name Bhṛṅgarīṭa from Śiva (VI.151.39ff).

Another wellknown *gaṇa* is Kīrtimukha. The *Śiva P.* states in detail the account of this *gaṇa*. The demon Jalandhara sent his messenger Rāhu to Śiva saying that Śiva should offer his wife (Pārvatī) to Jalandhara. Śiva getting furious, created a terrific being from the space between his eyebrows who rushed to eat Rāhu. This *gaṇa* of Śiva was large in size, having long arms, dry and rough body, with eyes shedding fiery flames. Rāhu was terrified and sought refuge to Śiva, who asked the *gaṇa* to leave Rāhu, who was a *brāhmaṇa*. The *gaṇa* left Rāhu but was worried about his food, not having his prey i.e. Rāhu. Śiva ordered that the *gaṇa* should eat his own flesh. The *gaṇa* obeyed Śiva's order and ate up his own body with only his head left. Being immensely pleased with the obedience of the *gaṇa*, Śiva said that the latter (the *gaṇa*) would be named 'Kīrtimukha', and being stationed as the door-keeper of Śiva, would always be worshipped, whenever Śiva would be worshipped (*Śiva P.* Rudrasaṁhitā, V Yuddhakhaṇḍa, 19.3ff-51). Kīrtimukha, the great *gaṇa* of Śiva is represented in sculptures by a trunkless head and is installed beside the door in front of Śiva's image.[7] Thus Kīrtimukha has been stationed at the entrance of Śiva temple.

The account of the *gaṇa* named Saṁvarta occurs in the *Sk.P.* (I.2.13.18-23). This *gaṇa* used to live in an ascetic manner near Varāṇasī, carrying a concealed Śivaliṅga. Remaining naked, steeped in dirt, subsisting on alms, he used to eat only from his palms. At night, people hiding themselves, used to place a corpse on the main road, which Saṁvarta would carry away.

The *gaṇa* Vīrabhadra was born from the head of Śiva to destroy the sacrifice of Dakṣa (*Sk.P.* I.1.33.99).[8] The *Sk.P.* says that Vīrabhadra in his former birth was a son of a Cāṇḍāla from a *brāhmaṇa* widow named Cañcalā. Though given to a detestable way of life, once, accidentally he observed fast on the Śivarātrī day and was born as King Vicitravīrya, the son of Citrāṅgada. And as in that birth, he was an ardent devotee of Śiva, he was born as the *gaṇa* Vīrabhadra (*Sk.P.* I.1.33.84ff).

The *Matsya P.* mentions a *gaṇa* Vīraka, who was having the jaws of a deer but had the motherly affection from Śiva's wife goddess Umā (*Matsya P.* 153.531ff).

The *Sk.P.* mentions the *gaṇeśa* (chief of the *gaṇas*) Puṣpadanta, who practised penance and established a Śivaliṅga (*Sk.P.* VII.1.180.1-3).

The *gaṇas* of Śiva in general are described in details by some of the Purāṇas. The *gaṇas* are conceived as thin and short, some of them tall, having a big belly, having the heads of tiger, elephant, goat, crocodile, pig, horse, donkey, fish etc., having many faces, eyes, bellies, black or tawny in colour, with flames issuing from their mouths, naked and thus looking ugly (*Matsya P.* 153.531cd-542; *Varāha P.* 90.7, 8; *Sk.P.* I.2.27.34 & 35). They have blue necks and black faces (Sk.P. V.2.77.20). Their boisterous nature is seen in their singing, dancing, running, making noise, laughing, prattling and shouting loudly (*Var. P.* 90.9). They are possessed of weapons and some of them fight taking clods of earth in their hands, others fight as boxers (*ibid.* 90.10). They can take any form or assume any amount of strength they like (*Sk.P.* V.2.77.21). They haunt the places of the *siddhas*, roads, old gardens, houses, the bodies of the demons, children or mad persons and drink heat, foam, smoke etc. and eat any intoxicating food (*Sk.P.* I.2.27.39, 40). The *Śiva P.* gives a long list of the *gaṇas*, some of the names therein being self-eloquent (*Śiva P.* II.20.11-25) e.g. Dundubhaḥ—'like a drum'; Vikṛtānanaḥ—'having deformed face'; Kākapadaḥ—'crow-footed'; Aśaniḥ—'thunderbolt' etc.

We have taken a detailed note of the individual *gaṇas* such as Andhaka and others and also the *gaṇas* as groups. About the individual *gaṇas*, as pointed out by Dange, sincere worship of Śiva with faithful austerity leads one to the favour of Śiva; and the highest favour is the position of *gaṇa*.[9] This falls under the sphere of devotion (*bhakti*), a mythological trait, which we have noted in the case of Kṛṣṇa or Viṣṇu also, when a devotee even by taking the name of the god is released from the cycle of birth and death. And the enemies of the god, constantly thinking about him, become one with him at the moment of death. This is in reality devotion (but) through enmity or opposition' (Virodhabhakti).

But what about the groups of the *gaṇas*? They are ugly and fierce to look at; are mighty, wrathful and destructive by nature; are noisy and boisterous and can be propitiated only with worship, as they are of the god Śiva.

When we turn to the *RV* and the *AV*, we find the terrestrial demons or goblins named *rakṣases*, who also have such grotesque appearance and destructive nature. These demons have the form of dogs, vultures, owls and other birds (*RV* VII.104.20-22). We find the most detailed account of the appearance of the *rakṣases* in the *AV*. Though they have mostly human form, they have frequently some kind of monstrous deformity, being three-headed, two-mouthed, bear-necked, four-eyed, five-footed, fingerless, with feet turned backwards or with horns on their hands (*AV* VIII.6; Hiraṇyakeśi G.S. II.3.7). Some of these dance round houses in the evening, bray like donkeys, make a noise in the forest, laugh aloud or drink out of skulls (*AV* VIII.6.10, 11, 14; *Hiraṇyakeśi G.S.* II.3.7).[10] These details mostly tally with those belonging to the *gaṇas* of Śiva. It seems that the Purāṇas have tailored the descriptions of the *gaṇas* of Śiva on these age-old details about the demons and evil spirits, the trait of Śaivite colour being their own.

The Vedic tradition (the *RV*-saṁhitā and the Brāhamaṇa-texts) has further helped the Purāṇas in forming the very concept of the *gaṇas* (groups), though the word *gaṇa* used in singular number means simply the ardent follower and attendant of Śiva. The *RV* mentions certain *gaṇas* or groups *viz.* Ādityas, Vasus, Rudras, Maruts, Aṅgirases, Ṛbhus and Viśve-devas.[11] Of all these, the striking *gaṇa* is of the Maruts—the Storm-gods. There is also the singing *gaṇa* of Bṛhaspati (*RV* IV.50.2, 5). Bṛhaspati (to whom the myth of Indra is transferred here) is said to have burst open with roar the enclosing cave of Vala with his well-praising and singing band-*gaṇena* (*ibid.* 5). Bṛhaspati is highly praised as the chieftain of (all) *gaṇas* (*ibid.* II.23.1).

The *gaṇa* of the Maruts is mentioned in the plural only. Their number is thrice sixty or thrice seven. They are the sons of Rudra and Pṛśni (a cow, probably a mottled storm-cloud). The Maruts moving in a group, being the sons of Rudra are themselves called Rudrāsaḥ (*RV* I.85.2), Rudragaṇa (*ibid.* I.39.4, 7) and sometimes Rudriyagaṇa (*ibid.* I.38.7; II.34.10). At times the Maruts show the malevolent traits of their father Rudra. Hence they are implored to ward off the lightning from their worshippers (*ibid.* VII.56.9); to avert their arrow and the stone, which they throw (*ibid.* I.172.2); their lightning (*ibid.* VII.57.4) and their cow-and-man-slaying bolt (*ibid.* VII.56.17). They can cause disasters (*ibid.* I.39.8). The main traits of the Maruts as found in the *RV viz.* helping a powerful god (always Indra and on some occasions Bṛhaspati), roaring, dancing and behaving in a fearful manner are carried on further in the Brāhmaṇa-texts. In the Vaiśvadeva-iṣṭi (in the Cāturmāsya-iṣṭis), a cake on seven potsherds is offered to the Maruts, as they are the people (*viśaḥ*) of the gods, who roam about entirely unimpeded (*Śat. Br.* II.5.1.12). In the Sākamedha-iṣṭi (in the Cāturmāsya-iṣṭis), a cake on seven potsherds is to be offered to the sportive (*krīḍinaḥ*) Maruts, for when Indra went forward to slay Vṛtra, the Maruts were sporting around him, singing his praises (*ibid.* II.5.3.20). The *Tait. Br.* states that when Indra had slain Vṛtra, he himself was apprehensive of his having (really) killed Vṛtra. The Maruts asking for themselves a boon (It was the first oblation, which was prepared for them), which was granted to them, sported i.e. danced, about on Vṛtra and thereby found out that he was dead (*Tait. Br.* I.6.7.4). The *Ait. Br.* says that when Indra had slain Vṛtra, all the deities left him, thinking that he had not laid him low. The Maruts alone, his true associates did not leave him (*Ait. Br.* III.16=12.5). The Maruts are identified with the clans-'*viśaḥ*' (*Śat. Br.* II.5.1.12; II.5.2.24, 27, 34). They are called *sāntapanāḥ* i.e. who scorch others. The *Śat. Br.* enjoins in the Sākamedha-iṣṭi a *caru* (a potful of boiled rice) to the Maruts, who are *sāntapanāḥ* (*Śat. Br.* II.5.3.3).

The Maruts with their prominent features and striking epithets (especially the epithet *viśaḥ*) and their constant association with Indra, the great warrior and the leader, remind us, of the set-up of the Aryan society and the political units of the Ṛgvedic period. Thus the *jana* was a category wider than the *grāma*, indicating a collection of many *grāmas.* In between these two was the unit *viś*. The king (*rājan*), the protector of the *jana* (*janasya gopā*) was the *viśpati* (the lord of the *viś* i.e. people).[12] Thus the chieftain or lord of the tribe or clan or the king, had a group of people, who used to be exclusively his followers and for whose protection he strived. The picture did not differ when it was transferred to the divine plane. As Eggeling has rightly pointed out, "....the identification of the common people with a whole class of comparatively inferior deities would naturally suggest itself. Hence we also find the Maruts, the constant companions and helpmates of Indra, the divine ruler, employed in a similar sense".[13]

In the religious thought of India, in the Puranic period, when the Vedic god Rudra gave place to Śiva, the fierce, boisterous and stormy *gaṇa* of the Maruts, with its destructive nature and having Rudra as their father, served as a model for the later *gaṇas* of Śiva. Though the Puranic Śiva was comparatively a much milder form of the Vedic Rudra, his *gaṇas* (who were not his sons but his devoted attendants) moreover inherited many prominent features of the *rakṣases*, mentioned in the *AV* as it is noted earlier. The *gaṇas* of Śiva stood unique, some of them enjoying the parental care and affection from Śiva and Pārvatī. Thus the concept of yore of *gaṇas* came to assume separate and independent position in the Śaiva religious thought of India.

About Viṣṇu when one thinks of his incarnations, *avataras* varying in numbers as seen in the *Mbh.*, Harivaṁśa and Purāṇas, require an explanation.

Broadly speaking the word *avatāra* signifies a new form. The Ṛgvedic Indra wanders about in many forms (*RV* VI.47.18). The Purāṇas have not restricted the idea of taking or assuming a new form only to Viṣṇu, but have extended it to Śiva. Thus Śiva, as occasion demanded, took the form of a deer (*Var. P.* 215.2ff); a frog (*Sk.P.* I.1.18.4d); a boar (*ibid.* V.3.19.41ff); a peacock (*ibid.* V.3.6.6-20); a tortoise (*ibid.* V.3.7.4ff); crane (*ibid.* V.3.8.1 ff).[14] The *Bhagavadgītā* in its tenth chapter has dealt with the *vibhūtis* of the Highest God. The note struck here at the end of the chapter clearly states that whatever is possessed of *vibhūti* or *śrī* or *ūrjita*, is produced from the part of God's lustre (*Bh.G.* X.40, 41). According to the Pāncarātra philosophy Viṣṇu's manifestations are of various kinds.[15]

A cursory glance at the number of *avatāras* and the exact names figuring there, results in giving interesting details. Thus we have — *Garuḍa P.* (I.1.14 ff-30ff)-22 *avatāras* of Viṣṇu with a note that Hari's *avatāras* are innumerable; *Brahmāṇḍa P.* (II.4.29-92ff)—10 *avatāras* springing from the fingers of goddess Lalitā; also (*ibid.* II.3.73.74 ff and 88ff)— 3 divine births of the Lord, who took birth in human form seven times; *Brahma P.* (chap. 213); *Var. P.* (chaps. 39-50)—various incarnations of Viṣṇu, the purpose of worship and also the mode of worship in different months, both as related to these incarnations; *Sk.P.* (V.3.151.4ff-27)-10 incarnations of Viṣṇu; also (*ibid.* II.9.18.17-

46)—incarnations exceeding no. 10, from Viṣṇu's own words; also (*ibid.* II.9.27.24ff)—16 *avatāras* of Hari, which are to be installed in the form of images in different quarters; *Agni P.* (II.2; III; IV.1-21)—some of the *avatāras* of Viṣṇu; *Matsya P.* (X.7.234-254)—3 celestial incarnations and 7 human incarnations; *Harivaṁśa* (I. chap. 42f)—the word used is *prādurbhāva* and not *avatāra* and 8 *prādurbhāvas* given; *Mbh.* (Śānti 339.103, 104)—9 incarnations of God; *Bhāg. P.* (III.17.31b)—many forms to favour the righteous; also (*ibid.* XI.4 whole chap.)—22 incarnations.

The concept of *avatāra* is dealt with on metaphysical plane by Huttington,[16] who says that *avatāra* signifies 'the divine descent into earthly form.' It symbolises, according to him, 'the passage from the unconditioned to the conditioned, from the infinite to the finite, from eternity to the temporal sphere.[17] However, we feel that primarily more important than metaphysics is the traditional belief regarding the potency of such creatures as fish, tortoise and boar, man-animal form as well as dwarf which occupy prime position in the first five *avatāras* (i.e. Matsya, Kaccha, Varāha, Nṛsiṁha and Vāmana). Huttington says that no direct reference in the Vedic literature, even the general concept of *avatāra* is found, though he sees the germs of several later stories, such as of Vāmana, even in the *RV*.[18] It has to be pointed out that the power of god to assume different forms can be taken as the first step which can lead to his actual descent to the terrestrial plane, which we call *avatāra* (fr. *ava* + √*tṛ*— 'to descend'). Thus the general concept of *avatāra* has a place in the Vedic literature. Devasthali has shown how the first five *avatāras* (noted above) are mentioned or referred to in the mythical accounts of the Brāhmaṇa-texts.[19]

Though we have mentioned the exact number of the *avatāras* given in the *Mbh.*, *Harivaṁśa* and Purāṇas, the well-known and commonly recognised *avatāras* are ten in number *viz.* fish (Matsya), Tortoise (Kaccha), Boar (Varāha), Man-lion

(Nṛsiṁha), Dwarf (Vāmana), Paraśurāma, Rāma, Kṛṣṇa, Buddha and Kalki. In all these *avatāras*, the god descends on earth with a particular mission which he has to perform and it is to save the earth from any calamity leading to the destruction of the earth, excepting the Buddha-*avatāra* whose inclusion in the list of the ten *avatāras* speaks of the note of assimilation, given priority by the ancient Indian thinkers. These ten *avatāras* are thus the arche types of the god's descent to the terrestrial plane and enjoy unfailing status, the later *avatāras* mentioned in the texts, noted before, stand as the corollaries of these.

We have said that the traditional beliefs have been at the basis of the first five mythical incarnations (*avatāras*). To deal mainly with these and the last one i.e. Kalki, which is also mythical in character. Paraśurāma, Rāma (Daśaratha's son) and Kṛṣṇa[20] and Buddha are humans and due to their extraordinary achievements and exploits are reckoned as the *avatāras* of the god.

The first incarnation 'Fish' can be seen in the *Śat. Br.* in the mythical account of Manu and his escape from the flood with the help of a fish. The mythical account comes here as an *arthavāda* for the ritual of Iḍā-offering (*Śat.Br.* I.8.1.12ff). The account is too well-known to have a detailed treatment here. With slight variation it occurs in the *Mbh.* (Vana chap. 187) and the Purāṇas (*Matsya P.* chaps. I and II; *Agni P.* chap. 1; *Padma P.* chap. XXXVI; *Bhāg. P.* VIII.24; *Kālika P.* XXXIV). The *Bhāg. P.* introduces a new feature. It mentions that in one of the nights of Brahmā during his repose, the whole universe was submerged in the primeval ocean. The demon Hayagrīva, at this time, came near and carried off the Vedas, which had slipped from Brahmā's mouth. To recover the lost Vedas, Viṣṇu assumed the form of a fish and saved Manu at the dissolution of the earth. When Brahmā awoke, Viṣṇu slew Hayagrīva and restored the Vedas to him (*Bhāg. P.* VIII.24 vv.6, 7 and 57 for Hayagrīva).

This story of the flood and Manu's subsequent escape at the hands of the great fish is generally taken to indicate the elements of the fish-incarnation. The story of the flood is universal. Apart from the traditions such as Babylonian, Hebrew, Transylvanian, Persian, eastern Asian, Australian and others, in India, the story of flood is told by the Bhils of the Central India, the jungle-tribes of Malwa, the Dravidian tribes of Raipur, the Mundas of Bengal, the Singphos, the Lushias, the Anals and the Ahoms of Assam.[22] Frazer opines that as the flood-story does not occur in the most ancient Sanskrit literature, but appears only in the books written long after the settlement of Aryans in India (we have noted the reference from the *Śat. Br.*), the Aryans might have learnt the flood-story from the aborigins.

The role of the fish as a saviour at the critical hour is an indispensable part of the flood-story. Several beliefs attached to fish have helped the hood of divinity to be fixed on this aquatic animal. Gonda suggests that the characteristics of this animal—as it symbolises growth because of its rapid reproduction—contributed to its becoming a manifestation of the High God Viṣṇu.[23] We feel that fish, as per the beliefs prevalent among folks, has stood as a symbol of fertility. These beliefs are at the basis of rituals, where fish figures prominently. It stands as a symbol of conjugal happiness. We note in the *Baudhāyana Gṛhyasūtra* (I.13) that on the fourth day of marriage, the newly married couple goes out of the village to pay respects to the Udumbara tree and pray for good fortune. On this occasion, fish are caught in fresh cloth and offered as a *bali* (offering) to the water-birds. In the same vein, *mīna* (fish) can be taken as the emblem of the god of love, who is called *mīnaketu* or *mīnaketana*. The goddess Vasudhārā, the goddess of plenty in ancient terracota, is associated with fish.[24] Most of the Vārāhī images hold a fish in one of their hands. *Vārāhī Tantra* describes five forms of Vārāhī. The last three of the 28 couplets describe Matsya Vārāhī[25]

Certain *brāhmaṇa* families in the state of Maharashtra, Surat and Mysore and certain royal families of Tripura and Orissa still retain the Matsya-tradition in the accounts of their origin and in royal insignias. Thus 'fish' carries with it the beliefs rooted in the tradition about its features of 'plenty' and 'progeny'—the touchstone of a creator-god. It is true that no other aquatic creature could be thought of as being capable of relieving Manu from the flood than the fish. But it is also possible to say that the appearance of fish as the first *avatāra* might be due its own importance rooted in tradition. Moreover the theory of evolution presupposes the first animals to be aquatic and this accounts for the *Matsya* (fish)-*avatāra.*

Tortoise is another aquatic animal (though it can remain alive on the earth for some time), which figures as the second *avatāra* of the god. This *avatāra* also can be traced to the Brāhmaṇa-texts. It is said that Prajāpati having become a tortoise created the beings (*Śat.Br.* VII.5.1.5). Prajāpati in the shape of a tortoise crept over the three worlds (*ibid.* VII.5.1.9). Tortoise is also said to be the sun (*ibid.* VII.5.1.6). This gets related to the worldwide belief that tortoise is a solar animal. The resemblance of the tortoise with the sun, is clear, the former being circular in form with the head, legs and tail standing for the rays of the sun. The folk-belief that 'a turtle will not die until sun-down' echoes the same idea.[26] The mythical account of the churning of the ocean for getting nectar, points out how the tortoise offered its valuable help to the gods and the Asuras, when they approached it (*Mbh.* Ādi 18.11, 12). The Purāṇas state that Viṣṇu himself takes the form of a huge tortoise to support the Mandara mountain (*Viṣṇu P.* I.9.88; *Bhāg.P.* VIII.6.8), which was made by the gods and the Asuras as a churning rod.

In the rite of Agnicayana (building of the Great Fire-altar), a live tortoise is buried in the lowest layer (*Śat. Br.* VII.5.1.1ff) and it is said to be the yonder sun (*ibid.* VII.5.1.6), Sun and Agni being the forms of one principle only namely 'Heat' as we have noted in the chapter on Sacrifice. The tortoise with its 'solar touch' could easily stand for the *avatāra* of the god Viṣṇu, who right from the *RV* is a solar god.[27]

The next incarnation is 'Boar', which is taken note of in details by Gonda.[28] This incarnation can be traced to the *Tait. Sam.*, where it is said that Prajāpati took the form of the boar, and raised the earth from the primeval waters (VII.1.5.1). In the Brāhmaṇa-texts also occurs this mythical account.[29] By the Puranic period, the boar is included in the list of the incarnations of Viṣṇu.[30] The *Sk.P.* refers to this incarnation at various places.[31] According to it, at one place it says that in the Vārāha-kalpa, Śiva assumed the form of a boar (*Sk.P.* V.3.19.41ff). It also says that Viṣṇu assumed the form of a boar in five ways (*Sk.P.* naming the five Varāhas V.3.189.14-17). In the *Bhāg.P.*, the mythical account of the demon Hiraṇyākṣa (the twin-brother of the demon Hiraṇyakaśipu) forms part of the account of the boar-incarnation. Finding nobody to combat with him, Hiraṇyākṣa with his mace went to Varuṇa, who directed him to Viṣṇu. On Varuṇa's suggestion, Hiraṇyākṣa went to the nether region (*rasātala*), where he saw the 'Great Boar' carrying the earth from the *rasātala*. In the combat between Hiraṇyākṣa and the Boar (Varāha), Hiraṇyākṣa met his death at the hands of Varāha (*Bhāg. P.* III. chaps.17-19).

It has to be taken into consideration that Varāha, a boar, has a religious and mythical tradition with it. The association of the boar with the earth is noted by the *AV* (XII.1.148). The belief that the boar deposits its strength in the earth which it kicks occurs in the *Kauśika Sūtra* (*Kau. S.* XV.2). It is enjoined that to have victory in battle, the earth dug up by a boar may be placed on the altar to have the boar's strength.[32] According to Gonda, the boar's usual habit of digging up the soil must have induced man to associate the animal with the fertility of the earth.[33] The Sūtras know well the importance of boar.[34]

Like other skins (or hides), the boar-skin stands for the boar, with its magical effect transferred to its skin. In the Rājasūya sacrifice, the king has to put on the shoes of boar's skin (*Śat.Br.* V.4.3.19). The *Tait.Br.* also prescribes for the king wearing of boar-skin shoes, saying that boar is the 'mettle' (*manyu*) of the animals, which the king places in himself in the Rājasūya rite (*Tait.Br.* I.7.9.4).

Thus like the earlier two *avatāras* (fish and tortoise), even the *avatāra* in the form of boar, has the firm basis of the folk-beliefs. Boar was thought to have miraculous powers, and so had its entry in the creation account. Even Prajāpati, the god of Sacrifice had to assume the form of a boar, Viṣṇu's entry as a boar from mythological point of view thus standing very late running through the *Mbh.* and the Purāṇas. These three *avatāras* are associated with water, as seen from the mythical accounts in which they figure. And this takes us to the beginning of the universe, when universe according to Indian tradition and in other traditions and mythologies, all the world over, comes out of water. The *RV* speaks about primeval waters (X.72.6; X.129.3). The *Tait. Sam.* states that waters were at the beginning (VII.1.5.1). According to the *Śat. Br.* water alone existed in the beginning. They thought of procreating (XI.1.6.1 ff). This same idea regarding primeval waters occurs in the Sumerian, Egyptian and Biblical traditions. The animals connected with water, already having folk-beliefs of yore woven around them, hence, naturally were taken to be the (first) incarnations of the god, the creator-god (here Viṣṇu). Pusalkar suggests for various *avatāras* various eras.[35] Rather than chronology, we feel that traditionally recognised order of the *avatāras* starts correctly from the sphere of waters, which are primeval waters.

The fourth *avatāra* is the Nṛsiṁha—Man-lion—*avatāra*, and is associated with land. Following the general Puranic trend, the *Bhāg. P.*, in connection with this *avatāra*, gives the mythical account of the demon Hiraṇyakaśipu and his death at the hands of the man-lion (*Bhāg.P.* VII.chaps.3-8). It relates how it was difficult to kill Hiraṇyakaśipu, who had become all powerful due to the boons granted to him by god Brahmā (*ibid.* VII.3.35-38). This part of the mythical account has its basis in the myth of the *asura* Namuci, which occurs in the *Śat.Br.* Indra himself had given a promise to Namuci the *asura* that the former would slay him neither by night nor by day, neither with staff nor with bow, neither with his palm nor with his fist, neither with the dry nor with the moist. Hence when Namuci carried away Indra's favourite drink Soma, Indra became helpless, being unable to counter-attack the *asura*. But Aśvins and Sarasvatī poured out foam of water to serve as a thunderbolt, for the foam was neither dry not moist. At the early day-break (it being neither night nor day), Indra struck off the head of Namuci (*Śat.Br.* XII.7.3.1-3).

Gonda fixes his attention on the pillar, from which Narasiṁha emerges to kill the demon Hiraṇyakaśipu. He states that the primary idea of the pillar is that of a sacrificial wooden post, made out of a tree such as Nyagrodha or Aśvattha etc., which is associated with Viṣṇu, his name being identified with sacrifice (*viṣṇurvai yajñaḥ*), at several places.[36] It has to be pointed out that according to the ancient Indian tradition, the sacrificial post is thought to embody Agni and Śākapūṇi has endorsed it as can be seen from Yāska's statement.[37] In fact, the sacrificial post (*yūpa*) fixed on the terrestrial plane in the sacrifice is understood to reach the region of the gods. The *Tait. Sam.* in the exposition of the Soma-sacrifice points out how the sacrificial stake touches all the three regions *viz.* the nether, earth and through mid-region heaven (*Tait.Sam.* VI.3.4.6, 7). Dange takes the concept of *yūpa* to that of *axis mundi.*[38] Hence the pillar or column from which the ferocious form of the Being—neither full man nor full animal—emerged (*Bhāg. P.* VII.8.18, 19), cannot be taken as the sacrificial post, as Gonda has maintained.

In the Nṛsiṁha form, the 'lion' is described with minute details (*ibid.* VII.8.20-22). *Siṁha* (lion) has been wellknown right from the *RV*, where Agni is called *siṁha* (*RV* I.95.5). The altar (*vedī*) is called *siṁhī* (*Vāj.Sam.* V.10). The *vedi* is identified with the earth. The overlord of the earth(=*vedī*=*siṁhī*)—the spirit of the earth—thus is a divinity in 'Man-lion' (Nṛsiṁha) form. In the *Bṛhajjābālopaniṣad,* (6.1) mentioned by Gonda,[39] a Narasiṁha standing on the bank of Bhavani is considered to be a divinity to protect or injure men. Here the concept of Nṛsiṁha is seen in the belief maintained by the people even in later ages.

The Nṛsiṁha-*avatāra* standing as the spirit of the earth reminds us of a couple of representations occurring in ancient Egypt. We have the concept of Aker, which stands as a symbol of the earth and is represented in the picture-script by two outfacing heads of lions bridged by two parallel lines.[40] Again the Egyptian Sphinx, having lion's head and man's body, towering high on the surface of the earth is no doubt the spirit of the earth.

Thus the spirit of the earth (in the Nṛsiṁha-*avatāra*) becomes a divine incarnation, in the sphere of mythology. In the later versions, of the mythical account of Nṛsiṁha-*avatāra*, the pillar from which the Man-lion emerges is shown to be that of the threshold of Hiraṇyakaśipu's palace. This is due to the importance attached to the threshold divinities, as seen in many ancient mythologies.[41] Nṛsiṁha (or Narasiṁha) in later tradition is attached to the Temple of Jagannātha, and in the living tradition is taken to be a deity, having malevolent traits, which will be dealt with further.

To turn to the 'Dwarf' (Vāmana) incarnation of Viṣṇu. The myth of Viṣṇu as a dwarf occurs in the *Śat.Br.* The gods and the *asuras* sprung from Prajāpati were striving for supremacy. Once when the gods faced defeat, the *asuras* taking hold of the whole earth began to divide it between themselves. The gods approached the *asuras* placing Viṣṇu ('dwarf') in the shape of the very sacrifice at their head and requested the *asuras* for a share in the earth. The *asuras* grudgingly agreed to give a share of the earth only as much as that Viṣṇu would lie upon. Having laid Viṣṇu down eastwards, the gods enclosed him on all the three sides with metres *viz.* Gāyatrī, Triṣṭubh and Jagatī. Having placed Agni on the east side, the gods went on worshipping and toiling with Viṣṇu (=Sacrifice) and obtained the entire earth (*Śat.Br.* I.2.5.1-7). The *Jaim.Br.* states a mythical account, explaining the cause of Viṣṇu's dwarfness. The gods (normally, as per belief) do not sleep. However, once, due to extreme toiling they closed their eyes. The *asuras*, seeking this opportunity, carried away their lustre, power and vigour. Viṣṇu noticed it. When the gods awakened, Viṣṇu told them what happened and sent them to waters for the search of their lustre, power and vigour. They observed a peak rising up from the surface of the waters. Having caught hold of that peak with the sacred utterances (Vyāhṛtis *viz.* Bhūḥ, Bhuvaḥ and Svar), they gave it to Viṣṇu. Having borne that peak of the gods' lustre, power and vigour, Viṣṇu under that weight was totally creeping. Hence is Viṣṇu a dwarf (*Jaim.Br.* III.354). It is the stature of the dwarf Viṣṇu that served as a precursor of the dwarf incarnation of Viṣṇu in the Epic and the Puranic mythologies. This form of Viṣṇu is deep-rooted in the Vedic ritualistic tradition. Thus in the Rājasūya sacrifice, at a rite—Triṣaṁyukta offering—in the offering to Viṣṇu, a dwarfish bull is the *dakṣiṇa* given, for the dwarf belongs to Viṣṇu (*Śat.Br.* V.2.5.4). The Vāmana(=Dwarf) incarnation of Viṣṇu is stated by the *Mbh.* (Vana 272.62-70). The Purāṇas deal with it (*Vām.P.* II.9.13ff; also *ibid.* 10.44-69; *Padma P.* I (Sṛṣṭikhaṇḍa).25), and the *Bhāg.P.* gives it at a great length (*Bhāg.P.* VIII.chaps. 18-23). This incarnation no doubt brings out prominently the extraordinary capacities of the god, as said by Gonda, who maintains that this incarnation reiterates the widespread belief in the miraculous abilities of those, who are considerably short of the usual size.[42]

The three steps taken by the dwarf Viṣṇu are to be traced to the *RV*, where Viṣṇu—the solar deity—traverses the whole sky in three steps (*tredhā vicakramāṇaḥ*) and is wide-striding (*urugāyaḥ*). One single hymn in the *RV* (I.154) very well presents this prominent trait of Viṣṇu, which hardly requires any more evidence. The *Śat.Br.* also speaks of these steps of Viṣṇu but these are obviously in the context of sacrifice. Thus to note—'Viṣṇu verily is the sacrifice. By striding he obtained for the gods that all-pervading power, which now belongs to him. By his first step he gained the earth, by the second the aerial expanse and by his last step the sky' (*Śat.Br.* I.9.3.9).

Now to speak about the dwarf form of Viṣṇu, which is no doubt important. Folk-literature abounds in tales, depicting the immesurable help rendered by a dwarf to the hero.[43] However the appearance of the dwarf (Vāmana) Viṣṇu in the form a *brahmacārin* is a point to be probed further. The *Mbh.* (Sabhā chap. 38 verses not given numbers; Vana 272.63-64) and the *Bhāg.P.* (VIII.18.14-19, 23-24) describe the *brahmacārī* Vāmana-Viṣṇu with his striking features. The extraordinary powers of a *brahmacārin* are spoken of in the *AV* (X.5.7, 12). These powers he attains due to his disciplined life, dedicated to the pursuit of knowledge (*vidyās*) in the house of the preceptor. The *Āśv.G.S.* speaks of a *snātaka* (one, who having completed his learning, has taken the final bath) as a 'Great Being'—*mahad bhūtam* (*Āśv.G.S.* III.9.8).[44] As the Vāmana *brahmacārin* had these miraculous powers, it was all the more difficult for king Bali to deny the former's request for having the land covering only his three steps, which apparently though small, were the three steps of the wide-striding (*urugāya*) Viṣṇu!

The last *avatāra* (which is as yet to come) is mentioned for the first time in the *Mbh.* (*Mbh.* Vana 190.93-97; 191.1-5). Here he appears as a *brāhmaṇa* called Kalki Viṣṇuyaśas, of great intelligence and prowess, who will exterminate all the evil-doers. This *avatāra*, though rarely worshipped, is the sublimation of the destroying power. He is said to appear at the end of the Kali Age, riding on a horse with his sword drawn (*Agni P.* for detailed description and the *Mbh.* Vana 190.93-97). According to Gonda, the horse on which Kalki rides throws light on Kalki's personality, the horse being an embodiment of Viṣṇu. According to him, the powers ascribed to the horse and the all-pervading powers of Viṣṇu may have contributed to this identification.[45] It has to be pointed out that from the Vedic ritualistic tradition itself, horse is taken to be associated and even (in rituals) identified with Prajāpati or the sun.[46] The *Mbh.* clearly states that Kalki, destroying all 'evil', and 'sin' will establish again the fourfold (*varṇa* and *āśrama*) system in the society. This is precisely the duty for which the king is ordained and to which he is bound by the 'Rājadharma' (*Manu Sm.* chap. VII). Hence the tenth *avatāra* in the form of Kalki, riding on a horse with a sword drawn is verily the representation of a human king, having the 'rod of punishment' in his hand. Manu speaks at great length of the necessity and the efficacy of the rod of punishment (Daṇḍa) wielded by a king (*Manu Sm.* VII.14ff). Kalki thus is a symbol of sturdy royalty, which will establish law and order at the end of the Kali age and then will start the Kṛta age. Jaiswal has rightly caught this image of a king in the Kalki *avatāra*.[47] We have made this point clear by making a reference to a detail from the *Kālacakra-tantra* in the 'Introduction'.

A note has to be taken of the cult of Jagannātha, as the deity is linked with Kṛṣṇa or Viṣṇu. In fact, the cult of Jagannātha is synthetic in character and stands as an excellent example of Indian way of assimilating and integrating various trends of thought.

There are four Māhātmyas (accounts) glorifying the Puruṣottama-kṣetra of Puri, which occur in the *Sk.P.* (Vaiṣṇava-khaṇḍa i.e. II, section 2), *Brahma P.* (chaps. 39-69), *Nārada P.* (Uttarakhaṇḍa chaps. 52-61) and *Padma P.* (seventh and the last section, chap. 18, 55 verses). The account given in the *Sk.P.*

is the oldest and the most important one and is referred to as the Puruṣottama-māhātmya. It consists of 49 chaptes, containing more than 3000 verses. To state broad outlines of the account-King Indradyumna of Avantī (of the Malwa region) sends Vidyāpati (his priest's brother) to search for the Puruṣottama-kṣetra, situated on the 'Blue Mountain' (Nīlādri or Nīlagiri) in a dense forest in Orissa. After long hours of wait and efforts, Vidyāpati gets the information about the Lord of the *kṣetra* (place) from an old Śabara, who is first reluctant to divulge the secret, which till then has been shared only by the members of his tribe. But he is reminded of a prophecy handed down from the older people of his tribe that the statue of Mādhava (the lord Puruṣottama) shall one day be covered with golden sand and disappear. Then a king named Indradyumna will come from Malwa and reinstall a new image of the God made of wood. So he takes Vidyāpati the *brāhmaṇa* emissary, to have a *darśana* of the deity Mādhava. Vidyāpati then returns to Avantī and everything happens as per the prophecy. But when the king (Indradyumna) sets out for the place of the Lord, he gets the bad news, on the borders of Orissa, that Lord Nīlamādhava has since disappeared. The distressed king is consoled by Nārada and on the advice of the latter, constructs first, a temple for Nṛsiṁha (the Primeval form of the Lord). At the end of the sacrificial ceremonies performed for the construction of this temple, to the great surprise of all, an extraordinary tree marked with auspicious signs is seen washed ashore. The tree is then put in a room (turned then into a workshop) and there comes a carpenter, who is the Lord himself. The carpenter enters the room with the wood of the sacred tree, doors are shut and loud music is played outside, so that the sound of fashioning the divine images may not be audible. The images are ready at the end of a fortnight. A divine voice is heard saying that only the descendants of the Śabara Viśvāvasu—the original worshipper of Nīlamādhava—should be entrusted the task of giving the final shape to the images. And thus finally there are the images, but of wood![48]

The account from the *Sk.P.* is given above in short and the other Purāṇas mentioned earlier follow in the foot-steps of the *Sk.P.*

In this connection, let us take into account the age-old legend, which though in oral form, can shed light on an hitherto unearthed detail. The legend states that in early times, Śabara Viśvāvasu used to worship the deity 'Nīlamādhava' in the form of a 'blue stone' (*'nīla'* means 'black' also) in the forest. Vidyāpati, the *brāhmaṇa* minister of the king Indradyumna with the help of the Śabara Viśvāvasu, could find out 'Nīlamādhava'. It is said that the Śabara (Viśvāvasu) could show 'Nīlamādhava' only at the request of his daughter Lalitā, who was in deep love with Vidyāpati. Once when Indradyumna appeared on the scene, 'Nīlamādhava' disappeared. But at the behest of Lord Viṣṇu, the king carved out the wooden image of the Lord at the place, now known as 'Guṇḍīcā ghara' (the house of Guṇḍīcā), Guṇḍīcā being the name of the king's loving wife. After the construction of this edifice, thus named after Guṇḍīcā, the wooden images were established there. The children born from the marriage of Lalitā (Śabara Viśvāvasu's daughter) with Vidyāpati (king's minister) were known as Pati Mahāpātras and the head of this group has come to be known as (Vidyā-)Pati Mahāpātra.[49] The descendants of the Śabara Viśvāvasu are known as Daitās. These Daitās (Śabaras) and Pati Mahāpātras (half-Śabaras), because of their age-old association with the deity Jagannatha, are employed as very important functionaries in the temple, carrying out important tasks.[50] In the process of evolution of Jagannātha, the deity is linked with Kṛṣṇa or Viṣṇu.

This account though mythical, gives a plausible reason for the association of the 'Śabara' and the 'half-Śabara' officials, with the temple rituals. Though an *arthavāda*, the account confirms the association of the deity Jagannātha with Śabaras, the aboriginals, who were acculturated with the Aryans from ancient times, as we have noted in the chapter on Tribes.

The real problem is of linking the wooden image (images) with that of Mādhava (or Nīlamādhava, as he was on the Nīlādri or Nīlagiri—Blue Mountain). Tripathi G.C. in his voluminous work on the Jagannatha Temple has dealt with this in details.[51] He has also criticised having examined the investigation of the Indradyumna legend made by R. Geib. Geib thinks that the events narrated in the legend reflect some sort of historical truth regarding the development of the Jagannātha Temple. He maintains that the stone statue of the Mādhava form of Viṣṇu was removed by some king from the Temple, because of the increasing popularity of the wooden images of Jagannātha (standing at the same time) in a Maṇḍapa at the Guṇḍīcāgṛha. The same king brought wooden statues of Jagannātha etc. in chariots with great pomp and show and installed them in the present Temple. The annual Car Festival is to commemorate this event.[52] Tripathi has taken a detailed note of Geib's stand-point and has supported his own counter stand-point taking a local survey with several evidences pertaining to the images and temples in Orissa.[53] For Geib's argument, he states that "to assert that in the Jagannātha cult we have to do with a process in which a Hinduistic deity (Mādhava) has been relinquished and replaced by a tribal wooden deity is putting the cart before the horse and does not exhibit a proper understanding of the religious spectrum of Orissa".[54] According to Tripathi, the motive of Mādhava in the story is simply an invention of the priestly class with a view to defend and explain the queer and unusual iconography of Jagannātha and the substance (wood) which it is made of.[55]

Taking into consideration the account from the *Sk.P.*, following it similar accounts given by three other Purāṇas and the age-old mythical account (or legend) handed down by the oral tradition, we note the following incidents, which are sequential—

1. Originally the image of Puruṣottama, may be in the form of a rude stock of stone, was at the Blue Mountain (Nīlādri or Nīlagiri), hence known to be in the form of a 'Blue Stone'. (In Sanskrit, *nīla* means 'black' also).
2. Initially it was worshipped by the Śabaras, who were tribals.
3. The deity and the place remained a 'tribal secret' for a long time, with the Śabaras.
4. A prophecy foretold the disappearance of the 'old' image and the installation of the 'new' image of the deity—a shift from the (sacred) 'stone' to the 'wooden' image.
5. King Indradyumna was the agent (chosen by the gods) to install and thus re-establish the new image of the deity (Lord Puruṣottama).
6. Prior to this, the king had to have a *darśana* of the 'Nṛsiṁha' form of the Lord on the Blue Mountain (situated near the Nīlakaṇṭheśvara temple, not very far off from the present Temple of Jagannātha). He had to perform a sacrifice and also construct a temple for Nṛsiṁha on the Blue Mountain, Nṛsiṁha being the 'Primeval Form' of the Lord.
7. Then were the four images (in wood) established—of Balarāma, Subhadrā, Jagannātha and Sudarśana.

For Tripathi as we noted earlier, the motive of Mādhava (itself) is simply an invention of the priestly class. He says—"The best and the most effective argument to encounter those who could not accept the iconography of Jagannātha as a matter of course, was to tell them that 'the present Jagannātha has not always been so; he was a blue Mādhava in old ages but has himself now incarnated in this new wooden form suitable to the present age.'[56]

We have already noted that the tribe of the Śabaras was acculturated in the Vedic-brahmanical Hindu society from very early times. Nevertheless like every tribe, even the Śabara tribe must have preserved its own tradition. This takes us to the stage of aniconism—'worship or veneration of an object that represents a god, without being an image of him,'[57] though not in the Hindu society, but prevalent in the lowest strata of the society at large. The rude stock of stone—'Blue Stone' (-'Nīlamādhava')-, kept at a secret place in the (Blue) Mountain recesses, might have been regarded by the Śabaras with veneration, as a god or a 'fetish'.[58] But some day, this stage of aniconism was crossed over to develop into the stage of presenting anthropomorphic images.[59] The prophecy handed down from the older people of the tribe to Śabara Viśvāvasu that the then existing 'stone' (image?) would disappeared and a new image mode of wood would come, indicates this stage. The prophecy serves as a mythological strategy used by the Puranic and old traditions to show this transit from the stage of aniconism to that of having images. Can we say that the images of Jagannātha etc. also can be traced to the Śabara origin and the Śabaras had the main part to play in this? Probably so! It is a patent fact that the images of Jagannātha etc. are somewhat unusual and are not suiting to the norms of Hindu iconography. Tripathi has directed our attention to the *calantī pratimā* (movable or portable image) of the main image, the latter fashioned in the classical Hinduistic manner and the earlier carried from one place to the other on certain occasions. He has pointed out to Virajā Ṭhākurāṇī having two images — one beautiful, anthropomorphic image, another a simple wooden pole, wrapped up in coloured stripes, when the goddess goes to visit the Goddess Bhagavati.[60] The Goddess Stambheśvarī is widely worshipped as a 'pole' in the eastern part of Orissa (Hence the name which is self-eloquent!). Tripathi just hints that Jagannātha is most probably yet another example of this phenomenon.[61] But as we have seen above, we can come to a most probable conclusion that both—Mādhava and Jagannātha—the two phases of the same deity—have come from the Śabara tribe.

The mythical account of the King Indradyumna figuring in the versions (*Sk.P.*, *Brahma P.* etc.) has to be taken as an *arthavāda*, serving as a link between Mādhava (Nīlamādhava—in the form of a 'stone') and Jagannātha (in the form of a somewhat crude image)—the two phases of one and the same deity—coming from the Śabara tribe. In this account we have the mention of the prophecy, remembered by the Śabara Viśvāvasu. We have dealt with "Curses, boons and oaths" in an earlier chapter. The prophecy falling in line with them, serves as a mythological tool, giving weightage to the *arthavāda*, and the *arthavāda* (account of King Indradyumna) used as a device by the Puranic tradition as well as the oral tradition is for justifying the very basis of the Jagannātha cult. Thus the images in the Jagannātha Temple, in spite of being 'unusual' are accepted and revered, and the cult of Jagannātha has, in holiness, fame and popularity, crossed all the limits. The Daitās[62] (Śabara descendants) and Pati Mahāpātras (reckoned as partially having Śabara origin) are associated with the tasks of the Jagannātha Temple, as noted earlier.[63] It has to be pointed out that the Temple of Jagannātha is the only temple in India, which, right from early times (possibly from the times of its very construction) has been open to persons belonging to any caste, including the lowest caste. Another speciality is partaking of the *Mahāprasāda* ('cooked rice', which is again unique, not found in any other temple) of the deity Jagannātha, without the least consideration of the caste of the person offering it. The cooked food is first offered to the god and then the same is distributed among the devotees, as we find the practice (of '*naivedya*') in any other temple. By way of *arthavāda*, the *Sk.P.* gives an account of a *brāhmaṇa*, who did not accept the *Mahāprasāda*, as it was cooked by others. The result was that he suffered from diseases and all his family-members including himself became dumb. But when he partook of the Mahāprasāda, he became free from these calamities (*Sk.P.* II.2.38.54-60).

The Mahāprasāda is also called *Kaivalya* and the area where it is sold is called *Kaivalyahāṭa*. From the word *Kaivalya*, meaning 'liberation' in Jainism and the suffix 'Nātha' (like that in the words Pārśvanātha, Neminātha etc.) in the name of Jagannātha, there have been efforts to trace the element of Jainism in the Jagannātha cult.[64] In the Daśāvatāra sculpture (depicting the ten incarnations of Viṣṇu) engraved in the Jagannātha Temple, Jagannātha is engraved in place of Buddha. The medieval writers of Oria literature have tried to depict Jagannātha as Buddha. But earlier to these, Indrabhūti, the preacher of the Vajrayāna (Tantrik) sect of Mahāyāna Buddhism, has paid salutation to Jagannātha in the introduction to his esoteric work *Jñānasiddhi*.[65]

In the account from the *Sk.P.*, we have seen that the king Indradyumna was asked to propitiate Nṛsiṁha and construct a temple in his honour, prior to going in for the installation of the images (in wood). Nṛsiṁha is the presiding deity of Navakalevara (fashioning the deities 'new' after a certain period), and plays a role in the rite of Vanayāga ('forest-sacrifice', performed to purify and sanctify the tree out of which the images are to be fashioned) and in the consecration ceremony. The images of Jagannātha etc. to this day are consecrated mainly with the 32-syllabic Mantrarāja of Nṛsiṁha and this, as well as the Pātāla-Nṛsiṁha are the Mantras with which the oblations are offered in the sacrificial fire. According to Tripathi, it is not improbable that Jagannātha was once actually worshipped with the Mantrarāja as Viṣṇu in his Nṛsiṁha aspect. This gains according to him, support from the fact that the now almost deserted temple of Nṛsiṁha in the precincts of the Jagannātha Temple is the ancient most of all in that complex and has yielded the oldest of all inscriptions.[66]

It is an established fact that in the process of evolution, Jagannātha came to be linked with Kṛṣṇa or Viṣṇu and his association with Nṛsiṁha, the latter being one of the incarnations of Viṣṇu can thus stand to reason. But Nṛsiṁha's figuring in the cult of Jagannātha and reverence paid to him as a presiding deity of certain rites and rituals of the Temple, invite explanation and hence require further probe. It is patently seen that the grotesque and fierce appearance of Narasiṁha (or Nṛsiṁha) make him stand apart from the other incarnations of Viṣṇu. Nṛsiṁha figures in an important account. In the detailed note of the goddesses, the mythical account of killing the demon Andhaka will be discussed. The *Matsya P.* (chap. 179) elaborately describes the whole episode and states how even the great god Śiva has to approach lord Nṛsiṁha, who helps him by creating a number of Mothers to control and frighten the Mothers created by Śiva himself, as Śiva could not control them. The *Agni P.* gives the Jvālāmālī mantra of Narasiṁha (Nṛsiṁha), where he is invoked for the destruction of beasts, ghosts and their possessions (*Agni P.* 306.18). A *stotra* ((prayer-song) named 'Viṣṇorapāmārjanastotra', which is regarded as a part of the *Viṣṇudharmottara P.* gives a long list of demonic groups that Narasiṁha rules.[67]

In Maharashtra (in India), Nṛsiṁha is regarded (mostly) as a fearful god, having malevolent characteristics and hence to be always pacified. The words generally used are 'Ugra', 'Vīra', 'Mahogra' etc. before the word Narasiṁha (as 'Ugranarasiṁha' etc., though very rarely 'Śāntanarasiṁha'). In the tradition of the Mahānubhāva sect[68] and also in the writings of some Marathi saint-poets,[69] Narasiṁha is regarded as belonging to the ghostly families. Hence reciting the chants of Narasiṁha is said to be a remedy against ghostly possession.[70] In many families in Maharashtra and Karnataka, Brahmapūjā (a Narasiṁha *vrata*) is observed on the Dīpāvalī day as an annual ritual with strict observances.[71]

Narasiṁha can be taken to be from the category of deities viz. Kṣetrapālas, Bālagrahas, Mātṛkās etc. Bālagrahas and Mātṛkās can be taken as having both the traits, benevolent and malevolent. And so is Kṣetrapāla, protecting a particular region (reminding us of the deity Vāstupuruṣa—the deity of the place of residence). Kṣetrapālas are worshipped in the form of aniconic stones, many times smeared with vermilion (*sindūra*). There are many Narasiṁha shrines like the above, with aniconic stone and no idol.[72] Dange states about Nṛsiṁha that the symbol of lion or the lion-headed man was depicted at the entrance of the dwelling or at a prominent place which may even be a pillar (at the entrance or inside), as a protector deity.[73] Two mythical accounts from Myanmar (Burma) can be pointed out in this connection,[74] where we have the figure of 'Manu Siṁha' (Manu—i.e. *manu*—'man', not Manu the law-giver) called so, not Nṛsiṁha. One account is of Siṁhabāhu, who not knowing, inadvertently killed his own father ('lion'); established a kingdom; gave the name Siṁhapura to the capital and built a temple at the entrance of which he established a 'Manu-Siṁha' to be worshipped as his father. Another account is of the two disciples of Moggalāna (himself Buddha's disciple)—Sohana and Uttara—who created the Manu-Siṁha to drive away the evil powers from the delivery-room of the queen of Taykala's king.

Thus Nṛsiṁha's mention in the mythical account from the *Sk.P.* and his prominent role in the rituals of the Jagannātha Temple, are here totally not because of the god's being the incarnation of Viṣṇu (and Viṣṇu linked to Jagannātha), but they occur here indicating the god Nṛsiṁha's distinct independent status rooted in tradition. Thus related to the Jagannātha Temple, is seen the assimilation of two cults—that of *Narasiṁha* (Nṛsiṁha), and the other that of Jagannātha, having the Śabara-origin, which is indigenous, and hence the major one.

The Purāṇas present a multitude of goddesses, who have independent existence and specific significance and power. Though the concept of goddess as such occurs in the *RV* as for ex. in Indrāṇī, she is simply the wife of Indra in the Vṛṣākapi hymn (*RV* X.86). We have Varuṇānī (*ibid.* I.22.12; II.32.8; V.46.8;

VII.34.22) and Agnāyī (*ibid.* I.22.12; V.46.8), the names of the goddesses being fashioned from those of their husbands, as are feminine nouns in Sanskrit, at times made from masculine stems. The wife of Rudra receives the oblations at the Śūlagava sacrifice under several names such as Rudrāṇī, Śarvāṇī and Bhavānī (Pār. G.S. III.8.10). But here we have entered the period of the Sūtras. Ambikā is regarded as the sister of Rudra in *YV*[75] and receives oblations in the Baliharaṇa ceremony mentioned in the Gṛhyasūtras.[76] Indrāṇī occasionally receives offerings (*Mait. Sam.* III.8.4; *Tait.Sam.* II.2.8.1). In the rite of Agnicayana (building the Great fire-altar), in the ritual of making ready the fire-pan (*ukhā*), the wives of the gods and Dhiṣaṇās the goddesses connected with Viśve-devāḥ (All-gods) are invoked (*Tait.Sam.* IV.1.6.1, 2; *Vāj.Sam.* XI.61). In the New-moon and Full-moon sacrifices (Darśapūrṇamāsa-*iṣṭis*), the Patnīsaṁyāja offerings are made to the wives of the gods, along with some gods; the deities are—Soma, Tvaṣṭṛ, wives of the gods as a group and Agni Gṛhapati. The *Ait.Br.* mentions Prāsahā the favourite wife of Indra (III.22=12.11) and in later mythology we have Śacī as Indra's wife (obviously from his name 'Śakra'—the lord of strength'). But Prāsahā and Śacī are not regarded as goddesses. About the Ṛgvedic goddesses Dawn (Uṣas) and Night (Rātrī)—as the natural phenomena underlying them are so patent that they cannot be considered on par with the goddesses, we have noted above from the Vedic context, who follow their husbands as per the practice in human life.

In the Purāṇas the goddesses are not merely the 'wives of gods', but they have an independent status.[77] Thus there are Mothers (*mātaraḥ*), Yoginīs, Śaktis and even Kumārīs. Yoginīs and Śaktis owe their origin to the Tantric tradition. Kumārī is described as being of eight years, sometimes twelve and even sixteen.[78]

The Mothers are many and can be broadly grouped in different types—

1. We have Brāhmī, Māheśvarī etc. and also those, who have taken their names from mythological deities. We have Sauparṇī (from Suparṇa—Garuḍa), Vaiṣṇavī, Vārāhī, Nārasiṁhī etc. (*Matsya P.* 179.9-11).
2. Those who have taken their names from beasts and birds. We have Biḍālī (from cat), Ulūkī (from owl), Gardabhī (from ass), Krauñcā (from heron), Śakunī (from bird etc.), (*Matsya P.* 179.12-19).
3. Those having names from trees—We have Aśvatthā (from Aśvattha tree) (*Matsya P.* 179.69); Bilvā (from Bilva tree) (*ibid.* 71); Kadambā (*Sk.P.* III.2.9.110).
4. Having names indicating their fierce and grotesque nature—Here are—Mahānāsā, Mahāmukhī, Alambākṣī, Kumbhakarṇī, Lohitāmukhī, Daṁṣṭrālā etc. (*Matsya P.* 179.21-23).
5. Those whose names indicate their origin from the folks of various strata of the society. We have Mātaṅgī (*Matsya P.* 179.27); Bhūtaḍāmarī (*ibid.* 31) etc.
6. Some are of well disposition, such as Subhgā, Nandinī (*Matsya P.* 179.14) etc.

Special mention has to be made of the following, they being unique. They are—

(i) Vaṭamātaraḥ— associated with the Vaṭa (banyan) tree. Some of the old goddesses as Brāhmī (Brahmāṇī), Parvatī etc. are identified with the Vaṭa tree (*Sk.P.* V.1.70.41, 43-44). At another place, the *Sk.P.* says that these goddesses are called Vaṭamātaraḥ, for they desire food at the Vaṭa tree (*ibid.* V.1.34.82 ab).

(ii) We have Carpaṭa-mātaraḥ, desiring to eat *'carpaṭa'*—*'capātī'* in Hindi, a thin round Indian cake (*ibid.* V.1.34.82cd);

(iii) Paula-mātaraḥ, desiring to eat *'paula'*—another type of Indian cake, called *'poḷi'* in Marathi[79] (*ibid.* V.1.34.83);

(iv) Taila-mātṛkāḥ—'Oil-mothers', to be given offerings of oil at night, for getting success in work (*ibid.* V.1.35.3).

It has to be pointed out that offering of thick *capātī or poḷī* (not made of wheat but of rice or the 'jawar' grains)—called *bhākarī* and preparations from green leafy vegetables has been the living tradition of India, when the two goddesses (called Gaurīs) come to stay in the house for three days in the Gaṇeśa festival in Maharashtra State. This offering is given on the very day of arrival and the next day, sixteen vegetables are used for the spicy preparations, and there are several sweets. The festival falls in the rainy season and so is the availability and importance of the green leafy vegetables! Again offering of oil to the goddess is still a practice in vogue, especially in villages.

From the details gathered from the Purāṇas, it becomes quite clear that there was a practice of establishing the images of the 'Mothers' in every habitat (may be at a central place or at various quarters) to protect people and to assure for them the general weal, including the gain of issues (*Sk.P.* III.2.16.4 ff).

The *Matsya P.* gives an interesting mythical account regarding the creation or 'birth' of these various Mothers, which tries to justify their appearance and established place in the tradition. When asked by the sages, the Sūta narrates the whole account, as follows. There was a demon named Andhaka who had become immortal due to his severe penance. Once he happened to see Pārvatī enjoying amorous sport with her husband Śiva (Mahādeva), and desired to carry her away. In the Avantī region in the Mahākāla-forest, he gave a tough fight to Śiva, who was sọ harassed as to release the terrible arrow Pāśupata by name targeting the demon. The arrow hit the demon only to create more havoc, for from the blood of the demon erupted hundreds and thousands of Andhakas. On being torn (by the arrows of Śiva), these gave rise again to terrible Andhakas, so as to make the whole world enveloped by these. The only remedy was to drink (lick) the blood of Andhakas. Hence Śiva created innumberable goddesses for this (*Matsya P.* 179.2-32). The goddesses carried out their task and were extremely satisfied. But there sprang forth again the series of Andhakas, the mere sight of which made god Śiva depressed and he went to lord Vāsudeva for succour. Lord Viṣṇu (Vāsudeva) created the demoness named 'Śuṣkarevatī,' who drank (licked) in a moment the entire blood of those Andhakas. As she went on drinking the blood, she became more and more dried up. (She was already 'Śuṣka'—dried Revatī). And thus were destroyed all the Andhakas by god Śiva, the main demon Andhaka ultimately asking pardon of Śiva, who as usual forgave the offender i.e. the demon (*ibid.* 34-40). But the terrible goddesses (created by Śiva) were reluctant to stop the killing, for which they were created. In spite of being warded off by Śiva they started gobbling up the three worlds. Śiva was in a fix. Having created the goddesses, how could he think of their destruction. The only way was to approach lord Viṣṇu. And this he did by meditating on the terrible form of Viṣṇu as 'Man-lion'—Nṛsiṁha. When lord Nṛsiṁha appeared before Śiva the latter praised him and told him about the havoc created by the goddesses. Lord Nṛsiṁha created from his limbs, the goddesses—Vāgīśvarī, Māyā, Bhavamālinī, Kālī and Śuṣkarevatī and then created thirty-two more from his other limbs (*ibid.* 41-74). Seeing these with their eyes wide with wrath, the group of 'Mothers' created earlier by lord Śiva sought refuge to Nṛsiṁha. The words of advice to these 'Mothers' are important for they bring out the very purpose of the cult of the Mothers (*Mātaraḥ*). Nṛsiṁha says—"As men and beasts (including all other creatures, birds etc.) take care of their little ones, so are you to take care of the people in this world"(*ibid.* 77-78). It is seen further that Nṛsiṁha has his own group of Mothers (*mātṛgaṇa*) and so has Śiva his own (*ibid.* 83-88). The *Matsya P.* here, at the end of the chapter (chap. 179), ends with a regular note of conciliation between the Śaivite and the Vaiṣṇavite faiths which states that when the image of Hara (Śiva) accompanied by the group of Mothers is established, lord Śiva himself offers worship to the image of Nṛsiṁha (*ibid.* 90). Such passages account for the temple-culture in India of having the images of the two faiths in the premises of one and the same temple though the main deity may be one of the two faiths.

All these goddesses (Mothers) are the aspects of the Mother-goddess, who is none other than Pārvatī—in origin the symbol of the Great Earth being Durgā.

In fact, the cult of the Mother-goddess has been an ever-inviting subject for study, and several scholars have written and been writing on it. It has to be stated that it has been a living tradition of India, the new goddesses being added to the old ones, getting their local habitat and name. The detailed information of Mother-goddesses, from villages, towns and also cities (areawise), the myths about them, their unique festivals and the offerings given to them, will not only be interesting but can also serve as a missing link to the old tradition of the Mother-goddess cult.

Here is recorded a living tradition of the goddess Meladī (called Meladī-Mā), whose temple is at a place named Sarā, in the district Zālāwaḍ, in Saurashtra (in India). The special feature about this goddess is that a woman even in her 'periods' can enter the sanctum sanctorum of the temple and can light a lamp. The word *mela* denotes 'dirt' and the story goes that the goddess Meladī-Mā was created from the 'dirt' of the nine goddesses, when they were dancing in the Navarātrī festival, the *'garabā-dance'* being a speciality, in Saurashtra and Gujarat regions. (The 'nine-day' festival is of Devī and is named Navarātrī.). It seems that the 'dirt' most probably is the reason for not objecting the entrance of the woman in her menstruation period in the sanctum sanctorum, for the goddess does not find in it any so-called impurity, she herself being from 'dirt'.[80] According to the Vedic and Puranic tradition, the menstruation period of the women is a third part of Indra's guilt of *brahmahatyā*, taken upon themselves by women on his request.

According to the *Tait. Sam.*, Indra smote the three heads of Tvaṣṭṛ's son Viśvarūpa, with his thunderbolt, but being afraid of the sin of *brahmahatyā* sticking to him, divided it among the following three—the earth, trees and women (II.5.1.2-5). The *Tait. Sam.* lays down several 'taboos' about the women in menses (II.5.1.5-7).

According to the Purāṇas, the sin of *brahmahatyā* sticking to Indra was for killing Vṛtra (Viśvarūpa's younger brother), of which he was afraid. Hence Bṛhaspati divided it among women, trees and rivers, which release it at certain periods, in the form of menstruation-fluid, gum and the yellowish flood water in the rainy season, respectively (*Sk.P.* I.1.16.41f). The *Sk.P.*, at another place, says that Brahmā gave half of this sin to women, which lasts for 'four' days (I.1.16.32). According to the *Brahmaṇḍa P.*, it was Viṣṇu who divided the sin (II.4.9.24-25).

According to the ancient thought as seen from the *Tait. Sam.* and the Purāṇas, even the face of a woman in the 'four' days in this period is not to be seen by anyone, entering a temple, thus standing there is then a far cry. But the *Var. P.* surprisingly gives its own independent view, which can support the living tradition of the practice of a mentstruating woman entering the temple of the Meladī-Mā and lighting a lamp there. The *Var. P.* says that a woman who is in her 'periods', devoted to god, may touch the idol of Viṣṇu (or any other god), or eat what she desires or decorate her body. The only condition is that she should propitiate Viṣṇu with the *mantra* —'I—a *rajasvalā* (in 'periods')—bow down to the highest god, who has no beginning, middle state or end, who is unborn and is ancient". Having uttered this *mantra*, whatever she does, is not polluted (*Var.P.* 142.7-10).

This view-point of the *Var. P.* is unique and must have paved the way for a reform in the old tradition. We get a glimpse of this in the life of Appaya Dikshit recorded by Harinarayan Dikshit in his book *Śrīmadappayadīkṣitacaritam*

(Devavani Parishad, Delhi, 1981, p.49). The author must have verified the incident from other sources. It is as follows. When the youngest daughter of Appaya Dikshit attained puberty, at the very 'first time', she asked her father, whether she should worship god Śiva in that state of her. Appaya Dikshit gave his consent. On knowing this through his wife, Tātācārya, the jealous rival of Appaya Dikshit, poisoned the mind of the ruling king against Appaya Dikshit. Appaya Dikshit was summoned to the court. He explained, taking the support of the ancient texts that the god was satisfied with the worship performed by a devotee in any state of his and not the worship done only formally. The king was satisfied and asked Appaya Dikshit to record his thoughts in a book. Thereafter Appaya Dikshit wrote the book *Śivārcanacandrikā* and the commentary *Bālacandrikā* on it.

Even among the Liṅgāyatas (a sect of the Hindus, carrying a small 'Śivaliṅga' woven in a thread and having it on their body as a necklace), known for their convictions about extreme purity, a woman in her 'periods' can enter a temple and can worship god Śiva. This practice prevalent among the Liṅgāyatas even in the present times is verified from a Liṅgāyata 'swāmī' (a priest of a '*matha*', which is a residential place of the followers as also of congregation for the purpose of prayers and rituals).

Thus the practice in the temple of Melaḍī-Mā of allowing a woman in her 'periods' to light a lamp and thus have entry into the sanctum sanctorum, has been sanctioned by the *Var. P.* and is still in vogue in the tradition of the temple in Saurashtra. The tale about the 'creation' of Melaḍī-Mā from the 'dirt' of the nine goddesses, is mythical and is an *arthavāda* supporting the holiness of the 'New Goddess' (Melaḍī-Mā), giving her a rightful place among the goddesses.

To come to the phenomenon of death, presented as the 'Lady Death', though not a goddess, having the same supreme power. The *Mbh.* presents the mythical account about her at two places— in the Droṇa *parvan* and the Śānti *parvan* which we have already taken note of in the first chapter, while dealing with the 'Eschatological' myths or mythical accounts. The occasion is to console Dharmarāja at the death of Abhimanyu.

Here is taken the same account from both the *parvans* of the *Mbh.* to point out the efficacy of creating the 'Lady Death'. To turn to the account again. The wrath in Brahmā's mind, seeing the ever-increasing number of human beings, gives rise to fire, with which Brahmā starts burning the whole universe. When Śiva approaches him in order to pacify him, Brahmā says that he does not desire that beings be not born on the earth, but he intends to have the process of destruction for the sake of the Earth. The very Earth being overpopulated has entreated upon him for this (lessening of her burden), lest she being overburdened, should plunge in waters (*Mbh.* Śānti 257.3-4). Then Śiva pleads that there be no extinction of human race and expresses his earnest desire that the beings be born again and again (*ibid.* 257.11; also *ibid.* 12— *yācāmi āvṛttijāḥ prajāḥ*). Brahmā heeds to Śiva's word of advice and absorbs the Fire, created by him. And from Brahmā's body is produced a woman having black, red and yellow colours and her tongue, mouth and eyes red. And she resorts to the southern quarter-the quarter of Nirṛti—Death (*Mbh.* Droṇa 52.18, 19). The woman is addressed as 'Mṛtyu' (Lady Death-Mṛtyudevatā!) by Brahmā, who tells her the very purpose of her being created. She weeps bitterly, being unable to bear the sorrow of such a cruel task of killing people. The rest of the account we have already noted in the first chapter, under "Eschatological".

The description of the 'Lady Death' in grotesque colours and horrible appearance indicates her of being a cruel goddess. But this 'cruelty' is given to her as a 'duty'. Brahmā tells her that the tears gathered by him in his hands (while she was weeping) would turn into various diseases, which would weaken the people and then she should take away their lives with 'austere impassivity' (*Mbh.* Droṇa 52.38-45), chap. 53; 54.1-44). One of the 'Household Tales' by Grimm Brothers points out that the diseases are regarded as the "Messengers of Death".[81]

Purāṇas mention some Tree-goddesses, which we have passingly referred to. Here we take into account some of these, which are still existing in the living tradition of India. The Purāṇas mention multitude of trees, prevalent in their times.[82] Some of these had attained great importance so as to become Tree-goddesses, which are mentioned as "Mothers" and are offered worship daily or on a particular day. This is obviously because of their medicinal value as also due to the beliefs attached to them. The mythical accounts woven in their respect, resorting to the principle of *arthavāda,* are only for glorifying them. We take here some of these for consideration, which are commonly found and have gathered much aura about them.

1. Udumbarī—from her resort at the Udumbara tree, the goddess of that name.

Among all trees, Udumbara (*Ficus glomerata*) has assumed a place of prime importance in the Vedic ritual. The oft-repeatedly occurring *arthavāda* about Udumbara is that it stands for strength and food. The mythical account occurring in the context of the Agnicayana rite (the rite of building the Great Fire-altar), runs as follows—The gods and the *asuras,* both sprung from Prajāpati vied with each other. All the trees went to the *asuras,* except the Udumbara, which did not forsake the gods. When the gods conquered the *asuras* and also the trees in their possession, they favoured the Udumbara tree by placing in it all the pith and essence of all those trees. Hence the Udumbara tree is always moist, full of milky sap and has fruit equal to that of all the other trees. The Udumbara tree is thus all food, acquired from all trees (*Śat. Br.* VI.6.3.2, 3). The *arthavāda*-account occurs in the context of the Agnicayana rite, when he (the sacrificer i.e. the priest on his behalf) has to offer Udumbara-stick on fire, while tending the fire in the fire-pan (*ukhā*). The Udumbara tree or the things made of its wood are several times spoken of in the Vedic ritual.[83] One such detail is of the branch of the Udumbara tree to be fixed as the central support of the sacrificial pendal in Vedic sacrifices (*Śat.Br.* III.6.1.1ff).

By the time we come to the Purāṇas, Udumbara or Audumbara seems to have become an important tree. The *Agni P.* (74.2) states that Gaṇa, Sarasvatī, Lakṣmī, Śiva's vehicle Nandī and the river Gaṅgā are to be worshipped at the root of the Audumbara tree. At a special ritual to be performed in the bright half of the Kārttika month, a person is advised to go to the Audumbara tree, after bath, wearing white garments, and draw at its foot a circle and in it a figure of a lotus with eight petals. In that he is advised to worship Brahmā, Viṣṇu, Śiva and Sarasvatī (*Sk.P.* II.4.11.2-7). This shows how the tree is regarded as associated with the important gods.

Noted above is the ritual of fixing the branch of the Udumbara tree (Audumbarī) in Vedic sacrifices. The *Sk.P.* has anthropomorphised this branch of the Udumbara tree as the daughter of a Gandharva called Parvata, and the name given is 'Audumbarī'. Audumbarī once laughed at Nārada, making a fun of his singing. Hence she was cursed by him to be a mortal. He also advised her that in that birth she should go to a sacrifice and point out a mistake in it. She was born in Camatkārapura as the daughter of the couple Satyabhāmā and Devaśarman. Once when she went to see the sacrifice performed by Brahmā, having remembered Nārada's words, she pointed out the mistake there in that a peg in the pendal was not in order. She was right and hence Brahmā released her from the curse of Nārada. He also granted her a boon. He said that from that time onwards, whenever a sacrifice would be performed on the earth, she (i.e. Audumbarī—the branch of the Audumbara tree) should be installed at a central place and then the *śaṅku* (peg) be fixed before the Audumbarī. Thus is the tradition of fixing the Audumbarī first and then the pegs for the pendal (*Sk.P.* VI.188.15-28). As in the ritual tradition in the Brāhmaṇa-texts, so in the Puranic tradition,

Audumbara or Udumbara tree and the things made of its wood are spoken of as having great significance.[84]

A special feature of the Udumbara tree is that small fruits cling right to the stem of the tree (not to the branches) and the stem oozes out milky sap. Due to this feature, it could come in line with other such trees that stand as the Mother-goddess trees, because the small fruits clinging to the stem of the tree resemble the teats. In some ancient mythologies there is a mention of such Mother-goddess trees. The Mexican Mother-goddess was Mayauel, who was believed to be a woman of four hundred breasts, and the gods due to her being fruitful, changed her into the Maguey plant. The wine of this plant is called 'pulque'.[85] The Mother-goddess is shown everywhere seated before or on the Maguey (Agave) plant.[86] The Greek goddess Artemis, believed to have four hundred breasts was the Fig-tree goddess, the fruits of the fig-tree (*Ficus*, of the mulberry family), regarded as teats in ancient times. The green part of the fig tree including the fruit distills a white milk-like juice in abundance. The fruits of this tree appear before the leaves and hence the tree was personified as "goddess of many breasts".[87] The ancient Egyptian goddess, in one of her forms, was the sycamore tree (a kind of fig tree). The sycamore tree has the similar feature in that the fruit all adhere to the stock of the tree and not to the end of the branches.[88]

It has to be pointed out that nowhere in the ritual-texts, the Udumbara tree is mentioned as a Mother-goddess tree. However when the tree is spoken of as 'strength and food', it is not simply a glorification of the tree through a ritual metaphor, but it echoes some mythological belief about this tree. The mention of the Udumbara tree or the things made from the Udumbara wood in the Vedic ritual vouchsafes for this. A ladle made of the Udumbara wood (*Tait.Br.* I.3.8.2); the seat of the Udgātṛ priest made of the Udumbara tree (*ibid.* I.2.6.5); the sacrificer king's mandatory dwelling in the wood full of the Udumbara trees, as required in the Viśvajit sacrifice (*Kaus. Br.* XXV.15); in the Rājasūya sacrifice, the water brought from different places for being sprinkled on the king, to be mixed in the Udumbara vessel (*Śat.Br.* V.3.4.2); in the Vājapeya sacrifice, the drink to be kept in a vessel made of the Udumbara wood (*ibid.* V.2.2.2) and also the seat of the sacrificer of the Udumbara wood (*ibid.* V.2.1.22, 23); a staff of the Udumbara wood to be handed over by the Adhvaryu priest to the sacrificer, undergoing the rite of consecration (*ibid.* III.2.1.32, 33); a post of the Udumbara wood to be in the middle of the *sadas* (*ibid.* III.6.1.2)—and several such *vidhis*, which strike a common note that the Udumbara tree stands for strength and food.

The Purāṇas also mention the use of the Audumbara wood as also vessels from it, to which we have already referred. But the *Matsya P.* has spoken of the Audumbara tree as a Mother-goddess—'Udumbarī'— created by god Mahādeva to drink the blood of the several Andhakas, born from the blood of the original demon Andhaka (*Matsya P.* 179.18), as per the account already seen. Here the Audumbara tree comes as a goddess-Mother-goddess-in the form of a Tree-goddess. The mythical account here mentioning several other goddesses having names from their physical features is simply an *arthavāda*. But the status of a goddess given to the Audumbara tree is a point to be probed further.

It has to be pointed out that not only the age-old ritual use of the things made of the Audumbara tree (i.e. its wood) and the mythological beliefs associated with the tree, but also the medicinal use of the tree, has contributed to the elevated position of the tree, so much so that it has reached the status of a Tree-goddess. The *Matsya P.* mentions also Aśvatthā (179.69) and Bilvā (179.71) as the 'Mothers" (here they being Tree-goddesses) together with Udumbarī (179.18), which will be seen further.

Even accepting that there have been many interpolations in the extant texts of the Purāṇas, it is accepted that in the major Purāṇas, the efforts to collect information on varied topics had started earlier than 6th century AD. The Indian science of medicine was certainly far developed prior to the Purāṇas. Right in the 1st century AD the *Caraka-saṁhitā* had wielded its influence on the society as regards food and drink.[89] The Purāṇas while prescribing medicines for various ailments and diseases,[90] had these texts from the stalwarts of Indian medicine (like Caraka and Suśruta the latter for surgery also) before them.[91] The trees, some of them having the age-old ritual-tradition at their back, but now proved useful from the medicinal point of view, were revered to such an extent as to get the status of a goddess i.e. Tree-goddess, and then included in the group of "Mothers." The Udumbara is but one of the examples of this process.[92]

To turn to Aśvatthā, mentioned as a Mother(-goddess). The Aśvattha tree (*Ficus religiosa*) is mentioned at several rituals and rites in the Brāhmaṇa-texts.[93] Here we note some of these. The fruits of the Aśvattha tree are to be used in the Mahābhiṣeka (Great Anointing) of the king, with the belief that the Aśvattha tree stands for the overlordship (*sāmrājyam*) of the trees (*Ait.Br.* VIII.16=39.2). The Aśvattha tree was born from brilliance and stands for the overlordship of the trees. As the sacrificial-king stands for the lordly power, by using the Aśvattha wood, he or the priest places brilliance (*tejaḥ*) and the overlordship (*sāmrājyam*) of the trees in the lordly power—*kṣatra* (*ibid.* VII.32=35.6). The Aśvattha tree is regarded as a resort of Prajāpati (*Tait. Br.* III.8.12.2) or Agni (*ibid.* I.1.3.9) for one year, when Prajāpati in one account and Agni in the other account took the form of a horse (Hence the name of the tree Aśvattha—'coming from *aśva* i.e. horse; *aśva*+√*sthā*—'to stand'>*ttha*). In the Puranic period, Aśvattha came to assume divine position.[94] The *Sk.P.* states that Aśvattha is the symbol of Viṣṇu, while Vaṭa that of Śiva, and when the idols of these gods are not obtained, they (these trees) should be worshipped as such (*Sk.P.* II.4.3.38). The *Padma P.* says that the very glace at the Aśvattha tree destroys sin. It identifies the tree with Bodhisattva and says that it is the resort of Viṣṇu (*Padma P.* Sṛṣṭikhaṇḍa 55.15-16). In fact all the three gods—Viṣṇu, Śiva and Brahmā—stay in it; Viṣṇu at the top (*ibid.* 55.20). The *Padma P.* points out that as the goddess Lakṣmī is said to stay at the tree on Saturday, the tree should be worshipped on Saturday (*Padma P.* Uttarakhaṇḍa 118.26). Thus when the *Mastya P.* (179.69) mentions Aśvatthā as one of the Mothers i.e. (Tree-goddess), it is the glorification of the tree, which is regarded as a seat of the god Viṣṇu.[95]

In connection with the Aśvattha tree, an interesting ritual detail from the *Tait. Br.* is to be noted. The *Tait. Br.* lays down churning of Agni from a stick of Aśvattha tree, the branches of which are intertwined in the interior of the Śamī tree (I.1.9.1—*śamīgarbhādagnim manthati* and Sāyaṇa on it). The *Sk.P.* makes use of this detail and alters it a bit in order to glorify the Aśvattha tree. It says that if a person does not have any one of the twelve types of son,[96] he should regard the Aśvattha tree as his son, to give sustenance to his ancestors after him. He should get the tree 'married' to a Śamī tree. The family would prosper as long as the Aśvattha tree would stand (*Sk.P.* VI.215.53-55). The point of the 'marriage' of the Aśvattha tree with the Śamī tree invites explanation. Does it mean that the Śamī tree is to be planted near the Aśvattha tree or only a branch of the Śamī tree is to be brought near the Aśvattha tree for a symbolic marriage? Anyway the basis of this is deep rooted in the ritual tradition, as we have noted above. The 'marriage' of a tree is still practised in the living tradition.[97]

To turn to the 'Mother' Bilvā (Tree-goddess), which is mentioned by the *Matsya P.* (179.71). In the Vedic ritual tradition, Bilva is one of the sacrificial trees.[98] A detail common about them is that they are green and thus fresh, for that is what constitutes their living element, by which they are vigorous and possessed of strength (*Śat. Br.* I.3.4.1). The Bilva tree (*Aegle marmelos*) should be one which gets fruits every year, which is a symbol of proper food. The tree should also be one which is covered with branches up to its roots and that is the symbol of prosperity (*Ait. Br.* II.1=6.1). Here the *Ait.Br.* enjoins a sacrificial post of the Bilva wood in the animal sacrifice. A stake from this tree is enjoined by the *Śat. Br.* in the Horse-sacrifice (*Śat.Br.* XIII.4.4.8).

The *Sk.P.* and the *Śiva P.*—the Śaivite Purāṇas—have much to say about the greatness of Bilva.[99] Lord Śiva is believed to stay at the root of the Bilva tree (*Śiva P.* Vidyeśvara-saṁhitā II.44). At the foot of this tree stays Girijā-Pārvatī and on the different parts of Bilva (branches, leaves, bark, central bark, thorns etc.), several goddesses are believed to stay namely Dākṣāyaṇī, Māheśvarī, Pārvatī, Kātyāyanī, Gaurī, Aparṇā, Durgā, Umā and crores of goddesses in the multiples of nine—all these being the aspects of one and the same goddess (*Sk.P.* VI.250.14-17). The tree thus becomes one of the 'Mothers', in the *Matsya P.* (179.71). In spite of this greatness attached to the Bilva tree, which could be traced to the Vedic ritual tradition, the tree got quite an elevated position in the Puranic period, more so by its medicinal use.[100]

A detailed note has already been taken of the Vaṭa tree (*Ficus indica*)[101] which in the Vedic ritual tradition is known as Nyagrodha (=Nyubja) and in the Epic and Puranic period also known as Rauhiṇa. Again already are mentioned the 'Vaṭamātaraḥ'—'those goddesses who desire food at the foot of the Vaṭa tree'. Here the tree itself seems to have been personified as a goddess. In the Puranic period, the tree got so much importance as to be an important part of the account of Satyavān and Sāvitrī and receive worship in the vow to be observed by married women. The vow is known as the 'Vaṭasāvitrīvrata.'

The *Sk.P.* mentions the goddess Kadambā, the personification of the tree itself. The tree Kadamba (*Nauclea cadamba*) is a tree with orange-coloured fragrant blossoms. There are hardly any mythological details about the tree. There could be other uses of the tree,[102] which must have made the *Sk.P.* (III.2.9.110) to mention it as the goddess Kadambā.

Here to note the tree Āmalaka or Āmalakī (*Emblic myrobalan, Emblica officinalis gaertn*), which in an account from the *Sk.P.* (V.2.28.45-55) is spoken of as a goddess. It says that a certain king observed the 'day'—Āmalakī Ekādaśī—the eleventh day in the bright half of the Māgha month- and slept in an open place. When enemies attacked him, this goddess (Āmalakī-Ekādaśī) came out of his body and killed all the enemies. The tree is also called Dhātrī and is said to have divine birth as from the drop of Brahmā's saliva (*Padma P.* Uttarakhaṇḍa 47.7-11) and according to the *Sk.P.* (II.4.12.13) from Brahmā's tears. Many gods are said to have their stay at the Dhātrī or Āmalakī tree and they are—Viṣṇu at its root; means at the top and many gods and sages at its branches and the joints thereof (*Sk.P.* II.4.12.21-23). When the fruits of this tree are enjoined to be worn at the neck, arms or even at the ears (*Padma P.* Brahmakhaṇḍa 22.20) and when even the thought of this tree is said to give the virtue of giving away many cows; its very touch giving twice the virtue and eating its fruit thrice that virtue (*Padma P.* Uttarakhaṇḍa 47.18-19), it is justified in pointing out that it is not simply belief but the medicinal value of the tree Āmalakī[103] that has made the tree so elevated in the Puranic period, that it has attained a divine status.[104]

Neem—The leaves of the Nimba tree (*Margosa*) are mentioned in the Purāṇas in some rituals as also for medicinal purposes.[105] The medicinal use of the Nimba tree for different purposes has made the tree attain the status of a goddess, especially in the villages and towns in India even in modern age.

The bitterness of the (Nimba) leaves, has made the tree associate with the funeral rite. This is obviously on the basis of sympathetic magic on the principle of 'Like produces like', death being a bitter fact of life, to be wiped of by biting the bitter leaves of the tree. The *Agni P.* (157.38) mentions this practice and the *Yājñ.Sm.* (III.12) enjoins it after attending a funeral. The leaves are to be placed at the door of such a house where death has occurred (*Agni P.* 158.57; *Garuḍa P.* I.106.7). The decoction of the leaves of the Nimba tree, oil prepared from them and their juice are useful from medicinal point of view.[106]

Nimba (Neem) tree is regarded as a Śītalādevī (Cooling Goddess) in the living tradition of India. Even to this day, in the villages or at times also in towns, curds and cooked rice (both 'cooling') as 'offering' are given to the goddess, when a child affected by chicken-pox or measles (such illness or epidemic) is being cured or is completely cured.[107] Neem tree is an excellent example of how the medicinal value of a tree makes it attain the position of a goddess.

Another such example is the plant Tulasī, which is medicinally important, though much mythology has been woven around it. This sacred basil (sweet-smelling plant), anthropomorphised, is said to have been born on the Full-moon-day of the Kārttika month (*Brahmavai. P.* Prakṛtikhaṇḍa 22.34). Hence this month (i.e. Kārttika) is regarded as special for the worship of Tulasī. On the 12th day in the bright half of the Kārttika month, the marriage of Kṛṣṇa (Viṣṇu) with the Tulasī plant is to be celebrated. The *Sk.P.* describes it in details. All the rituals in the Vedic Hindu marriage are given here, which are to be performed in this 'marriage of the god and the plant' (*Sk.P.* II.4.31.1-31). It has to be pointed out that it is still a practice followed in some families, not only in villages but also in the cities, in India, where *Tulasī-vivāha*' is a great festive occasion.

About the use of the Tulasī plant in the rituals of an Indian household, it can be said with certainty that no other member (tree, plant or grass) of the 'green world' can ever be able to stand in importance near the Tulasī plant.[108] A bath beneath a Tulasī plant; sprinkling of water with the Tulasī-leaf placed in it or by a Tulasī leaf (*Brahmavai P.* Prakṛtikhaṇḍa 21.38-41); the gift of a Tulasī leaf (*ibid.* 42); giving Tulasī-water at the last moment to a dying person (*ibid.* 43); dying with a Tulasī-leaf in hand (*ibid.*46); daily drinking of Tulasī-water (*ibid.* 44) etc. can be pointed out in this connection. There are many more such things and usages of the Tulsī-plant, in the daily life of an Indian man. They may appear to come under 'blind belief' or 'blind faith' in the sacredness of the Tulasī-plant. But the medicinal properties of this sacred basil set at naught all misgivings about it.[109] The Purāṇas are very well in the know of these medicinal properties of the plant.

The Purāṇas glorify the Tulasī plant, anthropomorphise it and make her (as a female) the wife of the demon Śaṅkhacūḍa. As the demon Śaṅkhacūḍa troubled the gods, they decided to do away with him. But they came to know that as long the wife of Śaṅkhacūḍa Tulasī was faithful to him, he was invincible. Viṣṇu then took the form of Śaṅkhacūḍa and seduced her (*Brahmavai. P.* Prakṛtikhaṇḍa 16.103ff; 17.1ff; 20.1ff). This mythical account is very much on the lines of a folktale, in which the hero, in order to vanquish the demon or kill him, first takes possession of the latter's secret power of survival. Here Tulasī has to be taken as the very 'power' (*śakti*) of Śankhacūḍa, which is taken away by Viṣṇu.

The *Brahmavai P.* (Prakṛtikhaṇḍa 6.32-48) gives another account where Lakṣmī is cursed by Sarasvatī to be both a tree and river on the earth. To the dejected Lakṣmī, Viṣṇu says that she should go to the earth (i.e. terrestrial region) and be born as the daughter of Dharmadhvaja; then become there a tree; then the wife of Śaṅkhacūḍa, who is Viṣṇu's own part; then Viṣṇu's own wife and become famous as (the plant) Tulasī; and later as a river, known as Padmāvatī. The account is given simply for the glorification of the plant, bringing in so many ideas distantly connected. This is the characteristic of the Purāṇa literature, which aims to reach the common masses, in order to justify the matter in hand.

Here we come to the 'rivers', the mythology woven around them, getting an upsurge in the Puranic period. In the context of Tīrthayātrā (Pilgrimage), dealt with in an earlier chapter we have seen that the *tīrthas* (holy places) mostly are on the banks of rivers, which themselves are regarded as holy. The principle of 'animism' working here has made the rivers 'living' and they are anthropomorphised[110] at least in concept, though no detailed anthropomorphic traits are described in their case. In the *Mbh.* and the Purāṇas occur several instances in this connection.

To have a glimpse at some of these. The river Narmadā became the wife of king Purukutsa (*Mbh.* Āśrama. 20.12, 13). The river Narmadā fell in love with one righteous King Duryodhana (not from the Kauravas), from whom she had a fair daughter Sudarśanā (*ibid.* Anu. 2.18f). Bhiṣma was the son of the river Gaṅgā. Śrutāyudha was the son of river Parṇāśā by Varuṇa (*ibid.* Droṇa 92.44f). In the Purāṇas, we have a number of such instances. The *Matsya P.* refers to the river Parṇāśā but the account varies from that in the *Mbh.* The river Parṇāśā favoured the issueless king Devavṛdha and became his wife (*Matsya P.* 44.51-56). The river Virajā, formerly was a cowherdess (*gopī*), who while sporting with Śrīkṛṣṇa when caught by Rādha, got herself turned into a river (*Brahmavai P.* Prakṛtikhaṇḍa 49.4-23).

The rivers are thought to be important as they have the flowing waters. The idea goes back to the Vedic ritual tradition. The Vasatīvarī waters (which are collected on the previous day), enjoined to be used in sacrifice, are to be brought from the flowing current of waters. The *Tait. Sam.* states that these waters are to be collected in the day-time, when they have the radiance or light of the sun in them (*Tait. Sam.* VI.4.2.2). The *Śat.Br.* states that if the waters are required to be collected after the sunset, he has to hold a firebrand or a piece of gold close above the waters. This is for having the effect of the yonder burning sun (*Śat. Br.* III.9.2.9) on waters, for both fire and gold are shining by nature. Fire is regarded as the other form of the sun and gold is said to be the seed of Agni. When Agni united with waters, his seed became gold (*Śat. Br.* II.1.1.5).

It is a fact of daily observation that the flowing waters are lukewarm for touch, as they catch the rays of the sun i.e. 'Heat'. In the Purāṇas, the concept developed further and Agni (Fire) came to be regarded as the husband of rivers. The *Brahmāṇḍa P.* states that Agni (Fire) called Śaṁsya married sixteen rivers, which include important rivers *viz.* Kāverī, Narmadā, Yamunā, Godāvarī etc. (*Brahmāṇḍa P.* I.2.12.13ff). According to the *Sk.P.* Agni, born from Brahmā's mind, propitiated Śiva at the river Narmadā and asked for a boon that the sixteen rivers including the Narmadā should be his wives and Śiva granted that boon (*Sk.P.* V.3.22.9, 11).

The rivers thus are important due their flowing waters, which have made the rivers divine. It is said that when Indra slew Vṛtra, the latter died on the waters. The pure part of the waters, which was fit for sacrifice and hence 'divine', was set free (*Tait. Sam.* V.4.2.3). The account indicates that this divine part is the flowing[111] waters.

The rivers mentioned in the Purāṇas are said to be 'divine', for the origin of these (some rivers existing in reality and some mythical) is traced to the gods. Here are some examples. The river Somavatī Śiprā (the river Somavatī joining with Śiprā and hence the new name!) formed from the moon ('Soma', so the river Somavatī), oozed out from the heat of Atri's penance (*Sk.P.* V.1.28.57-58); the river Gaṅgā from Viṣṇu's right toe and the river Sarayū from his left toe (*ibid.* II.8.1.45); the river Narmadā born as a beautiful girl (later on becoming a river) from the perspiration of Śiva and Pārvatī in their love-sports (*ibid.* V.3.5.29-30); the river Kiraṇā born from Sun's perspiration, while meditating on the goddess Maṅgalāgaurī (*ibid.* IV.59.107-109); the river Ānandā from Agni's tears, when he got back his daughter Suvarṇā (*Brahma P.* 128.73-74).[112]

Here to come to an important point *viz.* identification of a river with a cow, the Sanskrit word *payas* denoting both 'water' and 'milk'. The *Sk.P.* says that during the deluge, the sage Mārkaṇḍeya saw a cow in the midst of the vast ocean. She was in reality the river Narmadā sent by Śiva to rescue the sage (*Sk.P.* V.3.19.2-15).

This concept of a river-cow becomes all the more prominent in the mythical accounts about the origin of the river Godāvarī—'giver of cow' (*go*='cow'; √*da*—'to give'). The Purāṇas refer to the sage Gautama, bringing the Gaṅgā in the form of the river Godāvarī.[113] But the *Brahma P.* (chap. 74) and the *Śiva P.* (Rudrasaṁhitā chaps. 24-25) deal elaborately with the concept of the 'River-cow', through the mythical accounts about the river Godāvarī. These accounts have been coined to extol Śiva (Tryambakeśvara) and the mountain Brahmagiri, that is the source of the river Godāvarī.

According to the *Śiva P.* there occurred a terrible famine of long duration. So, Gautama, the husband of Ahalyā, who was staying there along with other sages and their families, practised austere penance to propitiate Varuṇa, who controlled water and rain. It has to be noted that in this later mythology, Varuṇa the Ṛgvedic sovereign god is reduced to have his sway only on a limited sphere of waters (mainly of ocean). Pleased with Gautama's austerities, Varuṇa appeared before him and advised him to dig a pit a cubit deep. When Gautama did this, the god filled it with fresh water. The peculiarity of this pit (which developed into a pond with steps), was that it would never go dry. Then Gautama watered his fields and reaped harvest. So did other sages. Once, as usual, when the students of Gautama (staying in the '*gurukula*'—hermitage) went to fetch water from the pond, the wives of other sages did not allow them to touch water. Even Gautama's wife Ahalyā also was treated in the same way. The incident was reported by

Ahalyā to her husband Gautama. Even the other sages came to know of it through their wives. But the sages became apprehensive of Gautama's displeasure, as they knew his prowess. So they sought the help of the god Gaṇeśa, who agreed to help them. He took the form of a black cow and the 'cow' entered Gautama's hermitage. As she began eating grains kept there, Gautama took a small stalk of corn and tried to drive away the 'cow' gently. But the moment he touched the 'cow' with the stalk, the 'cow' fell to the ground—dead! The other sages, who were on the watch, rushed to the spot and censured Gautama for committing the sin of killing a cow (*gohatyā*). When Gautama tried to stress his innocence and helplessness, they suggested to him two ways to mitigate the sin. One way was to go round the earth thrice announcing his sin, then practise penance for a month, and circumambulate the mountain Brahmagiri a hundred times.[114] The other way was to propitiate Śiva to send the river Gaṅgā, stationed in his matted locks, to Brahmagiri; then to take a dip in her waters and install one hundred 'Śivaliṅgas' at that place. Gautama chose the latter way. Gautama propitiated Śiva, who sent the Gaṅgā. The river Gaṅga first alighted from the heaven on a branch of the Audumbara tree (*Ficus glomerata*), that was on the Brahmagiri. As she came down on the earth at that spot, she came to be called Godāvarī—the 'Gaṅga of the South', still known by this name (*Śiva P.* IV Rudrasaṁhitā chaps. 24-25).

The *Brahma P.* (chap. 74) has a similar account and the context also is the same. The cause of the descent of Gaṅgā, however, shows a variation. According to the account, Pārvatī, dejected due to Śiva's overlooking her for Gaṅgā (as per Pārvatī's own conjecture!) and hence being jealous of Gaṅgā, wanted to send her away from Śiva. Pārvatī confided with her son Gaṅeśa about this dart pricking her mind. Gaṅeśa promised her his help. Taking the form of a sage, he went to Brahmagiri, talked to the sages there and hatched a plan. He asked his female attendant Jayā to take the form of a cow and asked her to enter the hermitage of Gautama. The rest of the account is the same as we have noted from the *Śiva P.* In both these accounts it is implied that the 'dead' cow was revived after the river was brought to Brahmagiri and water flowed over her. Even this day, at Tryambakeśvara, where Śiva is worshipped as the deity of the mountain, there is the stepped pond and the source of the Godāvarī river is the mountain Brahmagiri. It is also interesting to note that even this day, the decapitated image of a cow (just to show the cow 'killed' by Gautama) is kept at the source of the river on Brahmagiri and mini-cows of metal are offered there at Tryambakeśvara.[115]

The accounts noted from the two Purāṇas are the versions of the same mythical account, coined to extol Śiva and the mountain Brahmagiri, which is the source of the famous river Godāvarī. This river also called Gautamī, runs through Maharashtra and the Andhra regions of southern India. The Godāvarī river is called the 'Gaṅgā of South'. It has to be pointed out that in India, it is customary to call any river 'Gaṅgā.'

It has been noted earlier that the name 'Godāvarī' has a clear association with 'cow' etymologically. The two versions from the Purāṇas also clearly show that the 'cow' is at the centre of the main mythical account. Even the name Gautama is based on the word '*go*' ('cow'); otherwise any other name of that sage could have been there in the two accounts. The belief that the river is a 'cow' is very old and obtains even in *RV*, which at various places speaks of the flowing streams of water (including rain-water) as cows.[116] The god Apām-napāt is located in rivers.[117] He is called *nādya* fr. *nadī*—'river' (*RV* II.35.1) and is said to have a cow in his abode (*ibid.* II.35.7—this cow—*dhenuḥ* is *sudughā*—a milch cow). Thus he is in profuse waters, which are fertilising and rejuvenating.

That the river Godāvarī is inseparably connected to a cow goes deep in the folk-mind, as can be seen from a folktale current in the Andhra region. According to it, once a cow delivered a calf. But as soon as she delivered it, Garutmantaḍu (a hawk) carried it away. (Garutmantaḍu is the Andhra version of Garutmān or Garuḍa). The mother-cow was helpless. However, she pursued the shadow of the giant bird on the earth, as the bird flew into the sky taking with it the calf. Due to motherly affection, milk started flowing from the cow's teats. It gathered into a stream, which developed into a river. This river came to be called Godāvarī, as the cow generated it.[118] Another name for this river is 'Gostanadī'. Though this name is popular (in Andhra region), there can hardly be any doubt, that it is a corrupt folk-form of the original word *Go-stana-nadī*, for the river got formed from the teat (udder *stana*) of a cow (*go*).

Hitherto we have seen some of the important facets of the river-mythology from the Purāṇas. In the context of the Tīrthayātrā (pilgrimage), it is particularly noticed that practically all holy places (*tīrthas*) are situated on the banks of the rivers (chap. IV on this). The concept of a river as a cleansing agent goes back to the *RV*, where the deity 'Āpaḥ' is eulogied as taking away defilement and making the worshipper come out of them pure and cleansed (*RV* X.17.10). The waters are also invoked to cleanse from moral guilt, the sins of violence, cursing, and telling lies (*ibid.* I.23.22=X.9.8). All remedies, immortality and healing are contained in 'Waters'–Āpaḥ (*ibid.* X.9.5-7; I.23.19-21). The rivers are seen to have these same qualities and the point of pilgrimage has a focus on these. Anne Feldhaus, who has dealt with the point 'of religious meanings of rivers in Maharashtra' says that besides having the power of cleansing and that of making things wet, the rivers are important on one more matter and it is to combat the evil of drought and famine. She draws our attention to a dry area like the deccan plateau, dependent for moisture on a fickle monsoon, where water is (almost) always conceived as a blessing.[119] We have already dealt with the mythical incident regarding the river Godāvarī, which is said to have happened in the same region near the mountain Brahmagiri at Tryambakeśvara, where (monsoon) water had been a scarcity. We are here reminded of the division of regions made by the tradition as the 'Devamātṛka-*deśas*' (the regions subsisting on rains—Rain-god) and the 'Nadīmātṛka-deśas' (the regions subsisting on the rivers). In both the expressions, the word *mātṛ* is used showing that both—Rain as well as River—nourish the regions as a mother nourishes her children.

Thus like 'Āpaḥ' (waters) in the *RV*, the rivers are deified in the Purāṇas. Not being the simple reservoirs of water, they are in the possession of life-giving substance in the form of water running through them. In this sense they are reckoned as 'Mothers' and even in colloquial speech occasionally a river with her proper name has an appendage of a word '*mātā*' or *māī* or '*maiyyā* all meaning 'mother', as we have the names of rivers as 'Gaṅgāmaiyyā', Kṛṣṇāmāī, Pūrṇāmāī, lovingly coined for them.

Thus there are gods and also goddesses, which come under the banner of 'Mother-goddess'. There are Tree-goddesses and the sacred rivers, the latter rising to the status of 'Mother' and becoming the mainstay of the pilgrim-places, assuring the persons taking bath there the merit ('fruit') of manifold sacrifices. At times the old gods are gently set aside and the new gods get related to them through any mythological strategy such as curse, boon, etc.

The multi-ethnic ancient Indian society presents a multifaceted picture of those times, when following the track of the 'old' tenets, the 'new' ideas are introduced, appreciated and accepted. It has been a long journey, introducing changes suiting to the times, but not swerving from the 'old' norms. And in this, the narratives, long or short, occurring as *arthavādas* in the Vedic, Epic and Puranic literature, due to their functional value, have been of great help. This method of glorifying, justifying and convincing through *arthavāda* the matter in hand, has become so common a feature as to become an indispensable part of this literature.

Thus *arthavāda* or we can say the method of Arthavādaism is the right key to unfold the fine synthesis of 'old' and 'new', that has made the Indian Man.

NOTES AND REFERENCES

1. See E.W. Hopkins, *Epic Mythology*, Reprint, Motilal Banarsidass, Delhi, 1986 (Strassburg, 1915), p. 72f; and for shrines and temples of gods, *ibid.*, pp. 70-71f.
2. See Sadashiv A. Dange, *Ency. PBP*, Vol. V, pp. 1628-1633.
3. See Sadashiv A. Dange, *Ency. PBP*, Vol. III, Navrang, New Delhi, 1987, p. 889 n.3.
4. It is believed that there is only one temple in India dedicated to Brahmā and it is in Pushkar near Ajmer in Rajasthan State. However, as informed by P.P. Ramachandran, Mumbai, there are three Brahmā temples in Kerala— 1. At Thiruvallam on the outskirts of Trivandrum (Thiruvananthapuram). The temple is for Parashurama, Śiva and Brahmā, in three different locations; 2. At Mithranandapuram in the capital city (of Kerala), a Trimurti temple for Śiva, Viṣṇu and Brahmā. The Brahmā temple is a separate one; and 3. At Tirunavaya near Ponani in Malappuram. It is heard that there is a Brahmā temple at the place Kharepatan in the district Sindhudurg (Maharashtra State, India), as informed by Dr. Madhavi Narsalay, Mumbai. The author's student Sanjay Sharma in his Dissertation—"Mythology of Devabhūmi" has mentioned several small or big temples of god Brahmā, in Himachal Pradesh, which he has personally visited.
5. We have already discussed this curse-episode in the chapter on Curses, Boons and Oaths.
6. See Sadashiv A. Dange, *Ency. PBP*, Vol. II, p. 392f.
7. See M.K. Dhavalikar, "Kīrtimukha", Ananthacharya Indological Research Institute Series No. XI, *Proceedings* of the Seminar on 'Symbolism in Temple Art and Architecture', Bombay (Mumbai), 1992 pp. 85-90.
8. *Matsya P.* (71.11-13). From a drop of sweat from Śiva's head, was born the *gaṇa* Vīrabhadra, who was fierce and blazing, had many faces and could shatter the seven under-worlds.

9. See Sadashiv A. Dange, *Ency. PBP*, Vol. IV, p. 1313.
10. For details see A.A. Macdonell, *Vedic Mythology*, pp. 162-64.
11. *Ibid.*, pp. 77, 101; and for Daśagvas and Navagvas pp. 80, 141, 144, 170.
12. See Sadashiv A. Dange, *Cultural Sources from the Veda*, Bharatiya Vidya Bhavan, Bombay (Mumbai), 1977, p. 74.
13. *The Śatapatha Brāhmaṇa*, Pt. I, SBE, Vol. 12, Reprint, Motilal Banarsidass, Delhi, 1978 (1882), Intrn. pp. xviif.
14. For details see Sadashiv A. Dange, *Ency. PBP*, Vol. IV, pp. 1302-1303.
15. For Pāncarātra philosophy, see S.N. Dasgupta, *History of Indian Philosophy*, III, p. 38ff.
16. Ronald Huttington, "Avatāras and Yugas," *Purāṇa*, Vol. VI, No. 1, 1964, pp. 7-39.
17. *Ibid.*, p. 8f.
18. *Ibid.*, p. 12.
19. G.V. Devasthali, *Religion and Mythology of the Brāhmaṇas*, Poona University Publication, Poona, 1965, pp. 8-10.
20. Jayadeva in his 'Aṣṭapadī' at the beginning of his *Gītagovinda* (the best example of the lyrical poetry), however states Balarāma as the eighth *avatāra* and not Kṛṣṇa, the regularly mentioned eighth *avatāra*. This is rater unique. The idea might be that as Kṛṣṇa is the main character (described in human form) in the *Gītagovinda*, he cannot figure as an *avatāra*. Hence Balarāma gets a place there.
21. See J.G. Frazer, *Folklore in the Old Testament*, Vol. I, London, 1918, pp. 104-361; also a paper by Winternitz, published in 1901, *"Flutsagen des Altertums und der Naturvoelker"* (*Flood Legends in Antiquity and among Primitive people*), mentioned in *German Indologists*, Max Mueller Bhavan, New Delhi, 1981, p. 161f, in which he has compared the story of Manu with over 70 other legends concerning the deluge; also Suryakanta, *Flood Legend in Sanskrit Literature*, Delhi, 1950.
22. C.E. Luard (compiler), *The Jungle tribes of Malwa*, Lucknow, 1909, p. 17.
23. J. Gonda, *Aspects of Early Viṣṇuism*, Utrecht, 1954, p. 125.
24. See R.C. Agrawala, "Fish and Vārāhī in ancient Indian Sculpture", *Orissa Historical Research Journal*, Bhuvaneshvara, Vol. XII, No. 1, p. 1ff.

25. *Vārāhī Tantra* is a Sanskrit text written in Oriya script in the collection of Pundit Sadashiv Radha Sharma of Puri; also see J.N. Banerjea, "The Vārāhī Temple at Chaurashi," V.V. Mirashi Fel. Vol., Nagpur, 1965, p. 353f; also by the same author, *Development of Hindu Iconography*, 2nd edn., pp. 505-07.
26. See H.M. Hyatt, *Folk-lore of Adams County Illinois*, New York, 1935.
27. See A.A. Macdonell, *Vedic Mythology*, p. 38f.
28. J. Gonda, *op.cit.* pp. 129-145.
29. *Tait. Br.* I.1.3.5; *Śat. Br.* XIV.1.2.11 where the name of the boar is given as Emūṣa.
30. *Brahmāṇḍa P.* I.1.5.11ff; *Kūrma P.* I.6.3ff; *Brahma P.* 179.18cd-19ab; also *ibid.* 180.27cd-28ab; *Agni P.* IV.1ff.
31. *Sk.P.* II.1.36; V.1.52; V.3.19; V.3.189.
32. See A.B. Keith, *The Religion and Philosophy of the Veda and Upanishads*, HOS, Vol. 32, Reprint, Motilal Banarsidass, Delhi, 1989 (1925), p. 387.
33. J. Gonda, *op.cit.*, p. 132.
34. *Baudh. G.S.* IV.2.7; *Baudh. D.S.* I.5.12.6; *Gaut. D.S.* XXII.24.
35. A.D. Pusalkar, *Studies in Epics and Purāṇas*, Bharatiya Vidya Bhavan, Bombay (Mumbai), 1955, pp. 51-52.
36. J. Gonda, *op.cit.*, p. 105f.
37. *Nir.* VIII.18, see under "Vanaspati". The view of Śākapūṇi—*agniriti śākapūṇiḥ*. Also see K.R. Potdar, "Āprī-hymns", *Journal of the University of Bombay*, Sep. 1945, p. 35 ff.
38. Sadashiv A. Dange, "*Axis Mundi* and the Vedic *Yūpa*" *Gleanings from Vedic to Puranic Age*, ed. by Mrs. S.S. Dange, pp. 13-24.
39. J. Gonda, *op.cit.*, p. 106.
40. R.T. Rudle Clark, *Myth and Symbol in Ancient Egypt*, London, 1959, p. 141.
41. J.G. Frazer, *Folk-lore in the Old Testament*, Vol. III, London, 1918, p. 2ff.
42. J. Gonda, *op.cit.*, p. 145f.
43. See *Household-tales* of Grimm Brothers, Eng. Tr. by Margaret Hunt, 1864, 1884, "The Three Little Men in the Wood"; "Water of Life"; "The Golden Goose" etc.
44. Also see *Manu Sm.* II.69ff; *Yājñ. Sm.* I.15ff. We have here the rules and duties laid down for the '*brahmacārin*'. *The Bhār.G.S.* (II.18) and the *Hiraṇya. G.S.* (I.10.3) say that the sun shines taking the

lustre of the students, who have completed their study. The Hiraṇya. G.S. here says that the face of a *snātaka* radiates lustre, as it were.

45. See J. Gonda, *op.cit.*, pp. 147-150.
46. See Sindhu S. Dange, *Vedic Beliefs and Practices through Arthavāda*, Vol. I, pp. 182-185.
47. K.P. Jaiswal, "Historical Position of Kalki and his identification with Yaśodharman", *Indian Antiquary*, Vol. 46, 1917, p. 145 ff.
48. A mythical tale or a folktale (as it is circulated from mouth to mouth) about the wooden images, showing crudeness especially of their hands, has come down to the present author through her aunt (late Smt. Padmavati A. Page) who had visited the Jagannatha temple nearly hundred years ago. The tale says that the carpenter who was no other than the Lord himself had told the King Indradyumna not to disturb him in his work of making the images. As the work was taking a long time, Indradyumna lost his patience and broke open the door. The carpenter (the Lord) had disappeared (may be hearing the sound of the door!). And there were seen the three images with crude hands as an incomplete task!! The tale is no doubt an *arthavāda*, giving an aetiological explanation of the misshapen hands of the images.
49. See U.N. Dhal, "Rathayātrā—A Sacrificial Festival of Lord Jagannatha", *Sacrifice in India—Concept and Evolution*, (ed.) Sindhu S. Dange, Viveka Publications, Aligarh, 1987, p. 178.
50. Their significant role is at the time of Anavāsara—period of yearly recolouring of the deities after Snānayātrā on the full-moon day in the Jyeṣṭha month; Navakalevara—fashioning the deities anew; Rathayātrā; Vanayāga—for the collection of wood for the construction of chariots; and for making new images (of wood) at the time of Navakalevara. The Pati Mahāpātras carry out the most important and solemn ritual of shifting the Brahmapadārtha (immortal life substance) from the old image of Jagannatha to the new one at the time of Navakalevara.
51. G.C. Tripathi, *Communication with God*, Indira Gandhi National Centre for the Arts, New Delhi and Aryan Books International, New Delhi, 2004, pp. 8-13.
52. *Ibid.*, p. 10f.

53. *Ibid.*, pp. 11-13.
54. *Ibid.*, p. 13.
55. *Ibid.*
56. *Ibid.*
57. For "aniconism", See Chambers Twentieth Century Dictionary, Allied Publishers Pvt. Ltd., 9th Reprint 1983.
58. About the concept of *fetish*, see chapter III, note 126.
59. *ERE*, Vol. VII, p. 143a.
60. G.C. Tripathi, *op.cit.*, p. 12.
61. *Ibid.*, p. 13.
62. Tripathi takes the word "Daïta-s' to mean *'daityas'*. It may cause misconception about the tribe of the Śabaras, which are Aryanised from very early times. See G.C. Tripathi, *op. cit.*, p. 10. The word 'Daitas' leans towards the meaning 'devotees' attached to the temple, as pointed out by Brajkishore Swain, Puri.
63. See note 50 supra.
64. Pt. Nilakantha Das, "The Cult of Jagannātha", *Orissa Review* (Navakalevara Special), Vol. XXXIII, No. 12, July 1977, Bhubaneswar, pp. 1-9.
65. U.N. Dhal, "Ratha Yātrā—A Sacrificial Festival of Lord Jagannātha", *Sacrifice in India—Concept and Evolution* (Proceedings of the National Seminar, Uni. of Bombay (Mumbai), (ed.) S.S. Dange, Viveka Publications, Aligarh, p. 178, note 3.
66. G.C. Tripathi, *op.cit.*, p. 227.
67. See Pt. Divakar Sharma, *Bṛhadstotraratnākaraḥ*, Dhavale Prakashan, Reprint, Mumbai, 2008, p. 135.
68. R.C. Dhere, *Lokadaivatanche Vishva* (Marathi), Padmagandha Prakashan, 2nd ed., Pune, 2000, p. 128.
69. *Ibid.*, pp. 130-131.
70. *Ibid.*, p. 131.
71. M.A. Shirgaonkar, "Brahmapūjā-Narasiṁhapūja", *Prasada* (*Nṛsiṁha Daivata Viśeṣāṅka*), ed. by M.Y. Joshi, Prasada Prakashan, Pune, Aug. 1983, p. 57.
72. Dr. Madhavi Narsalay, Mumbai, has given the following information about the deity Narasiṁha—the family-deity from the side of her in-laws. It is in the form of a stone-slab (*śilā*—an aniconic stone only). No woman is allowed to go in the precincts

of the temple, except a girl below 12 years of age and a woman, above 60 years of age.

The present author is glad to mention the help rendered by her student Mrunalini Newalkar, who has studied for her dissertation *Narasiṁha Through Puranic Sources*, for the M. Phil. degree, University of Mumbai, 2012.

73. See Sadashiv A. Dange, *Towards Understanding Hindu Myths*, Aryan Books International New Delhi, 1996, p. 278.
74. For these accounts, see Ram Newaj, *Vedic-Puranic Sources and Burmese Myth and Ritual*, Ph.D. Thesis, University of Bombay (Mumbai), 1994, pp. 279-284.
75. *Vāj. Sam.* III.57; *Tait. Sam.* I.8.6.1-2; *Mait. Sam.* I.10.4.
76. *Baudh. G.S.* II.8.9; *Āgniv.G.S.* II.5.3; *Āpa. Ś.S.* VIII.18.1.
77. For detailed treatment of these, see Sadashiv A. Dange, *Ency. PBP*, Vol. II, p. 685-732, under "Goddesses" (General and Individual).
78. *Brahmavai. P.* Gaṇapatikhaṇḍa 34.22; Śrīkṛṣṇakhaṇḍa 1.26; Prakṛtikhaṇḍa 35.4-5; 44.23.
79. Here a practice prevalent in South India, noted by Whitehead, can be recalled. It is customary to offer boiled rice in many cases soaked with the blood of the victim and shout *"poli! poli!"* ("Food! Food!") at the festival in honour of the Mother-goddess. See Henry Whitehead, *The Village Gods of South India*, 2nd edn., Sumit Publications, Delhi, 1976 (1921), pp. 56, 66.
80. The said information was given to the author by her student Mrs. Hetal Kamdar, Mumbai, who worked on the topic "Melaḍī-Mā" for her dissertation.
81. See chapter I, note 35.
82. Sadashiv A. Dange, *Ency. PBP*, Vol. V, p. 1461f.
83. Sindhu S. Dange, "Trees, Plants and Varieties of Grass", *Vedic Beliefs and Practices through Arthavāda*, Vol. I, pp. 153-57, see under "Udumbara". For the things made from the Udumbara tree, *ibid.*, p. 155f.
84. Sadashiv A. Dange, *Ency PBP*, Vol. V, p. 1475f.
85. Donald Mackenzie, *Myths of Pre-Columbian America*, London, Year not given, p. 177.

    The botanical name of the plant Maguey is *Agava americana*, and the name 'pulque' of the wine is derived from the language of the natives of Chile.

86. *Ibid.*, p. 180. The plate given opposite of this page shows the milk-yielding tree with fruits in the form of teats.
87. *Ibid.*, p. 182f.
88. *Ibid.*, p. 183.
89. S.N. Dasgupta, *A History of Sanskrit Literature,* Classical Period, Vol. I, University of Culcutta (=Kolkata), 1947, Intrn., p. xciv.
90. Sadashiv A. Dange, *Ency. PBP*, Vol. III, pp. 1010-19.
91. See P.V. Sharma, *Āyurveda kā Vaijñānika Itihāsa* (Hindi) 8th edn., Chaukhamba Orientalia, Varanasi, 2005.
    * See pp. 1-7—The extant *Caraka-saṁhitā* has come down to us in three stages—
    (a) The original Saṁhitā of Ātreya Agniveśa—1000 BC;
    (b) Recension of Caraka—3rd cent BC to 2nd cent. BC (i.e. Maurya and Śuṅga period). It was Caraka's recension that made the original *Agniveśasaṁhitā* to get the name and fame as *Caraka-saṁhitā.*
    (c) Dṛḍhabala's recension of the *Caraka-saṁhitā*—4th cent. AD (i.e. Gupta period). Final Form.
    * See P.V. Sharma, *op.cit.*, pp. 86-87—The *Suśruta-saṁhitā* has also undergone four stages. The two important ones are—
    (a) The work by Kāśirāja Divodāsa, who is also known by the name Ādya Suśruta or Vṛddha Suśruta—1500 to 1000 BC.
    (b) Suśruta's recension of the original Saṁhitā, so perfect as to get the name Suśruta-saṁhitā—2nd cent. BC.
    Thus these two great works on Āyurveda were in full swing, when the Purāṇas came on the scene.
92. For the medicinal use of the Udumbara, *Caraka.*, Cikitsā. 7.87 p. 2669; 19.48 p. 3097; 30.36 p. 3472. *Suśruta.* Uttaratantram 45.23 p. 912; 49.22 p. 930.
93. Sindhu S. Dange, "Trees, Plants and Varieties of Grass", *Vedic Beliefs and Practices through Arthavāda,* Vol. I, p.143f, under "Aśvattha".
94. See Sadashiv A. Dange, *Ency. PBP,* Vol. V, pp. 1470-1472f, for Aśvattha."
95. For the medicinal use of the Aśvattha, *Caraka.* Cikitsā, 25.38 p. 3288; 25.52 p. 3293; 29.50 p. 3456.
    Suśruta. Cikitsā, 3.6 p. 471; 11.9 p. 530; 26.27 p. 603.

96. *Manu Sm.* IX. 158-178; *Yājñ. Sm.* II.128-131. To mention some of these—one's own, adopted, purchased, one who offers himself etc.

97. There is still a practice in the Tarai region of Nepal that prior to having a lay-out of a mango-groove, in the same area, very near to the groove, they dig a 'well'. After planting the tender shoots of mango-trees, they perform a ceremonious marriage of the 'well' with the 'mango-groove.'
See Shri Bhavani Bhikṣu, "Kūvā aur Āmaraī" (Hindi), *Rashtrabhāratī*, Sep. 1967, p. 402. Taking for support or as a base, this prevalent practice, the Bhikṣu has given here a tale, having a touch of pathos.

98. Sindhu S. Dange, *Vedic Beliefs and Practices through Arthavāda*, Vol. I, p. 142 for the names of the sacrificial trees.

99. Sadashiv A. Dange, *Ency. PBP.*, Vol. V, p. 1473 f.

100. For Bilva, see *Caraka.*, Cikitsā, 14.29, p. 2875; 15.37 p. 2942.
Suśruta, Uttaratantram, 28.7, p. 823; 30.3 p.824; 40.127 p. 879.

101. The medicinal uses of Vaṭa (also called Nyagrodha or Rauhiṇa) are already taken note of by us. See chap. IV, note 60.

102. There are medicinal uses of Kadamba. See *Caraka,* Cikitsā, 25.38; p. 3288; 25.39, p. 3290; 26.20, p. 3303.

103. For Āmalakī, see *Caraka*, Cikitsā, 1.7, p. 2291; (the first chapter is named (Abhayāmalakīya Rasāyanapāda") especially 1.22-24, pp. 22.74-2280; 1.25, p. 2281; 3.111, 139, p. 2476, 2496; 4.28, p. 2547; 14.61, p.2891; 17.41, p. 3027.
Suśruta, Cikitsā, 6.13, p.499; 11.8, p.530; Uttaratantram, 12.49, p.770; 52.36, p.947; 58.40, p. 969.

104. See Sadashiv A. Dange, *Ency. PBP*, Vol. V, p. 1469f.

105. For Nimba (Neem tree), *ibid.*, p. 1474 for details.

106. For Nimba (Neem) tree *Agni P.* 285.29-35; 286.9-10, 16; 287.86. Also see *Caraka*, Cikitsā, 2.3, p. 219; 3.22, 23, p. 2487; 7.57, p. 2655; 10.9, p. 527; 11.8, p. 531; 20.27, p. 569; 31.282, p. 863.

107. While giving bath to the child stricken with measles or chiken-pox, the Neem-leaves are dipped in the bath-water and they are also spread on the bed of the child. This is to give the cooling effect to the patient (i.e. the child), who can feel fresh.

108. See for detailed information, Sadashiv A. Dange, *Ency. PBP*, Vol. V, pp. 1481-1483f, under "Tulasī".

109. For Tulasī—*Caraka*, 2.2, p. 218; 4.2, p. 260; *Caraka*, Cikitsā, 18.24, p. 3043; 18.27, p. 3046; 18.43, p. 3054; 18.46; 18.61, p. 3063; Tulasī included in the class of Green plants—*ibid.*, 27.31, p. 1044.
Suśruta, Sūtra, 39.6, p. 149; Uttaratantram, 39.272, p. 862.
110. For details, see Sadashiv A. Dange, *Ency. PBP*, Vol. IV, pp. 1180-1181f.
111. The use of stagnant waters is denied in sacrifice, for they are seized by Varuṇa. By taking stagnant waters, he would cause Varuṇa to seize his sacrifice (*Tait. Sam.* VI. 4.2.4).
112. For details, see Sadashiv A. Dange, *Ency. PBP*, Vol. IV, pp. 1184-1187.
113. *Vāyu P.* I.45.104; *Matsya P.* 112.29; *Mārk P.* 56.26; *Kūrma P.* I.47.28-39; *Brahmāṇḍa P.* II.16.24-40; *Vām. P.* XIII.20-33.
114. Circumambulation of the Brahmagiri mountain is a practice popular even today.
115. See Anne Feldhaus, *Water and Womanhood*, Oxford University Press, 1995, photographs opposite of p. 64.
116. A.A. Macdonell, *Vedic Mythology*, p. 59f.
117. *Pañc. Br.* XXV.10.15—offering to Apām Napāt at the confluence of the rivers Dṛṣadvatī and Sarasvatī.
118. John Cain, "Native Custom of Godāvarī", *Indian Antiquary*, Vol. IV, 1875, p. 198.
119. Anne Feldhaus, *op.cit.* p. 184f.

Appendix A

SŪTA—CHRONICLER, COMPOSER AND NARRATOR.

The Sūta-tradition played a very vital role in the composition and preservation of the secular type of literature and also helped the assimilation of this type of literature with the Vedic ritual literature.

The representative of this tradition, *sūta* is mentioned as *rājakṛt* in the *AV* (III.5.7 ab), this being the oldest reference. In the Śatarudriya formula in the *YV*, Rudra is praised as a *sūta*, who does not harm or kill.[1] In the Rājasūya sacrifice (rejuvenation of the king), the sacrificer king has to offer oblations at the houses of the persons called *ratnin*, associated with the king and the ruling of the kingdom[2]. Among them figures the *sūta* (*Tait. Sam.* I.8.9.1; *Tait.Br.* I.7.3.4; *Śat.Br.* V.3.1.5). The commentators of the ritual-texts have rendered the word *sūta* as a charioteer or the guard of the horses, which rendering is accepted by some scholars.[3] Eggeling, however, opines that Sūta at the Vedic period, had the same connotation as was in the later period of the Epics. The business of *sūta* was to compose and sing the praise of the king, and also record important chronicles.[4] According to Weber, the *sūta* was an honorable person at the royal court and could see the king freely.[5] This shows that *sūta* must be very close to the ruler, in the Vedic period, as to be in a position to harm any one. This explains the ephithet of Rudra in the Śatarudriya formula as —'the *sūta*, who does not harm or kill,' signifying 'a good and righteous *sūta*. The *Mbh.* knows *sūta* as 'a strict adherent of the code of conduct'—*paramadhārmika* (*Mbh.* Śānti 12.47). He is mentioned as 'the son of Viśvamitra' (*Mbh.* Anu. 4.49.57c), which takes us to the mythical account of Śunaḥśepa (*Ait.Br.* VII.18=33.6). When Viśvāmitra adopted Sunaḥśepa as his son as per latter's desire, Viśvāmitra's sons elder than his son Madhucchandas did not approve of it. So Viśvāmitra cursed them to be Andhra, Puṇḍra, Śabara, Pulinda, Mūtiba etc. In the *Mbh.*, the list of the sons of Viśvāmitra starting from Madhucchandas, includes the *sūta* (*Mbh.* Anu. 4.50-59). Lomaharṣaṇa a *sūta* had a son named Ugraśravas, who is referred to as Sauti (fr. *sūta+iñ*—in the sense of the son of *sūta*) and who narrated the *Mbh.* to the sages including Śaunaka (*Mbh.* Ādi 1.5-21). In this context it is mentioned that the stories compiled in the *Mbh.* were narrated by Vyāsa and Vaiśampāyana. These stories were securely collected by Ugraśravas and the same were narrated by him to Śaunaka and other sages. According to the *Agni P.*, the *sūta* compiled the text of the Purāṇas due to the favour of Vyāsa (150.31). This shows that *sūta* was a person who committed to memory or maintained, the ancient records and narrations and often added to them. Thus he combined in himself the office of the chronicler, composer and narrator.

Though born of a mixed marriage of the *pratiloma* type.[6] the Purāṇas give him a place of prime importance. After the castes were fixed in the then society, there seems to have arisen a question about the exact status to be given to *sūta*. In this context, we note an interesting account narrated in the *Bhāg. P.* According to it, once the sages were performing a sacrifice of long duration (*sattra*) in the Naimiṣa forest. In that *sattra*, at the seat of Vyāsa (the chief compiler of the Purāṇas) was seated the *sūta* Romaharṣaṇa. When Balarāma came to attend the sacrificial session, Romaharṣaṇa did not rise from his seat, nor did he fold his hands to show respect to him. Balarāma flew into rage on seeing this honour bestowed on the *sūta* (the son of a mixed caste) and also *sūta's* behaviour which pricked him. Balarāma shot a pointed blade of *kuśa* grass at Romaharṣaṇa, which pierced the latter's vitals and killed him. The sages disapproved this rude behaviour of Balarāma, for they themselves had willingly offered the position of honour to Romaharṣaṇa till the conclusion of the sacrifice, giving him blessings of peaceful life. They declared that Balarāma was guilty of murder, which was nothing less than the killing of a *brāhamaṇa.* Thus Balarāma according to them had committed the sin of *brahmahatyā*, for the seat Romaharṣaṇa was adorning was the Brahmāsana. They advised Balarāma to undergo the prescribed expiation. Balarāma saw his folly and accepted the wish of the sages. The first thing he did was to seat the son of 'Romaharṣaṇa'—Sauti Ugraśravas— on the 'Brahmāsana' (*Bhāg. P.* X.78.20-40). As expiation, Balarāma roamed for one year, visiting the holy places (*ibid.* chap. 79).

This account can be purely mythical or may be regarded as having a grain of historical truth. But the account reveals certain points. The *sūta*, born of a *pratiloma* type of marriage was not regarded as a *brāhamaṇa.* However, as *Padma P.* (Sṛṣṭikhaṇḍa I.28) points out, he was respected as he was a veritable human record of social and religious events, and was extremely knowledgeable. Hence, at assemblies of narrations he was believed to be more important even than the *muni* and the *brāhmaṇa.* The *Agni P.*, at the very beginning states that the sages like Śaunaka welcomed the *sūta*, who came to the Naimiṣa forest during his wanderings for visiting various holy places, and said to him, "O *sūta*, you are worthy of worship to us. Impart to us the information which would render us endowed with knowledge" (1.2, 3). The *sūta* replied that he would speak what he knew from such sages as Paila and Śuka, when he happened to stay in the hermitage at Badarikā (*ibid.*

1.6). This makes it clear that the vocation and practice of *sūta* was to gather information from varied places.

At many places *sūta* is mentioned along with *māgadha*. The *Padma P.* (Bhūmikhaṇḍa 28.74) states that these two were born to praise, indicating their profession by birth. Even the *bandin* and the *cāraṇa* were singers of praise (*ibid.* 28.73). But they seem to have a status lower than the *māgadha.*

The *Arthaśāstra* of Kauṭilya makes a mention of the 'Paurāṇika' *sūta* (*Artha.* III.7.29), and about his salary (*ibid.* V.3.13). The word *paurāṇika* requires some explanation.[7] But it is in the sense of a person, who has studied the Purāṇa or Purāṇas. *Sūta* in later times was associated with the training of horses and elephants (*Vāyu P.* 62.32) and he also worked as a charioteer (*Agni P.* 151.15a). Probably there was a separate class of the *sūtas* (*Paurāṇika*), who studied, sang and explained the Purāṇa-texts as is indicated in the *Arthaśāstra*.

Though a bit lower than the *brāhmaṇa* the *sūta* was entitled for the rite of *upanayana* (initiation), could study the Vedas, give offerings into the fire in the morning and in the evening (*agnihotra*) and follow the rules meant for a *brāhmaṇa*. He was supposed to be well-versed in various *śāstras* (*Padma P.* Bhūmikhaṇḍa 28.69-71). the *Kūrma P.* also expects the *sūta* to know all the *śāstras* and lores (1.13.13).

It is interesting to see that the Purāṇas have tried to justify the status and importance of the *sūta* by means of mythical accounts of his birth. Thus the *sūta*, though a Paurāṇika, was Viṣṇu himself by his *māyā* (power), says the *Kūrma P.* (I.13.12). The *Vāyu P.* gives a mythical account, which is very interesting. It is said that king Pṛthu performed the Soma-sacrifice in honour of Bṛhaspati. Actually for the rite of pressing the shoots of the Soma-plant, the *mantra* in honour of Bṛhaspati was to be uttered; but through oversight, a *mantra* for Indra was uttered. Hence there happened a mixture of the Indra-*mantra* with the offering meant for Bṛhaspati. Bṛhaspati the priest of the gods was a *brāhmaṇa*, and Indra a *kṣatriya*. Hence *sūta* is of mixed birth, having the traits of both the gods. By nature *sūta* is Bṛhaspati, learned in tradition, allowed for the Vedic studies and respected even to the *brāhmaṇas,* but in the social order lower than the latter (*Vāyu P.* 62.135-142).

It is certain that the *sūtas* preserved the tradition of the common folks and mastered the art of collecting and preserving the myths and other stories of the populace, and mainly the Itihāsa-Purāṇa, along with *gāthās, nārāśaṁsīs* and at times even *ślokas.* The mythical accounts occurring in the Epics and Purāṇas come from the secular tradition, in which the *sūta* was the chronicler, composer and narrator.

NOTES AND REFERENCES

1. *Vāj. Sam.* XVI.18; *Tait. Sam.* IV.5.2.1; *Kāṭh. Sam.* XVII.2; *Mait. Sam* II.9.3.
2. For the important rite '*ratninām havīṁṣi*' in the Rājasūya sacrifice, see Sadashiv A. Dange, *Vedic Sacrifices—Early Nature,* Vol. II, pp. 306-315f.
3. A.A. Macdonell, and A.B. Keith, *Vedic Index of Names and Subjects,* under "Sūta".
4. J. Eggeling, *The Śatapatha Brāhmaṇa,* pt. III, SBE, Vol. 41, Delhi, 1989 (1894), p. 62 f.n. 1.
5. A.A. Macdonell, and A.B. Keith, *op.cit., loc.cit.*
6. Sūta was the one born to a *brāhmaṇa* woman from a *kṣatriya.* See *Manu Sm.* X.11, 17; *Yājñ. Sm.* I.93.
7. R.P. Kangle, takes the word *paurāṇika* as 'mentioned in the Purāṇa'. See R.P. Kangle, *The Kauṭiliya Arthaśāstra,* pt. II (Eng. Tr. with notes), University of Bombay (=Mumbai) Pub., 2nd ed., 1972 (1963), p. 215.

   On the face of it, this interpretation is not correct, for here the sense is of a person and not any matter concerning the Purāṇas. Again it is not warranted by grammar. Pāṇini and Kauṭilya were comparatively closer to each other chronologically. *Aṣṭādhyāyī* of Pāṇini lays down the suffix *ṭhak,* and the *vārttika* specifies this laying down in the context of *ākhyāna, ākhyāyikā, itihāsa* and *purāṇa,* having the *anuvṛtti* of the *Aṣṭā. Sūtra* IV.2.59—*tadadhīte tadveda,* meaning 'who has studied that' or 'who understands that'. Here the *anuvṛtti* of the suffix *aṇ* is debarred by the suffix *ṭhak* (i.e. *ika,* which makes the lengthening of the beginning vowel). Thus the word *paurāṇika* means a person who has studied the Purāṇa or Purāṇas.

Appendix B

PURANIC TREE-GODDESSES—
THEIR MEDICINAL BASIS

Some trees are reckoned as Tree-goddesses in the Purāṇas, as we have seen in chapter VI. Apart from the beliefs attached to them, these trees are important for their medicinal properties. The Purāṇas had before them the fully developed Indian Science of Medicine (Āyurveda), which was at its zenith from early times. The tree-goddesses mentioned in the Purāṇas are really the trees, which have the utmost medicinal value. As these trees, due to their medicinal uses help the people at large, they carry out the role of a 'Mother', reminding us of the advice given by Nṛsiṁha to 'Mothers' (*mātaraḥ*). He says that as men and beasts take care of their little ones, so the 'Mothers' (including Aśvatthā, Bilvā etc.) should take care of the people in this world (*Matsya P.* 179.77-78).

Though we have given the references from the *Caraka-saṁhitā* and the *Suśruta-saṁhitā* in Chapter VI (Notes), here we point out in short the medicinal uses of the trees-Sacred ones—which are the Tree-goddesses, called 'Mātaraḥ.'

1. Āmalakī (*Emblic myrobalan, Emblica officinalis gaertn*).
   (a) *Caraka*, Cikitsā 1.22-24, mixing the Āmalaka powder with other medicines, which are useful for increasing the level of intelligence, for preparing the 'Brāhmarasāyanakalpa'.
   (b) *Ibid.* 3.139, the decoction of the grapes fried in ghee and Āmalaka, followed by (*anupāna*) of milk, to be given to cause vomiting, for nullifying fever or bringing down the temperature.
   (c) *Ibid.* 3.111, for a patient suffering from fever, the liquid porridge from brown rice (*raktaśālī*), in which is mixed the powder of *pippalī*, Āmalaka etc.
   (d) *Ibid.* 14.61, for treating the ailment of 'piles', in the preparation of 'Abhayāriṣṭa', Āmalaka figures.
   (e) *Ibid.* 4.28, for treating the 'Raktapitta' (Bleeding Disorder), together with other ingredients, figures Āmalaka.
   (f) *Ibid.* 17.41, for treating 'Hiccoughs' (*Hikkā*), together with other ingredients, Āmalaka.
   (g) *Suśruta*, Cikitsā, 6.13, for treating the ailment of 'piles', in the 'Takrakalpa' (preparation of butter-milk), Āmalaka is used.
   (h) *Ibid.* Uttaratantram 12.49, for curing the blood oozing out, ointment made from the leaves and fruits of Āmalaka to be used.
   (i) *Ibid.* Uttaratantram 58.40, for difficulty in urination, the Āmalaka-juice to be given to the patient.
   (j) *Ibid.* Uttaratantram 52.36, for curing cough, Āmalaka-powder, to be boiled in milk and mixed with ghee to be given. It gives respite to coughing.
   (k) *Ibid.* Cikitsā 11.8, in treating *Prameha* (Diabetes). Āmalaka-juice, in which turmeric powder and honey are mixed, to be given.
2. Aśvattha (*Ficus religiosa*).
   (a) *Caraka*, Cikitsā 25.21, thick ointment, prepared with ghee, from the barks of the trees Nyagrodha,

Udumbara, Plakṣa, Vetasa (Bamboo), and Aśvattha, to be used as poultice in the inflammation of a wound.

(b) *Ibid.* 25.52, the powder prepared from the barks of the trees Kakubha (Arjuna tree) Udumbara etc., Aśvattha figuring there, for healing the wounds, which very soon get the new skin over them.

(c) *Ibid.* 29.50, a decoction of Aśvattha with honey mixed in it, for curing gout (*Vātarakta*) and even the severe *Tri-doṣas* (Derangement of the three humours of the body *viz Vāta, Pitta* and *Kapha*).

(d) Suśruta, Cikitsā 11.9, in the bilious disorders (*Paittika*), in one of the varieties of bile (*Pitta-*)-dominant diabetes, the decoction of Aśvattha to be used.

(e) *Ibid.* 3.6, the barks of several trees, Aśvattha figuring there, to be used as a bandage for a wound.

3. Bilva (*Aegle marmelos*).

(a) *Caraka*, Cikitsā 14.29, a person suffering from piles (*Arśa*) to be made to seat in the decoction of the Bilva-roots, to lessen his pain.

(b) *Ibid.* 15.37, the powder prepared from the Bilva and Citraka, and dried ginger, to be mixed with Biḍa-lavaṇa (a kind of salt) and to be partaken of with warm water in the ailment of Sāma (concerning the three humours of the body) and also in the ailment pertaining to *Vāta* with *Kapha.*

(c) *Suśruta,* Uttaratantram 30.3, Bilva figures in the preventive medicine (measures) in the 'Skanda' ailment-*Apasmāra* (epilepsy), a kind of ailment common to children, also *Ibid.,* 28.7, a garland of the Bilva thorns, together with the sprouts of other plants and trees to be placed round the neck of a child suffering from this ailment. [The word '*skanda*' from √*skand*— 'to leap upon, jump.' Skanda, the son of Śiva is also believed to be the leader of the demons of illness, that attack children.]

(d) *Ibid.* 40.27, in diarrhoea as well as in desentery, the pulp of the Bilva fruit, honey, liquorice (*Yaṣṭhimadhu*) and *Śarkarā* (candied sugar) mixed together, to be given to the patient in the liquid rice porridge.

4. Kadamba (*Nauclea cadamba*).

(a) *Caraka*, Cikitsā 25.38, the decoctions made from the trees Nyagrodha, Udumbara, Aśvattha etc., Kadamba included in them, for healing the wounds.

(b) *Ibid.* 25.39, the leaves of Kadamba tree serving as a bandage to a wound. Other trees also are mentioned here.

5. Nimba (*Margosa*).

(a) *Caraka*, Cikitsā 7.57, for all sorts of skin-diseases, the powder or decoction used, made from the products of seven or eight trees, among which the Nimba tree (Neem tree) figures.

(b) *Ibid.*, Sūtra 2.3, for causing vomiting, Nimba with other trees, figures.

(c) *Ibid.*, Cikitsā 3.22-23, in treating periodic fever (typhoid etc.), in the decoction made from herbal products, Nimba figures.

(d) *Suśruta*, Cikitsā 10.9, for curing skin-diseases, in the decoction figures Nimba, which (i.e. decoction), is to be licked in the morning.

(e) *Ibid.*, Cikitsā 11.8, in treating the ailment of diabetes, the five products of some trees (the products—barks, leaves, roots, fruits and flowers), including those of Nimba to be used, for preparing decoction. These five products are said be the 'killers' of all the disorders concerning urination.

(f) *Ibid.* 20.27, for treating the scalp-ulcers (*Aruṁśikā*), the Nimba tree to be made use of, sprinkling the water, containing Nimba (leaves) or giving bath (overhead bath) to the patient with that water.

(g) *Ibid.* 31.282, heat of fever to be lessened by making the patient vomit. By grinding Nimba leaves with some water and in the foam of that, mixing little honey, the mixture to be given to the patient, for causing vomiting.

6. Nyagrodha also called Rauhiṇa or Vaṭa i.e. Banian or Banyan (*Ficus indica*).

(a) *Caraka*, Sūtrasthāna 27.27, in the bilious form of diarrhoea (*Pittātisāra*), the decoctions made from the tender fresh leaves of trees such as Udumbara, Aśvattha, Plakṣa etc., in which Nyagrodha figures, to be given.

(b) *Ibid.* Cikitsā, 21.33, in a disease which causes 'dry spreading itch', ointment prepared from the young (i.e. fresh) branches of Nyagrodha and lotus-seeds, to be used.

(c) *Ibid.* Śārīra, 8.14, in the Puṁsavana rite, (which is to be performed in the third month of pregnancy under the Puṣya constellation), two fresh sprouts of Nyagrodha are to be dipped in curds together with two grains of *māṣa* or of white mustard and the mixture to be given to the pregnant woman.

(d) *Ibid.* Śārīra 8.20, the decoction from Nyagrodha etc. to be smeared to the lower part of the navel of a pregnant woman or to be sprinkled there. Even in the potion to be given to the pregnant woman, prepared from the sprouts of trees and plants, the sprouts of Nyagrodha figures. This is for the safe placement of the foetus.

(e) *Suśruta*, Śārīra 2.32, three or four drops of the milky juice of Lakṣmaṇā or Sahadevā or Viśvadevā (plants) or the sprouts of Nyagrodha (which have milky sap) to be instilled in the right nostril of the pregnant woman. This refers to the Puṁsavana rite, which is performed for getting a male issue.

(f) *Ibid.* Uttaratantram 44.30, in the treatment of anaemia (*Pāṇḍuroga*) the decoction prepared from the trees of the 'Nyagrodha category' to be used.

Ibid., 44.48, gives a list of the trees of Nyagrodha-varga.' These trees are having the milky juice or sap by way of exudation.

(g) *Ibid.* 38.49. The trees from the *Nyagrodhādigaṇa* are useful for curing the wounds, bleeding disorders etc.

(h) *Ibid.* 40.85, the bark of Nyagrodha etc. in the form of freshly pounded pulp (*kalka*) to be used in treating desentery (*Atisāra*).

(i)*Ibid.* Cikitsā 11.7, in treating diabetes (*Prameha*), the decoction from Nyagrodha etc. used (treatment having a lengthy process).

(j)*Ibid.* Sūtra 40.8, the trees Nyagrodha etc. useful to treat the patient suffering from the disorder of bile (*Pittasamśamana*).

(k) *Ibid.*, Cikitsā 24.11, the decoction prepared from the trees Nyagrodha etc. to be used when swelling is due to bile (*Pitta*).

The Nyagrodha tree being important, that whole class of trees is mentioned as 'Nyagrodhādi', i.e. 'Nyagrodha etc.'

7. Tulasī (the sweet smelling sacred basil).

(a) *Caraka*, Cikitsā 18.24, the mixture prepared from Tulasī with other ingredients to be licked for healing cough.

(b) *Ibid.*, 18.27, in treating cough, caused by the combined derangement of the three humours of the body, the smoke of several ingredients together with the Tulasī—sprouts (*mañjarīs*) is prescribed for being inhaled.

(c) *Ibid.* 18.46, for cough (Kāsa) caused due to Kapha with Vāta, the decoction of Daśamūla, adding Puṣkara, Hiṅgu etc. and the grounded Tulasī-leaves, to be sipped (intermittently).

(d) *Ibid.* 18.61, together with Pippalī etc., Tulasī cures all kinds of cough.

(e) *Caraka*. Sūtra 2.2, Tulasī mixture to be used for nasal-instillation.

(f) *Ibid.* Sūtra 4.2, Tulasī included in the 'Śvāsahara'-class i.e. 'Anti-asthamatic class'.

(g) *Ibid.*, Sūtra 27.31, Tulasī included in the 'Harita'-class.

(h) *Suśruta*, Uttaratantram 39.6, Tulasī with other ingredients used for purgatory medication through nose. These are called *Śirovirecanāni.*

8. Udumbara (*Ficus glomerata*).

(a) *Caraka*, Cikitsā 7.87, for treating vitiligo (*Śvitra*—white patches on the skin), in the juice of the fruits of Kāka-udumbara, jaggery to be mixed and to be partaken of.

(b) *Ibid.*, 30.36, for cleaning the vaginal passage, the oily milky substance of the Udumbara to be used.

(c) *Ibid.* 19.48, in treating desentery (*Raktātisāra*) the sprouts of Nyagrodha, Udumbara and Aśvattha to be pounded and to be boiled in quadruple water and the decoction thus made ready (with the basis of ghee) to be given.

(d) *Suśruta*. Uttaratantram 49.22, for suffering from thirstiness (*Tṛṣṇā*), the juice or decoction of the ripe Udumbara fruits with sugar to be partaken of.

(e) *Ibid.*, 45.23, in bleeding disorder (*Raktapitta*), the juice of Udumbara fruits to be sipped daily.

All these trees, being extremely useful from medicinal point of view and also having various beliefs attached to them, at times seen through mythical accounts, assumed the status of 'Tree-goddess' and were reckoned as 'Mothers', having the same importance as other 'Mothers' in the Puranic age.

Bibliography

SANSKRIT TEXTS

SAṀHITĀS

Atharvaveda-saṁhitā, ed. by S.D. Satawalekar, Aundh, V. Saṁvat 1995.

Kāṭhaka-saṁhitā, ed. by S.D. Satawalekar, Aundh, V. Saṁvat 1999.

Maitrāyaṇī-saṁhitā, ed. by S.D. Satawalekar, Aundh, V. Saṁvat 1998.

Ṛgveda-saṁhitā (with Sāyaṇa's comm.), ed. by Vaidika Samshodhana Mandala, Pune, 1933-1951.

Sāmaveda-saṁhitā, ed. by S.D. Satawalekar, Svādhyāya-maṇḍala, Pardi, 2nd edn., 1998.

Taittirīya-saṁhitā, ed. by S.D. Satawalekar, New Print, Saṁvat 2039, Anandashram, Pune, 1948.

Vājasaneyi-saṁhitā, ed. by Pt. Ramaswarup Sharma, Moradabad.

BRĀHMAṆA-TEXTS

Aitareya Brāhmaṇa, pt. I, 2nd edn., Anandashram, Pune, 1930; pt. II, 3rd edn., Anandashram, Pune, 1977.

Gopatha Brāhmaṇa, ed. by Jivananda Vidyasagar, Calcutta, 1891.

Jaiminīya Brahmaṇa, ed. by Raghuvira and Lokesh Chandra, Motilal Banarsidass, Delhi, 1986 (1954).

Kauṣītaki Brāhmaṇa (=*Śaṅkhāyana Brāhmaṇa*), Anandashram, Pune, 1911.

Pañcaviṁśa Brāhmaṇa (=*Tāṇḍya Mahābrāhmaṇa*), Kashi Sanskrit Series Chaukhambha, Benares, 1936.
Ṣaḍviṁśa Brāhmaṇa, ed. by B.R. Sharma, Kendriya Sanskrit Vidyapeeth, Tirupati, 1967.
Śatapatha Brāhmaṇa, Chaukhambha Sanskrit Samsthan, 2nd edn., Varanasi, 1984.
Taittirīya Brāhmaṇa, Anandashram, 3rd ed., Poona, 1979.

Āraṇyaka-Texts

Aitareya Āraṇyaka, Anandashram, 2nd edn., Poona, 1992.
Śāṅkhāyana Āraṇyaka, Anandashram, Pune, 1911.
Taittirīya Āraṇyaka, Calcutta, 1871.

Upaniṣad-Texts

Bṛhadāraṇyaka Upaniṣad
Chāndogya Upaniṣad
Kaṭha Upaniṣad
Kauṣītakibrāhmaṇopaniṣad
Praśna Upaniṣad
Śvetāśvatara Upaniṣad
All these Upaniṣads from *The Twenty-eight Upaniṣads*, compiled by Swami Dwarikaprasada Shastri, Pracya Bharati Prakashan, Varanasi, 1965.

Sūtra-Texts

Agniveśya Gṛhyasūtra, ed. by L.A. Ravi Verman, Trivandrum, 1940.
Āpastamba Dharmasūtra, ed. by A. Chinnaswami Shastri, published in Kashi Sanskrit Series, Benares, 1934.
Āpastamba Śrautasūtra, ed. by R. Garbe in Bib. Ind., 1882-1902.
Āśvalāyana Gṛhyasūtra, Anandashram, Poona, 1936; also tr. in Marathi and explained by Shivaramashastri Shintre, Mumbai, 1938.
Āśvalāyana Śrautasūtra, ed. by Ganesh Shastri in Anandshram Sanskrit Series, Poona, 1917.
Baudhāyana Dharmasūtra, ed. by Chinnaswami Shastri, published in Kashi Sanskrit Series, Benares, 1934.
Baudhāyana Gṛhyasūtra, ed. by R. Sham Shastri, Mysore, 1920.

Baudhāyana Śrautasūtra, ed. by W. Caland in Bib. Ind., 1904-23.
Bhāradvāja Gṛhyasūtra, ed. by Henriette J.W. Salomons, Leyden, 1913.
Bhāradvāja Śrautasūtra, ed. by Raghuvira (*Journal of Vedic Studies*), Lahore, 1935.
Gautama Dharmasūtra, ed. by I. Srinivasacharya, Mysore.
Hiraṇyakeśi Gṛhyasūtra, ed. by J. Kirste, Vienna, 1889.
Kāṭhaka Gṛhyasūtra, ed. by W. Caland, Lahore, 1925.
Kātyāyana Śrautasūtra, ed. by V. Sharma, Benares, Saṁvat 1987.
Kauśika Sūtra (The Kauśika Sūtra of Atharva Veda), ed. by M. Bloomfield, Motilal Banarsidass, Delhi, Reprint 1972 (1st ed. 1889 *JAOS*).
Lāṭyāyana Śrautasūtra, ed. by Ananda Chandra, Bib. Ind., Calcutta, 1872.
Mānava Gṛhyasūtra (with the comm. of Aṣṭāvakra), ed. by Ram Krishna Harshaji Shastri in GOS, Baroda, 1926.
Mānava Śrautasūtra, ed. by F.Knauer, St. Petersburg, 1900-1903.
Pāraskara Gṛhyasūtra, ed. by M.G. Bakre, Bombay, 1917.
Śaṅkhāyana Śrautasūtra, ed. by H. Hillebrandt, in Bib. Ind., Calcutta, 1886-89.
Vasiṣṭha Dharmasūtra, ed. by A.A. Führer, Bombay Sanskrit Series, 3rd edn., Poona, 1930.
Viṣṇu Dharmasūtra, ed. by J. Jolly, Calcutta, 1881.

Epics

Rāmāyaṇa, ed. by Chinnaswami Shastri and Subrahmanya Shastri, 2nd edn., Mylapore, Madras, 1958.
Mahābhārata, ed. with the comm. of Nīlakaṇṭha, Chitrashala Press, Pune; Crit. ed., BORI, Pune; and Gita Press, Gorakhpur.

Smṛti-Texts

Manusmṛti (with the comm. of Kullūka), Nirnayasagar, Bombay, 1946.
Yājñavalkyasmṛti (with the comm. Mitākṣarā), Nirnaysagar, Bombay, 1937.

Purāṇa-Texts

Agni Purāṇa, ed. by H.N. Apte, Anandashram, Poona, 1900.
Bhāgavata Purāṇa, Gita Press, Gorakhpur, Saṁvat 1997-2018.

Bhaviṣya Purāṇa, Venkateshwar Press, Bombay, 1959.
Brahma Purāṇa, ed. by H.N. Apte, Anandashram, Poona, 1895.
Brahmāṇḍa Purāṇa, Motilal Banarsidass, Delhi, 1985.
Brahmavaivarta Purāṇa, ed. by Vasudevashastri Marathe, Anandashram, Poona, 1935.
Garuḍa Purāṇa, ed. by Ramshankar Bhattacharya, Chaukhamba, Varanasi, 1964.
Kālikā Purāṇa, Venkateshwar Press, Bombay, Śaka 1829.
Kūrma Purāṇa, ed. by Anandaswarup Gupta, All India Kashiraj Trust, Varanasi, 1972.
Liṅga Purāṇa, Motilal Banarsidass, Delhi, 1980.
Mārkaṇḍeya Purāṇa, Nag Publishers, Delhi, year not given.
Matsya Purāṇa, Nag Publishers, Delhi, 1983.
Padma Purāṇa, Nag Publishers, Delhi, year not given.
Śiva Purāṇa, ed. by Ramtej Shastri Pandey, Varanasi, Saṁvat 2020.
Sāmba Purāṇa (*Śāmba-upapurāṇa*). The word 'Sāmba' or 'Śāmba', is used in tradition as identical.
Skanda Purāṇa, Nag Publishers, Delhi, 1982.
Vāmana Purāṇa, ed by Anandaswarup Gupta, All India Kashiraj Trust, Varanasi, 1968.
Varāha Purāṇa, The Asiatic Society, Calcutta, 1893.
Vāyu Puraṇa, Nag Publishers, Delhi, 1983.
Viṣṇu Purāṇa, Geeta Press, Gorakhpur, Sake 2045.
Viṣṇudharmottara Purāṇa

OTHER TEXTS

Arthasaṅgraha, ed. by S.M. Paranjape, Bombay, 1927.
Aṣṭādhyāyī
Aṣṭāṅgahṛdayam of Vāgbhaṭa, with the comms. Sarvāṅgasundarā of Aruṇadatta and Āyurvedarasāyana of Hemadri, ed. by Harishastri Paradkar, published by Rashtriya Sanskrit Sansthan, New Delhi.
Bhagavadgītā, with Śaṅkara's comm., Ashtekar and Company, 2nd ed., Poona, 1929.
Bṛhaddevatā
Caraka-saṁhitā by Agniveśa, revised by Maharṣi Caraka, and Dṛḍhabala, with the comms. Āyurvedadīpikā and Jalpakalpataru, annotated by Gangadhar Kaviratna Kaviraja,

ed. and revised by Narendranath Sengupta and Balaichandra Sengupta, Reprint, Rashtriya Sanskrit Sansthan, New Delhi, 2002.

Dhvanyāloka of Anandavardhana, with the comm. 'Locana', tr. in Hindi with notes by Jagannath Pathak, Chowkhamba Vidyabhavan, Varanasi, 6th edn., 1997.

Dūtavākyam, from *Bhāsanāṭakacakram*, ed. by C.R. Devadhar, Oriental Book Agency, 2nd edn., 1951.

Gītagovindam, Nirnayasagar Press, Bombay, 1937.

Kālacakratantram of Vajrayāna Buddhism.

Mīmāṁsānyāyaprakāśa, Government Oriental Series, BORI, Poona, 1937.

Nirṇayasindhu of Kamalākarabhaṭṭa, ed. by Narayanram Acharya, Nirnayasagar, Mumbai, 5th edn., 1949.

Nirkuta, Nirnayasagar, Bombay, 1930.

Pūrvamīmāṁsāsūtra of Jaimini, Anandashram, Poona.

Raghuvaṁśa, Nirnayasagar, Bombay, 1916.

Ṛgvidhānam, ed. by J. Shastri, Lahore, 1940.

Śrautapadārtha-nirvacana, author unnamed, published by Yudhishthira Mīmāṁsaka, 1st edn. (earlier editions, if any, not available), Bahalgarh (Sonepat-Haryana), 1984.

Suśruta-saṁhitā of Suśruta (Part-1), ed. with Āyurvedatattva-Sandīpikā, Hindi comm. by Kaviraja Ambikadatta Shastri, 7th edn., Chaukhamba Sanskrit Sansthan, Varanasi, 1989.

The Kauṭilīya Arthaśastra, ed. by R.P. Kangle, University of Bombay, Part I (Text), 2nd edn., 1969; Part II (Tr. and notes), 2nd edn., 1972.

Uttararāmacaritam of Bhavabhūti, with the comm. of Ghanaśyāma, with notes and Introduction by P.V. Kane, Nirnayasagar Press, Bombay, 1st edn., 1915.

Vārāhī Tantra

Vyavahāramayūkha, ed. by P.V. Kane, BORI, Poona, 1926.

OTHER BOOKS

Acharya Kala, 1993: *Puranic Concept of Dāna*, Nag Publishers, Delhi.

Bakre, Alka, 1998: *Religion in Social Flux* (as seen in the Main Purāṇa-s), Eastern Book Linkers, Delhi.

Barnett, L.D., 1922: *Hindu gods and Heroes*, London.

Barth, A. 1882: *Religion of India*, London.
Benedict, Ruth, 1930-1935: *Encyclopaedia of the Social Sciences.*
Bergaigne, A., 1969: *Vedic Religion*, Vol. I, Eng. Tr. by Paranjpe, V.G., Aryasamskriti Prakashan, Poona.
Bloch, Marc (tr. from the French by Manyon, L.A.), 1961: *Feudal Society*, Routledge & Kegan Paul, London.
Bloomfield, M., 1899: *The Atharvaveda*, Strassburg.
Bloomfield, M. (ed.), 1972 (1st edn., 1889-*JAOS*): *The Kauśika Sūtra of Atharva Veda*, Motilal Banarsidass, Delhi.
Buddha Prakash, 1966: *Ṛgveda and the Indus Valley Civilization*, VVRI, Hoshiarpur.
Caland, W (tr.) 1982 (Calcutta, 1931): *Pañcaviṁśa Brāhmaṇa*, 2nd edn., Sri Satguru Publications, Delhi.
Campbell, Joseph, 1973 (1949): *The Hero with a Thousand Faces*, Bollingen Series XVII, Princeton University Press, Princeton, New Jersy.
Charpentier, J., 1920: *Die Suparṇa-sage*, Uppsala.
Cook, James and King, James, 1776-1780: *A Voyage to the Pacific Ocean*, London (Vols. I & II by Cook, J. and Vol. III by King, J.).
Cowell, E.B. (ed.), Pali Text of the Jātakas from V. Fausböll, (Eng. Tr.), 1895-1907: Cambridge University Press.
Dandekar, R.N., 1979: *Vedic Mythological Tracts*, Ajanta Publications, Delhi.
Dange, Sadashiv A., 1969: *Legends in the Mahābhārata*, Motilal Banarsidass, New Delhi.
—, 1970: *Pastoral Symbolism from the Ṛgveda*, University of Poona, Poona.
—, 1971: *Vedic Concept of 'Field' and the Divine Fructification*, University of Bombay, Bombay.
—, 1973: *Hindu Dharma āṇi Tattvajñāna* (in Marathi), Shri Lekhan-Vachan Bhandar, Poona; 2016: 2nd edn., Continental Publication, Pune.
—, 1977: *Cultural Sources from the Veda*, Bharatiya Vidya Bhavan, Bombay.
—, 1979: *Sexual Symbolism from the Vedic Ritual*, Ajanta Publications, New Delhi.
—, 1987: *Puranic Myth and Culture*, Ajanta Publications, New Delhi.
—, 1986-1990: *Encyclopaedia of Puranic Beliefs and Practices*, Vols. I-V, Navrang, New Delhi.

—–, 1996: *Towards Understanding Hindu Myths*, Aryan Books International, New Delhi.
—–, 1997: *Myths from the Mahābhārata*, Vol. 1, *Quest for Immortality*, Aryan Books International, New Delhi.
—–, 2000: *Images from Vedic Hymns and Rituals*, Aryan Books International, New Delhi.
—–, 2000: *Vedic Sacrifices—Early Nature*, Vols. I & II, Aryan Books International, New Delhi.
—–, 2001: *Myths from the Mahābhārata*, Vol. 2, *Study in Patterns and Symbols*, Aryan Books International, New Delhi.
—–, 2001: *Myths from the Mahābhārata*, Vol. 3, *Probe in Early Dim History and Folklore*, Aryan Books International, New Delhi.
Dange, Sindhu S. 1980: *Bauddha Dharma āṇi Tattvajñāna* (in Marathi), Continental Prakashan, Pune; also *Jaina Dharma āṇi Tattvajñāna* (in Marathi), Continental Prakashan, Pune.
—–, 1984: *The Bhāgavata Purāṇa—Mytho-Social Study*, Ajanta Publications, Delhi.
—–, 1985: *Hindu Domestic Rituals, A Critical Glance*, Ajanta Publications, Delhi.
—–, (ed.), 1987: *Myths of Creation (Proceedings* of the Seminar), University of Bombay, Bombay (=Mumbai).
—–, (ed.), 1987: *Sacrifice in India—Concept and Evolution (Proceedings* of the National Seminar), Viveka Publications, Aligarh.
—–, 1989: *Etymologies and Flexible Forms from the Purāṇas*, Viveka Publications, Aligarh.
—–, 1996: *Aspects of Speech in Vedic Ritual*, Aryan Books International, New Delhi.
—–, (ed.), 2002: Gleanings from Vedic to Puranic Age (collected papers of Dr. Sadashiv A. Dange), Aryan Books International, New Delhi.
—–, 2005: *Vedic Beliefs and Practices through Arthavāda*, Vols. I & II, Aryan Books International, New Delhi.
Das, A.C., 1925: *Ṛgvedic Culture*, Calcutta.
Dasgupta, S.N., 1947: *A History of Sanskrit Literature*, Classical Period, Vol. I, University of Calcutta (=Kolkata), Intrn., p. xciv.
Davane, G.V., (tr. from French into English), 1985: *An Essay on the Myth of the Ṛbhus* by Félix Nève, Ajanta Publications, Delhi.
—–, 1995: *Perspectives in the Vedic and the Classical Sanskrit Heritage*, D.K. Print World (P) Ltd., New Delhi.

Devasthali, G.V., 1965: *Religion and Mythology of the Brāhmaṇas*, University of Poona, Poona (=Pune).

Dharmadhikari, T.N. (ed.), 1989: *Yajñāyudhāni*, Vaidika Samshodhana Mandala, Pune.

Dhere, R.C., 2000: *Lokadaivatanche Vishva* (Marathi), Padmagandha Prakashan, 2nd edn., Pune.

Dowson, J., 1953: *A Classical Dictionary of Hindu Mythology and Religion*, London.

Drury, Nama, 1981: *The Sacrificial Ritual in the Śatapatha Brāhmaṇa*, Motilal Banarsidass, Delhi.

Durkheim, Emile, 1915: *The Elementary Forms of Religious Life, London.*

Eggeling, J. 1988 (1885): *The Śatapatha Brāhmaṇa*, Part II, SBE Vol. 26, Reprint, Motilal Banarsidass, Delhi.

—–, 1989 (1894): The *Śatapatha Brāhmaṇa*, pt. III, SBE Vol. 41, Reprint, Motilal Banarsidass, Delhi.

—–, 1978 (1900): *The Śatapatha Brāhmaṇa*, pt. V, SBE Vol. 44, Reprint, Motilal Banarsidass, Delhi.

Elwin, Verrier, 1942: *The Agaria*, Oxford University Press, Reprint.

Feldhaus, Anne, 1995: *Water and Womanhood*, Oxford University Press.

Frazer, J.G., 1918: *Folklore in the Old Testament*, Vol. I, Vol. III, London.

—–, 1957 (first issued in St. Martin's Library), *The Golden Bough*, Vols. I & II, Abridged Edition, Macmillian and Company Ltd., London; also 1910 and further: *The Golden Bough*, Vols. I-VII, New York.

Gledner, K.F., 1978: *Der Rig-Veda*, HOS, Vol. 34, Cambridge (Massachusetts), London, 2nd Reprint.

Godrej, Pheroza J. and Punthakey Mistree, Firoza, 2002: *A Zoroastrian Tapestry* (Art, Religion and Culture), Mapin Publishing Pvt. Ltd., Ahmedabad.

Graves, Robert, 1968: *New Larousse Encyclopaedia of Mythology*, London, Paul Hamlin.

Gonda, J., 1954: *Aspects of Early Viṣṇuism*, Utrecht.

—–, 1965: *The Savayajñas* (Kauśikasūtra 60-68, Tr., Intrn. and Comm.), N.V. Noord-Hollandsche Uitgevers Maatschappu—Amsterdam.

Grimm, Wilhelm, 1964; 1984: *Household Tales*, Eng. Tr. by Margaret Hunt, Vols. I & II.

Hariappa, H.L., 1953: *Ṛgvedic Legends through the Ages*, Deccan College, Poona.

Hastings, James (ed.), 1967 (1908-1921): *Encyclopedia of Religion and Ethics*, Vols. I-XII+XIII Index, T.T. Clark, Edinburgh.

Hazra, R.C., 1958; 1963: *Studies in the Upa-Purāṇas*, Vols. I and II resp., Calcutta.

Heesterman, J.C., 1985: *The Inner Conflict of Tradition*, Oxford University Press, Delhi.

Held, G.J., 1935: *The Mahābhārata*, London, Amsterdam.

Hopkins, E.W., 1986 (Strassburg, 1915): *Epic Mythology*, Motilal Banarsidass, Delhi.

—–, year not mentioned: *Origin and Evolution of Religion*, Reprint, Bharatiya Vidya Prakashan, Delhi (place and year of the 1st edn., not given).

Horsch, Paul, 1966: *Die vedische Gāthā-und Śloka Literatur*, Francke Verlag, Bern.

Hubert, Henri and Mauss, Marcel, 1981 (1898): *Sacrifice: Its Nature and Functions*, tr. by W.D. Halls, Midway Reprint, The University of Chicago Press.

Hyatt, H.M., 1935: *Folklore of Adams County Illinois*, New York.

Joshi, Mahadevashastri (ed.), 1970: *Bhāratīya Saṁskṛti Kośa* (Marathi), Vol. 4, Pune.

Kane, P.V., 1974: *History of Dharmaśāstra*, Vol. II, Pt. I, 2nd edn., BORI, Poona.

—–, 1974: Vol. II, Pt. II, 2nd edn., BORI, Poona.

—–, 1973: Vol. IV, 2nd edn., BORI, Poona.

—–, 1974: Vol. V, Pt. I, BORI, Poona.

Keith, A.B. (tr.), 1967 (1914): *The Veda of the Black Yajus School entitled Taittiriya Sanhita*, pts. I & II, HOS, Vols. 18 & 19, 2nd issue, Motilal Banarsidass, Delhi.

—–, 1989 (1925): *The Religion and Philosophy of the Veda and Upanishads*, HOS, Vols. 31 & 32, Reprint, Motilal Banarsidass, Delhi.

Kirk, G.S., 1970: *Myth—Its Meaning and Functions in ancient and other Cultures*, Cambridge University Press.

—–, 1976 (1974): *The Nature of Greek Myths*, Reprint, Penguin Books Ltd., Harmondsworth Middlesex, England.

Kosambi, D.D., 1962: *Myth and Reality*, Popular Prakashan, Mumbai.

Lang, Andrew, 1913 (1887): *Myth, Ritual and Religion*, Longman's Green and Company, London.

Leeuw, G. van der, 1938: *Religion in Essence and Manifestation*, London.

Longherst, A.H., 1933: *Humpi Ruins*, Delhi.

Luard, C.E. (Compiler), 1909: *The Jungle Teribes of Malwa*, Lucknow.

Macdonell, A.A., 1988 (1917): *A Vedic Reader for Students*, Oxford University Press, 14th Impression, Madras.

—, 1995 (Strassburg, 1898): *Vedic Mythology*, Motilal Bararsidass, Reprint, Delhi.

Mocdonell, A.A. and Keith, A.B., 1912: *Vedic Index of Names and Subjects*, London.

Mackenzie, Donald, (no year mentioned): *Myths of Pre-Columbian America*, The George Gresham Publishing Company, London.

—, (no year mentioned): *Myths of Crete and Pre-Hellenic Europe*, The George Gresham Publishing Company, London.

Malinowski, Bronislaw, 1926: *Myth in Primitive Psychology*, London.

Meyer, J.J., 1954: *Sexual Life in Ancient India*, Calcutta.

Modi, J.J., 1937 (1922), *The Religious Ceremonies and the Customs of the Parsees*, Bombay.

Mukherji, R.K., 1948: *Ancient India*, Allahabad.

Munz, Peter, 1973: *When the Golden Bough Breaks*, Routledge and Kegan Paul, London and Boston.

Narsalay, Madhavi, 2015: *Epics and Mahapurāṇas on Vedic Sacrifice*, Aryan Books International, New Delhi.

Oldham, C.F., 1905: *The Sun and the Serpent*, London.

O'Flaherty, Wendy Doniger, 1982 (1975): *Hindu Myths*, Penguin Books, New York.

Pusalkar, A.D., 1955: *Studies in Epics and Purāṇas*, Bharatiya Vidya Bhavan, Bombay (Mumbai).

Patil, D.R., 1946: *Cultural History from the Vāyu Purāṇa*, Deccan College, Poona.

Potdar, K.R., 1953: *Sacrifice in the Ṛgveda*, Bharatiya Vidya Bhavan, Bombay.

Ram Gopal, 1959: *India of Vedic Kalpasūtras*, National Publishing House, Delhi.

Redfield, R. (ed.), 1992 (1925): *Magic, Science and Religion and Other Essays*, London.

Richter-Ushanas Elbert, 1997: *The Indus Script and the Ṛgveda*, Motilal Banarsidass, Delhi.

Rundle Clark, R.T., 1959: *Myth and Symbol in Ancient Egypt*, Thames and Hudson, London.

Sharma, Pt. Divakar, 2008: *Bṛhad(t)stotraratnākaraḥ*, Dhavale Prakashan, Reprint, Mumbai.

Sharma, P.V., 2005: *Āyurveda kā Vaijñānika Itihāsa* (Hindi), 8th edn., Chaukhamba Orientalia, Varanasi.

Sharma, U.C., 1975: *The Viśvāmitras and the Vasiṣṭhas*, Viveka Publications, Aligarh.

Shastri, A.M., 1991: *Varāhamihira and his Times*, Kusumanjali Prakashan, Jodhpur.

Shendge, Malati J., 1977: *The Civilised Demons—the Harappans in the Ṛgveda*, Abhinava Publications, New Delhi.

Shroeder, L.V., 1908: *Mysterium and Mimus in Ṛigveda*, Leipzig.

Smart, Ninian, 1996: *Dimensions of the Sacred—An Anatomy of the World's Beliefs*, London.

Smith, W.R., 1923: *Lectures on the Religion of the Semites*, Adam and Charles Black, London.

Strenski, Ivan, 2006: *Thinking about Religion*, Blackwell Publishing Ltd. Malden, MA, USA.

Sūryakanta, 1950: *Flood Legend in Sanskrit Literature*, Delhi.

Thomas, F.W., 1942: *Indianism and its Expansion*, University of Calcutta, Calcutta.

Thomas, P., *Epics, Myths and Legends of India*, 9th ed., Bombay.

Tilak, B.G., 1893: *Orion*, Pub. by Tilak Brothers, Poona.

Tripathi, G.C., 2004: *Communication with God*, Indira Gandhi National Centre for the Arts, New Delhi and Aryan Books International, New Delhi.

Turner, Jonathan A., 1995 (the first Indian edn., 1887): *The Structure of Sociological Theory*, Reprint, Rawat Publication, Jaipur.

Turner, W. (ed.), 1959: *Hamlet* (Intrn.), The Educational Publishiing Company, Bombay.

Tylor E.B., 1903 (1871): *Primitive Culture*, Vol. I, 4th edn., London; 1891: Vol. II, London.

Wadekar, M.L., 1996, 1997: *Devalasmṛti—Reconstruction and Critical Study*, Vols. I & II, Koshal Book Depot, Delhi.

Westermarck, E., 1901: *History of Human Marriage*, London.

—–, 1908: *Origin and Development of the Moral Ideas*, London.

—–, 1926: *A Short History of Human Marriage*, London.

Whitehead, Henry, 1976(1921): *The Village Gods, of South India*, 2nd edn., Sumit Publications, Delhi.

Winternitz, M., 1972 (University of Calcutta, 1927): *History of Indian Literature*, Vol. I, 2nd edn., Munshiram Manoharlal, New Delhi.

PH.D. THESES

(Mrs.) Guard, Nawaz R., 1991: *Ritual Drink in the Iranian and Indian Traditions (from Avestan and Indian Sources)*, Thesis, University of Bombay, Bombay.

(Mrs.) Londhe, Veena A., 1977: *The Cult and Lore of the Vedic Agni*, Thesis, University of Bombay.

Newaj Ram, 1994: *Vedic-Puranic Sources and Burmese Myth and Ritual*, Thesis, University of Bombay, Bombay (Mumbai).

Sharma, Naval Kishor, 1978: *Solar Lore in the Purāṇas with special reference to the Skanda Purāṇa*, University of Bombay, Bombay.

PAPERS

Agrawala, R.C., "Fish and Vārāhī in Ancient Indian Sculpture," *Orissa Historical Research Journal*, Bhuvaneshvara Vol. XII, No. 1.

Bhandarkar, D.R., 1921: "Foreign Elements in Hindu Population," *Indian Antiquary*, Vol. XL.

Bhavani Bhikṣu, (Sep.) 1967: "Kuvā aur Āmarāī" (Hindi,) *Rashtrabharati*.

Bloomfield, M., "The Frog-hymn", *JAOS*, Vol. XVII.

Cain, John, 1875: "Native Custom of Godāvarī", *Indian Antiquary*, Vol. IV.

Chakrabarti, Samiran Chandra, 1982: "A Study of the Pāriplava", *Indo-Iranian Journal*, 32, Kluwer Academic Publishers (Printed in the Netherlands).

Chatterji, Suniti Kumar (General President), 1953: "Address", *Proceedings*, All India Oriental Conference, XVII Session, Ahmedabad, published by the Local Secretary, XVII AIOC, Gujarat Vidyasabha, Ahmedabad.

Converse, H., 1974-1975: "The Agnicayana Rite: Indigenous Origins?", *History of Religions*, Vol. XIV, 2.

Dandekar, R.N., 1954: "The Mahābhārata: Origin and Growth", University of Ceylon Review, 12.

——, 1972-1973: "Comparative Religion and Mythology", Dialogue' 72/'73, for F. Max Mueller 150th Birth Anniversary, ed. by Heimo Rau, pub., by the Branches of Max Mueller Bhavan (in India).

Dange, Sadashiv A., (July) 1963: "Sāvitrī and the Banyan," *Purāṇa*, Vol. V, No. 2, All India Kashiraj Trust, Varanasi.

—–, (Sep. 1975): "Urvaśī—The Water-Belle (A fresh interpretation of *RV* X.95), *Journal of the Oriental Institute*, M.S. University of Baroda, Baroda, Vol. XXV-1.

—–, (year not given): "Urvaśī—The Weaver of the Web of Life, "*Śrījagannāthajyotiḥ*, Jagannath University Journal of Indology, Puri, No. 6.

—–, 1997: "Araru āṇi Nārmara" (Marathi), Vidarbha Samshodhana Mandala, Nagpur, *Annual No.*

—–, 1980: "Purūravas—A Research for Identity", *A Corpus of Indian Studies (Gaurinath Shastri Fel. Vol.)*, Sanskrit Pustak Bhandar, Calcutta.

—–, 1982: "The Riddle of the Black Antelope", *Abhinandana-Bhāratī (Prof. Krishna Kanta Handiqui Fel. Vol.)*, Kāmarūpa Anusandhāna Samiti (Assam Research Society), Gauhati.

—–, 1998: "Vāstupuruṣa", *Purāṇa-Itihāsa-Vimarśaḥ* (*Prof. S.G. Kantawala Fel. Vol.*), Bharatiya Vidya Prakashan, Delhi.

Dange, Sindhu S., (January) 1971: "The Earth-Cow and Pṛthu's Dart", *Purāṇa*, All India Kashiraj Trust, Varanasi, XIII-i.

—–, 1974: "Trikadrukebhiḥ Patati (*RV* X.14.16)—(An Interpretation)", *Proceedings* of the All India Oriental Conference, XVII Session, Kurukshetra.

—–, 1993: "Prāśitra in Myth and Ritual", *Prbhākara-Nārāyaṇa-Śrīḥ (Studies in Indology and Musicology), Dr. Prabhakar Narayan Kawthekar Fel. Vol.*, Pratibha Prakashan, Delhi.

—–, 1993: "The Severed Head in Myth and Ritual", *Amṛtamahotsava Vol. Annals* of the Bhandarkar Oriental Research Institute, Vols., LXXII & LXXIII (1991 & 1992), Pune (published in 1993).

—–, 1996: "Athithi: A Probe in Concept", *Studies in Indology* (*Prof. Mukund Madhav Sharma Fel. Vol.*), Sri Satguru Publications, Delhi.

—–, (July) 1998: "Sūta—The Paurāṇika", *Purāṇa*, All India Kashiraj Trust, Varanasi, Vol. XL, No. 2.

—–, 1998: "Animal Alter-morphs of Agni-Prajāpati", *Journal of the Asiatic Society of Bombay (Mumbai)*, Vol. 73 (New Series).

—–, 2006: "The Disappearing Sun—from Myth to Ritual," *Nyāya-Vasiṣṭha* (*Fel. Vol. of Prof. V.N. Jha*), ed. by Manabendu Banerjee, Sanskrit Pustak Bhandar, Kolkata.

—–, 2005-06: "Ṛgveda II.12 and the Sūta-tradition", *Śrījagannāthajyotiḥ, Jagannath University Journal of Indology*, Vol

X, Sri Vihar, Puri, Vishvavidyalaya Silver Jubilee Year.
—–, 2009: "Solar Eclipse and the 'Fourth' Mantra of Atri", *Journal of the Asiatic Society of Mumbai*, Mumbai, Vol. 82 for 2008 (New Series).
—–, 2009: "Women in Smṛtis: Issues of Inheritance", *History of Science, Philosophy and Culture in Indian Civilization*, Vol. IX, Part 2, *Women in Ancient and Medieval India*, ed., by Bhuvan Chandel, Centre for Studies in Civilizations, New Delhi.
—–, 2010: "Āraṇyakas—A Search for their Identity", *The Studies in the Āraṇyakas*, ed. by Dr. (Mrs.) Bhagyalata Pataskar, Adarsha Sanskrit Shodha Samstha (Vaidika Samshodhana Mandala), Pune.
—–, 2011: "Puranic Rules of Dharma and Human Rights for Śūdras and Women", *Dharmaśāstra and Human Rights*, ed. by Ujjwala Jha, New Bharatiya Book Corporation, Delhi.
Das, Pt. Nilakantha, (July) 1977: "The Cult of Jagannatha", *Orissa Review (Navakalevara Special)*, Vol. XXXIII, No. 12, Bhubaneswara.
Dhal, U.N., 1987: "Rathayātrā—A Sacrificial Festival of Lord Jagannatha", *Sacrifice in India—Concept and Evolution*, (ed.) Sindhu S. Dange, Viveka Publications, Aligarh.
Dharmadhikari, T.N., 1987: "Gavām-ayanam", *Sacrifice in India—Concept and Evolution*, (ed.) Sindhu S. Dange, Viveka Publications., Aligarh.
Dhavalikar, M.K., 1992: "Kīrtimukha", Ananthacharya Indological Research Institute Series, No. XI, *Proceedings* of the Seminar on 'Symbolism in Temple Art and Architecture', Bombay (Mumbai).
Eliade, Mercia, 1969: "Crisis and Renewal", *The Quest*, University of Chicago Press, Chicago.
Godbole, G.H., 1987: "Later Vedic and Brahmanical Accounts", *Myths of Creation* (ed.) Sindhu S. Dange, University of Bombay, Bombay (Mumbai).
Goldman, R.P., (July) 1969: "Mortal Man and Immortal Woman", *Journal of the Oriental Institute*, Baroda, Vol. XVIII, No. 4.
Hazra, R.C., 1955: "The Sāmba Purāṇa, a Saura work of Different Hands", *ABORI*, XXXVI, Pune.
Hopkins, E.W., "Indra as the God of Fertility", *JAOS*, Vol. XXXVI, New Haven, USA.

Huttington, Ronald, 1964: "Avatāras and Yugas", *Purāṇa*, All India Kashiraj Trust, Vol. VI, No. 1, Varanasi.

Jaiswal, K.P., 1917: "Historical Position of Kalki and his identification with Yaśodharman", *Indian Antiquary*, Vol. 46.

Kantawala, S.G., (July) 1961: "Matsya Purāṇa and Promiscuity," *Purāṇa*, All India Kashiraj Trust, Vol. III, No. 2, Varanasi.

Mahalingam, T.V., (April) 1965: "The Nāgas in History and Culture", *Journal of Indian History*, University of Kerala, Trivandrum, Vol. XLIII, Pt. I, Serial No. 127.

Mitra, Debala, "Foreign Elements in Indian Population", *The Cultural Heritage of India*, II.

Navathe, P.D., 1980: "On the Mīmāṁsā Doctrine of Ekavākyatā", *Proceedings* of the Winter Institute on Ancient Indian Theories of Sentence-Meaning, University of Poona, Pune.

Norman, Brown, (May) 1921: "Some Notes on the Rain-charms", *New Indian Antiquary*, Vol. II-2.

Parpola, Asko, "The Coming of the Aryans to Iran and India and the Cultural and Ethnic Identity of the Dasas", originally pub. by Finnish Oriental Society, Helsinki and later on published in *Studia Orientalia*, 64, Helsinki.

Potdar, K.R., (Sep.) 1945: "Āprī-hymns", *Journal of the University of Bombay*.

Ramaswami Shastri, K.S., "The Aryan Colonies of Kiṣkindhā and Laṅkā," *Indian Culture*, Vol. V.

Ramdas, G., 1925: "The Aboriginal Tribes in the Rāmāyaṇa", *Man in India*, Vol. V.

Rolland, Pierre, 1972: "A Study of a solemn Vedic ritual—The Mahāvrata", *Journal of Bihar Research Society*, Vol. 58.

Shirgaonkar, M.A., (Aug.) 1983: "Brahmapūjā—Narasiṁhapūjā", *Prasada (Nṛsiṁha Daivata Viśeṣāṅka)*, ed. by M.Y. Joshi, Prasada Prakashan, Pune.

Smith, W.R., 1875-1880: "Sacrifice", the long article in *Encyclopaedia of Britannica*, 9th edn.

Theroux, Paul, (July) 1992: "Under the Spell of the Trobriand Islands", *National Geographic*.

Wright, J.C., 1967: "Purūravas and Urvaśī," *BSOAS*, Vol. XXX.

Index

(Figures in the brackets indicate the numbers of the notes on those particular pages.)